The Collected Works of J. Krishnamurti

Volume IX

1955–1956

The Answer Is in the Problem

KENDALL/HUNT PUBLISHING COMPANY
2460 Kerper Boulevard P.O. Box 539 Dubuque, Iowa 52004-0539

Photo: J. Krishnamurti, ca 1955
Copyright © 1991 by The Krishnamurti Foundation of America
P.O. Box 1560, Ojai, CA 93024

Library of Congress Catalog Card Number: 90–62735

ISBN 0–8403–6260–9

Printed in the United States of America
10 9 8 7 6 5 4 3 2 1

Contents

Preface

Jiddu Krishnamurti was born in 1895 of Brahmin parents in south India. At the age of fourteen he was proclaimed the coming World Teacher by Annie Besant, then president of the Theosophical Society, an international organization that emphasized the unity of world religions. Mrs. Besant adopted the boy and took him to England, where he was educated and prepared for his coming role. In 1911 a new worldwide organization was formed with Krishnamurti as its head, solely to prepare its members for his advent as World Teacher. In 1929, after many years of questioning himself and the destiny imposed upon him, Krishnamurti disbanded this organization, saying:

Truth is a pathless land, and you cannot approach it by any path whatsoever, by any religion, by any sect. Truth, being limitless, unconditioned, unapproachable by any path whatsoever, cannot be organized; nor should any organization be forced to lead or to coerce people along any particular path. My only concern is to set men absolutely, unconditionally free.

Until the end of his life at the age of ninety, Krishnamurti traveled the world speaking as a private person. The rejection of all spiritual and psychological authority, including his own, is a fundamental theme. A major concern is the social structure and how it conditions the individual. The emphasis in his talks and writings is on the psychological barriers that prevent clarity of perception. In the mirror of relationship, each of us can come to understand the content of his own consciousness, which is common to all humanity. We can do this, not analytically, but directly in a manner Krishnamurti describes at length. In observing this content we discover within ourselves the division of the observer and what is observed. He points out that this division, which prevents direct perception, is the root of human conflict.

His central vision did not waver after 1929, but Krishnamurti strove for the rest of his life to make his language even more simple and clear. There is a development in his exposition. From year to year he used new terms and new approaches to his subject, with different nuances.

Because his subject is all-embracing, the *Collected Works* are of compelling interest. Within his talks in any one year, Krishnamurti was not able to cover the whole range of his vision, but broad applications of particular themes are found throughout these volumes. In them he lays the foundations of many of the concepts he used in later years.

The *Collected Works* contain Krishnamurti's previously published talks, discussions, answers to specific questions, and writings for the years 1933 through 1967. They are an authentic record of his teachings, taken from transcripts of verbatim shorthand reports and tape recordings.

The Krishnamurti Foundation of America, a California charitable trust, has among its purposes the publication and distribution of Krishnamurti books, videocassettes, films and tape recordings. The production of the *Collected Works* is one of these activities.

Amsterdam, Holland, 1955

✳

First Talk in Amsterdam

One is apt rather to think that what is going to be said will be Oriental and something which you have to struggle after to find. You need not struggle; but I think it is important, if we wish to understand each other, that we should first of all clear our minds of obvious conclusions. I feel that what I am going to say is neither Oriental nor Occidental. It is not something which, because I happen to have a brown skin, is being brought from India for Western people to believe in. On the contrary, I think there is no East or West when we are concerned with human problems. As we are concerned with human problems, surely we must look at them from no particular point of view, but comprehensively. If we look at our human problems from a Western point of view, or with the attitude of an Indian, with certain traditions, ideas, and beliefs, it obviously prevents the comprehension of the total process of our living. So it seems to me that it is very important not to assume anything, not to draw upon any conclusion or base our life on any suppositions or postulates. That is one of our greatest difficulties—to free the mind from any assumption, from any belief, from all the accretions of our own accumulated knowledge and all that we have learned. Surely, if we would understand anything, we must have a free mind, unburdened of any previous conclusions, unburdened of all belief. When the mind is so free, unhampered by the various conditionings which have been imposed on it, is it not possible that such a mind is then capable of understanding the immediate challenge of life, whatever it may be?

We are concerned, are we not?—not only here in Europe, but also in Asia and India—with a challenge that demands quite a different approach from any method tried before. We have to respond to the challenge of the present crisis, surely, with a total mind, not with a fragmented mind—not as Christians or Buddhists or Hindus or communists or Catholics or Protestants or what you will. If we do so approach the challenge from our own particular standpoint, we shall fail because the challenge is far too big, too great, for us to respond to it partially or with a mind conditioned as a Christian or Buddhist or Hindu. So it seems to me that it is very important to free the mind, and not to start from any premise, from any conclusion. Because if we do start with any conclusion, with any premise, we have already responded to the challenge according to our own particular conditioning. So what is important, if we are at all serious and earnest, is to ask ourselves whether the mind can be unconditioned, and not merely seek to condition it into a better, nobler pattern—communist or

1

socialist or Catholic or what you will. Most of us are concerned with how to condition the mind into a nobler pattern, but can we not rather ask ourselves whether the mind can really be unconditioned? It seems to me that if we are at all serious, that is the fundamental issue. At present we are approaching life, with its extraordinarily fundamental challenge, either as a Christian or as a communist or as a Hindu or as a Buddhist or what you will, and so our response is always conditioned, limited, narrow, and therefore our reaction to the challenge is very petty. Therefore there is always conflict; there is always sorrow, confusion. My response being inadequate, insufficient, incomplete, must create within me a sense of conflict, from which arises sorrow. Realizing that one suffers, one tries to find a better, a nobler pattern of action—politically or religiously or economically—but it is still, essentially, conditioned.

So surely, our problem is not the search for a better pattern offered by one or the other of the various political or religious groups. Nor can we return in our confusion to the past, as most people are apt to do when they are confused—go back to something which we know, or which we have heard or read of in books, which again is the constant pursuit, is it not, of a better, nobler pattern of thinking, of conditioning. What we are talking about here is an entirely different matter—which is, is it possible for the mind to be free, totally unconditioned? At present all our minds are conditioned from the moment we are born to the moment we die; our mind is shaped by circumstances, by society, by religion, by education, by all the various pressures and strains of life—moral, social, ethical, and all the rest of it. And, having been shaped, we try to respond to something new, but obviously such a response can never be complete. There is always a sense of failure, of guilt, of misery. So, our question

is then, is it not, whether the mind can be really free from all conditioning. And it seems to me that it is really a very fundamental issue.

And if we are at all earnest, not only for the time being, temporarily, but if we would maintain an earnestness to find out if the mind can be free from all conditioning—that requires serious attention. I do not think any book, any philosophy, any leader, any teacher is going to help us, for surely each one of us must find out for himself whether the mind can be free. Some will say, "Obviously it cannot," and others may assert that it can. But both the assertions will have very little meaning, will they not, because the moment I accept one or the other, that very acceptance is a form of conditioning. Whereas if I as an individual—if there is such a thing as an individual—if I as a human being try to find out for myself, to inquire earnestly whether it is at all possible to free the mind totally from conditioning, both the conscious as well as the unconscious, surely that is the beginning of self-knowledge. I do not know if I can uncondition the mind; I neither accept nor reject the possibility, but I want to find out. That is the only way to approach life, is it not? Because a mind that is already in bondage, either in the bondage of nationalism or in the bondage of any particular religion, or held in a particular belief, however ancient or modern—such a mind is obviously incapable of really searching out what is true. A mind that is tethered to any belief, whatever the belief be, a mind that is merely held by an experience, whatever that experience be—how can such a mind investigate, proceed to understand? It can only move within the circle of its own bondage. So, if one is at all serious—and the times surely demand seriousness—then each one of us must ask himself, "Is it possible for the mind to be free from all conditioning?"

Now, what does this conditioning mean, actually? What is the nature of this conditioning? Why is the mind so willing to fit itself into the pattern of a particular design—as of a nation or group or religion? So long as the 'me', the self, is important, is there not always some form of conditioning? Because, the self assumes various forms—it exists as the 'me' or the 'you', as the 'I', only when there is some form of conditioning. So long as I think of myself as a Hindu, that very thought is the outcome of the feeling of importance. So long as I identify myself with any particular racial group, that very identification gives importance to me. And so long as I am attached to any particular property, name, family, and so on, that very attachment encourages the 'me', which is the very center of all conditioning. So, if we are serious and earnest in our endeavor to find out if the mind is capable of freeing itself from all conditioning, surely, consciously there must be no identification with any religion, with any racial group; there must be freedom from all attachment. For where there is identification or attachment, there is no love.

The mere rejection of a belief, of a particular church or a particular religion or other conditioning is not freedom. But to understand the whole process of it, go into it deeply, consciously, that requires a certain alertness of mind, the nonacceptance of all authority. To have self-knowledge, knowledge of myself as a total human being—the conscious as well as the unconscious, not just one fragment of myself—I must investigate, proceed to understand the whole nature of myself, find out step by step—but not according to any pattern or any philosophy, not according to any particular leader. Investigation into myself is not possible if I assume anything. If I assume that I am merely the product of environment, investigation ceases. Or if I assume that I have within me a spiritual entity, the unfolding God, or what you will, that assumption has already precluded, stopped, further investigation.

Self-knowledge, then, is the beginning of the freedom of the mind. There cannot be understanding of oneself, fundamentally, deeply, if there is any form of assumption, any authority, either of the past or of the present. But the mind is frightened to let go of all authority and investigate because it is afraid of not arriving at a particular result. So the mind is concerned with achieving a result, but not with the investigation to find out, to understand. That is why we cling to authority—religious, psychological, or philosophical. Being afraid, we demand guides, authorities, scriptures, saviors, inspiration in various forms, and so the mind is made incapable of standing alone and trying to find out. But one must stand alone, completely, totally alone, to find out what is true. And that is why it is important not to belong to any group. Because truth is discovered only by the mind that is alone—not in the sense of being lonely, isolated; I do not mean that at all because isolation is merely a form of resistance, a form of defense.

Only the mind that has gone into this question of self-knowledge deeply, and in the process of investigation has put aside all authority, all churches, all saviors, all following—only such a mind is capable of discovering reality. But to come to that point is extremely arduous, and most of us are frightened. Because to reject all the things that have been put upon us, to put aside the various forms of religions, churches, beliefs, is the rejection of society, is to withstand society, is it not? He who is outside society, who is no longer held by society—only such a person is then capable of finding out what God is, what truth is. To merely repeat that one believes or does not believe in God or in truth has very little significance. You can be brought up as a child not to believe in God, as is being done, or as a child, be brought up to believe in God. They are both the same because both minds are conditioned. But to find out what is true—if there is such a thing as God—that requires freedom of the mind, complete freedom, which means unconditioning the mind from all the past.

This unconditioning is essential because the times demand a new creative understanding, not the mere response of a past conditioning. Any society that does not respond to the new challenge of a group or an individual obviously decays. And it seems to me that if we would create a new world, a new society, we must have a free mind. And that mind cannot come about without real self-knowledge. Do not say, "All this has been said by so-and-so in the past. We can never find out the totality of our whole self." On the contrary, I think one can. To find out, the mind must surely be in a state in which there is no condemnation. Because what I am is the fact. Whatever I am—jealous, envious, haughty, ambitious, whatever it be—can we not just observe it without condemnation? Because the very process of condemnation is another form of conditioning *what is*. If one would understand the whole process of the self, there must be no identification, condemnation, or judgment, but an awareness in which there is no choice—just observation. If you attempt it, you will see how extraordinarily difficult it is. Because all our morality, our social and educational training, leads us to compare and to condemn, to judge. And the moment you judge, you have stopped the process of inquiry, insight. Thus, in the process of relationship, one begins to discover what the ways of the self are.

It is important not to merely listen to what is being said and accept or reject it but to observe the process of our own thinking in all our relationships. For in relationship, which is the mirror, we see ourselves as we actually are. And if we do not condemn or compare, then it is possible to penetrate deeper into the whole process of consciousness. And it is only then that there can be a fundamental revolution—not the revolution of the communist or what you will, but a real regeneration in the deepest sense of that word. The man who is freeing himself from all conditioning, who is fully aware—such a man is a religious man, not the man who merely believes. And it is only such a religious man who is capable of producing a revolution in the world. Surely, that is the fundamental issue for all of us—not to substitute one belief for another belief, to join this group or that, to go from one religion to another, one cage to another. As individuals we are confronted with enormous problems, which can only be answered in the process of understanding ourselves. It is only such religious human beings—who are free, unconditioned—who can create a new world.

Several questions have been sent in. And in considering them, it is important to bear in mind that life has no answer. If you are merely looking for an answer to the various problems, then you will never find it; you will only find a solution that is suitable to you, that you like or dislike, that you reject or accept; but that is not the answer—it is only your response to a particular like or dislike. But if one does not seek an answer but looks at the problem, really investigates it, then the answer is in the problem itself. But you see, we are so eager to find an answer. We suffer; our life is a confusion of conflict, and we want to put an end to that confusion; we want to find a solution, and so we are everlastingly seeking an answer. Probably there is no answer in the way we want it answered.

But if we do not seek an answer—which is extraordinarily difficult, and which means to investigate the whole problem patiently, without condemnation, without accepting or rejecting, just investigate and proceed patiently—then you will find the problem it-self, in its unfolding, reveals extraordinary things. For that, the mind must be free; it must not take sides, choose.

Question: It is fairly obvious that we are the product of our environment, and so we react according to how we are brought up. Is it ever possible to break down this background and live without self-contradiction?

KRISHNAMURTI: When we say it is fairly obvious that we are the product of our environment, I wonder if we are really aware of such a fact? Or is it merely a verbal statement without much meaning? When we say that we are the product of the environment, is that so? Do you actually feel that you are the product of the whole weight of Christian tradition, conscious as well as unconscious, the culture, the civilization, the wars, the hatreds, the imposition of various beliefs? Are you really aware of it? Or, do you merely reject certain portions of that conditioning and keep others—those which are pleasant, profitable, which give you sustenance, strength? Those you keep, do you not, and the rest, which are rather unpleasant, tiresome, you reject. But, if you are aware that you are the product of environment, then you must be aware of the total conditioning, not merely those parts which you have rejected, but also those which are pleasant and which you want to keep.

So, is one truly aware that one is the product of the environment? And if one is aware, then where does self-contradiction arise? You understand the issue? Within ourselves we are in contradiction, we are confused, we are pulled in different directions by our desires, ideals, beliefs, because our environment has given us certain values, certain standards. Surely the contradiction is part of the environment; it is not separate from it.

We are part of the environment, which is, religion, education, social morality, business values, tradition, beliefs, various impositions of churches, governments, the whole process of the past—those are all superficial conditionings, and there are also the inward unconscious responses to those superficial conditionings. When one is aware of all that, is there a contradiction? Or does contradiction arise because I am only partially aware of the conditioning of the environment and assume that there are parts of me which are not conditioned, thereby creating a conflict within myself?

So long as I feel guilty because I do not conform to a particular pattern of thought, of morality, obviously there is contradiction; the very nature of guilt is contradiction. I have certain values, which have been imposed or self-cultivated, and so long as I accept those values, there must be contradiction. But cannot the mind understand that it is entirely the product of conditioning? The mind is the result of time, conditioning, experience, and therefore, invariably, there must be contradiction within itself. Surely, so long as the mind is trying to fit into any particular pattern of thought, of morality, of belief, then that pattern itself creates the contradiction. And when we say, "How am I to be free from self-contradiction?" there is only one answer—to be free from all thought which creates the pattern. Then only is it possible for the mind to be free from self-contradiction.

Please, if I may suggest, do not reject this—perhaps you have to think about it, go more deeply into it. It is something you have not heard before, and the obvious reaction is to say, "Well, it is nonsense," and throw it out. But if you would understand, if you will listen to it deeply, you will see that so long as the mind, which is the center of all thought, is trying to think in a certain pattern, there will be contradiction. If it is thinking exclusively in that pattern, then there is no contradiction for the moment, but as soon as it diverges, moves away at all from the pattern, there must be contradiction.

So, the question "How is one to be free from self-contradiction?" is obviously a wrong question. The question is: "How can the mind be free from all environmental influences?" The mind itself is the product of environment. So as long as the mind is battling against the environment, trying to shake it, trying to break away from it, that very breaking away is a contradiction, and therefore there is a struggle. But if the mind is observant, is aware that it is itself the product of environment, then the mind becomes quiet, then the mind no longer struggles against itself. And being quiet, still, then it will be free from environment.

Perhaps you will kindly think about this—not accept or reject, but see the truth of what is being said; and you cannot understand the truth of something if you are battling against it or defending it. Can we not see that the very nature of the mind is to contradict, to be a slave to environment?—because it is the product of time, of centuries of tradition, of fear, of hope, of inspiration, of stress and strain. Such a mind is conditioned, totally. And, when such a mind rejects or accepts, that very acceptance or rejection is the further continuance of conditioning. Whereas, when the mind is aware that it is totally conditioned, consciously as well as unconsciously, then it is still, and in that stillness there is freedom from conditioning. Then there is no contradiction.

The division between contradiction and complete integration cannot be drawn intellectually, verbally. Integration comes into being only when there is the total understanding of oneself. And that understanding of oneself does not come through analysis because the problem then arises: Who is the analyzer? The analyzer himself is condi-

tioned, obviously, and therefore that which he analyzes is also the result of conditioning.

So, what is important is not how to eradicate self-contradiction but to understand the whole process of the conditioning of the mind. That can only be understood in relationship, in our daily life—seeing how the mind reacts, observing, watching, being aware, without condemning. Then you will see how extraordinarily difficult it is to free the mind because the mind assumes so many things; it has deposited so many assertions, values, beliefs. When the mind is constantly aware, without judging, without condemning, without comparing, then such a mind can begin to understand the total process of itself and therefore become still. Only in that stillness of mind can that which is real come into being.

May 17, 1955

Second Talk in Amsterdam

It seems to me that one of the most difficult things to do is to listen to somebody with a quiet mind. I think most of us listen without giving our whole attention. I mean by attention a state in which there is no particular object upon which the mind is concentrated. Most of us already have many opinions, conclusions, and experiences, and we listen to another through this cross section of our own particular idiosyncrasies, through our own particular forms of habit of thought. So it is very difficult for most of us to understand what the other person is actually saying. Our opinions, our beliefs, our experiences all intervene, distract, and so warp and twist what the other one is saying. If we could put aside our particular opinions, our conclusions, and the various forms of our own idiosyncrasies, and listen attentively, then perhaps there would be an understanding between us.

After all, you are here, if I may point it out, to understand what is being said. And to understand, you must listen to what is actually being said, and not merely listen to opinions you may have about what is being said. You can form your opinions, if you must, afterwards. I do not think what is being said is really a matter of opinion. If it is a matter of opinion, then there will be contradiction, your opinion against another opinion. Opinion, I feel, has no significance when one is facing facts. You cannot have an opinion about a fact—either it is, or it is not.

So it seems to me that it is important to listen, not with opinions clouding the mind, but with a mind that is capable of patiently listening to the whole matter without forming a conclusion. Surely any form of conclusion is also an opinion and therefore restricts the mind. What we are going to talk about does not demand opinions. On the contrary, we must approach the subject of our inquiry tentatively, hesitatingly, without any hypothesis, without any conclusion. That is very difficult for most of us because we want to arrive, to get somewhere—either to bolster up, to strengthen, our own particular beliefs or to argumentatively enhance our own particular thought.

So, if I may suggest, these talks will be utterly futile, will have no meaning, if we enter into controversy, setting one opinion against another. Can we not together, you and I, endeavor to find out what is true? To find out, the mind must be somewhat energetic, somewhat purposive, and not merely clogged by opinion.

What we are going to discuss this evening is how the mind can be creative. That is, can we not find out if it is possible for the mind to be completely purified of all its inhibitions, conditionings, its various forms of fear, and social impositions so that the mind is not held, put into a frame, merely functioning mechanically? Can we discover for ourselves what it is to be creative? It seems to me that is one of the most fundamental questions of the present time, perhaps of all time. Because obviously, we are not creative; we are merely repeating patterns of thought, even though we may be making mechanical progress.

I do not mean by creativeness merely self-expression—writing a poem or painting a picture. I mean by that word something entirely different. Creativeness, reality, God, or what you will, must be a state of mind in which there is no repetition, in which there is no continuity through memory as we know it. God, or truth, must be totally new, unexperienced before—something which is not the product of memory, of knowledge, of experience. Because if it is the product of knowledge, it is merely a projection, a desire, a wish, and obviously that cannot be what is true or what is real. Reality must surely be something unimagined, unexpressed, totally new; and the mind which would discover such a reality must be unconditioned so that it is truly individual.

Obviously we are not truly individuals. We may each have a different name, different tendencies, a particular house, a particular bank account; we may each belong to a particular family, have certain mannerisms, belong to a certain religion—but that does not make for individuality. Our whole mind is the result of the environmental influences of a particular society, of a particular culture, of a particular religion; and so long as it belongs to any of these particularities, obviously the mind is not simple, is not innocent in its directness. Surely a clear, simple mind is essential if we are to find out what is real.

So, is it possible for you and me to find out together if one can liberate the mind from all this weight of influence, of tradition, of belief? Because it seems to me, that is the only purpose of living—to find what is reality. If we would make that discovery, we must first find out what it is that makes us conform. We are conforming all the time, are we not? Our whole life, our whole tendency—our education, our morality, all the sanctions of religion—is to make us conform. Our religion is essentially based on conformity. And surely a mind that conforms is not a free mind, a mind capable of inquiry. So can you and I inquire into the whole process of conformity, what it is that makes the mind yield to a particular pattern of society, of culture? We conform, do we not, because essentially we are afraid. Through fear we create authority—the authority of religion, the authority of a leader—because we want to be safe, secure, not so much physiologically perhaps, but essentially inwardly, psychologically, we want to be secure; and so we create a society which assures us outwardly of security.

This is a fact, a psychological fact, and not a thing to be debated or quarreled over. That is, I want to be secure; psychologically, inwardly, I want to be certain—certain of success, certain of achievement, certain of "getting there," wherever "there" may be. So to achieve, to arrive, to be something, I must have authority.

Please, it would be advisable, if these talks are to be at all worthwhile, that in listening you are really examining your own mind. The talk, the words are merely a description of the state of your own mind, and merely to listen to the words will have no meaning. But in the process of listening, if one is capable of looking within oneself and seeing the operation of one's own mind, then such descriptive listening will have significance. And I hope, if I may suggest it, that you are doing this, and not merely listening to my words.

Each one of us desires to be secure—in our relationships, in our love, in the things that we believe in, in our experiences; we want to be secure, certain, without any doubt. And since that is our inmost desire, psychologically, then obviously we must rely on authority. Surely that is the anatomy of authority, is it not, the structure of it; that is why the mind creates authority. You may reject the authority of a particular society, of a particular leader, or of a particular religion, but then you yourself create another authority. Then your own experiences, your own knowledge, become the guide. Because, the mind seeks always to be certain; it cannot live in a state of uncertainty. So it is always seeking certainty and thereby creating authority.

And that is what our society is based on, is it not, with its culture, with its knowledge, with its religions. It is essentially based on authority—the authority of tradition, of the priest, of the church, or the authority of the expert. So we become slaves to the experts because our intention is to be secure. But surely, if we would find something real, not merely repeat the words *God, truth,* which have no meaning when repeated—if we would make a discovery, the mind must be completely insecure, must it not, in a state of nondependency on any authority. That is very difficult for most of us because from childhood we are brought up to believe, to hold to some form of dependency; and if the leader, the guide, the teacher, the priest, fails, we create our own image of what we think is true—which is merely the reaction of our own particular form of conditioning.

So it seems to me that so long as the mind is shaped and controlled by society—not merely the environmental, educational, and cultural society, but the whole concept of authority, belief, and conformity—it obviously cannot find that which is true, and therefore it cannot be creative; it can only be imitative, repetitive. The problem therefore is not how to be creative but whether we can understand the whole process of fear—the fear of what the neighbor says, the fear of going wrong, the fear of losing money, the fear of loneliness, the fear of not coming up to the mark, of not being a success, in this world or in some other world. So long as there is any form of fear, it creates authority upon which the mind depends, and obviously such a mind is not capable of pursuing, investigating, putting aside everything to find out what it is to be truly creative.

So, is it not important to ask ourselves, each one of us, whether we are really individuals, and not merely assert that we are? Actually, we are not. You may have a separate body, a different face, a different name and family, but the inward structure of your mind is essentially conditioned by society; therefore, you are not an individual. Surely, only the mind that is not bound by the impositions of society, with all the implications involved, can be free to find out that which is true and that which is God. Otherwise, all we do is merely to repeat catastrophe; otherwise, there is no possibility of that revolution which will bring about a totally different kind of world. It seems to me that is the only important thing—not to what society, to what group, to what religion you should or should not belong, which has all become so infantile, immature, but for you to find out for yourself if the mind can be totally free from all the impositions of custom, tradition, and belief, and thereby be free to find out what is true. Then only can we be creative human beings.

There are several questions to be answered. And before I answer them, let us find out what we mean by a problem. A problem exists only when the mind desires to get somewhere, to achieve, to become something. It is "this," and it wants to transform itself into "that." Or, I am "here," and I must get "there." I am ugly, and I want to be beautiful, physiologically as well as psychologically. When the mind is concerned with the movement of "getting there," becoming something, then the problem arises, because then you have the question "How?" So we are always creating problems because our whole thinking process is based on the movement towards something—towards the ultimate, towards the final, towards being happy, towards the ideal.

But I think there is a different way of looking at it, which is not to proceed from *what is* towards something else but to proceed from *what is* not in any preconceived direction. Is it not possible to realize *what is*—that one is greedy, envious, or any of the various forms of passion and lust—and to start from that without the desire to change into something else? The moment there is the desire to change that into something else, you have the problem. Whereas to proceed from *what is* does not create a problem.

I hope I am making myself clear. We see what we are, if we are at all aware, and then we proceed to change it; we want to transform *what is* into something else and thereby create conflict, problems, and so on. But, if we proceed with *what is* without wanting to transform it, if we observe it, remain with it, understand it, then there is no problem.

So in answering these questions we are concerned, not with how to proceed in order to bring about a change, but rather to understand what actually is. If I understand what actually is, then there is no problem. A fact does not create a problem. Only an opinion about a fact creates a problem.

Question: Can there be religion without a church?

KRISHNAMURTI: What is religion? What is fact—not the ideal? When we say we are religious, that we belong to a certain religion, what do we mean by it? We mean that we hold to certain dogmas, beliefs, conclusions, certain conditionings of the mind. To us, religion is nothing more than that. Either I go to church, or I do not go to church; either I am a Christian, or I give up Christianity and join some other form of religion, assume some other set of beliefs, perform some other series of rituals, obeying certain dogmas, tenets, and so on. That is the actual fact. And, is that religion? Can a mind whose beliefs are the result of impositions, of conditioning by a particular society—can such a mind find what is God? Or can the mind which has been trained not to believe ever find God either?

Surely, a mind that belongs to any religion—that is, which belongs to any particular form of belief, is stimulated by any form of ritual, has dogmas, believes in various saviors—surely such a mind is incapable of being religious. It may repeat certain words, may attend church, may be very moral, very respectable; but surely such a mind is not a religious mind. A mind that belongs to a church of any kind—Hindu, Buddhist, Christian, or what you will—is merely conforming, being conditioned by its own environment, by tradition, by authority, by fear, by the desire to be saved. Such a mind is not a religious mind. But to understand the whole process of why the mind accepts belief, why the mind conforms to certain patterns of thought, dogmas, which is obviously through fear—to be aware of all that, inwardly, psychologically, and to be free of it—such a mind is then a religious mind.

Virtue, surely, is necessary only to keep the mind orderly, but virtue does not necessarily lead to reality. Order is necessary, and virtue supplies order. But the mind must go beyond virtue and morality. To be merely a slave to morality, to conformity, to accept the authority of the church, or of any kind—

surely such a mind is incapable of finding what is true, what is God.

Please do not accept what I am saying. It would be absurd if you accepted, because that would be another form of authority. But if you will look into it, look into your own mind, how it conforms, how it is afraid, what innumerable beliefs it has upon which it relies for its own security, therefore engendering fear—if one is aware of all that, then obviously, without any struggle, without any effort, all those things are put aside. Then truly, such a mind is in revolt against society, such a mind is capable of creating a religious revolution—not a political or economic revolution, which is not a revolution at all. A real revolution is in the mind— the mind that frees itself from society. Such freedom is not merely to put on a different kind of coat. Real revolution comes only when the mind rejects all impositions, through understanding. Only such a mind is capable of creating a different world, because only such a mind is then capable of receiving that which is true.

Question: How can I resist distraction?

KRISHNAMURTI: The questioner asks, "How can I not yield, give in, to any form of distraction?" That is, he wants to concentrate on something, and his mind is distracted, taken away; and he wants to know how he can resist it.

Now, is there such a thing as distraction? Surely the so-called distraction is obviously the thing in which the mind is interested; otherwise, you would not go after it. So, why condemn a thing by calling it a distraction? Whereas, if the mind is capable of not calling it distraction, but is pursuing each thought, being alert and aware of every thought that arises—not as a practice, but being aware of every thought that it is thinking—then there is no distraction, then there is no resistance.

It is much more important to understand resistance than to ward off distraction. We spend so much energy in resisting; our whole life is taken up in resisting, in defending, in wanting—"That is a distraction, and this is not," "This is right, and that is wrong." Therefore we resist, defend, build a wall in ourselves against something. Our whole life is spent that way, and so we are a mass of resistances, contradictions, distractions, and concentrations. Whereas, if we are able to look, be aware of all that we are thinking and not call it a distraction, not give it a name, saying, "This is good and this is bad," but just observe every thought as it arises, then we will find that the mind becomes not a battlefield of contradictions, of one desire against another, of one thought opposing another, but only a state of thinking.

After all, thought, however noble, however wide and deep, is always conditioned. Thinking is a reaction to memory. So why divide thought into distraction and interest? Because the whole process of thinking is a process of limitation, there is no free thinking. If you observe, you will see all thinking is essentially based on conditioning. Thinking is the result of memory, reaction; it is very automatic, mechanical. I ask you something, and your memory responds. You have read a book, and you repeat it.

So, if you go into this question of thinking, you will see there can never be freedom in thinking, freedom in thought. There is freedom only when there is no thinking—which does not mean going into a state of blankness. On the contrary, it requires the greatest form of intelligence to realize that all thinking is the reaction, the response to memory, and therefore mechanical. And it is only when the mind is very still, completely still, without any movement of thought, that there is a possibility of discovering something totally new. Thought can never discover anything new because thought is the projection of the past, thought is the result of time, of many, many days, and centuries of yesterdays.

Knowing all that, being aware of all that, the mind becomes still. Then there is a possibility of something new taking place, something totally unexperienced, unimaginable, not something which is a mere projection of the mind itself.

Question: What kind of education should my child have in order to face this chaotic world?

KRISHNAMURTI: This is really a vast question, isn't it, not to be answered in a couple of minutes. But perhaps we can put it briefly, and it may be gone into further afterwards.

The problem is not what kind of education the child should have but rather that the educator needs education, the parent needs education. (Murmur of laughter) No, please, this is not a clever remark for you to laugh at, be amused at. Do we not need a totally different kind of education?—not the mere cultivation of memory, which gives the child a technique, which will help him to get a job, a livelihood, but an education that will make him truly intelligent. Intelligence is the comprehension of the whole process, the total process of life, not knowledge of one fragment of life.

So the problem is really: Can we, the grown-up people, help the child to grow in freedom, in complete freedom? This does not mean allowing him to do what he likes, but can we help the child to understand what it is to be free because we understand ourselves what it is to be free?

Our education now is merely a process of conformity, helping the child to conform to a particular pattern of society in which he will get a job, become outwardly respectable, go to church, conform, and struggle until he dies. We do not help him to be free inwardly so that as he grows older, he is able to face all the complexities of life—which means helping him to have the capacity to think, not teaching him what to think. For this, the educator himself must be capable of freeing his own mind from all authority, from all fear, from all nationality, from the various forms of belief and tradition, so that the child understands—with your help, with your intelligence—what it is to be free, what it is to question, to inquire, and to discover.

But you see, we do not want such a society; we do not want a different world. We want the repetition of the old world, only modified, made a little better, a little more polished. We want the child to conform totally, not to think at all, not to be aware, not to be inwardly clear—because if he is so inwardly clear, there is danger to all our established values. So, what is really involved in this question is how to bring education to the educator. How can you and I—because we, the parents, the society, are the educators—how can you and I help to bring about clarity in ourselves so that the child may also be able to think freely, in the sense of having a still mind, a quiet mind, through which new things can be perceived and come into being?

This is really a very fundamental question. Why is it that we are being educated at all? Just for a job? Just to accept Catholicism or Protestantism, or communism or Hinduism? Just to conform to a certain tradition, to fit into a certain job? Or is education something entirely different?—not the cultivation of memory, but the process of understanding. Understanding does not come through analysis; understanding comes only when the mind is very quiet, unburdened, no longer seeking success and therefore being thwarted, afraid of failure. Only when the mind is still, only then is there a possibility of under-standing, and having intelligence. Such education is the right kind of education, from which obviously other things follow.

But very few of us are interested in all that. If you have a child, you want him to have a job; that is all you are concerned with—what is going to happen to his future. Should the child inherit all the things that you have—the property, the values, the beliefs, the traditions—or must he grow in freedom, so as to discover for himself what is true? That can only happen if you yourself are not inheriting, if you yourself are free to inquire, to find out what is true.

May 19, 1955

Third Talk in Amsterdam

I think it would be wise if we could listen to what we are going to consider with comparative freedom from prejudice, and not with the feeling that what is being said is merely the opinion of a Hindu coming from Asia with certain ideas. After all, there is no division in thought; thought has no nationality, and our problems, whether Asiatic, Indian, or European, are the same. We can, unfortunately, conveniently divide our problems as though they were Asiatic and European, but in fact we have only problems. And if we would tackle them, not from any one point of view, but understand them totally, go into them profoundly, patiently, and diligently, it is first necessary to comprehend the many issues that confront each one of us. So, if I may suggest, it would be wise if we could dissociate ourselves for the time being from any nationality, from any particular form of religious belief, even from our own particular experiences, and consider fairly dispassionately what is being said.

It seems to me that there must be a total revolution—not mere reform, because reforms always breed further reforms, and there is no end to that process. But I feel it is important when we are confronted with an enormous crisis—as we are—that there should be a total revolution in our minds, in our hearts, in our whole attitude towards life. That revolution cannot be brought about by any outside pressure, by any circumstances, by any mere economic revolution, nor by leaving one form of religion to join another. Such adjustment is not revolution; it is merely a modified continuity of what has been. It seems to me that it is very necessary at the present time, and perhaps at all times, if we would understand the enormous challenge we are confronted with, that we approach it totally, with all our being—not as a Dutchman with a European culture, or a Hindu with certain beliefs and superstitions, but as a human being stripped of all our prejudices, our nationalities, our particular forms of religious conviction. I feel it is important that we should not indulge in mere reformation, because all such reform is merely an outward adjustment to a particular circumstance, to a particular pressure and strain; and that adjustment obviously does not bring about a different world, a different state of being, in which human beings can live at peace with each other. So it seems to me that it is very important to put aside all consideration of reformation—political, economic, social, or what you will—and bring about a total inward revolution.

Such a revolution can only take place religiously. That is, when one is really a religious person—only then is it possible to have such a revolution. Economic revolution is merely a fragmentary revolution. Any social reform is still fragmentary, separative; it is not a total reformation. So, can we consider this matter, not as a group, or as a Dutchman, but as individuals?—because this revolution obviously must begin with the individual. True religion can never be collective. It must be the outcome of individual endeavor, individual search, individual liberation and freedom. God is not to be found collectively. Any form of collectivism in search can only be a conditioning reaction. The search for reality can only be on the part of the individual. I think it is very important to understand this because we are always considering what is going to be the response of the mass. Do we not always say, "This is too difficult for the mass, for the general public," and do we not seek every form of excuse that we can find in order not to alter, not to bring about a fundamental revolution within ourselves? We find, do we not, innumerable excuses for indefinite postponement of direct individual revolution.

If you and I can separate ourselves from collective thinking, from thinking as Dutchmen or Christians or Buddhists or Hindus, then we can tackle the problem of bringing about a total revolution within ourselves. For it is only that total revolution within oneself which can reveal that which is of the highest. It is enormously difficult to separate ourselves from the collective because we are afraid to stand alone, we are afraid to be thought different from others, we are afraid of the public, what another says. We have innumerable forms of self-defense.

To bring about a revolution, a fundamentally radical change, is it not important that we should consider the process of the mind? Because, after all, that is the only instrument we have—the mind that has been educated for centuries, the mind that is the result of time, the mind that is the storehouse of innumerable experiences, memories. With that mind, which is essentially conditioned, we try to find an answer to the innumerable problems of our existence. That is, with a mind that has been shaped, molded by circumstances, a mind that is never free, with a process of thinking which is the outcome of innumerable reactions, conscious or unconscious, we hope to solve our problems. So it seems to me that it is very important to understand oneself, because self-knowledge is the beginning of this radical revolution of which I am talking.

After all, if I do not know what I think and the source of my thought, the ways I function—not only outwardly, but deep down, the various unconscious wounds, hopes, fears, frustrations—if I am not totally aware of all that, then whatever I think, whatever I do, has very little significance. But to be aware of that totality of my being requires attention, patience, and the constant pursuit of awareness. That is why I think it is essential for those of us who are really serious about these things, who are endeavoring to find out the answer to our innumerable problems, that we should understand our own ways of thinking and break away totally from any form of inward constriction, imposition, and dogma, so as to be able to think freely and search out what is true.

This requires, does it not, a freedom from all authority—not to follow, not to imitate, not to conform inwardly. At present, our whole thinking, our whole being, is essentially the result of conformity, of training, of molding. We comply, we adjust, we accept, because we are deeply afraid to be different, to stand alone, to inquire. Inwardly we want assurance, we want to succeed, we want to be on the right side. So we build various forms of authority, patterns of thought, and thereby become imitative human beings, outwardly conforming because inwardly we are essentially frightened to be alone.

This aloneness, this detachment, is surely not contrary to relationship with the collective. If we are able to stand alone, then possibly we shall be able to help the collective. But if we are only part of the collective, then obviously we can only reform, bring about certain changes in the pattern of the collective. To be truly individual is to be totally outside of the collective because we under-

stand what the whole implication of the collective is. Such an individual is capable of bringing about a transformation in the collective. I think it is important to bear this in mind since most of us are concerned with the so-called mass, the collective, the whole group. Obviously the group cannot change itself—it has never done so historically, or now. Only the individual who is capable of detaching himself totally from the group, from the collective, can bring about a radical change, and he can only detach himself totally when he is seeking that which is real. That means he must be really a religious person— but not the religion of belief, of churches, of dogmas, of creeds. Only one who is free from the collective can find out what is true. And that is extraordinarily difficult, for the mind is always projecting what it thinks to be religion, God, truth.

So it is very important to understand the whole process of oneself, to have knowledge of the 'me', the self, the thinker; because, if one is so capable of regarding one's whole process of living, one can free the mind from the collective, from the group, and so become an individual. Such an individual is not in opposition to the collective—opposition is merely a reaction. But as the mind understands both the conscious and the unconscious process of itself, then we will see that there is quite a different state—a state which is neither of the collective nor of the separate entity, the individual; he has gone beyond both and therefore is capable of understanding that which is true. The individual who is not in opposition to the collective in his search for truth is really a revolutionary.

And it seems to me that to be a true revolutionary is the essential thing. Such individuals are creative, able to bring about a different world. Because after all, our problems, whether in India, America, Russia, or here, are the same—we are human beings, we want to be happy. We want to have a mind that is capable of deep penetration and that is not merely satisfied with the superficiality of life. We want to go into this most profoundly, individually, to find out that which is the eternal, the everlasting, the unknown. But that thing cannot be found if we are merely pursuing the pattern of conformity. That is why it is important, it seems to me, that there should be some of us who are really earnest, not merely listening with curiosity or just as a passing fancy, but who are really essentially concerned with bringing about transformation in the world so that there can be peace and happiness for each one of us. For this, it seems to me, it is very important that we should cease to think collectively and should as human beings—not as mere repetitive machines of certain dogmas and beliefs—find out, inquire, search out for ourselves, what is true, what is God.

In that discovery is the solution to all our problems. Without that discovery, our problems multiply; there will be more wars, more misery, more sorrow. We may have peace temporarily, through terror. But if we are individuals, in the right sense of that word, seeking that which is real—which can only be found when we understand the whole process, conscious as well as unconscious, of our own thinking—then there is a possibility of such a revolution, which is the only revolution that can bring about a happier state for man.

Question: In Holland there are many people of goodwill. What can we really do in order to work for peace in the world?

KRISHNAMURTI: Why do you restrict the people of goodwill to Holland? (Laughter) Don't you think there are people of goodwill all over the world?

But you see, peace doesn't come about by goodwill; peace is something entirely different. It is not the cessation of war. Peace is a state of the mind; peace is a cessation of the effort to be something, peace is the denial of ambition, the ending of the desire to achieve, to become, to succeed. We think peace is merely the gap, the interval, between two wars. And probably, through the terror of the hydrogen bomb, we shall have peace of some kind or other. But surely, that is not peace. There is peace only when you have no separative nationalities and sovereignties, when you do not consider somebody else as inferior in race, or somebody else as superior, when there are no divisions in religions—you a Christian, and another a Hindu or Buddhist or Muslim.

Peace can only come about when you as an individual work for peace. This does not mean gathering yourselves into groups and working for peace; then what you create will be merely a conformity to a pattern called peace. But to bring about lasting peace is surely something entirely different. After all, how can a man who is ambitious, struggling, competitive, brutal—how can such a man bring about peace in the world? You may say, "What will happen to me if I am not ambitious? Will I not decay? Must I not struggle?" It is because we are ambitious, because we have struggled and pushed each other aside in our desire for achievement, success, that we have created a world in which there are wars.

I think if we could really understand what it is to live without ambition, without this everlasting desire to succeed—either in business, in schools, in the family—if we could really understand the psychological content of ambition, with all the implications that are involved, then we would abandon this meaningless activity. The ambitious man is not a happy man; he is always afraid of frustration, burdened by the misery of effort and struggle. Such a man cannot create a peaceful world. Also, those who believe in a particular form of church—the communist, the Catholic, the Protestant, the Hindu—they are not peaceful people; they can never bring about peace in the world because they are in themselves divided, broken, torn. It is only the integrated human being, he who understands this division and all its corruption—it is only such a human being who can bring about peace.

But we do not want to give up our cherished hopes, our fancies, our beliefs. We want to carry all that into the world of peace. We want to create a world of peace with all the elements that are destructive. Therefore you never have peace. It is only the mind which has understood itself, which is quiet, which does not demand, which is not seeking success, which is not trying to become or to be somebody—it is only such a mind that can create a world in which there is peace.

Question: Is there life after death?

KRISHNAMURTI: I see you are much more interested in that than in the previous question! It is extraordinary how we are interested in death. We are not interested in living, but we are interested in how we are going to die and if there is something after.

Let us go into the problem, if you will, seriously, because it is an enormous problem. To understand the whole implication of the question, one must approach it very carefully, wisely. You cannot approach it wisely if you have any belief about it, if you say—because you have read about it or you have a hope or intuition or a longing for it—that there is life after death. Surely, if you would understand the problem, you must approach it afresh, anew, in a state of mind which is inquiring and not believing, a state of mind which says, "I do not know, but I want to find out,"—not a mind which says there is, or there is not, a continuity after death. Surely, that is fairly obvious. I think that is the first step towards finding out the truth about death

and afterwards; that is the only way to approach any problem, especially a human problem—to say, "I do not know, but I want to find out." To say this is very difficult because most of us have read so much, we have so many desires, so many hopes, so many longings, we are so afraid and therefore already have many conclusions, many beliefs—all telling us that there is some kind of continuity, some kind of life after death. So we have already preconceived what it is; your own fears dictate what it should be.

So, to find out the truth of the matter, is it not important that first there must be freedom from all knowledge concerning death? After all, death is the unknown, and to find out, one must enter into death while living. Please listen. One must have the capacity to enter that which we call death while we are capable of breathing, thinking, acting. Otherwise, if you die—through disease, through accident—then you become unconscious, and there is no understanding of what lies after. But actively to be able while living, with full consciousness, to understand the whole problem of what death is requires astonishing energy, capacity, inquiry.

First, what is it that we are afraid of in death? Surely we are afraid, are we not, of ceasing to be, not having continuity. That is, I either cease to be or I hope to continue. When this thing called the body, the organism, the mechanism, dies, through various forms of disease, accident, or what you will, there is fear of 'me' not continuing. The 'me' is the various qualities, the virtues, the idiosyncrasies, the experiences, the passions, the values which I have cultivated, the memories which I have cherished, and those memories which I have put aside—all that is the 'me', surely. The 'me' that is identified with property, with a house, with a family, with a friend, with a wife, with a husband, with experiences, which has cultivated certain virtues, which wants to do something, which wants to fulfill, which has innumerable memories, pleasant or unpleasant—that 'me' says, "I am afraid, I want an assurance that there is a form of continuity."

Now, that which continues without breaking cannot ever be creative, can it? Creativeness comes into being only when there is the cessation of continuity. If I am merely the result of past yesterdays, and continue to be still the same pattern in the future, it is merely the repetitive form of a certain pattern of thought, a continuity of memory. And such a continuity in time obviously cannot find that which is beyond time. The mind thinks in terms of time—time being yesterday, today, and tomorrow—and such a mind cannot possibly conceive of a state when there is no tomorrow. So it says, "I must have continuity." It can only think in terms of time, and therefore it is everlastingly frightened of death because there may be the cessation of what has been.

The question "Is there life after death?" is really very immature, is it not? Because if one understands the whole process of oneself, the 'me', it is not very important whether you live or do not live afterwards. After all, what is the 'me' except a bundle of memories? Please follow this. The 'me' is merely a bundle of memories, values, experiences. And that 'me' wants to continue. You may say that the 'me' is not the only thing that is—that there is a spiritual entity in that 'me'. If there is a spiritual entity in that 'me', that spirit has no death; it is timeless and beyond time; it cannot be conceived of, it cannot be thought of, it does not know fear. That may be or it may not be. But we are frightened, and what frightens us is the cessation of the 'me' that is the product of time. So as long as I think in terms of time and death and fear, there can never be the discovery of that which is beyond time.

Unfortunately, we want a categorical answer, yes or no, to the question whether there is life after death. If I may point out, such a categorical answer is really quite an immature demand because life has no categorical answer, yes or no. It requires enormous penetration, insight, inquiry, to find out what is that state of mind which is beyond death. That is far more important than merely to inquire if there is life after death. Even if there is, what of it? You will be just as miserable, just as unhappy, in conflict and misery, struggling to fulfill, and all the rest of it. But if you will understand the whole process of the self, the 'me', and let the mind free itself from its own considerations, from its own bondages, and therefore be still, then you will find the question of death has very little significance. Then death is part of living. While we are concerned with living, there is no death. Life is not an ending and a beginning. Life cannot be understood if there is fear of death, or anxiety to find out what lies beyond.

All this requires enormous maturity and totality of thinking. But we are too impatient, we are too anxious, we want to have an immediate answer, we do not want to sit down and inquire—not through books, not through some authority, but to inquire within ourselves. To penetrate the many layers of our own consciousness and find out what is the truth requires patience, serious endeavor, and a constancy of intention.

Question: We are used to prayer. I have heard it said that meditation, as practiced in the East, is a form of prayer. Is this right?

KRISHNAMURTI: Do not let us bother about what the East practices or does not practice. Let us consider meditation and prayer and see if there is a difference.

What do we mean by prayer? Essentially, is it not supplication, a petition, a demand to something which we consider higher? I have a problem, I am miserable, I suffer; and I pray for an answer, for a meaning, a significance. I am in trouble and worn out with anxiety, and I pray. That is, I ask, I demand, I beg, I petition. And obviously, there is an answer, and we attribute it to something extraordinarily high; we say it is from God. But is it? Or, is it the response of the deep unconscious?

Please, do not brush this aside, thinking that I am merely repeating psychoanalytical things. We are trying to inquire. Surely, God must be something totally beyond the demands of my particular worries, of my particular wounds and frustrations and hopes. God, or truth, must be something totally outside of time, unimaginable, unknowable by the mind that is conditioned, that is suffering. But if I can understand what is sorrow and how sorrow comes into being, then there is no petition, then the understanding of sorrow is the beginning of meditation.

Prayer is entirely different from meditation. Prayer is the repetition of certain words that bring quietness to the mind. If you repeat certain words, phrases, obviously it quietens the mind. And in that quietude there may be certain responses, a certain alleviation of suffering. But suffering returns again because sorrow has not been fully fathomed and understood. So, suffering is the problem, not whether you should pray or not. The man who suffers is anxious to find an answer, an alleviation, a cessation of his sorrow, so he looks to somebody—maybe a medical doctor, or to a priest, or to "something beyond." But he has not solved the fundamental problem of sorrow, so any answer that he may receive surely cannot be from the most supreme; it must be from the unconscious depths of the collective, or from himself.

The understanding of sorrow is the beginning of meditation because without understanding the whole process of sorrow, of desire, of struggle, of the innumerable efforts that we make to achieve, to succeed—

without understanding the whole process of the self, the 'me'—sorrow is inevitable. You may pray as much as you will, go to church, repeat on your knees, but so long as the self, that seed of sorrow, is not understood, the mere repetition of words is nothing more than self-hypnosis. Whereas, if one begins to understand the process of sorrow by watching—without condemning, without judging—observing in the mirror of relationship all our words and our gestures, our attitudes, our values, then the mind can go deeper and deeper into the whole problem. Such a process is meditation.

But there is no system of meditation. If you meditate according to a system, you are merely following another pattern of thinking, which will only lead to the result which that pattern offers. But if you are able to be aware of every thought, every feeling, and so uncover the various layers of consciousness, both the outward and the inward, then you will see that such meditation brings about a quietness of the mind, a state in which there is no movement of any kind, a complete stillness—which is not of death. It is only then that one is capable of receiving that which is eternal.

May 22, 1955

Fourth Talk in Amsterdam

I think if each one of us could seriously inquire into what it is that we are each seeking, then perhaps our endeavor to find something lasting may have some significance. For surely, most of us are seeking something. Either the search is the outcome of some deep frustration or it is the outcome of an escape from the reality of our daily life, or the search is a means of avoiding the various problems of life. I think our seriousness depends on what it is we are seeking. Most of us, unfortunately, are very superficial, and we do not perhaps know how to go deeply, to dig profoundly, so as to reach something more than the mere reactions of the mind.

So I think it is important to find out what it is that we are seeking, each one of us, and why we are seeking—what the motive is, the intention, the purpose, that lies behind this search. I think in discovering what it is that we are seeking, and why we are seeking, we may be able to discover, each one of us, how to go very deeply into ourselves. Most of us, I feel, are very superficial; we just remain struggling on the surface, not being able to go beyond the mere superficial responses of pleasure and pain. If we are able to go beyond the surface, then we may be able to find out for ourselves that our very search may be a hindrance.

What is it that we are seeking? Most of us are unhappy, or we are frustrated, or some desire is urging us to move forwards. For most of us, I think, the search is based on some kind of frustration, some kind of misery. We want to fulfill, in some form or another, at different levels of our existence. And when we find we cannot fulfill, then there is frustration—in relationship, in action, and in every form of our emotional existence. Being frustrated, we seek ways and means to escape from that frustration; and so we move from one hindrance to another, from one blockage to another, always trying to find a way to fulfill, to be happy.

So our search—though we may say we are seeking truth or God or what you will—is really a form of self-fulfillment. Therefore it invariably remains very superficial. I think it is important to understand this profoundly. Because I do not think we will find anything of great significance unless we are capable of going very deeply into ourselves. We cannot go very deeply into ourselves if our search is merely the outcome of some frustration, the desire for an answer which will bring about a superficial response of happiness. So I think

it is worthwhile to find out what it is that each one of us wants, seeks, gropes after. Because on that depends what we find. And if there is no frustration, no misery, only a sense of finding a haven where the mind can rest, where the mind can find a refuge from all disturbance, then also such a search will inevitably lead to something superficial, passing, and trivial.

Now is it possible for us, for each one of us, to find out what it is that we are seeking and why we seek? In the process of our search we acquire knowledge, gather experience, do we not, and according to that gathering, that accumulation, our experiences are shaped. Those experiences then in turn become our guide. But all such experience is essentially based on our desire to be secure in some form or another, in this world or in an imaginary world or in the world of heaven, because our mind demands, seeks, searches out, a place where it will not be disturbed. In the process of this seeking there is frustration, and with frustration there is sorrow.

Now, is there ever any security for the mind? We may seek it, we may grope after it; we may build a culture, a society, which assures physical security at least, and we may thereby find some kind of security in things, in property, in ideas, in relationship; but, is there such a thing as security for the mind—a state of mind in which there will be no disturbance of any kind? And, is that not what most of us are seeking, in devious ways, giving it different terms, different words? Surely, a mind that is seeking security must always invite frustration. We have never inquired, most of us, whether there can be security for the mind—a state in which there is no disturbance of any kind. And yet, if we look deeply into ourselves, that is what most of us want, and we seek to create that security for ourselves in various forms—in beliefs, in ideals, in our attachments and our relationship with people, with property, with family, and so on.

Now, is there any security, any permanency, in the things of the mind? The mind, after all, is the result of time, of centuries of education, of molding, of change. The mind is the result of time and therefore a plaything of time—and can such a mind ever find a state of permanency? Or, must the mind always be in a state of impermanency?

I think it is important to go into this and to understand that most of us are seeking, not knowing what we want. The motive of the search is far more important than that which we are seeking, for if that motive is for security, a sense of permanency, then the mind creates its own hindrances, from which arise frustration and therefore sorrow and suffering. Then we seek further escapes, further means of avoiding pain, and so invite more sorrow. That is our state; that is the complex existence of our everyday life. Whereas, if we could remain with ourselves, if we could look to find out what the motive is of our search, of our struggle, then perhaps we would find the right answer. It is like accumulating knowledge—knowledge may give a certain security, but a man who is filled with knowledge obviously cannot find that which is beyond the mind.

So, is it not important to find out what it is that we are seeking, and why we seek, and also to inquire whether there can be an end to all seeking? Because, search implies effort, does it not?—the constant inquiry, the constant struggle to find. Can one find anything through effort? By "anything" I mean something more than the mere reactions of the mind, the mere responses of the mind, something other than the things that the mind itself has created and projected. Is it not important for each one of us to inquire if there is ever an end to the search? Because, the more we search, the greater the strain, the ef-fort, the dilemma of not finding, and the frustration.

Please let us consider this carefully. Do not let us say, "What will happen to us if there is no seeking?" Surely, if we seek with a motive, then the result of that search will be dictated by the motive, and so it will be limited; and from that limitation there is always frustration and sorrow, and in that we are all caught. So, is there existence without seeking? Is there a state of being without this constant becoming? The becoming is the struggle, the conflict; and that is our life. Is it not important for each one of us to find out whether there is a state in which this process of constant strife, constant conflict within ourselves, the contradictions, the opposing desires, the frustrations, the misery, can come to an end?—but not through some form of an invention or an image of the mind.

That is why it is so important to have self-knowledge—not the knowledge that one learns from books, from the hearsay of another, or from listening to a few talks, but to be constantly aware, just to observe, without choice, what is actually going on within the mind—observing all the reactions, to be alert in our relationships so that all the ways of our search, of our motives, of our fears, of our frustrations, are revealed. Because, if we do not know the origin of our thinking, the motive of our action, what the unconscious drive is, then all our thinking must inevitably be superficial and without very great significance. You may have superficial values; you may mouth that you believe in God, that you are seeking truth, and all the rest of it; but without knowing the inward nature of your own mind, the motive, the pursuit, the unconscious drive— which is all revealed as one observes oneself in the mirror of relationship—there is only sorrow and pain.

And I think that process of observation is seriousness. It is not giving oneself up to any particular idea, to any belief, to any dogma, or being caught in some idiosyncrasy; that is not seriousness. To be serious implies the awareness of the content of one's own mind—just to observe it without trying to distort it—as when one sees one's face in the mirror; it is what it is. So, likewise, if we can observe our thoughts, our feelings, our whole being, in the mirror of relationship, of everyday activity, then we will find that there is no frustration of any kind. So long as we are seeking fulfillment in any form, there must be frustration. Because fulfillment implies the pursuit and the exaggeration of the self, the 'me'; and the 'me', the self, is the very cause of sorrow. To understand the whole content of that 'me', the self—all the layers of its consciousness with its accumulations of knowledge, of likes and dislikes—to be aware of all that, without judgment, without condemnation, is to be really serious.

That seriousness is the instrument with which the mind can go beyond the limitations of itself. After all, we want to find, do we not, a sense of something greater than the mere inventions of the mind, something which is beyond the mind, something which is not a mere projection. If we can understand the mind—the mind which is in me and in you, with all its subtleties, its deceptions, its various forms of urges—in that very understanding there is an ending of its binding activities.

It is only when the mind no longer has any motive that it is possible for it to be still. In that stillness, a reality which is not the creation of the mind comes into being.

Question: A man fully occupied is kept busy day and night in his own subconsciousness with practical problems which have to be solved. Your vision can only be realized in the stillness of self-awareness. There is hardly any time for stillness; the immediate is too urgent. Can you give any practical suggestion?

KRISHNAMURTI: Sir, what do we mean by "practical suggestion"? Something that you should do immediately? Some system that you should practice in order to produce a stillness of the mind? After all, if you practice a system, that system will produce a result; but it will only be the result of the system, and not your own discovery, not that which you find in being aware of yourself in your contacts in daily life. A system obviously produces its own result. However much you may practice it, for whatever length of time, the result will always be dictated by the system, the method. It will not be a discovery; it will be a thing imposed on the mind through its desire to find a way out of this chaotic, sorrowful world.

So what is one to do when one is so busy, occupied night and day, as most people are, with earning a livelihood? First of all, is one occupied the whole of the time with business, with a livelihood? Or does one have periods during the day when you are not so occupied? I think those periods when you are not so occupied are far more important than the periods with which you are occupied. It is very important, is it not, to find out what the mind is occupied with. If it is occupied, consciously occupied, with business affairs all the time—which is really impossible—then there is obviously no space, no quietness, in which to find anything new. Fortunately, most of us are not occupied entirely with our business, and there are moments when we can probe into ourselves, be aware. I think those periods are far more significant than our periods of occupation, and if we allow it, those moments will begin to shape, to control, our business activities, our daily life.

After all, the conscious mind, the mind that is so occupied, obviously has no time for any deeper thought. But the conscious mind is not the whole entirety of the mind; there is also the unconscious part. And, can the conscious mind delve into the unconscious? That is, can the conscious mind, the mind that wants to inquire, to analyze—can that probe into the unconscious? Or, must the conscious mind be still in order for the unconscious to give its hints, its intimations? Is the unconscious so very different from the conscious? Or, is the totality of the mind the conscious as well as the unconscious? The totality of the mind as we know it, conscious and unconscious, is educated, is conditioned, with all the various impositions of culture, tradition, and memory. And perhaps the answer to all our problems is not within the field of the mind at all; it may be outside it. To find that which is the true answer to all the complex problems of our existence, of our daily struggle, surely the mind, the conscious as well as the unconscious, must be totally still, must it not?

And the questioner wants to know, when he is so busy, what shall he do? Surely he is not so busy—surely he does amuse himself occasionally? If he begins to give some time during the day, five minutes, ten minutes, half-an-hour, in order to reflect upon these matters, then that very reflection brings longer periods in which he will have time to think, to delve. So I do not think mere superficial occupation of the mind has much significance. There is something far more important—which is, to find out the operation of the mind, the ways of our own thinking: the motives, the urges, the memories, the traditions, in which the mind is caught. And we can do that while we are earning our livelihood so that we become fully conscious of ourselves and our peculiarities. Then I think it is possible for the mind to be really quiet, and so to find that which is beyond its own projections.

Question: All my life I have been dependent for happiness on some other person or persons. How can I develop the capacity to live with myself and stand alone?

KRISHNAMURTI: Why do we depend on another for our happiness? Is it because in ourselves we are empty and we look to another to fill that emptiness? And, is that emptiness, that loneliness, that sense of extraordinary limitation, to be overcome by any capacity? If it is to be overcome—that emptiness—through any system or capacity or idea, then you will depend on that idea or on that system. Now, I depend perhaps on a person. I feel empty, lonely—a complete sense of isolation—and I depend on somebody. And if I develop or have a method which will help me to overcome that dependence, then I depend on that method. I have only substituted a method for a person.

So, what is important in this is to find out what it means to be empty. After all, we depend on someone for our happiness because in ourselves we are not happy. I do not know what it is to love; therefore, I depend on another to love me. Now, can I fathom this emptiness in myself, this sense of complete isolation, loneliness? Do we ever come face to face with it at all? Or, are we always frightened of it, always running away from it? The very process of running away from that loneliness is dependence. So can my mind realize the truth that any form of running away from *what is* creates dependence, from which arises misfortune and sorrow? Can I just understand that—that I depend on another for my happiness because in myself I am empty, and therefore I depend. That dependence causes misery. Running away in any form from that emptiness is not a solution at all—whether we run away through a person, an idea, a belief, or God, or meditation, or what you will. To run away from the fact of *what is* is of no avail. In oneself there is insufficiency, poverty of being. Just to realize that fact and to remain with that fact—knowing that any movement of the mind to alter the fact is another form of dependence—in that, there is freedom.

After all, however much you may have of experience, knowledge, belief, and ideas, in itself, if you observe, the mind is empty. You may stuff it with ideas, with incessant activity, with distractions, with every form of addiction, but the moment one ceases any form of that activity, one is aware that the mind is totally empty. Now, can one remain with that emptiness? Can the mind face that emptiness, that fact, and remain with that fact? It is very difficult and arduous because the mind is so used to distraction, so trained to go away from *what is,* to turn on the radio, to pick up a book, to talk, to go to church, to go to a meeting—anything to enable it to wander away from the central fact that the mind in itself is empty. However much it may struggle to cover up that fact, it is empty in itself. When once it realizes that fact, can the mind remain in that state, without any movement whatsoever?

I think most of us are aware—perhaps only rarely since most of us are so terribly occupied and active—but I think we are aware sometimes that the mind is empty. And, being aware, we are afraid of that emptiness. We have never inquired into that state of emptiness, we have never gone into it deeply, profoundly; we are afraid, and so we wander away from it. We have given it a name—we say it is "empty," it is "terrible," it is "painful"; and that very giving it a name has already created a reaction in the mind, a fear, an avoidance, a running away. Now, can the mind stop running away, and not give it a name, not give it the sig-

nificance of a word such as *empty* about which we have memories of pleasure and pain? Can we look at it, can the mind be aware of that emptiness without naming it, without running away from it, without judging it, but just be with it? Because, then that is the mind. Then there is not an observer looking at it; there is no censor who condemns it; there is only that state of emptiness—with which we are all really quite familiar, but which we are all avoiding, trying to fill it with activity, with worship, with prayer, with knowledge, with every form of illusion and excitement. But when all the excitement, illusion, fear, running away stops, and you are no longer giving it a name and thereby condemning it, is the observer different then from the thing which is observed? Surely by giving it a name, by condemning it, the mind has created a censor, an observer, outside of itself. But when the mind does not give it a term, a name, condemn it, judge it, then there is no observer, only a state of that thing we have called "emptiness."

Perhaps this may sound abstract. But if you will kindly follow what has been said, I am sure you will find that there is a state which may be called emptiness but which does not evoke fear, escape, or the attempt to cover it up. All that stops when you really want to find out. Then, if the mind is no longer giving it a name, condemning it, is there emptiness? Are we then conscious of being poor and therefore dependent, of being unhappy and therefore demanding, attached? If you are no longer giving it a label, a name, and thereby condemning it—the state which is perceived, is it any longer emptiness, or is it something totally different?

If you can go into this very earnestly, you will find that there is no dependence at all on anything—on any person, on any belief, on any experience, any tradition. Then, that which is beyond emptiness is creativeness—

the creativity of reality, not the creativity of a talent or capacity, but the creativity of that which is beyond fear, beyond all demand, beyond all the tricks of the mind.

Question: Will evolution help us to find God?

KRISHNAMURTI: I do not know what you mean by evolution, and what you mean by God. I think this is a fairly important question to go into because most of us think in terms of time—time being the distance, the interval, between what I am and what I should be, the ideal. What I am is unpleasant, something to be changed, to be molded into something which it is not. And to shape it, to give it respectability, to give it beauty, I need time. That is, I am cruel, greedy, or what you will, and I need time to transform that into the ideal—the ideal may be called what you will, that is not of great importance. So, we are always thinking in terms of time.

And the questioner wants to know if through time that which is beyond time can be realized. We do not know what is beyond time. We are slaves to time; our whole mind thinks in terms of yesterday, today, or tomorrow. And being caught in that, the questioner wants to know if the ideal can be reached through the process of time. There is obviously some form of evolution, growth—from the simple car to the jet plane, from the oil lamp to electricity, the acquiring of more knowledge, more technique, developing and exploiting the earth, and so on. Obviously, technologically there is progress, evolution, growth. But, is there a growth or evolution beyond that? Is there something in the mind which is beyond time—the spirit, the soul, or whatever you like to call it? That which is capable of growth, of evolving, becoming, obviously is not part of the eternal, of something which is beyond time; it is still in time. If the soul, the spiritual entity, is capable of

growth, then it is still the invention of the mind. If it is not the invention of the mind, it is of no time; therefore, we need not bother about it. What we do have to be concerned with is whether through time the inward nature, the inward being, changes at all.

The mind is obviously the result of time; your mind and my mind are the result of a series of educations, experiences, cultures, a variety of thoughts, impressions, strains, stresses, all of which has made us what we are now. And with that mind we are trying to find out something which is beyond time. But surely God, or truth, or whatever it is must be totally new, must be something inconceivable, unknowable by the mind, which is the result of time. So, can that mind, which is the result of time, of tradition, of memory, of culture, can that mind come to an end?—voluntarily, not by being drilled, not by being put into a straitjacket. Can the mind, which is the result of time, bring about its own end?

After all, what is the mind? Thought—the capacity to think. And thinking is the reaction of memory, of association, of the various values, beliefs, traditions, experiences—conscious or unconscious; that is the background from which all thought springs. Can one be really aware of all that and thereby enable thought to come to an end? Because thought is the result of time, and thinking obviously cannot bring about or reveal that which is beyond itself. Surely, only when the mind, as thought, as memory, comes to an end, only when it is completely, utterly still, without any movement—then alone is it possible for that which is beyond the responses of the mind to come into being.

May 23, 1955

Fifth Talk in Amsterdam

Perhaps you would kindly listen to rather a difficult problem with which I am sure most of us are concerned. It is a problem we are all confronted with—the problem of change—and I feel one must go into it rather fully to understand it comprehensively. We see that there must be change. And we see that change implies various forms of exertion of will, effort. In it is also involved the question of what it is we are changing from and what it is we want to change to. It seems to me that one must go into it rather deeply and not merely be contented with a superficial answer. Because the thing that is involved in it is quite significant and requires a certain form of attention, which I hope you will give.

For most of us it is very important to change; we feel it is necessary for us to change. We are dissatisfied as we are—at least, most of the people are who are at all serious and thoughtful—and we want to change; we see the necessity of change. But I do not think we see the whole significance of it, and I would like to discuss that matter with you. If I may suggest it, please listen, not with any definite conclusion, not expecting a definite answer, but so that by going into the matter together, we may understand the problem comprehensively.

Every form of effort that we make in order to bring about a change implies, does it not, the following of a certain pattern, a certain ideal, the exertion of will, a desire to be achieved. We change, either through circumstances, forced by environment, through necessity, or we discipline ourselves to change according to an ideal. Those are the forms of change that we are aware of—either through circumstances which compel us to modify, to adjust, to conform to a certain pattern, social, religious, or family, or we discipline ourselves according to an ideal. In that discipline there is a conformity, the effort to conform to a certain pattern of thought, to achieve a certain ideal.

The change that is brought about through the exertion of will—with this process we are, most of us, familiar. We all know of this change through compulsion, change through fear, change made necessary by suffering. It is a modification, a constant struggle in order to conform to a certain pattern which we have established for ourselves, or which society has given us. That is what we call "change," and in that we are caught. But, is it change? I think it is important to understand this, to somewhat analyze it, to go into the anatomy of change, to understand what makes us want to change. Because all this implies, does it not, either conscious or unconscious conformity, conscious or unconscious yielding to a certain pattern, through necessity, through expediency. And we are content to continue in modified change, which is merely an outward adjustment—putting on, as it were, a new coat of a different color, but inwardly remaining static. So I would like to talk it over, to find out if that effort really brings about a real change in us.

Our problem is how to bring about an inward revolution which does not necessitate mere conformity to a pattern, or an adjustment through fear, or making great effort, through the exertion of the will, to be something. That is our problem, isn't it? We all want to change; we see the necessity of it unless we are totally blind and completely conservative, refusing to break the pattern of our existence. Surely most of us who are at all serious are concerned with this—how to bring about in ourselves and thereby in the world a radical change, a radical transformation. After all, we are not any different from the rest of the world. Our problem is the world problem. What we are, of that we make the world. So, if as individuals we can understand this question of effort and change, then perhaps we shall be able to understand if it is possible to bring about a radical change in which there is no exertion of will.

I hope the problem is clear. That is, we know that change is necessary. But into what must we change? And how is that change to be brought about? We know that the change which we generally think is necessary is always brought about through the exertion of will. I am "this," and I must change into something else. The "something else" is already thought out, it is projected—it is an end to be desired, an ideal which must be fulfilled. Surely that is our way of thinking about change—as a constant adjustment, either voluntarily, or through suffering, or through the exertion of will. That implies, does it not, a constant effort, the reaction of a certain desire, of a certain conditioning. And so the change is merely a modified continuity of what has been.

Let us go into it. I am something, and I want to change. So I choose an ideal, and according to that ideal I try to transform myself, I exert my will, I discipline, I force myself; and there is a constant battle going on between what I am and what I should be. With that we are all familiar. And the ideal, what I think I should be—is it not merely the opposite of what I am? Is it not merely the reaction of what I am? I am angry, and I project the ideal of peace, of love, and I try to conform myself to the ideal of love, to the ideal of peace; and so there is a constant struggle. But the ideal is not real; it is my projection of what I would like to be—it is the outcome of my pain, my suffering, my background. So the ideal has no significance at all; it is merely the result of my desire to be something which I am not. I am merely struggling to achieve something which I would like to be, so it is still within the pattern of self-enclosing action. That is so, is it not? I am "this," and I would like to be "that," but the struggle to be something different is still within the pattern of my desire.

So, is not all our talk about the necessity of change very superficial unless we first uncover the deep process of our thinking? So long as I have a motive for change, is there a real change? My motive is to change myself from anger into a state of peace. Because, I find that a state of peace is much more suitable, much more convenient, more happy; therefore, I struggle to achieve that. But it is still within the pattern of my own desire, and so there is no change at all—I have only gathered a different word, *peace* instead of *anger,* but essentially I am still the same. So, the problem is, is it not, how to bring about a change at the center, and not to continue this constant adjustment to a pattern, to an idea, through fear, through compulsion, through environmental influence. Is it not possible to bring about a radical change at the very center itself? If there is a change there, then naturally any form of adjustment becomes unnecessary. Compulsion, effort, a disciplining process according to an ideal, is then seen as totally unnecessary and false because all those imply a constant struggle, a constant battle between myself and what I should be.

Now, is it possible to bring about a change at the center?—the center being the self, the 'me' that is always acquiring, always trying to conform, trying to adjust, but remaining essentially the same. I hope I am making the problem clear. Any conscious deliberate effort to change is merely the continuity, in a modified form, of what has been, is it not? I am greedy, and if I deliberately, consciously, set about to change that quality into nongreed, is not that very effort to be nongreedy still the product of the self, the 'me', and therefore there is no radical change at all? When I consciously make an effort to be nongreedy, then that conscious effort is the result of another form of greed, surely. Yet on that principle all our disciplines, all our attempts to change, are based. We are either consciously changing or submitting to the pattern of society, or being pushed by society to conform—all of which are various forms of deliberate effort on our part to be something or other. So, where there is conscious effort to change, obviously the change is merely the conformity to another pattern; it is still within the enclosing process of the self, and therefore it is not a change at all.

So can I see the truth of that; can I realize, understand, the full significance of the fact that any conscious effort on my part to be something other than what I am only produces still further suffering, sorrow, and pain? Then follows the question: Is it possible to bring about a change at the center without the conscious effort to change? Is it possible for me, without effort, without the exertion of will, to stop being greedy, acquisitive, envious, angry, what you will? If I change consciously, if my mind is occupied with greed and I try to change it into nongreed, obviously that is still a form of greed because my mind is concerned, occupied, with being something. So, is it possible for me to change, at the center, this whole process of acquisitiveness, without any conscious action on the part of my mind to be nonacquisitive?

So, our problem is: Being what I am—acquisitive—how is that to be transformed? I feel I understand very well that any exertion on my part to change is part of a self-conscious endeavor to be nongreedy, nonacquisitive—which is still acquisitiveness. So what is to be done? How is the change at the center to be brought about? If I understand the truth that all conscious effort is another form of acquisitiveness, if I really understand that, if I fully grasp the significance of it, then I will cease to make any conscious effort, will I not? Consciously, I will stop exercising my will to change my acquisitiveness. That is the first thing. Because, I see that any conscious effort, any action of will, is another form of acquisitiveness; therefore, understanding that

completely, there is the cessation of any deliberate practice to achieve the nonacquisitive state.

If I have understood that, what happens? If my mind is no longer struggling to change acquisitiveness—either through compulsion, through fear, through moral sanctions, through religious threats, through social laws, and all the rest of it—then what happens to my mind? How do I then look at greed? I hope you are following this because it is very interesting to see how the mind works. When we think we are changing, trying to adjust, trying to conform, disciplining ourselves to an ideal, actually there is no change at all. That is a tremendous discovery; that is a great revelation. A mind occupied with nonacquisitiveness is an acquisitive mind. Before, it was occupied with being acquisitive; now it is occupied with nonacquisitiveness. It is still occupied, so the very occupation is acquisitiveness.

Now, is it possible for the mind to be nonoccupied? I hope you are following this because, you see, all our minds are occupied—occupied with something, occupied with God, with virtue, with what people say or don't say, whether someone loves you or doesn't love you. Always the mind is occupied. It was occupied before with acquisitiveness, and now it is occupied with nonacquisitiveness—but it's still occupied. So, the problem is really: Can the mind be unoccupied? Because if it is not occupied, then it can tackle the problem of acquisitiveness and not merely try to change it into nonacquisitiveness. Can the mind which has been occupied with acquisitiveness, can it, without turning to nonacquisitiveness—which is another occupation of the mind—put an end to all occupation? Surely it can, but only when it sees the truth that acquisitiveness and nonacquisitiveness are the same state of occupation. So long as the mind is occupied with something, obviously there cannot be a change. Whether it is occupied with God, with virtue, with dress, with love, with cruelty to animals, with the radio—they're all the same. There is no higher occupation or lower occupation; all occupation is essentially the same. The mind, being occupied, escapes from itself; it escapes through greed, it escapes through nongreed. So can the mind, seeing all this complex process, put an end to its own occupation?

I think that is the whole problem. Because, when the mind is not occupied, then it is fresh, it is clear, it is capable of meeting any problem anew. When it is not occupied, then, being fresh, it can tackle acquisitiveness with a totally different action. So our question, our inquiry, our exploration, then is—can the mind be unoccupied? Please do not jump to conclusions. Do not say it must then be vague, blank, lost. We are inquiring; therefore, there can be no conclusion, no definite statement, no supposition, no theory, no speculation. Can the mind be unoccupied? If you say, "How am I to achieve a state of mind in which there is no occupation?" then that "how to achieve" becomes another occupation. Please see the simplicity of it and, therefore, the truth of the whole matter.

It is very important for you to find out how you are listening to this, how you are listening to these statements. They are merely statements, which you should neither accept nor reject; they are simply facts. How are you listening to the fact? Do you condemn it? Do you say, "It is impossible"? Do you say, "I don't understand what you are talking about; it's too difficult, too abstract"? Or, are you listening to find out the truth of the matter? To see the truth without any distortion, without translating the fact into your own particular terminology or your own fancy—just to see clearly, just to be fully conscious of what is being said, is sufficient. Then you will find that your mind is no

longer occupied; therefore, it is fresh and so, capable of meeting the problem of change entirely, totally differently.

Whether change is brought about consciously or unconsciously, it is still the same. Conscious change implies effort, and unconscious endeavor to bring about a change also implies an effort, a struggle. So long as there is a struggle, conflict, the change is merely enforced, and there is no understanding; and therefore it is no longer a change at all. So, is the mind capable of meeting the problem of change—of acquisitiveness, for example— without making an effort, just seeing the whole implication of acquisitiveness? Because, you cannot see the whole content of acquisitiveness totally so long as there is any endeavor to change it. Real change can only take place when the mind comes to the problem afresh, not with all the jaded memories of a thousand yesterdays. Obviously, you cannot have a fresh, eager mind if the mind is occupied. And the mind ceases to be occupied only when it sees the truth about its own occupation. You cannot see the truth if you are not giving your whole attention, if you are translating what is being said into something which will suit you, or translating it into your own terms. You must come to something new with a fresh mind, and a mind is not fresh when it is occupied, consciously or unconsciously.

This transformation really takes place when the mind understands the whole process of itself; therefore, self-knowledge is essential—not self-knowledge according to some psychologist or some book, but the self-knowledge that you discover from moment to moment. That self-knowledge is not to be gathered up and put into the mind as memory because if you have gathered it, stored it up, any new experience will be translated according to that old memory. So self-knowledge is a state in which everything is observed, experienced, understood, and put away—not put away in memory, but cast aside so that the mind is all the time fresh, eager.

Question: The world in which we live is confused, and I too am confused. How am I to be free of this confusion?

KRISHNAMURTI: It is one of the most difficult things to know for oneself, not merely superficially but actually, that one is confused. One will never admit that. We are always hoping there may be some clarity, some loophole through which there will come understanding, so we never admit to ourselves that we are actually confused. We never admit that we are acquisitive, that we are angry, that we are this or that; there are always excuses, always explanations. But to know, really, "I am confused"—that is one of the most important things to acknowledge to oneself. Are we not all confused? If you were very clear, if you knew what is true, you wouldn't be here, you wouldn't be chasing teachers, reading books, attending psychological classes, going to churches, pursuing the priest, the confession, and all the rest of it. To know for oneself that one is confused is really an extraordinarily difficult thing.

That is the first thing—to know that one is confused. Now, what happens when one is confused? Any endeavor—please follow this —any endeavor to become nonconfused is still confusion. (Murmur of amusement) Please, listen quietly, and you will see. When a confused mind makes an effort to be nonconfused, that very effort is the outcome of confusion, is it not? Therefore, whatever it does, whatever pursuit, whatever activity, whatever religion, whatever book it picks up, it is still in a state of confusion; therefore, it cannot possibly understand. Its leaders, its priests, its religions, its relationships must all

be confused. That is what is happening in the world, is it not? You have chosen your political leaders, your religious leaders, out of your confusion.

If we understand that any action arising out of confusion is still confused, then, first we must stop all action—which most of us are unwilling to do. The confused mind in action only creates more confusion. You may laugh, you may smile, but you really do not feel that you are confused and that therefore you must stop acting. Surely, that is the first thing. If I have lost myself in a wood, I don't go round chasing all over the place; I just stop still. If I am confused, I don't pursue a guide, keep asking someone how to get out of confusion. Because any answer he gives and I receive will be translated according to my confusion; therefore, it will be no answer at all. I think it is most difficult to realize that whenever one is confused, one must stop all activity, psychologically. I am not talking of outward activity—going to business and all the rest of it—but inwardly, psychologically, one must see the necessity of putting an end to all search, to all pursuits, to all desire to change. It is only when the confused mind abstains from any movement that out of that stopping comes clarity.

But it is very difficult for the mind, when it is confused, not to seek, not to ask, not to pray, not to escape—just to remain in confusion and inquire what it is, why one is confused. Only then will one find out how confusion arises. Confusion arises when I do not understand myself, when my thoughts are guided by the priests, by the politicians, by the newspapers, by every psychological book that one reads. Contradiction—in myself and in the people I am trying to follow—arises when there is imitation, when there is fear. So it is important, if we would clear up confusion, to understand the process of confusion within oneself. For that, there must be the stopping of all pursuits, psychologically.

It is only then that the mind, through its own understanding of itself, brings about clarity so that it is aware of the whole process of its own thoughts and motives. Such a mind becomes very clear, simple, direct.

Question: Will you please explain what you mean by awareness.

KRISHNAMURTI: Just simple awareness! Awareness of your judgments, your prejudices, your likes and dislikes. When you see something, that seeing is the outcome of your comparison, condemnation, judgment, evaluation, is it not? When you read something, you are judging, you are criticizing, you are condemning or approving. To be aware is to see, in the very moment, this whole process of judging, evaluating, the conclusions, the conformity, the acceptances, the denials.

Now, can one be aware without all that? At present all we know is a process of evaluating, and that evaluation is the outcome of our conditioning, of our background, of our religious, moral, and educational influences. Such so-called awareness is the result of our memory—memory as the 'me', the Dutchman, the Hindu, the Buddhist, the Catholic, or whatever it may be. It is the 'me'—my memories, my family, my property, my qualities—which is looking, judging, evaluating. With that we are quite familiar, if we are at all alert. Now, can there be awareness without all that, without the self? Is it possible just to look without condemnation, just to observe the movement of the mind, one's own mind, without judging, without evaluating, without saying, "It is good," or "It is bad"?

The awareness which springs from the self, which is the awareness of evaluation and judgment, always creates duality, the conflict of the opposites—that *which is* and that 'which should be'. In that awareness there is judgment, there is fear, there is evaluation, condemnation, identification. That is but the awareness of the 'me', of the self, of the 'I', with all its traditions, memories, and all the rest of it. Such awareness always creates conflict between the observer and the observed, between what I am and what I should be. Now, is it possible to be aware without this process of condemnation, judgment, evaluation? Is it possible to look at myself, whatever my thoughts are, and not condemn, not judge, not evaluate? I do not know if you have ever tried it. It is quite arduous because all our training from childhood leads us to condemn or to approve. And in the process of condemnation and approval, there is frustration, there is fear, there is a gnawing pain, anxiety, which is the very process of the 'me', the self.

So, knowing all that, can the mind, without effort, without trying not to condemn—because the moment it says, "I mustn't condemn," it is already caught in the process of condemnation—can the mind be aware without judgment? Can it just watch, with dispassion, and so observe the very thoughts and feelings themselves in the mirror of relationship—relationship with things, with people, and with ideas? Such silent observation does not breed aloofness, an icy intellectualism—on the contrary. If I would understand something, obviously there must be no condemnation, there must be no comparison—surely, that is simple. But we think understanding comes through comparison so we multiply comparisons. Our education is comparative, and our whole moral, religious structure is to compare and condemn.

So, the awareness of which I am speaking is the awareness of the whole process of condemnation, and the ending of it. In that there is observation without any judgment—which is extremely difficult; it implies the cessation, the ending, of all terming, naming. When I am aware that I am greedy, acquisitive, angry, passionate, or what you will, is it not possible just to observe it, to be aware of it, without condemning?—which means putting an end to the very naming of the feeling. For when I give a name, such as *greed*, that very naming is the process of condemning. To us, neurologically, the very word greed is already a condemnation. To free the mind from all condemnation means putting an end to all naming. After all, the naming is the process of the thinker. It is the thinker separating himself from thought—which is a totally artificial process—it is unreal. There is only thinking; there is no thinker; there is only a state of experiencing, not the entity who experiences.

So, this whole process of awareness, observation, is the process of meditation. It is, if I can put it differently, the willingness to invite thought. For most of us, thoughts come in without invitation—one thought after another; there is no end to thinking; the mind is a slave to every kind of vagrant thought. If you realize that, then you will see that there can be an invitation to thought—an inviting of thought and then a pursuing of every thought that arises. For most of us, thought comes uninvited; it comes any old way. To understand that process, and then to invite thought and pursue that thought through to the end, is the whole process which I have described as awareness; and in that there is no naming. Then you will see that the mind becomes extraordinarily quiet—not through fatigue, not through discipline, not through any form of self-torture and control. Through awareness of its own activities, the mind becomes astonishingly quiet, still, creative— without the action of any discipline or any enforcement.

Then, in that stillness of mind comes that which is true, without invitation. You cannot invite truth; it is the unknown. And in that silence there is no experiencer. Therefore, that which is experienced is not stored, is not remembered as "my experience of truth." Then something which is timeless comes into being—that which cannot be measured by the one who has experienced, or who merely remembers a past experience. Truth is something which comes from moment to moment. It is not to be cultivated, not to be gathered, stored up, and held in memory. It comes only when there is an awareness in which there is no experiencer.

May 26, 1955

London, England, 1955

--- ✳ ---

First Talk in London

Though we have many problems, and each problem seems to produce so many other problems, perhaps we can consider together whether the wisest thing to do is not to seek the solution of any problem at all. It seems to me that our minds are incapable of dealing with life as a whole; we deal, apparently, with all problems fragmentarily, separately, not with an integrated outlook. Perhaps the first thing, if we have problems, is not to seek an immediate solution for them but to have the patience to inquire deeply into them and discover whether these problems can ever be solved by the exercise of will. What is important, I think, is to find out, not how to solve the problem, but how to approach it. Because, without freedom, every approach must be restricted; without freedom, every solution—economic, political, personal, or whatever it be—can only bring more misery, more confusion. So I feel it is important to find out what is true freedom, to discover for oneself what freedom is.

There is only one freedom—religious freedom; there is no other freedom. The freedom that the so-called welfare state brings, the economic, national, political, and various other forms of freedom that one is given surely are not freedom at all, but only lead to further chaos and further misery—which is obvious to anyone who observes. So

I think we should spend all our time, energy, and thought in inquiring as to what is religious freedom—whether there is such a thing. That inquiry requires a great deal of insight, energy, and perseverance if we are to carry the investigation right through to the end and not be turned aside by any attraction. I think it would be worthwhile if we could, all of us, concentrate on this problem—what it is to be religiously free. Is it possible to free the mind—that is, our own minds, the individual mind—from the tyranny of all churches, from all organized beliefs, all dogmas, all systems of philosophy, all the various practices of yoga, all preconceptions of what reality or God is, and, by putting these aside, thereby discover for oneself if there is a religious freedom? For surely, religious freedom alone can offer, ultimately and fundamentally, the solution to all our problems, individual as well as collective.

This means, really, can the mind uncondition itself? Because the mind, our own mind, is after all the result of time, of growth, of tradition, of vast experience—not only experience in the present, but the collective experience of the past. So the question is not how to ennoble our conditioning, how to better it—which most of us are attempting to do—but rather to free the mind entirely from all conditioning. It seems to me that the real issue is not what religion to belong to, what system or philosophy to accept, or what discipline to practice in order to realize something which is beyond the mind—if there is something beyond the mind—but rather to find out, to discover for oneself, by our own individual understanding, investigation, and self-knowledge, whether the mind can be free. That is the greatest, the only revolution—to free the mind from all conditioning.

After all, to find something which is eternal—if there is such a thing—the mind must not think in terms of time; there must be no accumulation of the past, for that breeds time. The very experiences that one gathers must be shed because they manufacture, they build up, time. Surely, our mind is the result of time; it is conditioned by the past, by the innumerable experiences, memories, which we have gathered and which give to us a continuity. So, can one be really free, religiously—in the deepest sense of that word *religion?* Because religion obviously is not the rituals, the dogmas, the social morality, going to church every Sunday, practicing virtue, the good behavior which leads to respectability—surely all that is not religion. Religion is something much more, something utterly different from all that.

If one would find what it is to be religiously free, I think the whole problem of will, desire, with its intentions, its pursuits, its purposes, its innumerable projections—in all of which the mind is caught—must be understood. So it seems to me that our problems, whatever they are, can be dissolved totally only by burning away the process of will—which may sound completely foreign to a Western mind, and even to the Eastern mind. Because, after all, the so-called religion that we generally accept is essentially based on the process of becoming, is it not?—of ultimately reaching a certain state which is either projected or invented. We may experience a new state at rare moments, but then we pursue those rare moments—

which also implies, does it not, the cultivation of the will to be, to become something, in which is the process of time. If the mind would seek something which is beyond time, beyond the limitations of our own experience, which is essentially based on the conditioning of action, thought, feeling—if we would find something beyond all that, surely our mind, which is made up of so many pursuits and desires, must come to an end. Which means really, does it not, the understanding of the whole process of the mind as being conditioned. After all, a mind that is conditioned, shaped, molded in the particular culture of any form of society, obviously cannot find that which is beyond all thinking. And the discovery of finding that which is beyond is the revolution, the true religion.

So what is significant is not whether you are a Christian, a Buddhist, a Hindu, whether you are a follower, changing from one religion to another to satisfy your particular vanity, accepting certain forms of rituals and discarding the old ones—you know the sensations that one gets from attending religious ceremonies—all this, it seems to me, is detrimental, completely useless for a mind that would find out what is true. But to relinquish this pursuit through the action of will surely only breeds further conditioning, and I think it is important to understand this. Because, we are used to exerting effort to achieve a result. That is why we practice; we practice certain virtues, pursue a certain form of morality, and all this indicates, does it not, an effort on our part to arrive somewhere.

I wish we could really think about this, discuss it, investigate it together—how to really free the mind from all conditioning, and whether it is possible to uncondition the mind either through the action of will or through analysis of the various processes of thought and their reactions, or whether there is a totally different way of looking at this, whereby there is merely an awareness which burns away all the processes of thought at the very root. All thinking obviously is conditioned; there is no such thing as free thinking. Thinking can never be free; it is the outcome of our conditioning, of our background, of our culture, of our climate, of our social, economic, political background. The very books that you read and the very practices that you do are all established in the background, and any thinking must be the result of that background. So if we can be aware—and we can go presently into what it signifies, what it means, to be aware—perhaps we shall be able to uncondition the mind without the process of will, without the determination to uncondition the mind. Because the moment you determine, there is an entity who wishes, an entity who says, ''I must uncondition my mind.'' That entity itself is the outcome of our desire to achieve a certain result, so a conflict is already there. So, is it possible to be aware of our conditioning, just to be aware?—in which there is no conflict at all. That very awareness, if allowed, may perhaps burn away the problems.

After all, we all feel there is something beyond our own thinking, our own petty problems, our sorrows. There are moments, perhaps, when we experience that state. But unfortunately, that very experiencing becomes a hindrance to the further discovery of greater things because our minds hold on to something that we have experienced. We think that it is the real, and so we cling to it, but that very clinging obviously prevents the experiencing of something much greater.

So, the question is: Can the mind which is conditioned look at itself, be aware of its own conditioning without any choice, be aware without any comparison, without any condemnation, and see whether in that awareness the particular problem, the particular thought, is not burned away totally at the root? Surely any form of accumulation, either of knowledge or experience, any form of ideal, any projection of the mind, any determined practice to shape the mind—what it should be and should not be—all this is obviously crippling the process of investigation and discovery. If one really goes into it and deeply thinks about it, one will see that the mind must be totally free from all conditioning for religious freedom. And it is only in that religious freedom that all our problems, whatever they be, are solved.

So I think our inquiry must be not for the solution of our immediate problems but rather to find out whether the mind—the conscious as well as the deep unconscious mind in which is stored all the tradition, the memories, the inheritance of racial knowledge—whether all of it can be put aside. I think it can be done only if the mind is capable of being aware without any sense of demand, without any pressure—just to be aware. I think it is one of the most difficult things—to be so aware—because we are caught in the immediate problem and in its immediate solution, and so our lives are very superficial. Though one may go to all the analysts, read all the books, acquire much knowledge, attend churches, pray, meditate, practice various disciplines, nevertheless, our lives are obviously very superficial because we do not know how to penetrate deeply. I think the understanding, the way of penetration, how to go very, very deeply, lies through awareness—just to be aware of our thoughts and feelings, without condemnation, without comparison, just to observe. You will see, if you will experiment, how extraordinarily difficult it is, because our whole training is to condemn, to approve, to compare.

So it seems to me that our problem—which is really timeless—is to find out for ourselves, to directly experience what it means to free the mind from all conditioning. It is comparatively easy to be free of nationality, to be free of the inherited racial qualities, to be free of certain beliefs, dogmas, and not to belong to any particular church or religion—those are comparatively easy things for anyone who has thought about these matters and who is at all earnest and serious. But it is much more difficult to go further, to go beyond. We think we have done a great deal if we throw off some of the superficial layers of culture, whether Western or Eastern. But to penetrate beyond, without illusion, without deceiving oneself, is extremely difficult. Most of us have not the energy. I am not talking of the energy which comes through abstinence, through denial, through asceticism, through control—those bring a wrong kind of energy which distorts observation—but I'm talking of that energy which comes when the mind is no longer seeking anything at all, is no longer in need of search, in need of discovery, in need of experiencing, and is therefore a really still mind. Only such a mind can find out, for it is only such a still mind that can receive something which is not of its own projection. A still mind is the free mind, and such a mind is the religious mind.

So can we really consider this—not as a collective group experiencing something, which is comparatively easy, but as individuals—can we really inquire and find out for ourselves to what degree and depth we are conditioned? And can we not be aware of that conditioning without any reaction to it, without condemning it, without trying to alter it, without substituting a new conditioning for the old, but be aware so easily and deeply that the very process of conditioning—which is, after all, the desire to be secure, the desire to have permanency—is burned away at the root? Can we discover that for ourselves—not because someone else has talked about it—and be aware of it directly so that the very root, the very desire to be secure, to have permanency, is burned away? It is this

desire to have permanency, either in the future or in the past, to hold on to the accumulation of experience, that gives one the sense of security—and cannot that be burned away? Because it is that which creates conditioning. This desire, which most of us have, to know and in that very knowing to find security, to have experience which gives us strength—can we wipe away all that?—not by volition, but burn it all away in awareness so that the mind is free from all its desires and that which is eternal can come into being.

I think that is the only revolution—not the communist or any other form of revolution. They do not solve our problems; on the contrary, they increase them, they multiply our sorrows—which again is very obvious. Surely the only true revolution is the freeing of the mind from its own conditioning, and therefore from society—not the mere reformation of society. The man who reforms society is still caught in society, but the man who is free of society, being free from conditioning, he will act in his own way, which will act again upon society. So our problem is not reformation, how to improve society, how to have a better welfare state, whether communist or socialist or what you will. It is not an economic or political revolution, or peace through terror. For a serious man these are not the problems. His real problem is to find out whether the mind can be totally free from all conditioning, and thereby perhaps discover in that extraordinary silence that which is beyond all measurement.

There are several questions, and before I answer them I think it is important to find out what we mean by a problem. A problem exists, does it not, only when the mind is occupied. Please listen and, if I may suggest it, do not jump to conclusions, because we are trying to investigate the whole thing together. When the mind is occupied, whether it is with God, with the kitchen, with a person, or with an idea, a virtue—all such occupation surely creates problems. If I am occupied with the discovery of God, or of truth, then it becomes a problem because then I go round asking, begging, trying to find out which method is the best, and so on. So the real question is not about the problem itself but rather why is the mind occupied? Why does the mind seek occupation? I am not talking of the daily occupation of business and all the rest of it but of this psychological occupation of the mind—which has relation to our daily life. Because whether we are occupied with God, with truth, with love, with sex, or with the affairs of the kitchen or of the nation, all occupations are the same; there are no "noble" occupations. The mind seeks occupation, does it not?—it wants to be occupied with something; it is frightened not to be occupied. Try some time to see how busily you are occupied with your own problems, and find out what would happen if you were not so occupied. You will soon discover how frightened the mind is not to have any occupation! All our culture, all our training, tells us that the mind must be occupied, and yet it seems to me the very occupation creates the problem. Not that there are no problems—there are problems, but I think it is the occupation with the problem which prevents the understanding of it. It is really very interesting to watch the mind, to watch one's own mind and discover how incessantly it is occupied with something or other— there is never a moment when it is quiet, unoccupied, empty, never a space which has no limit.

Being so occupied, our problems ever increase, and the mere solution of one particular problem, without understanding the whole process of the occupation of the mind, merely creates other problems. So can we not understand this peculiar insistence of the mind, on its part, to be occupied—whether with ideas, with speculations, with knowledge, with delusions, with study, or with its own virtue and its own fears? To be free of all that, to have an unoccupied mind, is quite arduous because it means, really, the cessation of all this reaction of memory, which is called thinking.

Question: I am very attached, and I feel it is very important to cultivate detachment. How am I to have this sense of freedom from attachment?

KRISHNAMURTI: Is our problem detachment? Or, is it attachment?—being attached brings pain; therefore, we desire to be unattached. If we can look at the whole process of attachment, not just superficially, but go into the whole significance of it, the depth of it, then perhaps there will be something entirely different from that which we call detachment.

Why are we attached to anything—to property, to people, to ideas, to beliefs?—you know the innumerable forms of attachment to so many things. Why are we attached? Is there not a sense of fear if we are not attached to something—to my friend, to an idea, to an experience that is over, to a son, to a brother, to a mother, to a wife who is dead? Do we not feel that we are disloyal, that we have no love, if we are not attached? And also, is there not that extraordinary fear of not being something through attachment? That is the problem, not how to cultivate detachment. If you cultivate detachment, the cultivation itself becomes a problem.

Please see this. I am attached. That attachment is the outcome of fear, of various forms of loneliness, emptiness, and so on. I am aware of that, and I know this pain of attachment, so I try to cultivate detachment. My mind is occupied with detachment and how to arrive at that detachment, and that very process becomes a problem, does it not? I want to achieve detachment, and so the mind, being occupied with the result, with an idea called detachment, makes the achievement of it into a problem; then there is the conflict—"I am attached, I must be detached"—there is pain, and so there is a constant striving to arrive at a particular state in which there is no pain, no fear. But if I can look at attachment, be aware of it, not ask how to get rid of the pain, or struggle to understand the whole implication of attachment, but just be aware of it as one is aware of the sky—that it's cloudy, dark with rain, or blue—then there is no problem; then the mind is not occupied with attachment or its opposite, detachment. When the mind is so aware, it sees the whole significance of attachment. But you cannot see the whole inward significance of attachment if there is any form of condemnation, any form of comparison, judgment, evaluation.

If you will experiment with this, you will see. Merely to cultivate detachment becomes so very superficial. If you are detached, then what? But when there is awareness, you will see that where there is attachment, there is no love; where there is attachment, there is the desire for permanency, for security, for self-continuance—which doesn't mean we should pursue self-destruction. And seeing that, then the problem of attachment becomes extraordinarily significant and wide. Merely to run away from attachment because so much pain is involved can only lead to superficial love, superficial thinking. And most of us who are practicing virtue—the virtue of detachment, of nongreed, of nonviolence—do lead superficial lives—the life of idea, the life of words.

If one is aware of the whole problem of attachment, one will begin to find out the extraordinary depths of it, how the mind is attached to the experience of yesterday with its pain or with its pleasure, how the mind clings to it. One cannot be free of the experience of both the pleasure and the pain until one is really aware. In that awareness in which there is no choice, no reaction, the mind can go very deeply. The mere practice of any virtue can only lead to respectability which is what most people desire, for respectability identifies us with society. We all desire to be recognized as being something—great or little, this or that—and to that idea we are attached. We may want to detach ourselves from people because it causes pain while the idea to which we are attached does not. But to really understand this whole problem of attachment—to tradition, to nationality, to custom, to a habit, to knowledge, to opinion, to a savior, to all the innumerable beliefs and nonbeliefs—we must not be satisfied merely to scratch the surface and think we have understood the problem of attachment when we are cultivating detachment. Whereas if we do not try to cultivate detachment—which only becomes another problem—if we can just look clearly at attachment, then perhaps we shall be able to go very deeply and discover something entirely different, something which is neither attachment nor detachment.

Question: I have studied many systems of philosophy and the teachings of the great religious leaders. Have you anything better to offer than what we know of already?

KRISHNAMURTI: I wonder why you study, why you read philosophy, why you read the sayings of religious leaders. Do you think the knowledge which you have learned, read of, will get you anywhere? Perhaps in a discussion, to show off your cleverness or erudition, it might be useful. But will accumulated knowledge—except in the scientific world—lead man, you or me, to find out what is real, what is truth, what is God, the eternal?—without which life has very little meaning. Surely, to find that which is the eternal, all knowledge must go, must it not? All the sayings of the Buddha, the Christ, of everyone—must not all that be put aside? If it is not, then you are merely seeking, are you not, your own projections or the projection of your church; it is really your own conditioning to which you are responding.

Surely you must cease to be a Christian, a Hindu, a Buddhist, or a practicer of yoga—you must totally cease all that, must you not, for something which is beyond to come into being—if there is something beyond. Just to say there is something beyond and accept it and hope to achieve it, thereby making a problem of it, is obviously very superficial. But can we take a journey "not knowing," not having any encouragement, not having any support, being neither a Christian, a Buddhist, nor a Hindu, which are only labels indicating a conditioned mind? To set aside all "knowing" is the only problem—not "Have I anything better to offer?" For surely one must be alone—not isolated, not alone in knowledge, alone in experience, because all knowledge, all experience, is a hindrance to the discovery of that which is real. The mind must be free from all conditioning, alone, to find out. The more you practice, the more you accumulate, the more you discipline, shape, twist, struggle, the less the understanding of that *which is*.

I am not talking of some Indian philosophy of negation, of doing nothing, whereas you all have the Western idea of doing something; I am not talking of that. What we are talking of is entirely different. The mind must be made innocent, fresh. It cannot be fresh and innocent if there is accumulation of knowledge, or the mere repetition of the words of a teacher, or the end result of some practice. Cannot the mind be aware of its own conditioning—not only the superficial conditioning, but all the symbols, the ideologies, the philosophies, images, all those things deep down which condition the

mind? To be aware of all that and to be free of it—such freedom is religious freedom. It is that freedom which brings about revolution—the only revolution that can transform the world.

June 17, 1955

Second Talk in London

I think it would be rather worthwhile if we could go into a problem thoroughly with that awareness of which we were speaking yesterday and see if one can go through the whole process—not theoretically, but actually—and discover for oneself the truth of what is being said. For that, it seems to me very important to know how to listen. Most of us do not really listen. We have various theories, reactions, responses, which actually block the real listening. I would like to discuss a problem which I think is quite complex and which therefore needs an attention in which there is neither the struggle to understand nor the attitude of merely listening to an explanation. Let us rather actually follow the issue, being alert and aware, and so explore, uncover, the whole problem.

Our culture is based on envy, and we are the product of that culture. Envy exists not only in social matters where there is competition with one another to achieve a result, a certain position, to gain power, and so on; but also inwardly, so-called spiritually, there is this acquisitive urge. I think most of us are aware of it. The urge to arrive, to grasp, to understand, to be, to gain a goal, to find happiness, God, or what you will—all these are obviously the process of acquisition, the urge of envy. Society, as it develops, is going more and more to control the acquisitive instinct outwardly through legislation, but inwardly there is no legislation which can control it. And it seems to me that this acquisitive instinct is one of the major issues because in it is involved the whole process of effort. If we can really go into this and see if one can actually be free from this urge to find a haven, a refuge, spiritually to become something, then I think we shall have solved an enormous problem—perhaps the only problem.

After all, when we seek reality, or God, we sometimes wish to give up the world with its competition, its divisions, its class warfare, and all the rest of it, and we then try to become monks, or sannyasis. But there is no abandonment of this process of acquisition even though we become hermits, even though we renounce the world. There is still this desire to "become something," to follow somebody in order to realize, in order to find truth; there is always this sense of envy, of acquisitiveness, of gain. On that whole process our culture, socially and spiritually, is based. All our efforts are directed towards acquiring either virtue or goods or property or a state of happiness, a state of bliss—in which is involved this constant endeavor, constant striving, the struggle to be something. I think that is a fact, and I think most of us are aware of it.

Now, can we be aware of this whole issue, not only consciously, but deep down in the unconscious, and so be free of this urge? Because so long as there is this striving, however beneficial it may be at one level, it becomes detrimental, a hindrance, at another. All of us are trained, educated, to compete, inwardly as well as outwardly, and so there is no love of anything for its own sake but only a sense of something to be achieved. Surely it is important to find out if the mind can be free from all this acquisitive pursuit.

After all, seeking to become virtuous is a form of envy, is it not? And can we discuss that? So long as the mind is caught in any form of envy, achieving, gaining a goal, pursuing a result, searching for heaven, peace, or reality, there must be a constant accumula-

tion of various forms of memory, which actually deter one from the discovery of the real. Essentially we are afraid, are we not, to be what we are; we want to change what we are, and in the process of changing, the whole problem arises of the "how." Our desire is to change in order to be something else, and so we are constantly inquiring as to a method—how to achieve, how to be nonviolent, and so on.

The issue is that our culture is acquisitive—which means essentially envious; our culture is based on envy. Socially one can see that very easily. But inwardly, so-called spiritually, intellectually, deep down, the same thing prevails—envy is the basis of our search. Because I am unhappy, in sorrow, I want to change that, to escape into another state, and so the problem arises of how to arrive at that other state. So we pursue different teachers, listen to various talks, read religious books, try to reform, try to discipline ourselves—always in order to achieve a result. If we can be aware of all that, then I think perhaps we shall understand a state in which there is no effort at all.

Can we actually discuss this?

Question: Is it wrong to try and improve ourselves? What are we doing here listening to you if we are not trying to improve?

KRISHNAMURTI: That is really a good question if we can go into it. What is self-improvement?

First of all, if there is to be improvement we must understand what the self is, must we not? We think it is permissible, right, that there should be self-improvement. But what do we mean by the self, the 'me'? Is there a 'me', a self, that is constant, that can be improved, a thing which has actual continuity?—not just the continuity that we wish to have, but in reality is there a continuity of the 'me' apart from the continuity of the physical organism with its particular name, its particular qualities, living in a certain place and in certain relationships, having a job, and so on? Apart from that, is there a 'me' that continues?

Audience: Yes. No.

KRISHNAMURTI: Surely it is not merely a matter of opinion, yes or no. If we are to find out, we must not jump to any conclusions. We must not take an opinion or a wish to be a fact. We want to find out if there is a 'me' that can improve, be added to, if there is a permanent entity that goes on improving, improving. Or, are there contradictory desires, urges, compulsions—one dominating the other, and that which dominates wishes to continue, suppressing the other desires? Or, is there only a state of flux, a constant change without any permanency, and the mind, realizing this impermanency, this flux, this transiency, wishes to have something permanent, which it calls the self, and wishes that self to continue by improving itself?

When we talk about self-improvement, 'myself' becoming better, nobler, less this and more that—surely that is all a process of thinking, is it not? There is no permanent 'me' except for the desire to have permanency. So, is there an improvement of 'me'; can I improve myself? What does it mean to "improve"?—from what to what? I am greedy; I want to improve, to be nongreedy. I am envious, irritable, whatever it is, and I wish to change that into something else. I make great efforts, discipline myself, follow certain meditations, and so on and so on, trying to improve myself all the time; but I never ask the basic question: What is the 'me' that wants to improve? Who are these two entities, the one that observes and wishes to change, and that which is observed?

Am I making myself clear?

Audience: Yes. Yes.

KRISHNAMURTI: So, when I say, "I must improve myself," what is the entity that says, "I must improve"? And is there an entity, a 'me', that is different from the observer?
(Pause)
Let us discuss this and go into it. I am greedy, envious, and I want to improve, to put away envy. In that there are two entities, are there not?—the one that is envious and the other that wants to free itself from envy.

Comment: Not necessarily—there is only one entity.

KRISHNAMURTI: Let us see. What is the actual process? I am envious, and I feel it is not the right thing; there is pain in it, it is immoral, and I wish to change the envy, or whatever it is. Those are the two states within me. But they are both within the same field of thought, are they not? The 'me' that is greedy, and the 'me' that wishes to change—both are 'me', are they not?

Comment: The minute you decide to change, you are greedy no longer.

KRISHNAMURTI: We are not at present discussing how or what to change. When we talk of improving ourselves, is there actually an improvement or merely a change from one coat to another, substituting one set of words and feelings for another?

Comment: There is no improvement unless you carry your ideal into action.

KRISHNAMURTI: Most of us pursue ideals—"the good," "the beautiful," "what is true," "nonviolence," and so on. And we know why we pursue them—because we hope through ideals to change ourselves.

Ideals act as a lever and urge us to change ourselves, to become more perfect. That is an actual fact, is it not?

Take violence: I am violent, and so I have the ideal of nonviolence. And I pursue that ideal, try to practice it, I am constantly thinking about it, trying to change myself and the ways of my thinking in order to conform to the ideal which I have established for myself. But, have I actually changed?—or have I merely substituted one set of words for another? Is violence changed through an ideal?

(Pause)

What is important, surely, is not the ideal but the actual, the understanding of *what is.* The important thing is to understand my state of violence, from whence it arises, what are the causes, and so on—and not to try to achieve a state of nonviolence. Is that not so? Is it not extremely difficult for most of us to give up ideals, to wipe them all away, and be concerned with actually *what is?* If you are only concerned with *what is,* then is there any form of self-improvement?

Question: Do all these things disappear if we discuss them? (Laughter)

KRISHNAMURTI: We are not concerned, are we, with how to make things disappear. We want to find out, do we not, how to transform something like greed without conflict.

Question: Being concerned with what is— *let us say, with violence—does that not give strength to the violence?*

KRISHNAMURTI: Does it? Please, let us go into this. All of us here, apparently, are great idealists; we accept ideals as a means of changing ourselves. So can we proceed from that, slowly?

Question: Is not an ideal good or bad according to the way you use it? You can buy things that are good or bad with your power, your money—and the same with your ideals.

KRISHNAMURTI: I thought this was an old subject, long ago brushed away, but I see it is not. Why do we have ideals?

Comment: Largely because we have been educated to have ideals.

KRISHNAMURTI: Even if you had not been educated to a certain pattern of thinking, would you not create ideals for yourself?

Comment: God gave us a brain to think with and with it we have made ideals to help ourselves forward.

KRISHNAMURTI: Let us go into this matter slowly, step by step, and find out at least one thing this evening—why we have ideals. Let us see if ideals have any significance at all in our lives—deeply, not superficially—and the whole implication of what is involved in ideals. Have they really any significance? If not, can we put them completely aside and perhaps look at things entirely differently?

Comment: It gives us great pleasure to think of the ideal.

Question: Are not ideals an approach to the light? Are we not attracted upwards without even knowing it?

Comment: Surely, we are dissatisfied with what we are and are trying to get away from it. If what we are gives us pain, then we try to get away from pain to something that gives us pleasure and happiness.

KRISHNAMURTI: That is so, is it not? We are dissatisfied with what we are and we want to get away from that, we want to be free from that state of dissatisfaction. That is our concern, is it not?—and not the ideal. Our concern is: We are dissatisfied with what we are.

Comment: I don't think it is. I am perfectly satisfied with what I am. I don't see why one shouldn't be. (Laughter)

KRISHNAMURTI: If I am perfectly satisfied with what I am, then there is no problem, no issue. But surely most of us are dissatisfied.

Question: Do we not have ideals because in every human being there is a divine spark?

KRISHNAMURTI: Sir, what does that mean? How do we know? I am dissatisfied with what I am—that is the general state with most of us. I am ugly and I want to become beautiful; I am greedy and I want to be non-greedy because greed involves pain; I am attached and I want to be detached because attachment breeds sorrow. It is all a form of dissatisfaction with *what is,* is it not? We hope through our dissatisfaction to achieve a change, a result; we want to wipe away dissatisfaction. If we can just concentrate on that issue now, perhaps we shall understand everything.

I am dissatisfied with what I am. Does that dissatisfaction arise because I am comparing myself with something else? You understand the question? I am dissatisfied with myself because I have seen you being happy, satisfied. You have something which I have not got, and I would like to get it.

Question: If we stop all that, if we are aware of that, if we know that "I am what I am"—then what have we left to go after, to build up, to strive for? Then, why are we frustrated?

KRISHNAMURTI: I think if we could go a little bit slowly and not jump to any conclusions, then perhaps we shall be able to get at the root of this problem.

It has been said that we have ideals because we are divine. But I do not know if I am divine. People may have told me that there is a spark of divinity in me, but I do not know anything about it, do I?—I merely repeat it. I want to find out for myself if there is such a thing as divinity. And I cannot find that out if my mind is dissatisfied because, being dissatisfied, I may myself create an idea of divinity which will satisfy me. Being dissatisfied psychologically, inwardly, my whole search is to find satisfaction. So I create a truth, a state, a reality, a bliss, a haven which will satisfy me; therefore, it is only my own creation. But if I can understand why I am dissatisfied, the whole process and the content of dissatisfaction, then perhaps I shall understand something much greater instead of merely clinging to a creation of my own desire.

So, let us please keep to this point: We are dissatisfied. Now, our problem is, being dissatisfied, how am I to find satisfaction? I may put it very crudely, but that is the actual fact.

Comment: (Standing up and brandishing Bible) I find satisfaction by reading God's word. I was converted, and since I've read God's word I'm satisfied and I don't want anything else.

KRISHNAMURTI: Yes, sir. We are all seeking satisfaction. You will find satisfaction in the Bible, in a book; I may find satisfaction in a drink. You may find satisfaction in power, position, prestige, money; and I may find satisfaction in self-improvement. So, we all are seeking satisfaction. Is that not so?

Audience: Yes. Yes.

KRISHNAMURTI: We are seeking satisfaction through the achievement of an ideal, through a belief. You may find it in one way, and I may find it in another; yours may be a so-called noble way, and mine may be a so-called low way. But the urge, the drive, the tendency, is to find a state of satisfaction which will never be disturbed. Is that not what we want?

Audience: Yes. Yes.

Question: But is not that urge smoothed out directly we get beyond ourselves? Like listening to music—it takes us away from ourselves and from life's limitations.

KRISHNAMURTI: Surely that is merely a theory—if we did "this," "that" would happen. It is a supposition. But the actual fact is that we are dissatisfied and are seeking satisfaction. That is why you are listening to me, is it not? You hope to find something by listening. You are dissatisfied, you are searching, you are unhappy, frustrated, in contradiction, and you want to find a way out of this mess, this chaos; and so you listen, hoping to find a way out.

Now, I am suggesting that we should first find out why there is dissatisfaction, and not concern ourselves with how to transform it into satisfaction. Actually, what does being dissatisfied mean?

Comment: It is because we do not have the understanding of supreme consciousness.

KRISHNAMURTI: Oh, sir! How can a mind which is so disturbed, which is so anxious, which is so frustrated, which is constantly demanding, wanting—how can such a mind think of a supreme consciousness or any of those ideals? They may be all nonsense. The actual fact is that I am disturbed. Why cannot we start from there? I am dissatisfied; how am I to find satisfaction? That is our problem, is it not?

Audience: Yes. Yes.

Question: Sir, isn't satisfaction the same as the self which is disturbed?

KRISHNAMURTI: We will investigate, sir. Please, let us go slowly, step by step. I am dissatisfied, and you are.

Comment: I am dissatisfied with what I am. If I knew what I am, I should be much happier—but I do not know what I am.

KRISHNAMURTI: That is the whole problem, is it not? I am unhappy, and I want to find happiness. I am in a state of misery, frustration, and I want to find fulfillment.

Audience: Why?

KRISHNAMURTI: Please—let us first see the fact, and not say, "Why?" We will go into that. But is that the fact?
(Pause)

Audience: Yes, it is.

KRISHNAMURTI: So the next thing we are concerned with is how to bring about a change. I am unhappy, and I want to be happy. How is that change to be brought about?

Comment: By being happy.

KRISHNAMURTI: Sir, if you say to an unhappy man, "Be happy," it has no meaning, has it?

Question: I can see there is dissatisfaction within myself and that by getting away from it, my mind is escaping.

KRISHNAMURTI: That is so, is it not? I have never understood the whole process of dissatisfaction, but I merely want to escape from it, I want to get away from it, to take flight from it, deny it. I am dissatisfied, I am unhappy, I am violent; I do not like that state, so I want to change it. And I have the ideal as a means of bringing about a change in me, or I pursue someone who will show me the way to be satisfied, how to be happy. Which means, really, I have not understood the state in which I am but am denying it. Surely that is so. I am denying the state in which I am because I am pursuing a state which I think will give me satisfaction, give me happiness, put an end to my frustration. Whereas, if we had no escape, if we would put away all ideals and face the fact that we are dissatisfied, then we could proceed. But so long as I am escaping from the fact that I am dissatisfied by trying to become satisfied, there is bound to be frustration. So I want to understand that state of dissatisfaction with all its implications, and not try to change it into something else.

Do we understand this? And can we, in talking it over together, free the mind from the ideal and face the fact that I am violent?—not ask how to be nonviolent, which is merely an escape from the fact. Can I look at the fact?

(Pause)

Question: What do you mean by "looking at the fact"?

KRISHNAMURTI: Can we now go into that? How do I actually face the fact that I am violent? What does it mean to look at something? It means, can I look at myself without condemning myself? Can I look at the fact of violence without introducing the desire not to be violent? The very word *violence* has a condemnatory significance, has it not? You are following this?

Audience: Yes. Yes.

KRISHNAMURTI: That is, I become aware that I am violent, envious. And to me, what is important is to understand that state and not try to change it. Because the very desire to change is an escape from the fact. Unless that is very clear, we cannot proceed further.

(Pause)

The difficulty here is that each one is pursuing his own thoughts, his own way of translating what is being said. Can we look at this one issue together, very simply? I am envious. I have been told from childhood that it is wrong, and I have been conditioned to condemn it; so I am dissatisfied with it. I have read in books, I have been told, that one must live in peace, in a state of love, and all the rest of it. So, I am trying to change what I am into what I should be. The 'should be' is the ideal, is it not?—which is an escape from what I am. I think that is fairly clear. So first let us put aside the ideal altogether. For most of us, that is the most difficult thing to do.

The mind must be free from the ideal first. Perhaps I am dissatisfied because of the ideal. Perhaps I feel I should be something noble, and because I am not, I am dissatisfied. Or, is dissatisfaction something inherent, quite apart from comparison? You understand the problem?

Audience: Yes.

KRISHNAMURTI: So do I know dissatisfaction only through the comparison of the ideal with what I am? And if there were no comparison at all, would I still be dissatisfied? If I did not think in terms of the 'more' or the 'less', would there be dissatisfaction? Is dissatisfaction inherent in my thinking, in my being? I know of the ideal, I am being taught about it, and also I want to improve, become something greater—therefore I am dissatisfied. But so long as I am thinking in terms of time—which is, the becoming something in the future—there must be dissatisfaction, surely? So, can the mind be free from all comparison?

You are listening to me, are you not, because you want to achieve a state which I have talked about. Whether I have achieved it or not is not important. You want to achieve that state. Why? Because, you are dissatisfied, you are unhappy, frustrated, you are nothing and you want to be something. And this effort to get from the state in which you are to the state which you think you should achieve is called a process of growth, is it not?

Audience: Yes.

KRISHNAMURTI: But if I can understand the actual state in which I am, then perhaps this whole idea of becoming something, this whole idea of demanding time in order to grow, may be irrelevant, may be utterly false. I think it is. So the problem then is that I am dissatisfied—and I am no longer concerned with how to achieve satisfaction because I see it as an escape from the actual fact of dissatisfaction, of unhappiness, of frustration. The actual fact is that I am frustrated because I am seeking fulfillment. Is that not so? I am seeking fulfillment, therefore I am frustrated.

So I ask myself if there is such a thing as fulfillment at all. You understand? So long as I am seeking fulfillment, there is the accompanying fear of not fulfilling. So, is it not right to find out for oneself whether there is fulfillment at all?—not how to fulfill, how to wipe away the frustration in which I am caught. Because so long as I am seeking fulfillment in any form, there must be frustration. Surely, that is a fact.

Now, why do I seek fulfillment?—in my son, through a job, and all the other ways; we know what it means without too much description. There may be no fulfillment at all, and if we seek fulfillment, there is frustration, from which arises sorrow. If I can find out the truth—whether there is fulfillment at all—then perhaps I can be free from frustration. So, is there fulfillment? That is the whole question. Is that clear?

Audience: Yes.

KRISHNAMURTI: In our daily life there is the urge to fulfill. And with that urge go frustration, grief, sorrow, envy, and all the rest of it—with which we are all familiar. So there is always a lack, a sense of insufficiency, is there not? I may fulfill in one direction and yet be miserable in another. It goes on indefinitely, and so frustration is a continual process. So, my problem then is to find out the truth—whether there is fulfillment. And, why do we want to fulfill?

Comment: Because we are afraid of a state of not being fulfilled; we are afraid to stay unfulfilled.

KRISHNAMURTI: Let us investigate, look into ourselves. Fulfillment is a state of transiency; the urge is constantly changing. There is no permanent state of fulfillment, is there? So, why is there this urge to fulfill?

Comment: Because we long for permanency.

KRISHNAMURTI: So because in ourselves we are not permanent, because there is nothing in us which is enriching, because we are inwardly poor, sorrowing, therefore we seek fulfillment, we try to gather, to be something. That is the root of it, is it not? Do we see that?

(Pause)

Audience: Yes.

KRISHNAMURTI: Now, let us proceed from that. We are confused, we are lonely, inwardly we are insufficient—that is the fact. Every action away from that fact is an escape, is it not? And it is one of the most difficult things to do, not to escape. Because, to look at the fact, to consider it, to be aware of it, implies no condemnation of the fact, no comparison, no evaluation. So can we, not theoretically but actually, experience the thing we are talking of? Because then we will see that it is possible to be totally free from this sense of insufficiency, from this root cause of misery.

Question: Do you mean that we should be satisfied as we are? (Sh! Sh!)

KRISHNAMURTI: No, sir—that only leads to stagnation, to immobility, to death. I am showing that any interpretation of the fact is either based on satisfaction or dissatisfaction.

So, can I look at that fact of inward insufficiency without comparing, without judging? Can I look at it without fear? Is it not fear of the fact that is making me do all these things, making me pursue the ideal? Can we understand now that it is fear that is making us compare?—fear of something which we do not know. We have given it the name of insufficiency, of loneliness, of misery, of confusion; and having given a name to it, we have thus condemned it and run away from the fact. When we do not condemn, do not judge, do not evaluate and compare, then we are left only with fear. Is that clear, so far?

Audience: Yes. Yes.

KRISHNAMURTI: Fear of what? You understand the question? I am afraid of a state which I call "insufficiency." I do not know that state; I have never really looked at it, but I am afraid of it. Being afraid of it, I run away from it. But now I am not running away through comparison or through ideals because I see the falseness of escape. So I am left only with fear of something about which I do not know. Is that not so?

Audience: Yes.

KRISHNAMURTI: If you are following this actually—not verbally, not intellectually, not descriptively—you will see for yourself the process of this unfolding, and the depths into which one can go. Then I no longer have ideals; they have no meaning any more. I am no longer striving to achieve. The fact is, I am afraid of something about which I do not know, but if I stop running away from it, then I am left with the fact and the fear. If I pursue the fear, if I ask the question, "How am I to get rid of fear?" then that is another escape from the fact, is it not? So, I am now concerned with the understanding of *what is,* and I see that giving a name to a thing as "emptiness," as "loneliness," as "insufficiency," has actually created the fear. Giving it a label has brought about the reaction of fear to that label.

So, can the mind be aware of the thing without condemning, without judging, without escaping, and without giving it a name? This is extraordinarily difficult because most of us are so conditioned to pursue the ideal that it prevents us from looking at the actual fact. We are not capable of looking at the fact when there is comparison, when the mind gives it a label, a name. But when there is no naming of the fact, no escaping from it through ideals, through comparison, through judgment, then what is there left? Is there anything which can be called insufficiency? Is there that urge to fulfill which breeds frustration?

(Pause)

So we begin to find out how the mind has been incapable of looking at anything without all this confusing, contradictory process. Only when the mind is capable of abandoning it all—not through any effort, but because it sees the truth of all this—only then is there the cessation of envy, the complete cessation. Such a mind is no longer caught by society, by any particular culture—for all our culture is based on envy. Then we will find that the mind is no longer seeking because there is nothing more to seek. Then such a mind is really quiet.

Merely repeating what has been said has no meaning at all. But to actually experience this through self-knowledge and not to accumulate that which has been experienced—because accumulation distorts all further experience—to be aware of all this gives truth, gives that extraordinary freedom which comes through complete aloneness. The mind that is completely alone, uncontaminated, not escaping, is capable of receiving that which is true.

June 18, 1955

Third Talk in London

It seems to me that, especially in religious matters, our search is very superficial. We do not seem to be able to go beyond the surface depths. Most of us spend our days in search-ing for some reality that our conditioned thinking either projects or can only superficially comprehend. Is it not a problem with most of us, how to search really very deeply, to go beyond the superficial depths, to be free of all psychologists, of all prophets, teachers, saviors, Masters, and disciplines so that we as individuals can really find out for ourselves what is true? And we do not seem to be able to do it because we are always looking for support, for confirmation from those who we think have already found, or who have been pointed out to us by the various religions. We have no confidence in our own capacity to find out. If we can have confidence in our own capacity, then perhaps we shall be free to find out for ourselves what is true—that which is beyond the measure of the mind.

Now, how is one to have this capacity? Because, if one has it, then one is free, one is liberated from all following, from all authority, from this sense of imitation, of conformity to the pattern laid down by any particular religion or philosophy. If we have this capacity to search really profoundly, to go to the very depths of our being, without distortion, without the fear of not discovering, of not finding a result, then perhaps we can be free of all culture, whether of the East or of the West. Because culture, it seems to me, does not help us to find reality—that which is beyond measure, that which is beyond time. Western or Eastern influence has so conditioned us, so shaped our minds, that we think only in the pattern of our own culture.

I do not think culture will ever help us. On the contrary, I think we must be free of all culture, totally—which means to be free from the desire to be recognized by society. The man who is capable of going to the very depth of things, he alone is the true individual. At present we are the mass, the collective, the result of culture, of tradition, of all the various beliefs and conditioned experiences. Surely it is only when we are free of all that, that we are truly individual, and it is only then that reality can come into being.

So, how is one to have this capacity which will set us free from all authority in spiritual matters so that we are true individuals, capable of finding out for ourselves, never asking for encouragement, for confirmation, for support? I think that is a fundamental question. We rarely ask fundamental questions, and if we do ask them, we are easily satisfied with superficial answers, with the words of another. So, can you and I have this capacity—not in the process of time, which is again an evasion—but can you and I have it immediately? Can one go beyond the superficial level? What is it that prevents me from being so clear that I understand the whole, the totality of my being? In the very process of understanding how my being is the result of tradition, of time, of culture, of fear, of experience, can I not set all that aside so that the mind is fresh, clear, and able to find out, to perceive directly? I am sure most of us must have asked this question. Can the mind be free, not depending on another, whoever it be, not depending on any system or any path? If you pursue a system, a path, then obviously you will have the result of that system, of that path, but you are no longer an individual, a true seeker. A true seeker must obviously be free. So what is it that is preventing this extraordinary capacity to pursue very deeply and not be satisfied with superficial explanations and beliefs?

One of the reasons is, is it not, that we move, that we think, from accumulation to accumulation. Where there is accumulation, there must be imitation. Every experience leaves a residue as memory, and from that memory we act, we gather, we strengthen ourselves. There is never a moment when the mind is really free, but always there is the residue of yesterday's experiences. It is this memory—the result of years of accumulation—which prevents the capacity to be clear, direct. So the mind is never free. I do not know if you have noticed how every experience leaves a residue, a result, and round that result all further experience is translated, gathered, accumulated, and held. So memory, as experience, as tradition, as knowledge, is the burden which prevents us from having this capacity to be free, to be completely individual, to discover for ourselves.

Being born a Hindu or a Christian naturally the mind is conditioned in a particular symbology, in various ideas of what reality is, what meditation is; and through that conditioning the mind experiences and so further strengthens its own conditioning. The Christian will always hold in spiritual matters to the vision of Christ or the Virgin Mary—and the Hindu does the same in his own way. To be totally free, not superficially but completely—which means when there is no form of imitation, when there is no sense of conformity psychologically, inwardly—only then, surely, one has this capacity to search, to find out.

If you have followed this, the obvious question is: How am I to free myself from all the accumulation of the past, from all my conditioning? There is no "how"; there is only the discovery of the truth without asking "how to be free." Because if our whole attention is given to the discovery of what is true, then that very perception, that very listening to that which is true, liberates. So long as we think in terms of belief, of illusion, of things we would wish to be, we are incapable of listening, giving our whole attention. Our beliefs, our traditions, our symbols prevent the actual listening to any truth. It seems to me the only important thing is to give attention; complete attention is the complete good. Attention with an object in view is no longer attention—it is exclusion.

Therefore, if we can listen, not in order to gain something—such attention becomes exclusive, narrow, limited—but listen with our whole being, totally, without any object, then we will see that we will never ask the "how," the method, the system, the philosophy, the discipline. In that state of complete attention there is no contradiction within ourselves, there is no battle between the conscious and the unconscious—it is a total attention. And so there is no need to go through all the psychoanalytical process, delving into memory after memory, in order to be free.

So can we, you and I who are listening, actually experience without each experience leaving a residue? You understand the problem? If I experience something and it leaves a memory, that memory conditions future experiences, and so that which is measureless can never be experienced. That *which is* is timeless, and memory is of time. Whether it is the superficial memory of a certain incident or the memory of an experience that one has had on rare occasions when one has perhaps felt, known, something beyond the measurement of the mind, something eternal—whatever it be, we are forever clinging to that experience, and so it prevents the mind from experiencing further, more profoundly. So long as experience leaves a mark of memory, which is time, that which is eternal can never be experienced. So the mind must die to itself from moment to moment of all experience. Surely only in that state is it creative.

And can one have the capacity to penetrate deeply? I think one can, but only when we are not satisfied with explanations, when we are no longer fed with words, when we no longer depend on other people's experiences, when we are not looking to anybody, when we are taking the journey completely alone, having shed all tradition, all culture, all belief, and above all, all knowledge—because a mind that is cluttered with knowledge can only experience that which it knows. So can you and I, not theoretically, not just for the moment because you are listening to a talk, but actually, directly, put aside all the inherited racial accumulation, cease to be English or Hindu, cease to have religion in the sense of orthodoxy, dogmas, symbols? If we cling to all these, we are no longer seekers; then we are merely pursuing satisfaction, the pleasure of an experience, which the conditioned mind demands.

And I think this capacity is not of time. If we look to time, then we shall again be caught in the method. But to see the importance, feel the importance, be aware of the necessity of complete inward freedom, see the truth of it—then that very perception, that very listening with full attention, brings the capacity.

Question: I want my child to be free. Is true freedom incompatible with loyalty to the English tradition of life and education?

KRISHNAMURTI: This is what they say in India too—can I be a Hindu, with loyalty to my country, and yet be free to find God? Can I still be a Hindu, a Buddhist, a Christian, and yet be free? Can you? One may have a passport, a piece of paper for traveling, but that need not make one a Hindu. Surely freedom is totally incompatible with any nationality, any tradition. There is the American way of life, the English way of life, the Russian way of life, and the Hindu way of life. Each one says, "Our way is the only way," and clings to it; and yet we all talk of freedom, peace.

I think all this has to go if we are to bring about a different world, a world which is ours, a world in which there is no communism or socialism or capitalism or Hinduism or Christianity. The earth is our world in which to live undivided, to live happily, to live freely. But it cannot be our world so long as there are Englishmen, Hindus, Germans, communists, and so on—that way it can never be free. This freedom can only come about when we are really religious, when each one of us is really an individual in the true sense.

When we are religiously free, then we can create a world which is ours and so give a different kind of education—not merely condition the child to a particular culture, encase him in a particular system, train him to be a communist or atheist or Catholic or Protestant or Hindu; such individuals are not free; therefore, they are not really religious; they are merely conditioned, and they create such misery. So if we are to create a totally different world, there must be a religious revolution—not the going back to some belief, or going forward to some achievement, but freedom from all tradition, all dogma, all symbols, all belief, so that one is truly an individual, free to find, to search out, that which is measureless.

Question: The Western mind is trained to contemplate on object, the Eastern mind to meditate on subject. The first leads to action, the other to the negation of action. It is only by the integration of these two directions of perception within the individual that a total understanding of life can emerge. What is the key to that integration?

KRISHNAMURTI: Why do we divide the human being as of the West or of the East? Is there not a different approach to this problem altogether?—not merely an attempt to integrate action with meditation. I think such an integration is an impossibility. Perhaps there may be a different approach to the problem altogether instead of this attempt to integrate action with a state of mind which is aloof, which merely observes, contemplates.

We have divided life as action and nonaction, and therefore we seek integration. But if we do not divide ourselves at all, if we can eliminate from our thinking this whole issue of the Orient as against the Occident and look at the problem differently—then, in seeking reality, the mind becomes creative, and in the very perception of that which is real, there is action, which is contemplation—there is no division.

To the Western mind, the Orient with its mysticism and all that stuff is foreign. Because of the cold climate in the West, because of the various forms of industrial revolution and all the rest of it, you must be active, you must bother with a lot of clothing. In the East, where there is a very warm climate and very little clothing is needed, one has time, leisure; and there is the old tradition that one must go away from society to find. Here, you are concerned entirely with reform—better conditions, better living. So, how can the two be integrated? Both approaches may be false—and surely they must be when one gives exaggerated importance to the one and denies the other.

But if we try to find, seeking not as a group of Christians but as individuals, having no authority in our search for reality, then that very search itself is creative, and that very creativeness brings about its own action. If we do not seek that religious freedom, all reform leads only to further misery—which is being shown everywhere. You may have peace through terror, but there will still be inward wars with each other—competition, ruthlessness, the search for power by the group or by the individual. Only those people who are religious in the deepest sense of the word, who have shed all spiritual authority, who do not belong to any church, any group, who have not identified themselves with any particular doctrine, who are seeking everlastingly, timelessly asking and never accumulating any experience—only such people are truly creative. Such a mind is the only religious and therefore revolutionary mind, and it will act without dividing itself as the contemplative or the active because such a one is a total being.

Question: I am afraid of death. I have lived a very rich and full life intellectually, artistically, and emotionally. Now that I am approaching death, all that satisfaction is gone, and I am left with nothing but the religious beliefs of my childhood—such as purgatory, hell, and so on—which now fill me with terror. Can you give me any reassurance?

KRISHNAMURTI: And I think the next question is also concerned with death, so I will read that too.

Question: I am a young man, until a few weeks ago in perfect health and enjoying life to the full. An accident has injured me fatally, and the doctors only give me a few months to live. Why should this happen to me, and how am I to meet death?

KRISHNAMURTI: I think most of us, whether we are young or old, are afraid of death. The man who wants to finish his work, he is afraid of death, because he wants to achieve a result. The man who is making a successful career does not want to be cut off in the middle of it, so he is afraid of death. The man who has lived fully, with all the richness of this world, he also is afraid of death. So what is one to do? You see, we never ask fundamental questions. The person who has lived richly, fully, has never asked the question. His rich and full life was very superficial because underneath, deep down, all the traditions of Christianity, of Hinduism, or what you will were there, hidden, lying dormant; and when his life is not being

lived richly, fully, the sediments of the past come to the top, and he is afraid of purgatory, or he invents a heaven which will be satisfactory.

So there are in the unconscious the sediments of our culture, of our racial fears, and so on. And while we are active, thoughtful, healthy, it seems to me it is a necessity to inquire into the very depths of our being in order to find out and eradicate all these deposits, sediments, of tradition, of fear so that when death does come, we are capable of looking at it. Which means, really, that we should be able to ask a fundamental question now, and not be satisfied with superficial answers. There are those who believe in reincarnation; they say they will live the next life, that there is a continuity, there is no annihilation; and they are happy in that belief. But they have not solved the problem; they are merely satisfied with words, with explanations. Or, if you are very intellectual, you say, "Death is inevitable, it is part of existence. As I am born, I shall die. Why make an issue of it?" They have not solved the problem either.

Most of us are afraid, only we cover it up with beliefs, with explanations, with rationality. And there is the man who says, "I am only young, why should I be cut off? I want to live, see the richness of life. And why should it happen to me?" When anyone says, "Why should it happen to me?" obviously it means, "It should happen not to me but to you." So we are all concerned with this issue. Now, can we search into it?

Please, will you experiment with what I am saying?—not merely listen, but really experience this now by actually following the description and applying it to yourself. The description is merely the door through which you are looking, but you have to look. If you do not look, the description, the door, has very little value. So, we are going to look, and find out for ourselves the truth of this problem—but not by seeking explanations, not by changing one belief for another, not by substituting the Christian belief in heaven for the Hindu belief in reincarnation, and so on.

The fact is, there is death; the organism comes to an end. And the fact is, there may or may not be a continuity. But I want to know now, while I am healthy, vital, and alive, what it is to live richly, and I also want to find out now what it means to die—not wait for an accident or a disease to carry me off. I want to know what it means to die—living, to enter the house of death. Not theoretically, but actually, I want to experience the extraordinary thing it must be—to enter into the unknown, cutting off all the known.

Not to meet with the known, not to meet a friend on the other side—that is what is frightening us. I am afraid to let go of all the things I have known: the family, the virtue that I have cultivated, the property, the position, the power, the sorrow, the joy, everything that I have gathered, which is all the known—I am afraid to let all that go, totally, deep down, right from the depths of my being, and to be with the unknown, which is, after all, death. Can I, who am the result of the known, not seek to move into something also known, but enter something which I do not know, something which I have never experienced? Books have been written about death, various religions have taught of it; but those are all descriptions, those are all the things known. Death, surely, is the unknown as truth is the unknown, and the mind that is burdened with the known can never enter into that realm of the unknown.

So the question is: Can I put away all the known? I cannot put it away by will. Please, follow this. I cannot put away the known by will, by volition, because that entails a maker of the will, an entity who says, "This is right and this is wrong; this I want and this I do not want." Such a mind is acting from the known, is it not? It says, "I want to enter that extraordinary thing which is death, the unknowable, and so I must relinquish the known." Such a person then searches the various corners of his mind in order to push aside the known. This action allows the entity who deliberately pushed away the known to remain. But as that entity is itself the result of the known, it can never experience or enter that extraordinary state. Is this not clear?—that so long as there is an experiencer, that experiencer is the result of the known; and then that experiencer wishes to understand that which is the not-known, the unknown. Whatever efforts he may make towards that, his experience will still be within the field of the known. So the problem then is: Can the experiencer cease, totally? Because, he is the actor, he is the urge, he is the seeker, he is the entity who says, "This is the known, and I must move towards the unknown." And surely any action, any movement on the part of the observer, the experiencer, is still within the field of the known.

So, can the mind, which is the result of the known, which is the result of time—can that mind enter into the unknown? Obviously it cannot. So any explanation of death, any belief, is still the outcome of the known. Therefore can I, can my mind, denude itself totally of all the known? There is no answer. It depends on you. You have to find out, you have to inquire, you have to delve into this problem. Fundamental questions have no yes or no for an answer. You have to posit the fundamental question and wait for it to unfold itself. It cannot unfold itself if you are merely seeking an answer, an explanation. This is the fundamental question: Can I, who am the result of the known, enter into the unknown, which is death? If I want to do it, it must be done while living, surely, not at the last moment. At the last moment the mind is not capable of looking, understanding; it is diseased, tired, exhausted; it has very little consciousness. But while one is active, full of consciousness, alert, aware—can one not find out? While living, to enter the house of death is not just a morbid idea; it is the only solution. While living a rich, full life— whatever that means—or while living a miserable, impoverished life, can we not know that which is not measurable, that which is only glimpsed by the experiencer in rare moments?

So can you and I put away the known? You understand the depths of the problem? The mind clings to every pleasurable experience and wants to avoid the unpleasant. This accumulation of the pleasant is the known, and the avoidance of the unpleasant is also the known. Can the mind die from moment to moment to everything that it experiences, and never accumulate? Because if there is accumulation, then there is the experiencer always looking from that accumulation; that accumulation itself is the experiencer; therefore, he can never know what is beyond the known. I think it is very important for each one of us to understand this deeply because then knowledge, then discipline, then belief and dogma, the pursuit of teachers and gurus, and all the rest of it, have no meaning at all. For the disciplines, the methods, are all the known—things to be practiced and ends to be gained.

Can we see the totality of all that, giving our whole attention to it?—not in order to gain the unknown, for such attention is merely exclusion, a form of greed. Can we be aware that so long as there is any movement of the mind, that movement is born of time, of the known, and such a movement towards the unknown can never enter that field of freedom? If we can, then the mind, seeing the truth of it, becomes completely motionless. It is no longer seeking, asking, searching out because it understands that any searching, asking, is from the known. Only when the mind is totally still is it possible for the unknown to be.

June 19, 1955

Fourth Talk in London

It seems to me that one of the most difficult problems is this question of how to bring about a fundamental change in ourselves. We often think the transformation of the individual is not important, but that we should rather be concerned with the mass, with the whole. I think that is quite a mistaken idea. I think transformation must begin with the individual—if there is such an entity as the individual. There must be a fundamental change in you and me.

One can see that any conscious change is no change at all. The deliberate process of bringing about self-improvement, the deliberate cultivation of a particular pattern or form of action does not bring about a real change at all, for it is merely a projection of one's own desire, of one's own background, as a reaction. Yet we are most of us concerned over this question of change because we are groping, we are confused. And those of us who are at all given to seriousness must vitally inquire into this question of how to bring about a change in ourselves. The difficulty, it seems to me, lies in understanding the fact that any form of change in a conditioned mind gives only a different conditioning, not a transformation. If I, as a Hindu or a Christian or what you will, try to change within that pattern, it is no real change at all; it is only perhaps a seemingly better, more convenient, more adaptive conditioning, but fundamentally it is not a change. I think one of the greatest difficulties we are confronted with is that we think we can change within the pattern. Whereas, surely, for a mind which is conditioned by society, by any form of culture, to bring about a conscious change within the pattern is still a process of conditioning. If that is very clear, then I think our inquiry to find out what transformation is, how it is possible to bring about a radical change in ourselves, becomes very interesting, a vital issue. Because culture—that is, the society about us—can never produce a religious man; it can breed ''religion,'' but it cannot bring about a religious man.

Now, if I may somewhat go off the point—most of us have a strong reaction to that word *religion*. Some like it; the very word gives them a sense of emotional satisfaction; others are repelled by the word. But I think it is important to find out how to truly listen to what is being said. How does one listen? You hear the word religion, and either you like it or you dislike it. That very word acts as a barrier to further understanding, to further exploration, because one reacts to the word. But can one listen without that reaction? For if we can listen without any reaction, without our prejudices, our peculiarities, our idiosyncrasies, our beliefs coming in the way, then I think we can go very far. But it is very arduous to put our prejudices aside and give complete attention to something that is being said. Attention becomes narrow, exclusive, when it is merely concentrated on a particular idea. Most of us have ideas, certain prejudices, and so long as we are thinking along those lines, we may pay so-called attention, but it is really only a form of exclusion—which is not attention at all.

What I am suggesting is that to really listen, one must be aware of one's own prejudices, one's own emotional and neurological reactions to a particular word, like *God, religion, love,* and so on, and put those reactions aside. If one can so listen, attentively, not looking for any particular idea which may tally with one's own, or any which may go contrary to one's own, then I think these talks will be worthwhile.

So, as I was saying, culture can only produce religions, not a religious man. And I think it is only the religious man who can really bring about a radical change within himself. Any change, any alteration within the conditioned mind of a particular culture is no real change; it is merely a continuation of the same thing modified. I think that is fairly obvious, if one thinks about it—that so long as I have the pattern of a Hindu, a Christian, a Buddhist, or what you will, any change I bring about within that pattern is a conscious change, still part of the pattern, and therefore no change at all. Then the question arises: Can I bring about a change through the unconscious? That is, either I start consciously to change the pattern of my living, the way I think, to remove consciously my prejudices—which is all a deliberate process of effort in the pursuit of a determined object, ideal—or I try to bring about a change by delving into the unconscious.

Surely, in both these approaches is involved the problem of effort. I see I must change—for various reasons, for various motives—and I consciously set about changing. Then I realize, if I think about it at all, that it is not a real change, and so I delve into the unconscious, go into that very deeply, hoping through various forms of analysis to bring about a change, a modification, or a deeper adjustment. And now I ask myself whether this conscious and unconscious effort to change does bring about a change at all? Or, must one go beyond the conscious as well as the unconscious to bring about a radical change? You see, both the conscious desire as well as the unconscious urge to change imply effort. If you go into it very deeply, you will see that in trying to change oneself into something else, there is always the one who makes the effort and also that which is static, that upon which the effort is exerted. So in this process of desire to bring about a change—whether it is conscious or unconscious—there is always the thinker and the thought, the thinker trying to change his thought—the one who says, "I must change," and the state which he desires to change. So, there is this duality, and we are always, everlastingly, trying to bridge this gap through effort. I see in myself that there is, in the conscious as well as in the unconscious, the maker of the effort and that which he wishes to change. There is a division between that which I am and that which I wish to be. Which means there is a division between the thinker and the thought, and so there is a conflict. And the thinker is always trying to overcome that conflict, consciously or unconsciously.

We are quite familiar with this process; it is what we are doing all the time; all our social structure, our moral structure, our adjustments, and so on, are based on that. But does that bring about a change? If not, then must not a change come about at a totally different level which is not in the field either of the conscious or of the unconscious? Surely the whole field of the mind, the conscious as well as the unconscious, is conditioned by our particular culture. That is fairly obvious. So long as I am a Hindu, a Buddhist, a Christian, or what you will, the very culture in which I have been brought up conditions my whole being. My whole being is the conscious as well as the unconscious. In the field of the unconscious are all the traditions, the residue of all the past of man, inherited as well as acquired; and in the field of the conscious I am trying to change. Such change can only be according to my conditioning, and therefore can never bring about freedom. So transformation, obviously, is something which is not of the mind at all; it must be at a different level altogether, at a different depth, at a different height.

So, how am I to transform? I see the truth—at least, I see something in it—that a change, a transformation, must begin at a level which the mind as the conscious or the unconscious cannot reach because my consciousness as a whole is conditioned. So, what am I to do? I hope I am making the problem clear. If I may put it differently: Can my mind, the conscious as well as the unconscious, be free of society?—society being all the education, the culture, the norm, the values, the standards. Because if it is not free, then whatever change it tries to bring about within that conditioned state is still limited and therefore no change at all. If I see the truth of that, what is the mind to do? If I say it must become quiet, then that very "becoming quiet" is part of the pattern; it is the outcome of my desire to bring about a transformation at a different level.

So, can I look without any motive? Can my mind exist without any incentive, without any motive to change or not to change? Because, any motive is the outcome of the reaction of a particular culture, is born out of a particular background. So, can my mind be free from the given culture in which I have been brought up? This is really quite an important question. Because if the mind is not free from the culture in which it has been reared, nurtured, surely the individual can never be at peace, can never have freedom. His gods and his myths, his symbols and all his endeavors are limited, for they are still within the field of the conditioned mind. Whatever efforts he makes, or does not make, within that limited field, are really futile in the deepest sense of that word. There may be a better decoration of the prison—more light, more windows, better food—but it is still the prison of a particular culture.

So, can the mind, realizing the totality of itself, not just the superficial layers or certain depths—can the mind come to that state when transformation is not the result of a conscious or unconscious effort? If that question is clear, then the reaction to the problem arises—how is one to reach such a state? Surely the very question "how?" is another barrier. Because the "how" implies the search for and practice of a certain system, a method, the "steps" towards that fundamental, deep, inevitable transformation at a new level. You understand? The "how" implies the desire to reach, the urge to achieve; and that very attempt to be something is the product of our society, which is acquisitive, which is envious. So we are caught again.

So, what is the mind to do? I see the importance of change. And I see that any change at any level of the conscious or unconscious mind is no change at all. If I really understand that, if I have grasped the truth of it—that so long as there is the maker of the effort, the thinker, the 'I' trying to achieve a result, there must be a division and hence the desire to bring about an abridgment, an integration between the two, which involves conflict—if I see the truth of that, then what happens?

Here is the problem: Do I see that any effort I make within the field of thinking, conscious as well as unconscious, must entail a separation, a duality, and therefore conflict? If I see the truth of that, then what happens? Then have I, has the conscious or unconscious mind, to do anything? Please, this is not some Oriental philosophy of doing nothing or going into some kind of mysterious trance. On the contrary, this requires a great deal of thought, penetration, and inquiry. One cannot come to it unless one has gone through the whole process of understanding the conscious as well as the unconscious, not by merely saying, "Well, I won't think, and then things will happen." Things won't happen. That is why it is very important to have self-knowledge. Not self-knowledge according to some philosopher or some psychoanalyst,

great or little—that is mere imitation; it is like reading a book and trying to be that book; that is not self-knowledge. Self-knowledge is actually discovering in oneself the process of one's thinking, feeling, motives, responses—the actual state in which we are, not a desired state.

That is why it is very important to have self-knowledge—of whatever we are: ugly, good, bad, beautiful, joyous, the whole of it—to know one's superficial conditioning as well as the deeper unconscious conditioning of centuries of tradition, of urges, compulsions, imitations, to know, to actually experience the whole totality through self-knowledge. Then I think we will find that the conscious as well as the unconscious mind no longer makes any movement to achieve a change, but a change comes about, a transformation comes about, at a totally different level—at a height, a depth, which the conscious as well as the unconscious mind can never touch. The transformation must begin there, not at the conscious or unconscious level, which is the product of a culture.

That is why it is very important to be free of society through self-knowledge. And I think then, when this whole process of recognition by society has ceased, when the mind is no longer concerned with reform of any kind—then there is a radical transformation which the conscious or the unconscious mind cannot touch, and from that transformation a different society, a different state, can be brought about. But that state, that society, cannot be conceived of—it must come from the depths of self-discovery. So it seems to me that what is important is this inquiry into the self, the 'me', and to know the self as it is, with its ambitions, envies, aggressive demands, deceptions, the division as the high and the low—to uncover it so that not only the conscious mind is revealed but also the unconscious, the storehouse of past tradition, the centuries of deposits of all kinds of experiences. Knowing the totality of that is the ending of it. Then the mind, not being concerned with society, with recognition, with reformation, even with the changing of itself, finds that there is a change, that there is a transformation which is not the outcome of a purposeful effort to produce a result.

Question: I am an artist and very much concerned with the technique of painting. Is it possible that this very concern hinders the true creative expression?

KRISHNAMURTI: I wonder why most of us, including the artist, are so concerned with technique. We are all asking how—how am I to be more happy, how am I to find God, how am I to be a better artist, how am I to do this or that? We are all concerned with the "how." I am violent; I want to know how to be nonviolent. Being so concerned with technique, and as the world offers nothing but that, we are caught in it. We pursue the technique because we want results. I want to be a great artist, engineer, musician; I want to achieve fame, notoriety. My ambition drives me to seek the method.

Can an artist, or any human being if he is pursuing a technique, really be an artist? Whereas, if one loves the very thing one is doing, then is one not an artist? But we do not understand what that word means. Can I love a thing for itself, for its own sake, if I am ambitious, if I want to be known? If I want to be the best painter, the best poet, the greatest saint, if I am seeking a result, can I then really love a thing for itself? If I am envious, if I am imitative, if there is any fear, any competition, can I love that which I am doing?

If I love a thing, then I can learn the technique—how to mix colors or what you will. But now, we do not have this sense of real love of a thing. We are full of ambition, envy; we want to be a success. And so we are learning techniques and losing the real thing—not losing it, because we have never had it. At present our whole mind is given to acquiring a technique which will get us somewhere. If I love what I am doing, surely then there is no problem, there is no competition, is there? I am doing what I want to do—not because it gives me any publicity; to me that is not important. What is important is to totally love what one is doing, and that very love is then the guide.

If the parent wants his son to follow in his footsteps, to be something, if the parents try to fulfill themselves in their children, then there is no love; it is merely self-projection. The very love of the child will bring its own culture, will it not? But unfortunately we do not think in these ways. And so there is this whole problem, this astonishing development of technique.

Question: I am entirely occupied with the ordinary cares, joys, and sorrows of daily life. I am quite aware that my mind is exclusively taken up with action, reaction, and motive, but I cannot go beyond these. Since reading your books and hearing you speak, I see that there is another and a completely different way of living, but I cannot find the key which will unlock the door of my cramped, narrow abode and lead me into freedom. What am I to do?

KRISHNAMURTI: I wonder if we *are* aware what our minds are occupied with! As the questioner says, the mind is only occupied with superficial things—earning a livelihood, parenthood, all the rest of it. But do we know what our mind is occupied with at a deeper level? Apart from the daily occupations, do we know what our mind is occupied with at a different level, the unconscious? Or, are our conscious minds so occupied during the day, all the time, that we do not know what the unconscious is occupied with? Are we aware of what we are occupied with apart from the daily routine, daily existence?

For most of us, our occupation is with the daily process of living, and we are concerned with how to bring about a change in that—a better adjustment, more happiness, less of this and more of that. To hold on to superficial happiness, to put away certain things that cause us pain, to avoid certain stresses, strains, to adjust ourselves to certain relationships, and so on—that is our whole occupation.

Now, can we let that occupation alone—let it go on, on the surface, and find out deep down what our mind is unconsciously occupied with? We all see that there must be some kind of adjustment on the surface, but are we concerned with the deeper occupation of the mind? Do I know, and do you know, what the deeper mind is occupied with? Surely we should find out because that occupation may translate itself into the superficial occupations and adjustments with their joys and sorrows, their miseries and trials. So unless you and I know the deeper occupations of the mind, mere alteration at the surface has very little meaning.

Surely all superficial occupation must come to an end if I am to find the other. If my mind is occupied all the time with superficial adjustments, putting the picture straight which someone else has made askew, always concerned about the things of the home, about my children, about my wife, about what society thinks and doesn't think, about my neighbor's opinion, and so on—can that mind, which is already occupied, discover the deeper occupation of itself? Or, must not the superficial occupation come to an end? That is, can we let it go on, adjust itself without force, but also inquire deeply into what our mind is occupied with at a deeper level?

What is it occupied with at a deeper level? Do you and I know? Or do we merely conjecture about it or think someone else can tell us? Surely I cannot find out unless I am not totally occupied with the superficial adjustments. That is, there must be release from the superficial to find out. But we dare not release, we dare not let go, because we do not know what is below; we are frightened, we are scared. That is why most of us are occupied. Deep down there may be complete loneliness, a sense of deep frustration, fear, agonizing ambition, or what you will—for of that we are not fully conscious. But being a little conscious, or being slightly aware, we are frightened of all that. So we are concerned with the room, the pictures, the lampshades, who comes and goes, the parties; we read books, listen to the radio, join groups—you know, the whole wretched business. All that may be an escape from the deeper issue. And to examine the deeper issue, there must be the letting go of the room and the contents of the room. Unfortunately, we want the room, and the discovery of the other is something we never allow ourselves to experience.

It is not a question of trying to reach the deeper level. Trying is always a question of time. If I want to inquire into the deeper issue, and I see the necessity of letting the superficial things alone, then there is no trying. I do not try to open the door and consciously make a move to get out of the house. I know I must get out, and I get out—the door is there. There is no attempt to reach that door; you are not thinking in terms of trying. Understanding and action are simultaneous. But such integration cannot take place if you are merely concerned with the surface level.

Question: Is there any real significance in dreams? What happens during sleep?

KRISHNAMURTI: I think it would be good if we could go into this question very deeply. So, if I may suggest, do not merely listen to the description but actually experience what is being said. Then perhaps we can go together into the significance of this whole process of sleeping and dreaming.

During the day, the waking hours, we are so occupied with our worries, with our miseries, with our little joys, the job, the livelihood, the passing fashions, and all the rest of it, that we never receive any intimation, any hint of the deeper things; the superficial mind is too busy, too active. So when we sleep we begin to dream, and you can see that the dreams take various forms, various symbols, which contain the intimations, the hints. Then, realizing that these dreams have some kind of significance, we seek interpretations in order to translate them into our daily life. So the interpreter becomes very important, and we gradually begin to depend on others, psychologically. Or else we interpret for ourselves according to our own likes and dislikes, and so again we are caught.

Is it possible not to dream at all? The expert psychologists say it is impossible—that though we may not remember it, there is always a dream process going on. But can I, can you and I receive the intimations, the hints, in the waking hours during the day when the mind is alert?—at least, supposed to be alert. That is, can my mind not let a single thought go by—please listen—not let a single thought go by without knowing all the contents of that thought? Which does not mean I must be so concentrated that I will not let one thought escape me; you cannot be so concentrated. Thought will escape you, but there will be other thoughts.

So, can one play with a thought—I'm using the word *play* deliberately—and find out the whole content of it?—the motive, the reaction, and the further reaction of that motive. Which means, to have no condemnation

of that thought, no justification, no comparison, no evaluation, but just to observe that thought as it arises. Can we watch each thought, as it goes by, so that the mind becomes aware of the depths of each thought and begins to purge itself of all the contents of its own thoughts?—and there are not very many thoughts either. And, when the mind has finished watching thought, pursuing thought, then can it invite thought? So that all the thoughts that are hidden, accumulated in the dark, can be brought out, examined, looked at, gone into—again, without condemnation, without evaluation—just looked at so as to know the whole business of it.

I am not describing a method. Please do not translate this as a method to empty the mind so as not to dream. Because all dreams, as we said, are mere intimations, hints, which will become unnecessary if during the waking consciousness we are extraordinarily alert, alive, aware of all the inward things. Then what happens when one does go to sleep? As the conscious mind has uncovered all the unconscious intimations, hints, warnings, and gone deeply into the unconscious during the day, it has become fatigued and quiet. So there is no contradiction, no conflict, between the conscious and the unconscious; there is a quietude. Then the mind can go beyond, can reach something which the conscious and the unconscious mind can never reach.

I do not know if you have ever experimented with this just for the fun of it—not for any result, not in order to find a state of consciousness which is not touched, corrupted, by any human being; then it becomes a bargaining, a trade. But if one can really without any motive just find out, then sleep has a great deal of significance. What I am saying has nothing to do with the astral plane and all that stuff, the imaginations and peculiarities of our particular conditioning—all that must obviously go. Everything that one has acquired, learned, must totally disappear. Then only is it possible, during that state which we call sleep, for something to come into being which the mind cannot possibly perceive; and on waking the mind is made new. A source has come into being which is not the product of our ambitions, envies, desires, and pursuits.

I think it is very important to understand all this. And to understand it, one must have self-knowledge—how the mind works during the day, its motives, its actions and reactions—so that at the end of the day the conscious mind becomes very quiet. Then, the contradiction between the conscious and the unconscious having been understood, the mind becomes really still—not made still. The mind that is made still is a dead mind, a corrupt mind. But the mind that is still through understanding, the mind that comes to stillness because of self-knowledge—such a mind in sleep can perhaps reach something, or rather, something else can reach the mind which the mind itself cannot pursue. Then, it seems to me, such a sleep has significance in the waking hours.

But that requires great delving, and not clinging to anything that one has discovered. Because if you are tied to your own knowledge, or to the knowledge of others, you cannot go very far. There must be the dying to everything that one has accumulated, to every experience that one has rejoiced in or put aside. It is only then that something which is beyond the mind can touch it.

June 24, 1955

Fifth Talk in London

One of our problems, it seems to me, amongst so many others, is this dependence—dependence on people for our happiness, dependence on capacity, the dependence that leads the mind to cling to something. And the question is: Can the mind ever be totally free from all dependence? I think that is a fundamental question and one which we should be constantly asking ourselves.

Obviously, superficial dependence is not what we are talking about, but at the deeper level there is that psychological demand for some kind of security, for some method which will assure the mind of a state of permanency; there is the search for an idea, a relationship, that will be enduring. As this is one of our major problems, it seems to me it is very important to go into it rather deeply, and not respond superficially with an immediate reaction.

Why do we depend? Psychologically, inwardly, we depend on a belief, on a system, on a philosophy; we ask another for a mode of conduct; we seek teachers who will give us a way of life which will lead us to some hope, some happiness. So we are always, are we not, searching for some kind of dependence, security. Is it possible for the mind ever to free itself from this sense of dependence? Which does not mean that the mind must achieve independence—that is only the reaction to dependence. We are not talking of independence, of freedom from a particular state. If we can inquire without the reaction of seeking freedom from a particular state of dependence, then we can go much more deeply into it. But if we are drawn away at a tangent in search of independence, we shall not understand this whole question of psychological dependence of which we are talking.

We know we depend—on our relationships with people or on some idea or on a system of thought. Why? We accept the necessity for dependence; we say it is inevitable. We have never questioned the whole issue at all, why each one of us seeks some kind of dependence. Is it not that we really, deep down, demand security, permanency? Being in a state of confusion, we want someone to get us out of that confusion. So, we are always concerned with how to escape or avoid the state in which we are. In the process of avoiding that state, we are bound to create some kind of dependence, which becomes our authority. If we depend on another for our security, for our inward well-being, there arise out of that dependence innumerable problems, and then we try to solve those problems—the problems of attachment. But we never question, we never go into the problem of dependence itself. Perhaps if we can really intelligently, with full awareness, go into this problem, then we may find that dependence is not the issue at all—that it is only a way of escaping from a deeper fact.

May I suggest that those who are taking notes should refrain from doing so. Because, these meetings will not be worthwhile if you are merely trying to remember what is said for afterwards. But if we can directly experience what is being said now, not afterwards, then it will have a definite significance; it will be a direct experience, and not an experience to be gathered later through your notes and thought over in memory. Also, if I may point it out, taking notes disturbs others around you.

As I was saying, why do we depend, and make dependence a problem? Actually, I do not think dependence is the problem; I think there is some other deeper factor that makes us depend. And if we can unravel that, then both dependence and the struggle for freedom will have very little significance; then all the problems which arise through dependence will wither away. So, what is the deeper issue? Is it that the mind abhors, fears, the idea of being alone? And does the mind know that state which it avoids? I depend on somebody, psychologically, inwardly, because of a state which I am trying to avoid but which I have never gone into, which I have never examined. So, my dependence on a person—for love, for encouragement, for guidance—becomes immensely important, as do all the many problems that arise from it. Whereas, if I am capable of looking at the factor that is making me depend—on a person, on God, on prayer, on some capacity, on some formula or conclusion which I call a belief—then perhaps I can discover that such dependence is the result of an inward demand which I have never really looked at, never considered.

Can we, this evening, look at that factor?—the factor which the mind avoids, that sense of complete loneliness with which we are superficially familiar. What is it to be lonely? Can we discuss that now and keep to that issue, and not introduce any other problem?

I think this is really very important. Because so long as that loneliness is not really understood, felt, penetrated, dissolved—whatever word you may like to use—so long as that sense of loneliness remains, dependence is inevitable, and one can never be free; one can never find out for oneself that which is true, that which is religion. While I depend, there must be authority, there must be imitation, there must be various forms of compulsion, regimentation, and discipline to a certain pattern. So, can my mind find out what it is to be lonely and go beyond it?—so that the mind is set totally free and therefore does not depend on beliefs, on gods, on systems, on prayers, or on anything else.

Surely, so long as we are seeking a result, an end, an ideal, that very urge to find creates dependence, from which arise the problems of envy, exclusion, isolation, and all the rest of it. So can my mind know the loneliness in which it actually is, though I may cover it up with knowledge, with relationship, amusement, and various other forms of distraction? Can I really understand that loneliness? Because, is it not one of our major problems, this attachment and the struggle to be detached? Can we talk this over together, or is that too impossible?

So long as there is attachment, dependence, there must be exclusion. The dependence on nationality, identification with a particular group, with a particular race, with a particular person or belief, obviously separates. So it may be that the mind is constantly seeking exclusion as a separate entity and is avoiding a deeper issue which is actually separative—the self-enclosing process of its own thinking, which breeds loneliness. You know the feeling that one must identify oneself as being a Hindu, a Christian, belonging to a certain caste, group, race— you know the whole business. If we can, each of us, understand the deeper issue involved, then perhaps all influence which breeds dependence will come to an end, and the mind will be wholly free.

Perhaps this may be too difficult a problem to discuss in such a large group?

Question: Can you define the word alone, *in contrast to* loneliness?

KRISHNAMURTI: Please—we are surely not seeking definitions, are we? We are asking if each one of us is aware of this loneliness— not now, perhaps, but we know of that state, and we know, do we not, that we are escaping from this state through various means and so multiplying our problems. Now can I, through awareness, burn away the root of the problem so that it will never again arise, or if it does, I will know how to deal with it without causing further problems?

Question: Does that mean we have to break unsatisfactory bonds?

KRISHNAMURTI: Surely that is not what we are discussing, is it? I do not think we are

following each other. And that is why I am hesitant as to whether it is possible to discuss this problem in so large a group.

We know, do we not, that we are attached. We depend on people, on ideas. It is part of our nature, our being, to depend on somebody. And that dependence is called love. Now I am asking myself, and perhaps you also are asking yourselves, whether it is possible to free the mind—psychologically, inwardly—from all dependence. Because I see that through dependence many, many problems arise—there is never an ending to them. Therefore I ask myself, is it possible to be so aware that the very awareness totally burns away this feeling of dependence on another, or on an idea, so that the mind is no longer exclusive, no longer isolated, because the demand for dependence has totally ceased?

For example, I depend on identification with a particular group; it satisfies me to call myself a Hindu or a Christian; to belong to a particular nationality is very satisfactory. In myself I feel dwarfed. I am a nobody, so to call myself somebody gives me satisfaction. That is a form of dependence at a very superficial level perhaps, but it breeds the poison of nationalism. And there are so many other deeper forms of dependence. Now, can I go beyond all that so that the mind will never depend psychologically, so that it has no dependence at all and does not seek any form of security? It will not seek security if I can understand this sense of extraordinary exclusion, of which I am aware and which I call loneliness—this self-enclosing process of thinking which breeds isolation.

So the problem is not how to be detached, how to free oneself from people or ideas, but can the mind stop this process of enclosing itself through its own activities, through its demands, through its urges? So long as there is the idea of the 'me', the 'I', there must be loneliness. The very essence, the ultimate self-enclosing process, is the discovery of this extraordinary sense of loneliness. Can I burn that away so that the mind never seeks any form of security, never demands?

This can only be answered, not by me, but by each one of us. I can only describe, but the description becomes merely a hindrance if it is not actually experienced. But if it reveals the process of your own thinking, then that very description is an awareness of yourself and of your own state. Then, can I remain in that state? Can I no longer wander away from the fact of loneliness but remain there without any escape, without any avoidance? Seeing, understanding, that dependence is not the problem but loneliness is, can my mind remain without any movement in that state which I have called loneliness? It is extraordinarily difficult because the mind can never be with a fact; it either translates it, interprets it, or does something about the fact; it never is with the fact.

Now, if the mind can remain with the fact without giving any opinion about the fact, without translating, without condemning, without avoiding it, then is the fact different from the mind? Is there a division between the fact and the mind, or is the mind itself the fact? For example, I am lonely. I am aware of that, I know what it means; it is one of the problems of our daily existence, of our existence altogether. And I want to tackle for myself this question of dependence and see if the mind can be really free—not just speculatively or theoretically or philosophically, but actually be free of dependence. Because, if I depend on another for my love, it is not love. And I want to find out what that state is which we call love. In trying to find it out, obviously all sense of dependence, security in relationship, all sense of demand, desire for permanency may go, and I may have to face something entirely different. So in inquiring, in going within myself, I may come upon this thing called loneliness. Now, can I

remain with that? I mean by "remain," not interpreting it, not evaluating it, not condemning it, but just observing that state of loneliness without any withdrawal. Then, if my mind can remain with that state, is that state different from my mind? It may be that my mind itself is lonely, empty, and not that there is a state of emptiness which the mind observes.

My mind observes loneliness and avoids it, runs away from it. But if I do not run away from it, is there a division, is there a separation, is there an observer watching loneliness? Or, is there only a state of loneliness, my mind itself being empty, lonely?—not, that there is an observer who knows that there is loneliness.

I think this is important to grasp—swiftly, not verbalizing too much. We say now, "I am envious, and I want to get rid of envy," so there is an observer and the observed; the observer wishes to get rid of that which he observes. But is the observer not the same as the observed? It is the mind itself that has created the envy, and so the mind cannot do anything about envy.

So, my mind observes loneliness; the thinker is aware that he is lonely. But by remaining with it, being fully in contact—which is, not to run away from it, not to translate and all the rest of it—then, is there a difference between the observer and the observed? Or is there only one state, which is, the mind itself is lonely, empty? Not that the mind observes itself as being empty, but the mind itself is empty. Then, can the mind, being aware that it itself is empty, and that whatever its endeavor, any movement away from that emptiness is merely an escape, a dependence—can the mind put away all dependence and be what it is, completely empty, completely lonely? And if it is in that state, is there not freedom from all dependence, from all attachment?

Please, this is a thing that must be gone into, not accepted because I am saying it. It has no meaning if you merely accept it. But if you are experiencing the thing as we are going along, then you will see that any movement on the part of the mind—movement being evaluation, condemnation, translation, and so on—is a distraction from the fact of *what is,* and so creates a conflict between itself and the observed.

This is really—to go further—a question of whether the mind can ever be without effort, without duality, without conflict, and therefore be free. The moment the mind is caught in conflict, it is not free. When there is no effort to be, then there is freedom. So can the mind be without effort—and therefore free?

Question: I am now able to accept problems on my own behalf. But how can I stop myself suffering on my children's behalf when they are affected by the same problems?

KRISHNAMURTI: Why do we depend on our children? And also, do we love our children? If it is love, then how can there be dependence, how can there be suffering? Our idea of love is that we suffer for others. Is it love that suffers? Or is it that I depend on my children, that through them I am seeking immortality, fulfillment, and all the rest of it? So I want my children to be something, and when they are not that, I suffer. The problem may not be the children at all; it may be me. Again we come back to the same thing—perhaps we do not know what it is to love. If we did love our children, we would stop all wars tomorrow, obviously. We would not condition our children. They would not be Englishmen, Hindus, Brahmins, and non-Brahmins; they would be children.

But we do not love, and therefore we depend on our children; through them we hope to fulfill ourselves. So when the child, through whom we are going to fulfill, does something which is not what we demand, then there is sorrow, then there is conflict.

Merely putting a question and waiting for an answer has very little meaning. But if we can observe for ourselves the process of this attachment, the process of seeking fulfillment through another, which is dependence and which must inevitably create sorrow—if we can see that as a fact for ourselves, then there may be something else, perhaps love. Then that relationship will produce quite a different society, quite a different world.

Question: When one has reached the stage of a quiet mind and has no immediate problem, what proceeds from that stillness?

KRISHNAMURTI: Quite an extraordinary question, is it not? You have taken it for granted that you have reached that still mind, and you want to know what happens after it. But to have a still mind is one of the most difficult things. Theoretically, it is the easiest, but factually, it is one of the most extraordinary states, which cannot be described. What happens you will discover when you come to it. But that coming to it is the problem, not what happens after.

You cannot come to that state. It is not a process. It is not something which you are going to achieve through a practice. It cannot be bought through time, through knowledge, through discipline, but only by understanding knowledge, by understanding the whole process of discipline, by understanding the total process of one's own thinking, and not trying to achieve a result. Then, perhaps, that quietness may come into being. What happens afterwards is indescribable; it has no word and it has no "meaning."

You see, every experience, so long as there is an experiencer, leaves a memory, a scar. And to that memory the mind clings, and it wants more and so breeds time. But the state of stillness is timeless; therefore, there is no experiencer to experience that stillness.

Please, this is really, if you wish to understand it, very important. So long as there is an experiencer who says, "I must experience stillness," and knows the experience, then it is not stillness; it is a trick of the mind. When one says, "I have experienced stillness," it is just an avoidance of confusion, of conflict—that is all. The stillness of which we are talking is something totally different. That is why it is very important to understand the thinker, the experiencer, the self that demands a state which it calls stillness. You may have a moment of stillness, but when you do, the mind clings to it and lives in that stillness in memory. That is not stillness; that is merely a reaction. What we are talking of is something entirely different. It is a state in which there is no experiencer, and therefore such silence, quietness, is not an experience. If there is an entity who remembers that state, then there is an experiencer; therefore, it is no longer that state.

This means, really, to die to every experience with never a moment of gathering, accumulating. After all, it is this accumulation that brings about conflict, the desire to have more. A mind that is accumulating, greedy, can never die to everything it has accumulated. It is only the mind that has died to everything it has accumulated, even to its highest experience—only such a mind can know what that silence is. But that state cannot come about through discipline because discipline implies the continuation of the experiencer, the strengthening of a particular intention towards a particular object, thereby giving the experiencer continuity.

If we see this thing very simply, very clearly, then we will find that silence of the mind of which we are talking. What happens after that is something that cannot be told, that cannot be described, because it has no "meaning"—except in books and philosophy.

Question: If we have not experienced that complete stillness, how can we know that it exists?

KRISHNAMURTI: Why do we want to know that it exists? It may not exist at all; it may be my illusion, a fancy. But one can see that so long as there is conflict, life is a misery. In understanding conflict, I will know what the other means. It may be an illusion, an invention, a trick of the mind—but in understanding the full significance of conflict, I may find something entirely different.

My mind is concerned with the conflict within itself and without. Conflict inevitably arises so long as there is an experiencer who is accumulating, who is gathering, and therefore always thinking in terms of time, of the 'more' and the 'less'. In understanding that, in being aware of that, there may come a state which may be called silence—give it any name you like. But the process is not the search for silence, for stillness, but rather the understanding of conflict, the understanding of myself in conflict.

I wonder if I have answered the question—which is, how do I know that there is silence? How do I recognize it? You understand? So long as there is a process of recognition, there is no silence.

After all, the process of recognition is the process of the conditioned mind. But in understanding the whole content of the conditioned mind, then the mind itself becomes quiet, there is no observer to recognize that he is in a state which he calls silence. Recognition of an experience has ceased.

Question: I would like to ask if you recognize the teaching of the Buddha that right understanding will help to solve the inner problems of man, and that inner peace of the mind depends entirely on self-discipline. Do you agree with the teachings of the Buddha?

KRISHNAMURTI: If one is inquiring to find out the truth of anything, all authority must be set aside, surely. There is neither the Buddha nor the Christ when one wishes to find what is true. Which means, really, the mind must be capable of being completely alone, and not dependent. The Buddha may be wrong, Christ may be wrong, and one may be wrong oneself. One must come to the state, surely, of not accepting any authority of any kind. That is the first thing—to dismantle the structure of authority. In dismantling the immense structure of tradition, that very process brings about an understanding. But merely to accept something because it has been said in a sacred book has very little meaning.

Surely, to find that which is beyond time, all the process of time must cease, must it not? The very process of search must come to an end. Because if I am seeking, then I depend—not only on another, but also on my own experience, for if I have learned something, I try to use that to guide myself. To find what is true, there must be no search of any kind—and that is the real stillness of the mind.

It is very difficult for a person who has been brought up in a particular culture, in a particular belief, with certain symbols of tremendous authority, to set aside all that and to think simply for himself and find out. He cannot think simply if he does not know himself, if there is no self-knowledge. And no one can give us self-knowledge—no teacher, no book, no philosophy, no discipline. The self is in constant movement; as it lives, it must be understood. And only through self-knowledge, through understanding the process of my own thinking, observed in the mirror of every reaction, do I

find out that so long as there is any movement of the 'me', of the mind, towards anything—towards God, towards truth, towards peace—then such a mind is not a quiet mind; it is still wanting to achieve, to grasp, to come to some state. If there is any form of authority, any compulsion, any imitation, the mind cannot understand. And to know that the mind imitates, to know that it is crippled by tradition, to be aware that it is pursuing its own experiences, its own projections—that demands a great deal of insight, a great deal of awareness, of self-knowledge.

Only then, with the whole content of the mind, the whole consciousness, unraveled and understood, is there a possibility of a state which may be called stillness—in which there is no experiencer, no recognition.

June 25, 1955

Sixth Talk in London

I think it is important to find out for oneself what it is that we are seeking and why we are seeking it. If we can go into this rather deeply, I think we will discover a great many things involved in it. Most of us are seeking some kind of fulfillment. Being discontented, we want to find contentment—either in some relationship or by fulfilling certain capacities or by searching for some kind of action that will be completely satisfying. Or, if we are not of that disposition, then we generally seek what we think is the truth, God, and so on. Most of us are seeking, searching, and if we could each find out for ourselves what it is that we are seeking, and why we seek, I think it would reveal a great deal.

Being discontented with ourselves, with our environment, with our activities, our particular job, most of us want a better job, a better position, a better understanding, wider activities, a more satisfying philosophy, a capacity that will be entirely gratifying. Outwardly, that is what we want, and when that does not satisfy us, we go a little deeper; we pursue philosophy, go in for reform, gather together in various groups to discuss, and so on—and still there is discontent.

It seems to me that it is important to find out whether the motive for our search is to understand discontent, or to find satisfaction. Because if it is satisfaction that we are seeking, at any level, then obviously our minds become very petty. Whereas there may perhaps be a discontent without an object, discontent in itself, which is not the urge to achieve a result, to get somewhere. I think that most of us, being dissatisfied in our relationships, in our ways of life, in our attitudes, in the values that we have, are trying to shake them all off and find a different set of values, different relationships, different ideas, different beliefs; but behind it all there is this urge to be satisfied. I think it would be important if we could find out for ourselves whether there is such a thing as a discontent which has no motive, which is not the outcome of some frustration—because that very discontent without motive may be the quality that is necessary.

At present when we seek, our search is the outcome of dissatisfaction, discontent, and our motive is to find gratification in some form or another. Especially when we talk about truth, or God, we are, are we not, seeking some state of mind which will be completely satisfying. Whether the mind is extensive, clever, has much capacity or little, if it is seeking satisfaction—however subtle—then its gods, its virtues, its philosophies, its values, are bound to be petty, small, shallow.

So, is it possible for the mind to be free of all search? Which means, really, to be free of that discontent which has the motive of finding satisfaction. Because however clever the mind is, however intelligent, and whatever virtues it has cultivated, surely if it is merely

seeking gratification in any form, it is incapable of grasping what is true. Surely all the thinking process is petty, is very limited. After all, thinking is the result of accumulated memory, of association, of experience, according to our conditioning; thinking is the reaction of that memory, thinking is the response of a conditioned mind. When that conditioning creates dissatisfaction, then any outcome of that dissatisfaction is surely still conditioned. Our search remains so utterly futile while it is based on a discontent which is merely the reaction to a particular conditioning.

If one sees that, then, the question arises as to whether there is any other form of discontent—whether there is a discontent which is not canalized, which has no motive, which is not seeking a fulfillment. It may be that discontent without any motive, the discontent which is not the response to a conditioning, is the one essential. At present our thinking, our search, has a motive, and that motive is based on our demand to find some permanent state of complete satisfaction where there will be no disturbance of any kind—which we call peace, which we call God or truth, and all our purpose in seeking is to gain that state.

So, search for most of us is based on the demand for satisfaction, the demand for a state of permanency in which we shall never be disturbed. And can such a mind, thinking from a motive of finding satisfaction, ever discover what is true? It seems to me that one must understand for oneself the whole process of why one seeks, and not be satisfied by any chosen word, by any chosen end or target, however ennobling, inspiring, or ideal it may seem. Because surely, the very way of the self, the 'me', is this constant process of discontent directed towards a fulfillment; that is all we know. When there is no fulfillment, there is frustration, and then come the many problems of how to overcome that frustration. So, the mind seeks a state in which there will be no frustration, no sorrow. Therefore our very search for so-called truth may be merely the fulfillment, the expansion, of the self, of the 'me'. And so we are caught in this vicious circle.

If one is aware of all this completely, to-tally, then there is no sense of fulfillment in any belief, in any dogma, in any activity, or in any particular state. The search for fulfill-ment implies sorrow, frustration; and seeing the truth of that, the mind then is no longer seeking.

I think there is a difference between the attention which is given to an object, and at-tention without object. We can concentrate on a particular idea, belief, object—which is an exclusive process, and there is also an at-tention, an awareness, which is not exclusive. Similarly, there is a discontent which has no motive, which is not the outcome of some frustration, which cannot be canalized, which cannot accept any fulfillment. Perhaps I may not be using the right word for it, but I think that that extraordinary discontent is the es-sential. Without that, every other form of dis-content merely becomes a way to satisfac-tion.

So can the mind, being aware of itself, knowing its own ways of thinking, put an end to this demand for self-fulfillment? And, when that comes to an end, can one remain without seeking and be completely in a state of void, with neither hope nor fear? Must not one arrive at that state when there is com-plete cessation of all seeking?—for then only is it possible for something to take place which is not the product of the mind.

After all, our thinking is the result of time, of many yesterdays; and through time, which is thinking, we are trying to find something which is beyond time. We are using the mind, the instrument of time, to find something which cannot be measured.

So can the mind totally cease for something else to take place? Which does not mean, surely, a state of amnesia, a state of blank-ness, a state of thoughtlessness. On the con-trary, it requires a great deal of alertness, an awareness in which there is no object nor an entity who is aware.

I think this is important to understand. At present when we are aware, simply, daily, there is in that awareness condemnation, judgment, evaluation; that is our normal awareness. When we look at a picture, imme-diately the whole process of condemnation, comparison, evaluation, is taking place, and we never see the picture because the screen of the evaluating process has come between. Can one look at that picture without any evaluation, without any comparison? Similar-ly, can I look at myself, whatever I am—all the mistakes, miseries, failures, sorrows, joys—and see it all without evaluation, just be aware of it without introducing the screen of condemnation or comparison? If the mind is capable of doing this, then we will find that that very awareness burns away the root of any particular problem.

When the mind is so aware, so totally aware, then there is no search; the mind is no longer comparing, seeking satisfaction, think-ing in terms of achievement. Then, is not the mind itself timeless? So long as the mind is comparing, condemning, judging, is condi-tioned, then it is in time; but when all that has totally ceased, then is not the mind itself that state which may be called the eternal? In that there is no observer, no experiencer who has associations, who has memories, who is seeking—which is all the product of time. So long as the experiencer is seeking, trying to fulfill, trying to gather experience, more knowledge, trying to find vaster fields in which to live, he is creating time, and whatever his actions are, they will always be in the field of time.

That which is measureless can never be found by the experiencer, by the seeker. It is only in that state in which the mind is no longer seeking, when the mind is not cultivating through search an end to be achieved—only then is it possible for reality to come into being.

Question: I am very interested in what you are saying and feel full of enthusiasm. What can I actually do about it?

KRISHNAMURTI: Enthusiasm soon fails. If you are merely inspired by what is being said, that inspiration will disappear, and you will seek another form of inspiration or another sensation. But if what is being said is part of your own discovery, the result of your own inward inquiry, then it is yours, it is not another's. But if it is another's, then you have the whole complicated, tiresome, corroding process of building authority and worshiping authority. If you have listened and if you have understood, then naturally you will do something about it; but if you are merely enthusiastic, "inspired," then you will join groups, form societies, organizations—which will become another hindrance.

After all, what is it that we are talking about? I am not saying anything new. We are only trying to understand how to look at ourselves, how to observe the whole process of consciousness—that which we are. To understand oneself, there must be self-knowledge, an awareness in which there is no condemnation, comparison, judgment—just the capacity to be aware, to know the way of our thought, the way of the self; and that needs no authority, surely. It is for you as an individual to find out for yourself.

The difficulty is that we want encouragement, we want companionship; we want to be told that we are doing very well; we want to meet others thinking along the same lines—which are all distractions. This is something that must be done entirely by yourself. You will find, if I may suggest, as you go deeper and deeper into the whole issue, that you will discover for yourself a state which will act of its own accord—you do not have to do anything. If you discover something real, that truth will operate of itself. But we want to operate on the truth; we want to do something about it. So we begin to condition ourselves further by every kind of experience in order to satisfy our own particular vanity through action.

But I think there is an activity which comes into being that is not the result of hearing a few talks or reading some books; it is an activity which comes into being because you yourself have experienced a state beyond the mind. But if you cling to that experience and try to act from it because you think you have understood something, then it becomes your own impediment.

Question: How can we have peace in this world?

KRISHNAMURTI: First of all let us see if anybody can give us peace. Politicians cannot give peace. There will be no peace while there are nationalists, while there are armies, separate governments, barriers of race and, above all, barriers of belief, barriers of religion—at least, so-called religion. There may be peace through terror, but surely that is not peace. Peace is something entirely different, is it not? Peace is the cessation of inward violence—that violence which expresses itself through ambition, through competition. And, are you and I willing to give up our ambitions? To be as nothing?

Peace is a state of mind, is it not, which cannot be bought. And how is one to come to this inward sense of peace? Not through self-hypnosis, not by saying, "I will be peaceful," and practicing the virtue of nonviolence. That is merely a process of hypnotizing oneself into a certain state. So can one actually, inwardly, psychologically, put aside all nationality, all sense of ambition, all sense of comparing oneself with somebody else?—for all those things breed violence and envy. Only then is it possible, surely, to have a world which can be called ours.

It is not our world now. Western civilization is opposed to Eastern civilization, and there is either the English world or the American world or the communist world and so on. It is not our world, yours and mine, to live in. And that world of ours cannot come into being if any one of us has any sense of nationality, any sense of competition, of trying to achieve a result, becoming something. So long as I am trying to become something, there is violence—which expresses itself in competition, in ruthlessness. So is it possible for you and me, actually, not theoretically, to be as nothing?—not as an escape because my ambitions have not been fulfilled and therefore I try to become nothing, or because I have no opportunities for my capacities and therefore I try to become peaceful, but because I understand the whole process, the inward nature, of violence.

If I love something for itself there is no need for competition, is there? If I love what I am doing, not because of what it is going to bring me—the reward, the punishment, the achievement, the notoriety, and all the rest of it—but for its own sake, then all sense of competition has been rooted out of me because I am no longer concerned with who is greater and who is less. Because we do not think in these terms, we have violence. There may be pacts, legislation perhaps, which will bring superficial peace, but inwardly we are seeking, inwardly we are competing, struggling, trying to express ourselves, to be something. And so long as that violence exists, there will be no peace, do what you will.

To have peace, there must be deep understanding of the ways of the self, the 'me'

that is competing, trying to become something. It is very difficult to understand that and to let go of it. All our tradition, all our education, our social culture, everything, has conditioned us to be something, and we think that if we are nothing, we shall be destroyed. In fact, we are destroying ourselves because we are trying to be something, either as a group, an individual, a nation, or a class; that is what is actually happening. We are destroying ourselves because we all demand to be something. But if we can understand the whole process of this urge to be something, then perhaps in being nothing, we may find a different way of living which may be the only true way.

But this requires a total revolution—not the communist or any other kind of outward revolution, but a complete inward revolution in which there is no division as your religion and my religion, your belief and my belief. Then this is our world to live in. From that feeling that the world is ours, a totally different kind of culture, of government, of power, can come into being.

Question: You say that if one thinks out completely a thought that arises, it will not take root, and one is therefore free of it. But even when I have done so to the best of my ability, the thought crops up again. How then can I deal with it?

KRISHNAMURTI: You try to think out a thought completely because you want to get rid of it, do you not? Is that not the reason why you try to think out a thought completely? For the questioner says, "I cannot get rid of it, it recurs again and again." So he is concerned with getting rid of a particular thought; that is the motive of his examination. Therefore he is not thinking it out completely at all because all he wants is to be rid of a particular thought which is tiresome, which is painful. If it is pleasant, obviously he will keep it; therefore, there is no problem; it is the unpleasant thought that he wants to get rid of. So that is his motive for thinking it out. And if he is concerned with a particular thought only with the idea of getting rid of it, he is already condemning it, is he not? He merely opposes a thought with the desire to remove it. So how can he understand the thought completely when his intention is to put it away?

So, what is important is not how to think out a thought completely but to understand that you cannot think completely if there is any sense of condemnation—which is fairly obvious, is it not? If I want to understand a child, I must study the child, I must not condemn him, I must not say, "This child is better than that child," or identify myself with the child. I must watch him—when he is playing, when he is weeping, crying, eating, sleeping. So, can my mind watch a particular thought without naming it? Because, the very naming of a particular thought is already condemning it.

This is rather a complex process, but if you will kindly listen, I am sure you will get the significance of it. Let us say I am greedy, envious, and I want to understand that envy completely, not merely get rid of it. Most of us want to get rid of it and try various ways of doing that, for various reasons, but we are never able to get rid of it; it goes on and on indefinitely. But if I really want to understand it, go to the root of it completely, then I must not condemn it, surely. The very word *envy* has a condemnatory sense, I feel; so can the mind dissociate the feeling which is called envy from the word? Because, the very terming, giving a name to that feeling as envy, with that very word I have condemned it, have I not? With the word *envy* is associated the whole psychological and religious significance of condemnation. So, can I dissociate the feeling from the word? If the mind is capable of not associating the

feeling with the word, then is there an entity, a 'me', who is observing it? Because the observer is the association, surely, is the word, is the entity who is condemning it.

Let us go into this a little bit more. Please, if I may suggest, watch your own minds in operation; do not listen to me merely intellectually, verbally, but examine any particular feeling of envy or of violence with which you are familiar, and go into it with me.

Let us say, I am envious. The ordinary response to that is either justifying it or condemning it. I am justifying when I say to myself, "I am not really envious. My desire to become somebody is part of culture, a part of my society, and without it I shall be a nobody." Or I condemn it because I feel it is not spiritual, or for whatever reasons there may be. So, I approach that feeling which I call envy, either justifying it or condemning it. Now, if I do neither—which is extremely difficult because it means I have to free the mind from all my conditioning of the past, of the culture in which I have been brought up—if the mind is free of that, then the mind also must be free of the word because that very word *envy* implies condemnation. You understand? Now, my mind is made up of words, of symbols, of ideas; those symbols, ideas, words, are 'me'. And can there be a feeling of envy when there is no verbalization, when there is the cessation of all that is associated with the 'me', which is the very essence of envy? So, is envy ever experienced when that 'me' is absent?—because that 'me' is the very essence of condemnation, verbalization, comparison.

To think out a thought completely, go to the very root of it, there must be an awareness in which there is no sense of condemnation, justification, and all the rest of it, nor any sense of trying to overcome a problem. Because if I am merely trying to dissolve a problem, then my attention is focused on the dissolution of it, and not on the understanding of the problem. The problem is the way I think, the way I act; and if I condemn my way, the way I am, it obviously blocks further investigation. If I say, "I must not be this, and I must be that," then there is no understanding of the ways of the 'me', whose very nature is envy, acquisitiveness.

The question is: Can I be so deeply aware without any sense of condemnation or comparison?—for then only is it possible to think out a thought completely.

Question: You appear to dismiss yoga as useless, and I agree with you that yoga is often practiced as a method to escape from what is. *But if we avoid the artificial fixing of the mind on a chosen object, and allow our so-called meditation to take the form of an inquiry over the whole field of* what is, *without expecting any particular answer, this surely is what you recommend. Do you not think also that we may be able to do this difficult thing more easily if we have learned to quieten the body and the breathing?*

KRISHNAMURTI: The questioner wants to know, really, how to meditate—whether quietening the body and steadying the breath will not help in meditation—which is the process of inquiring over the whole field of *what is* and not running away from it. So let us find out how to meditate.

Now, if you will kindly listen without focusing your attention on any particular sentence, on any particular phrase of the answer, we can inquire together into the whole question of how to meditate. To me, the "how" is not the problem at all. The problem is: What is meditation? If I do not know what is meditation, the mere inquiry how to meditate has no significance. So my inquiry is not how to meditate, what method to follow, how to be aware of *what is* without escaping, how to sit quietly, how to repeat certain words, and so on. We are not discussing all that. If I

know what meditation is, then the question of how to meditate will not be an issue, surely.

Now, what is meditation? As we do not know what meditation is, we have no idea how to begin; so we must approach it with an open mind, must we not? Do you understand? You must come to it with a free mind which says, "I do not know," and not with an occupied mind which is asking, "How am I to meditate?" Please, if you will really follow this—not hold on to what I am saying, but actually experience the thing as we go along—then you will find out for yourself the significance of meditation.

We have so far approached this problem with an attitude of asking how to meditate, what systems to follow, how to breathe, what kind of yoga practices to do, and all the rest of it—because we think we know what meditation is and that the "how" will lead us to something. But do we know what meditation is, actually? I do not, nor, I think, do you. So we must both come to the question with a mind that says, "I do not know"— though we may have read hundreds of books and practiced many yoga disciplines. You do not know actually. You only hope, you only desire, you only want, through a particular pattern of action, of discipline, to arrive at a certain state. And that state may be utterly illusory; it may be only your own wish. And surely it is; it is your own projection, as a reaction from the daily existence of misery.

So, the first essential is not how to meditate but to find out what is meditation. Therefore the mind must come to it without knowing—and that is extremely difficult. We are so used to thinking that a particular system is essential in order to meditate—either the repetition of words, as prayer, or the taking of a certain posture, or fixing the mind on a particular phrase or on a picture, or breathing regularly, making the body very still, having complete control of the mind;

with these things we are familiar. And we believe these things will lead us to something which we think is beyond the mind, beyond the transient process of thought. We think we already know what we want, and we are now trying to compare which is the best way. That issue of "how" to meditate is completely false. But, can I find out what meditation is? That is the real question. It is an extraordinary thing to meditate, to know what meditation is, so let us find out.

Surely meditation is not the pursuit of any system, is it? Can my mind entirely eliminate this tradition of a discipline, of a method?—which exists not only here but also in India. That is essential, is it not, because I do not know what meditation is. I know how to concentrate, how to control, how to discipline, what to do; but I do not know what is at the end of it—I have only been told, "If you do these things, you will get it," and because I am greedy, I carry out those practices. So can I, to find out what meditation is, eliminate this demand for a method?

The very going into all this is meditation, is it not? I am meditating the moment I begin to inquire what is meditation—instead of how to meditate. The moment I begin to find out for myself what is meditation, my mind, not knowing, must reject everything that it knows—which means I must put aside my desire to achieve a state. Because the desire to achieve is the root, the base, of my search for a method. I have known moments of peace, quietness, and a sense of 'otherness', and I want to achieve that again, to make it a permanent state—so I pursue the "how." I think I already know what the other state is and that a method will lead me to it. But if I already know what the other is, then it is not what is true; it is merely a projection of my own desire.

My mind, when it is really inquiring what meditation is, understands the desire to achieve, to gain a result, and so is free from it. Therefore it has completely set aside all authority because we do not know what meditation is, and no one can tell us. My mind is completely in a state of 'not-knowing'; there is no method, no prayer, no repetition of words, no concentration, because it sees that concentration is only another form of achievement. The concentration of the mind on a particular idea, hoping thereby to train itself to go further by exclusion, implies again a state of 'knowing'. So, if I do not know, then all these things must go. I no longer think in terms of achieving, arriving. There is no longer a sense of accumulation which will help me to reach the other shore.

So, when I have done that, have I not found what meditation is? There is no conflict, no struggle; there is a sense of not accumulating—at all times, not at any particular time. So, meditation is the process of complete denudation of the mind, the purgation of all sense of accumulation and achievement—which is the very nature of the self, the 'me'. Practicing various methods only strengthens that 'me'. You may cover it up, you may beautify it, refine it, but it is still the 'me.' So, meditation is the uncovering of the ways of the self.

And you will find, if you can go deeply into it, that there is never a moment when meditation becomes a habit. For habit implies accumulation, and where there is accumulation, there is the process of the self asking for more, demanding further accumulation. Such meditation is within the field of the known and has no significance whatsoever except as a means of hypnotizing oneself.

The mind can only say, "I do not know"—actually, not merely verbally—when it has wiped away, through awareness, through self-knowledge, this whole sense of accumulation. So meditation is dying to one's accumulations—not achieving a state of silence, of quietness. So long as the mind is capable of accumulating, then the urge is always for more. And the 'more' demands the system, the method, the setting up of authority—which are all the very ways of the self. When the mind has completely seen the fallacy of that, then it is in a constant state of 'not-knowing'. Such a mind can then receive that which is not measurable and which only comes into being from moment to moment.

June 26, 1955

Ojai, California, 1955

✳

First Talk in The Oak Grove

Throughout the world we have many grave problems, and even though welfare states may be created, and the politicians may bring about a superficial peace of coexistence—with economic prosperity in a country of this kind where there is booming production and the promise of a happy future—I do not think that our problems can so easily be solved. We want these problems to be solved, and we look to others to solve them—to religious teachers, to analysts, to leaders—or else we rely on tradition, or we turn to various books, philosophies. And I presume that is why you are here—to be told what to do. Or you hope that through listening to explanations, you will comprehend the problems that each one of us is confronted with. But I think you will be making a grave mistake if you expect that by casually listening to one or two talks, without paying much attention, you will be guided to the comprehension of our many problems. It is not at all my intention merely to explain verbally or intellectually the problems that we are confronted with; on the contrary, what we shall attempt to do during these talks is to go much deeper into the fundamental issue which makes all these problems so complicated, so infinitely painful and sorrowful.

Please have the patience to listen without being carried away by words, or objecting to one or two phrases or ideas. One must have immense patience to find out what is true. Most of us are impatient to get on, to find a result, to achieve a success, a goal, a certain state of happiness, or to experience something to which the mind can cling. But what is needed, I think, is a patience and a perseverance to seek without an end. Most of us are seeking; that is why we are here, but in our search we want to find something, a result, a goal, a state of being in which we can be happy, peaceful; so our search is already determined, is it not? When we seek, we are seeking something which we want, so our search is already established, predetermined, and therefore it is no longer a search. I think it is very important to understand this. When the mind seeks a particular state, a solution to a problem, when it seeks God, truth, or desires a certain experience, whether mystical or any other kind, it has already conceived what it wants; and because it has already conceived, formulated what it is seeking, its search is infinitely futile. And it is one of the most difficult things to free the mind from this desire to find a result.

It seems to me that our many problems cannot be solved except through a fundamental revolution of the mind, for such a revolution alone can bring about the realization of that which is truth. Therefore, it is important to understand the operation of one's own mind, not self-analytically or introspectively, but by being aware of its total process; and that is what I would like to discuss during these talks. If we do not see ourselves as we are, if we do not understand the thinker—the entity that seeks, that is perpetually asking, demanding, questioning, trying to find out, the entity that is creating the problem, the 'I', the self, the ego—then our thought, our search, will have no meaning. As long as one's instrument of thinking is not clear, is perverted, conditioned, whatever one thinks is bound to be limited, narrow.

So our problem is how to free the mind from all conditioning, not how to condition it better. Do you understand? Most of us are seeking a better conditioning. The communists, the Catholics, the Protestants, and the various other sects throughout the world, including the Hindus and Buddhists, are all seeking to condition the mind according to a nobler, a more virtuous, unselfish, or religious pattern. Everyone throughout the world, surely, is trying to condition the mind in a better way, and there is never a question of freeing the mind from all conditioning. But it seems to me that until the mind is free from all conditioning, that is, as long as it is conditioned as a Christian, a Buddhist, a Hindu, a communist, or whatnot, there must be problems.

Surely, it is possible to find out what is real, or if there is such a thing as God, only when the mind is free from all conditioning. The mere occupation of a conditioned mind with God, with truth, with love, has really no meaning at all, for such a mind can function only within the field of its conditioning. The communist who does not believe in God thinks in one way, and the man who believes in God, who is occupied with a dogma, thinks in another way; but the minds of both are conditioned; therefore, neither can think freely, and all their protestations, their theories and beliefs have very little meaning.

So religion is not a matter of going to church, of having certain beliefs and dogmas. Religion may be something entirely different; it may be the total freeing of the mind from all this vast tradition of centuries, for it is only a free mind that can find truth, reality, that which is beyond the projections of the mind.

This is not a particular theory of mine, as we can see from what is happening in the world. The communists want to settle the problems of life in one way, the Hindus in another, and the Christians in still another; so their minds are conditioned. Your mind is conditioned as a Christian, whether you will acknowledge it or not. You may superficially break away from the tradition of Christianity, but the deep layers of the unconscious are full of that tradition; they are conditioned by centuries of education according to a particular pattern; and surely, a mind that would find something beyond, if there is such a thing, must first be free of all conditioning.

So during these talks we are not discussing self-improvement in any way, nor are we concerned with the improvement of the pattern; we are not seeking to condition the mind in a nobler pattern, nor in a pattern of wider social significance. On the contrary, we are trying to find out how to free the mind, the total consciousness, from all conditioning, for unless that happens, there can be no experiencing of reality. You may talk about reality, you may read innumerable volumes about it, read all the sacred books of the East and of the West, but until the mind is aware of its own process, until it sees itself functioning in a particular pattern and is able to be free from that conditioning, obviously all search is in vain.

So it seems to me of the greatest importance to begin with ourselves, to be aware of our own conditioning. And how extraordinarily difficult it is to know that one is conditioned! Superficially, on the upper levels of the mind, we may be aware that we are conditioned; we may break away from one pattern and take on another, give up Christianity and become a communist, leave Catholicism and join some other equally tyrannical group, thinking that we are evolving, growing towards reality. On the contrary, it is merely an exchange of prisons.

And yet that is what most of us want—to find a secure place in our ways of thinking. We want to pursue a set pattern and be undisturbed in our thoughts, in our actions. But it is only the mind that is capable of patiently observing its own conditioning and being free from its conditioning—it is only such a mind that is able to have a revolution, a radical transformation, and thereby to discover that which is infinitely beyond the mind, beyond all our desires, our vanities and pursuits. Without self-knowledge, without knowing oneself as one is—not as one would like to be, which is merely an illusion, an idealistic escape—without knowing the ways of one's thinking, all one's motives, one's thoughts, one's innumerable responses, it is not possible to understand and go beyond this whole process of thinking.

You have taken a lot of trouble to come here on a hot evening to listen to the talk. And I wonder if you do listen at all. What is listening? I think it is important to go into it a little, if you do not mind. Do you really listen, or are you interpreting what is being said in terms of your own understanding? Are you capable of listening to anybody? Or is it that in the process of listening, various thoughts, opinions, arise so that your own knowledge and experience intervene between what is being said and your comprehension of it?

I think it is important to understand the difference between attention and concentration. Concentration implies choice, does it not? You are trying to concentrate on what I am saying, so your mind is focused, made narrow, and other thoughts intervene; so

there is not an actual listening but a battle going on in the mind, a conflict between what you are hearing and your desire to translate it, to apply what I am talking about, and so on. Whereas, attention is something entirely different. In attention there is no focusing, no choice; there is complete awareness without any interpretation. And if we can listen so attentively, completely, to what is being said, then that very attention brings about the miracle of change within the mind itself.

What we are talking about is something of immense importance because unless there is a fundamental revolution in each one of us, I do not see how we can bring about a vast, radical change in the world. And surely, that radical change is essential. Mere economic revolution, whether communistic or socialistic, is of no importance at all. There can be only a religious revolution, and the religious revolution cannot take place if the mind is merely conforming to the pattern of a previous conditioning. As long as one is a Christian or a Hindu, there can be no fundamental revolution in this true religious sense of the word. And we do need such a revolution. When the mind is free from all conditioning, then you will find that there comes the creativity of reality, of God, or what you will, and it is only such a mind, a mind which is constantly experiencing this creativity, that can bring about a different outlook, different values, a different world.

And so it is important to understand oneself, is it not? Self-knowledge is the beginning of wisdom. Self-knowledge is not according to some psychologist, book, or philosopher but it is to know oneself as one is from moment to moment. Do you understand? To know oneself is to observe what one thinks, how one feels, not just superficially, but to be deeply aware of *what is* without condemnation, without judgment, without evaluation or comparison. Try it and you will see how extraordinarily difficult it is for a mind that has been trained for centuries to compare, to condemn, to judge, to evaluate, to stop that whole process and simply to observe *what is;* but unless this takes place, not only at the superficial level, but right through the whole content of consciousness, there can be no delving into the profundity of the mind.

Please, if you are really here to understand what is being said, it is this that we are concerned with and nothing else. Our problem is not what societies you should belong to, what kind of activities you should indulge in, what books you should read, and all that superficial business, but how to free the mind from conditioning. The mind is not merely the waking consciousness that is occupied with daily activities, but also the deep layers of the unconscious in which there is the whole residue of the past, of tradition, of racial instincts. All that is the mind, and unless that total consciousness is free right through, our search, our inquiry, our discovery, will be limited, narrow, petty.

So the mind is conditioned right through; there is no part of the mind which is not conditioned, and our problem is: Can such a mind free itself? And who is the entity that can free it? Do you understand the problem? The mind is the total consciousness with all its different layers of knowledge, of acquisition, of tradition, of racial instincts, of memory; and can such a mind free itself? Or can the mind be free only when it sees that it is conditioned and that any movement from this conditioning is still another form of conditioning? I hope you are following all this. If not, we shall discuss it in the days to come.

The mind is completely conditioned—which is an obvious fact if you come to think about it. It is not my invention, it is a fact. We belong to a particular society; we were brought up according to a particular

ideology with certain dogmas, traditions; and the vast influence of culture, of society, is continually conditioning the mind. How can such a mind be free, since any movement of the mind to be free is the result of its conditioning and must therefore bring about further conditioning? There is only one answer. The mind can be free only when it is completely still. Though it has problems, innumerable urges, conflicts, ambitions, if—through self-knowledge, through watching itself without acceptance or condemnation—the mind is choicelessly aware of its own process, then out of that awareness there comes an astonishing silence, a quietness of the mind in which there is no movement of any kind. It is only then that the mind is free because it is no longer desiring anything; it is no longer seeking; it is no longer pursuing a goal, an ideal—which are all the projections of a conditioned mind. And if you ever come to that understanding, in which there can be no self-deception, then you will find that there is a possibility of the coming into being of that extraordinary thing called creativity. Then only can the mind realize that which is measureless, which may be called God, truth, or what you will—the word has very little meaning. You may be socially prosperous, you may have innumerable possessions, cars, houses, refrigerators, superficial peace, but unless that which is measureless comes into being, there will always be sorrow. Freeing the mind from conditioning is the ending of sorrow.

There are many questions here, and what is the function of asking a question and receiving an answer? Do we solve any problem by asking a question? What is a problem? Please follow this, think with me. What is a problem? A problem comes into being only when the mind is occupied with something, does it not? If I have a problem, what does it mean? Let's say that my mind is occupied from morning till night with envy, with jealousy, with sex, or what you will. It is the occupation of the mind with an object that creates the problem. The envy may be a fact, but it is the occupation of the mind with the fact that creates the problem, the conflict. Isn't that so?

Let's say I am envious, or I have a violent urge of some kind or another. The envy expresses itself; there is conflict, and then my mind is occupied with the conflict—how to be free of it, how to resolve it, what to do about it. It is the occupation of the mind with envy that creates the problem, not envy itself—which we will go into presently, the whole significance of envy. Our problem, then, is not the fact but occupation with the fact. And can the mind be free from occupation? Is the mind capable of dealing with the fact without being occupied with it? We shall examine this question of occupation as we go along. It is really very interesting to watch one's mind in operation.

So, in considering these questions together, we are trying to liberate the mind from occupation, which means looking at the fact without being occupied with it. That is, if I have a particular compulsion, can I look at that compulsion without being occupied with it? Please, you watch your own peculiar compulsion of irritability or whatever it be. Can you look at it without the mind being occupied with it? Occupation implies the effort to resolve that compulsion, does it not? You are condemning it, comparing it with something else, trying to alter it, overcome it. In other words, trying to do something about your compulsion is occupation, is it not? But can you look at the fact that you have a particular compulsion, an urge, a desire, look at it without comparing, without judging, and hence not set going the whole process of occupation?

Psychologically, it is very interesting to observe this—how the mind is incapable of looking at a fact like envy without bringing in the vast complex of opinions, judgments, evaluations with which the mind is occupied— so we never resolve the fact but multiply the problems. I hope I am making myself clear. And I think it is important for us to understand this process of occupation because there is a much deeper factor behind it, which is the fear of not being occupied. Whether a mind is occupied with God, with truth, with sex, or with drink, its quality is essentially the same. The man who thinks about God and becomes a hermit may be socially more significant; he may have a greater value to society than the drunkard, but both are occupied, and a mind that is occupied is never free to discover what is truth.

Please don't reject or accept what I am saying; look at it, find out. If each one of us can really attend to this one thing, give our full attention to the whole process of the mind's occupation with any problem without trying to free the mind from occupation, which is merely another way of being occupied—if we can understand this process completely, totally, then I think the problem itself will become irrelevant. When the mind is free from occupation with the problem, free to observe, to be aware of the whole issue, then the problem itself can be solved comparatively easily.

Question: All our troubles seem to arise from desire, but can we ever be free from desire? Is desire inherent in us, or is it a product of the mind?

KRISHNAMURTI: What is desire? And why do we separate desire from the mind? And who is the entity that says, "Desire creates problems; therefore, I must be free from desire"? Do you follow? We have to understand what desire is, not ask how to get rid of desire because it creates trouble or whether it is a product of the mind. First we must know what desire is, and then we can go into it more deeply. What is desire? How does desire arise? I shall explain and you will see, but don't merely listen to my words. Actually experience the thing that we are talking about as we go along, and then it will have significance.

How does desire come into being? Surely, it comes into being through perception or seeing, contact, sensation, and then desire. Isn't that so? First you see a car, then there is contact, sensation, and finally the desire to own the car, to drive it. Please follow this slowly, patiently. Then, in trying to get that car, which is desire, there is conflict. So in the very fulfillment of desire there is conflict, there is pain, suffering, joy, and you want to hold the pleasure and discard the pain. This is what is actually taking place with each one of us. The entity created by desire, the entity who is identified with pleasure, says, "I must get rid of that which is not pleasurable, which is painful." We never say, "I want to get rid of pain and pleasure." We want to retain pleasure and discard pain, but desire creates both, does it not? Desire, which comes into being through perception, contact, and sensation, is identified as the 'me' who wants to hold on to the pleasurable and discard that which is painful. But the painful and the pleasurable are equally the outcome of desire, which is part of the mind—it is not outside of the mind—and as long as there is an entity which says, "I want to hold on to this and discard that," there must be conflict. Because we want to get rid of all the painful desires and hold on to those which are primarily pleasurable, worthwhile, we never consider the whole problem of desire. And when we say, "I must get rid of desire," who is the entity that is trying to get rid of something? Is not that entity also the outcome of desire? Do you understand all this?

Please, as I said at the beginning of the talk, you must have infinite patience to understand these things. To fundamental ques-

tions, there is no absolute answer of yes or no. What is important is to put a fundamental question, not to find an answer, and if we are capable of looking at that fundamental question without seeking an answer, then that very observation of the fundamental brings about understanding.

So our problem is not how to be free from the desires which are painful while holding on to those which are pleasurable but to understand the whole nature of desire. This brings up the question: What is conflict? And who is the entity that is always choosing between the pleasurable and the painful? The entity whom we call the 'me', the self, the ego, the mind, which says, "This is pleasure, that is pain; I will hold on to the pleasurable and reject the painful"—is not that entity still desire? But if we are capable of looking at the whole field of desire, and not in terms of keeping or getting rid of something, then we shall find that desire has quite a different significance.

Desire creates contradiction, and the mind that is at all alert does not like to live in contradiction; therefore, it tries to get rid of desire. But if the mind can understand desire without trying to brush it away, without saying, "This is a better desire and that is a worse one, I am going to keep this and discard the other"; if it can be aware of the whole field of desire without rejecting, without choosing, without condemning, then you will see that the mind is desire; it is not separate from desire. If you really understand this, the mind becomes very quiet; desires come, but they no longer have impact; they are no longer of great significance; they do not take root in the mind and create problems. The mind reacts; otherwise, it is not alive, but the reaction is superficial and does not take root. That is why it is important to understand this whole process of desire in which most of us are caught. Being caught, we feel the contradiction, the infinite pain of it, so we struggle against desire, and the struggle creates duality. Whereas, if we can look at desire without judgment, without evaluation or condemnation, then we shall find that it no longer takes root. The mind that gives soil to problems can never find that which is real. So the issue is not how to resolve desire but to understand it, and one can understand it only when there is no condemnation of it. Only the mind that is not occupied with desire can understand desire.

August 6, 1955

Second Talk in The Oak Grove

Perhaps it might be worthwhile, first of all, to talk over together what we mean by listening. You are here, apparently, to listen to and to understand what is being said, and I think it is important to find out how we listen because understanding depends on the manner of listening. As we listen, do we discuss with ourselves what is being said, interpreting it according to our own particular opinions, knowledge, and idiosyncrasies, or do we just listen attentively without any sense of interpretation at all? And what does it mean to pay attention? It seems to me quite important to differentiate between attention and concentration. Can we listen with an attention in which there is no interpretation, no opposition or acceptance, so that we understand totally what is being said? It is fairly obvious, I think, that if one can listen with complete attention, then that very attention brings about an extraordinary effect.

Surely, there are two ways of listening. One can superficially follow the words, see their meaning, and merely pursue the outward significance of the description; or one can listen to the description, to the verbal statement, and pursue it inwardly—that is, be aware of what is being said as a thing that one is directly experiencing in oneself. If one

can do the latter—that is, if through the description one is able to experience directly the thing that is being said—then I think it will have great significance. Perhaps you will experiment with that as you are listening.

Throughout the world there is immense poverty, as in Asia, and enormous wealth, as in this country; there is cruelty, suffering, injustice, a sense of living in which there is no love. Seeing all this, what is one to do? What is the true approach to these innumerable problems? Religions everywhere have emphasized self-improvement, the cultivation of virtue, the acceptance of authority, the following of certain dogmas, beliefs, the making of great effort to conform. Not only religiously, but also socially and politically, there is the constant urge of self-improvement: I must be more noble, more gentle, more considerate, less violent. Society, with the help of religion, has brought about a culture of self-improvement in the widest sense of that word. That is what each one of us is trying to do all the time—we are trying to improve ourselves, which implies effort, discipline, conformity, competition, acceptance of authority, a sense of security, the justification of ambition. And self-improvement does produce certain obvious results; it makes one more socially inclined; it has social significance and no more, for self-improvement does not reveal the ultimate reality. I think it is very important to understand this.

The religions that we have do not help us to understand that which is the real because they are essentially based, not on the abandonment of the self, but on the improvement, the refinement of the self, which is the continuity of the self in different forms. It is only the very few who break away from society, not the outward trappings of society, but from all the implications of a society which is based on acquisitiveness, on envy, on comparison, competition. This society conditions the mind to a particular pattern of thought, the pattern of self-improvement, self-adjustment, self-sacrifice, and only those who are capable of breaking away from all conditioning can discover that which is not measurable by the mind.

Now, what do we mean by effort? We are all making effort; our social pattern is based on the effort to acquire, to understand more, to have more knowledge, and from that background of knowledge, to act. There is always an effort of self-improvement, of self-adjustment, of correction, this drive to fulfill, with its frustrations, fears, and miseries. According to this pattern, which we all know and of which we are a part, it is perfectly justified to be ambitious, to compete, to be envious, to pursue a particular result; and our society, whether in America, in Europe, or in India, is essentially based on that.

So does society, does culture in this widest sense, help the individual to find truth? Or is society detrimental to man, preventing him from discovering that which is truth? Surely, society as we know it, this culture in which we live and function, helps man to conform to a particular pattern, to be respectable, and it is the product of many wills. We have created this society; it has not come into being by itself. And does this society help the individual to find that which is truth, God—what name you will, the words do not matter—or must the individual set aside totally the culture, the values of society, to find that which is truth? Which does not mean—please let us remember this very clearly—that he becomes antisocial, does what he likes. On the contrary.

The present social structure is based on envy, on acquisitiveness, in which is implied conformity, acceptance of authority, the perpetual fulfillment of ambition, which is essentially the self, the 'me' striving to become something. Out of this stuff society is made, and its culture—the pleasant and the unpleasant, the beautiful and the ugly, the whole field of social endeavor—conditions the mind. You are the result of society. If you were born and trained in Russia through their particular form of education, you would deny God, you would accept certain patterns, as here you accept certain other patterns. Here you believe in God; you would be horrified if you did not; you would not be respectable.

So everywhere society is conditioning the individual, and this conditioning takes the form of self-improvement, which is really the perpetuation of the 'me', the ego, in different forms. Self-improvement may be gross, or it may be very, very refined when it becomes the practice of virtue, goodness, the so-called love of one's neighbor, but essentially it is the continuance of the 'me', which is a product of the conditioning influences of society. All your endeavor has gone into becoming something, either here, if you can make it, or if not, in another world; but it is the same urge, the same drive to maintain and continue the self.

When one sees all this—and I am not necessarily going into every detail of it—one inevitably asks oneself: Does society or culture exist to help man to discover that which may be called truth or God? What matters, surely, is to discover, to actually experience something far beyond the mind, not merely to have a belief, which has no significance at all. And do so-called religions, the following of various teachers, disciplines, belonging to sects, cults, which are all, if you observe, within the field of social respectability—do any of those things help you to find that which is timeless bliss, timeless reality? If you do not merely listen to what is being said, agreeing or disagreeing, but ask yourself whether society helps you, not in the superficial sense of feeding you, clothing you, and giving you shelter, but fundamentally—if you are actually putting that question directly to yourself, which means that you are applying what is being said to yourself so that it becomes a direct experience and not merely a repetition of what you have heard or learned, then you will see that effort can exist only in the field of self-improvement. And effort is basically part of society, which conditions the mind according to a pattern in which effort is considered essential.

It is like this. If I am a scientist, I must study, I must know mathematics, I must know all that has been said before, I must have an immense accumulation of knowledge. My memory must be heightened, strengthened, and widened. But such a memory, such knowledge, actually prevents further discovery. It is only when I can forget the total acquisition of knowledge, wipe away all the information that I have acquired, which can be used later—it is only then that I can find something new. I cannot find anything new with the burden of the past, with the burden of knowledge, which is again an obvious psychological fact. And I am saying this because we approach reality, that extraordinary state of creativity, with all the burden of society, with the conditioning of a given culture, and so we never discover anything new. Surely, that which is the sublime, the eternal, must always be new, timeless, and for the new to come into being, there cannot be any endeavor in the field in which effort is exercised as self-improvement or self-fulfillment. It is only when such effort totally ceases that the other is possible.

Please, this is really very important. It is not a question of gazing at your navel and going into some kind of illusion but of understanding the whole process of effort in society—this society of which you are the product, which you have built, and in which effort is essential because otherwise you are lost. If you are not ambitious, you are destroyed; if you are not acquisitive, you are trodden on; if you are not envious, you cannot be an executive or a big success. So you are constantly making effort to be or not to be, to become something, to be successful, to fulfill your ambition; and with that mentality, which is the product of society, you are trying to find something which is not of society.

Now, if one wishes to find that which is truth, one must be totally free from all religions, from all conditioning, from all dogmas, from all beliefs, from all authority which makes one conform, which means, essentially, standing completely alone, and that is very arduous; it is not a hobby for a Sunday morning when you go for a pleasant drive to sit under the trees and listen to some nonsense. To find out what is truth requires immense patience, gentleness, hesitancy. The mere studying of books has no value, but if as you listen you can be completely attentive, then you will see that this very attention frees you from effort so that without movement in any direction the mind is capable of receiving something which is extraordinarily beautiful and creative, something which is not to be measured by knowledge, by the past. It is only such a person who is really religious and revolutionary because he is no longer part of society. As long as one is ambitious, envious, acquisitive, competitive, one is society. With that mentality, which is extraordinarily difficult to be free of, one seeks God, and that search has no meaning at all because it is merely another endeavor to become something, to gain something. That is why it is very important to understand one's relationship to society, to be aware of all the beliefs, dogmas, tenets, superstitions that one has acquired, and to throw them off—not with effort, because then you will again be caught in it, but just to see these things for what they are and let them go, like the autumnal leaf that withers and is blown away, leaving the tree naked. It is only such a mind that can receive something which brings measureless happiness to life.

In discussing with you some of these questions, I am obviously not answering them because we are trying to find out together the significance of the question. If you are merely listening for an answer to the question, I'm afraid you will be disappointed because then you are not interested in the problem but are only concerned with the answer—as most of us are. I feel it is very important to ask fundamental questions and to keep on asking them without trying to find an answer, because the more you persist in asking fundamental questions, demanding, inquiring, the sharper and more aware the mind becomes. So what are the fundamental questions? Can anyone tell you what they are, or must you find out for yourself? If you can find out for yourself what are the fundamental questions, your mind has already altered; it has already become much more significant than when it asks a petty question and finds a petty answer.

Question: Juvenile delinquency in this country is increasing at an alarming rate. How is this mounting problem to be solved?

KRISHNAMURTI: There is obviously revolt within the pattern of society. Some revolts are respectable, others are not, but they are always within the field of society, within the limits of the social fence. And surely, a society based on envy, on ambition, cruelty, war, must expect revolt within itself. After all, when you go to the cinema, the movies, you see a great deal of violence. There have been two enormous global wars, representing total violence. A nation which maintains an army must be destructive of its own citizens. Please listen to all this. No nation is peaceful as long as it has an army, whether it is a defensive or an offensive army. An army is both offensive and defensive; it does not bring about a peaceful state. The moment a culture establishes and maintains an army, it is destroying itself. This is historically a fact. And on every side we are encouraged to be competitive, to be ambitious, to be successful. Competition, ambition, and success are the gods of a particularly prosperous society such as this, and what do you expect? You want juvenile delinquency to become respectable, that's all. You do not tackle the roots of the problem, which is to stop this whole process of war, of maintaining an army, of being ambitious, of encouraging competition. These things, which are rooted in our hearts, are the fences of society within which there is revolt going on all the time on the part of both the young and the old. The problem is not only that of juvenile delinquency; it involves our whole social structure, and there is no answer to it as long as you and I do not step totally out of society—society representing ambition, cruelty, the desire to succeed, to become somebody, to be on top. That whole process is essentially the egocentric pursuit of fulfillment, only it has been made respectable. How you worship a successful man! How you decorate a man who kills thousands! And there are all the divisions of belief, of dogma—the Christian and the Hindu, the Buddhist and the Muslim. These are the things that are bringing about conflict; and when you seek to deal with juvenile delinquency by merely keeping the children at home, or disciplining them, or putting them in the army, or having recourse to the various solutions offered by every psychologist and social reformer, you are surely dealing very superficially with a fundamental question. But we are afraid to tackle fundamental questions because we would become unpopular, we would be termed communists or God knows what else, and labels seem to have extraordinary importance for most of us. Whether it is in Russia, in India, or here, the problem is essentially the same, and it is only when the mind understands this whole social structure that we shall find an entirely different approach to the problem, thereby perhaps establishing real peace, not this spurious peace of politicians.

Question: I have gone from teacher to teacher seeking, and now I have come to you in the same spirit of search. Are you any different from all the others, and how am I to know?

KRISHNAMURTI: Now, you are really seeking, and what does it mean to seek? Do you understand the question? You are obviously seeking something, but what? Essentially, you are seeking a state of mind which will never be disturbed and which you call peace, God, love, or whatever it be. Is it not so? Our life is disturbed, anxious, full of fear, darkness, upheaval, confusion, and we want to escape from all that; but when a confused man seeks, his search is based on confusion, and therefore what he finds is further confusion. Are you following this?

First of all, then, we must inquire why we seek and what it is we are seeking. You may go from teacher to teacher, each teacher offering a different method of discipline or meditation, some foolish nonsense; so what is important, surely, is not the teacher and what he offers, but what it is you are seeking. If you can be very clear about what you are seeking, then you will find a teacher who will offer you that. If you are seeking peace, you will find a teacher who will offer you that which you seek. But that which you seek may not be true at all. Do you understand? I may want perfect bliss, which means an undisturbed state of mind in which there will be complete quietness, no conflict, no pain, no inquiry, no doubt; so I practice a discipline which some teacher offers, and probably that very discipline produces its own result, which I call peace. I might just as well take a drug, a pill, which will have the same ef-fect—only that's not respectable, whereas the other is. (Laughter) Please, it is not a laughing matter; this is what we are actually doing.

So, that which you are seeking, you will find, obviously, if you are willing to pay for it. If you put yourself in the hands of another, follow some authority, discipline, control yourself, you will find what you want, which means that your desire is dictating your search; but you are really not aware of the motivation of your search at all, and then you ask me what my position is and how you are to know whether what I am saying is true or false. Having gone to various teachers and been caught, burned, you now want to try this. But I am not telling you anything; actually I am not telling you anything at all. All that I am saying is to know yourself deeper and deeper, see yourself as you actually are, which nobody can teach you; and you cannot see yourself as you are if you are bound by beliefs, by dogmas, by superstitions, fears.

Sirs, for a mind that cannot stand alone, search will have no meaning at all. To stand alone is to be uncorrupted, innocent, free of all tradition, of dogma, of opinion, of what another says, and so on. Such a mind does not seek because there is nothing to seek; being free, such a mind is completely still without a want, without movement. But this state is not to be achieved; it isn't a thing that you buy through discipline; it doesn't come into being by giving up sex, or practicing a certain yoga. It comes into being only when there is understanding of the ways of the self, the 'me', which shows itself through the conscious mind in everyday activity, and also in the unconscious. What matters is to understand for oneself, not through the direction of others, the total content of consciousness, which is conditioned, which is the result of society, of religion, of various impacts, impressions, memories—to understand all that conditioning and be free of it. But there is no "how" to be free. If you ask how to be free, you are not listening.

Say, for example, I am telling you that the mind must be totally unconditioned. Now, how do you listen to a statement of that kind? With what attention are you listening to it? If you are watching your own mind, which I hope you are, you will see that you are inwardly saying, "How impossible this is," or "It cannot be done," or "Conditioning can only be modified," and so on. In other words, you are not listening to the statement attentively but you are opposing it with your own opinions, with your own conclusions, with your own knowledge; therefore, there is no attention.

The fact is that the mind is conditioned, whether as a communist, a Catholic, a Protestant, a Hindu, or whatever it be, and either we are unaware of this conditioning or we accept it or we try to modify it, ennoble it, change it; but we never put the question: Can the mind be totally free from conditioning? Before you can really put that question attentively to yourself, you must first be aware that your mind is conditioned, as it obviously is. Do you understand what I mean by conditioning? Not the superficial conditioning of language, gesture, costume, and all the rest of it, but conditioning in a much deeper, more fundamental sense. The mind is conditioned when it is ambitious, not only in this world, but ambitious to become something spiritual. This whole endeavor of self-improvement is the result of conditioning, and can the mind be totally free from such conditioning? If you really put that question to yourself, attentively, without seeking an answer, then you will find the right answer, which is not that it is possible or impossible, but something entirely different takes place.

So it is important to find out how we pay attention to these talks. If you don't pay attention, I assure you it is a waste of time for you to come here every weekend. It may be pleasant to drive to Ojai, but it's hot. Whereas, if you can pay direct attention to what is being said, which is not to remember something you have read, or to oppose opinion by opinion, or to take notes and say, "I'll think about it later," but actually to put the given question to yourself immediately, while you are listening, then that very actuality of attention brings about the right answer.

Question: It is now a well-established fact that many of our diseases are psychosomatic, brought on by deep inner frustrations and conflicts of which we are often unaware. Must we now run to psychiatrists as we used to run to physicians, or is there a way for man to free himself from this inner turmoil?

KRISHNAMURTI: Which raises the question: What is the position of the psychoanalysts? And what is the position of those of us who have some form of disease or illness? Is the disease brought on by our emotional disturbances, or is it without emotional significance? Most of us are disturbed. Most of us are confused, in turmoil, even the very prosperous who have refrigerators, cars, and all the rest of it; and as we do not know how to deal with the disturbance, inevitably it reacts on the physical and produces an illness, which is fairly obvious. And the question is: Must we run to psychiatrists to help us to remove our disturbances and thereby regain health, or is it possible for us to find out for ourselves how not to be disturbed, how not to have turmoil, anxieties, fears?

Why are we disturbed, if we are? What is disturbance? I want something, but I can't get it, so I'm in a state. I want to fulfill through my children, through my wife, through my property, through position, success, and all the rest of it, but I am blocked, which means that I am disturbed. I am ambitious, but somebody else pushes me aside and gets ahead; again I am in chaos, in turmoil, which produces its own physical reaction.

Now, can you and I be free of all this turmoil and confusion? What is confusion? Do you understand? What is confusion? Confusion exists only when there is the fact plus what I think about the fact: my opinion about the fact, my disregard of the fact, my evasion of the fact, my evaluation of the fact, and so on. If I can look at the fact without the additive quality, then there is no confusion. If I recognize the fact that a certain road leads to Ventura, there is no confusion. Confusion arises only when I think or insist that the road leads somewhere else—and that is actually the state that most of us are in. Our opinions, our beliefs, our desires, ambitions, are so strong, we are so weighed down by them, that we are incapable of looking at the fact.

So, the fact plus opinion, judgment, evaluation, ambition, and all the rest of it, brings about confusion. And can you and I, being confused, not act? Surely, any action born of confusion must lead to further confusion, further turmoil, all of which reacts on the body, on the nervous system, and produces illness. Being confused, to acknowledge to oneself that one is confused requires, not courage, but a certain clarity of thought, clarity of perception. Most of us are afraid to acknowledge that we are confused, so out of our confusion we choose leaders, teachers, politicians; and when we choose something out of our confusion, that very choice must be confused, and therefore the leader must also be confused.

Is it possible, then, to be aware of our confusion, and to know the cause of that confusion, and not act? When a confused mind acts, it can only produce further confusion; but a mind that is aware that it is confused and understands this whole process of confusion need not act because that very clarity is its own action. I think this is rather difficult for most people to understand because we are so used to acting, doing; but if one can watch action, see what its results are, observe what is happening in the world politically and in every direction, then it becomes fairly obvious that so-called reformatory action is merely producing more confusion, more chaos, more reforms.

So can we individually be aware of our own confusion, of our own turmoil, and live with it, understand it, without wanting to get rid of it, push it away, or escape from it? As long as we are kicking it, condemning it, running away from it, that very condemnation, running away, is the process of confusion. And I do not think any analyst can solve this problem. He may temporarily help you to conform to a certain pattern of society which he calls normal existence, but the problem is much deeper than that, and no one can solve it except yourself. You and I have made this society; it is the result of our actions, of our thoughts, of our very being, and as long as we are merely trying to reform the product without understanding the entity that has produced it, we shall have more diseases, more chaos, more delinquency. The understanding of the self brings about wisdom and right action.

August 7, 1955

Third Talk in The Oak Grove

I think one of our greatest difficulties is that of communication. I want to say something, naturally, with the intention that you should understand it, but each one of us interprets the words he hears according to his own peculiar background, and so with a large audience like this it is extremely difficult to convey exactly what one intends.

I would like to discuss this evening something that I consider quite important, and that is the whole problem of the cultivation of virtue. One can see that without virtue the mind is quite chaotic, contradictory, and without having a quiet, orderly mind in which there is no conflict, one obviously cannot go much further. But virtue is not an end in itself. The cultivation of virtue leads in one direction, and being virtuous leads in another. Most of us are concerned with the cultivation of virtue because, even though only superficially, virtue does give a certain poise, a certain quietness of mind in which there is not this incessant conflict of contradictory desires. But it seems to me fairly obvious that the mere cultivation of virtue can never bring about freedom, but only leads to respectable tranquillity, the sense of order, of control, which arises from shaping the mind to conform to a certain social pattern which is called virtue.

So, our problem is to be good without trying to be good. I think there is a vast difference between the two. Being good is a state in which there is no effort, but we are not in that state. We are envious, ambitious, gossipy, cruel, narrow, petty minded, caught in various forms of stupidity, which is not good; and being all that, how can one come to a state of mind which is good without making an effort to be good? Surely, the man who makes an effort to be virtuous is not virtuous, is he? A person who tries to be humble obviously has not the least understanding of what humility is. And not being humble, is it possible to have the sense of humility without the cultivation of humility?

I do not know if you have thought about this problem at all. One can see very well that there must be virtue. It is like keeping the room tidy, but having a tidy room is not at all important in itself. To make virtue an end in itself obviously has social benefits; it helps you to be a so-called decent citizen who lives according to a certain pattern, whether here, in India, or in Russia. But isn't

it very important for the mind to be orderly without enforcement, without discipline, and to forget it so that it is not all the time restrained, disciplined, cultivating conformity?

After all, what is it we are seeking? What is it that each one of us is in search of, not theoretically, abstractly, but actually? And is there any difference between the search of the man who is seeking satisfaction through knowledge, through God, and that of the man who is seeking to be wealthy, to fulfill his ambition, or who seeks satisfaction through drink? Socially there is a difference. The man who is seeking satisfaction through drink is obviously an antisocial being, whereas the man who seeks satisfaction by joining a religious order, becoming a hermit, and so on, is socially beneficial—but that's all.

So, does what we are seeking actually bring about contentment, however serious we are in our search? And we are serious, are we not? The hermit, the monk, the man who is pursuing various forms of pleasure, each in his own way is very serious. And does that constitute earnestness? Is there earnestness when there is a search to acquire something? Do you understand my question? Or, is there earnestness only when there is no seeking of an end?

After all, you who are here must be somewhat earnest; otherwise, you wouldn't have taken the trouble to come. Now, I am asking myself, and I hope you are asking yourself, what it means to be earnest because on that depends, I think, what I am going to explain a little later. If you are here seeking contentment, or to understand some past experience, or to cultivate a certain state of mind which you think will give you tranquillity, peace, or to experience that which you call reality, God, you may be very earnest; but should you not question that earnestness? Is it earnestness when you are seeking something which is going to give you pleasure or tranquillity?

If we can really understand this whole process of seeking, understand why we seek and what we seek—and that process can be understood only through self-knowledge, through awareness of the movement of our own thinking, of our own reactions and responses, of our various urges—then perhaps we shall find out what it is to be virtuous without disciplining ourselves to be virtuous. You see, I feel that as long as the mind is held in conflict, though we may suppress it, though we may try to run away from it, discipline it, control it, shape it according to various patterns, that conflict remains latent in the mind, and such a mind can never be really quiet. And it is essential, it seems to me, to have a quiet mind because the mind is our only instrument of understanding, of perception, of communication, and as long as that instrument is not completely clear and capable of perception, capable of pursuit without an end, there can be no freedom, no tranquillity, and therefore no discovery of anything new.

So, is it possible to live in this world—where there is so much turmoil, anxiety, insecurity—without effort? That is one of our problems, is it not? To me, that is a very important question because creativity is something that comes into being only when the mind is in a state of no effort. I am not using that word *creativity* in the academic sense of learning creative writing, creative acting, creative thought, and all that stuff; I am using it in an entirely different sense. When the mind is in a state where the past, with its cultivation of virtue through discipline, has wholly ceased—it is only then that there is a timeless creativity, which may be called God, truth, or what you like. So, how can the mind be in that state of constant creativity?

When you have a problem, what happens? You think it out, you wallow in it, you fuss over it, you get wildly excited about it; and the more you analyze it, dig into it, polish it, worry about it, the less you understand it. But the moment you put it away from you, you understand it—the whole thing is suddenly very clear. I think most of us have had that experience. The mind is no longer in a state of confusion, conflict, and therefore it is capable of receiving or perceiving something totally new. And is it possible for the mind to be in that state so that it is never repetitive but is experiencing something new all the time? I think that depends on our understanding of this problem of the cultivation of virtue.

We cultivate virtue; we discipline ourselves to conform to a particular pattern of morality. Why? Not only in order to be socially respectable, but also because we see the necessity of bringing about order, of controlling our minds, our speech, our thought. We see how extraordinarily important that is, but in the process of cultivating virtue, we are building up memory, the memory which is the 'me', the self, the ego. That is the background we have, especially those who think they are religious—the background of constantly practicing a particular discipline, of belonging to certain sects, groups, so-called religious bodies. Their reward may be somewhere else, in the next world, but it is still a reward; and in pursuing virtue, which means polishing, disciplining, controlling the mind, they are developing and maintaining self-conscious memory, so never for a moment are they free from the past.

If you have ever really disciplined yourself, practiced not being envious, not being angry, and so on, I wonder if you have noticed that that very practice, the very disciplining of the mind leaves a series of memories of the known? This is rather a difficult problem we are discussing, and I hope I am making myself clear. The whole process of saying, "I must not do this," breeds or builds up time, and a mind that is caught in time can obviously never experience something which is timeless, which is the unknown. Yet the mind must be orderly, free of contradictory desires—which does not mean conforming, accepting, obeying.

So, if you are at all earnest, in the sense in which I am using that word, this problem must inevitably arise. Your mind is the result of the known. Your mind is the known; it is shaped by memories, by reactions, by impressions of the known; and a mind that is held within the field of the known can never comprehend or experience the unknown, something which is not within the field of time. The mind is creative only when it is free from the known—and then it can use the known, which is the technique. Am I making myself clear, or is it all as clear as mud? (Laughter)

You see, we are so bored that we constantly read, acquire, learn, go to churches, perform rituals, and we never know a moment which is original, pristine, innocent, completely free from all impressions; and it is that moment that is creative, that is timeless, everlasting, or whatever word you like to use. Without that creativity, life becomes so insipid, stupid, and then all our virtues, our knowledge, our pursuits, our amusements, our various beliefs and traditions have very little meaning. As I was saying the other day, society merely cultivates the known, and we are the result of that society. To find the unknown, it is essential to be free of society—which doesn't mean that you must withdraw into a monastery and pray from morning till night, everlastingly disciplining yourself, conforming to a certain belief, dogma. Surely, that does not bring about the release of the mind from the known.

The mind is the result of the known; it is the result of the past, which is the accumulation of time; and is it possible for such a mind to be free from the known without effort so that it can discover something original? Any effort it makes to free itself, any search in order to find, is still within the field of the known. Surely, God or truth must be something totally unthought of; it must be something entirely new, unformulated, never discovered, never experienced before. And how can a mind which is the result of the known ever experience that? Do you follow the problem? If the problem is clear, then you will find the right way of approaching it, which is not a method.

That's why it is important to find out if one can be good, in the complete sense of the word, without trying to be good, without making an effort to get rid of envy, of ambition, of cruelty, without disciplining oneself to stop gossiping—you know, the whole mass of strictures which we impose upon ourselves in order to be good. Can there be goodness without the attempt to be good? I think there can be only if each one of us knows how to listen, how to be attentive—now. There is goodness only when there is complete attention. See the truth that there can be no goodness through endeavor, through effort, just see the truth of that—and you can see the truth of it only if you are giving complete attention to what is being said. Forget all the books you have read, the things that you have been told of, and give complete attention to the statement that there can be no virtue as long as there is endeavor to be virtuous. As long as I am trying to be nonviolent, there is violence; as long as I am trying to be unenvious, I am envious; as long as I am trying to be humble, there is pride. If I see the truth of that, not intellectually or verbally, which is merely to hear the words and agree with them, but very simply and directly, then out of that comes goodness. But the difficulty is that the mind then says, "How can I keep that state? I may be good while sitting here listening to something which I feel is true, but the moment I go out, I am again caught in the stream of envy.'' But I don't think that matters—you'll find out.

Our culture, our society, is based on envy, on various forms of acquisitiveness, whether it is the acquisition of knowledge, of experience, of property, or what you will. And to be free of all that doesn't require endeavor, effort, but seeing the whole implication of effort. A man who is acquiring knowledge is not peaceful, he is caught in effort. It is only when the mind is totally without effort that it is peaceful, which is really an extraordinary state, and I think anybody can have it who gives his heart, his whole attention to the matter. A mind that is not toiling, that is not trying to become something socially or spiritually, that is completely nothing—it is only such a mind that can receive the new.

Question: Some philosophers assert that life has purpose and meaning while others maintain that life is utterly haphazard and absurd. What do you say? You deny the value of goals, ideals, and purposes; but without them, has life any significance at all?

KRISHNAMURTI: Has what the philosophers say a great significance to each one of us? Some intellectuals say there is meaning, significance to life, while others say it is haphazard and absurd. Surely, in their own way, negatively or positively, both are giving significance to life, are they not? One asserts, the other denies, but essentially they are both the same. That is fairly obvious.

Now, when you pursue an ideal, a goal, or inquire what is the purpose of life, that very inquiry or pursuit is based on the desire to give significance to life, is it not? I do not know if you are following all this.

My life has no significance, let us suppose, so I seek to give significance to life. I say, ''What is the purpose of life?'' because if life has a purpose, then according to that purpose, I can live. So I invent or imagine a purpose, or by reading, inquiring, searching, I find a purpose; therefore, I am giving significance to life. As the intellectual in his own way gives significance to life by denying or asserting that it has purpose and meaning, we also give significance to life through our ideals, through our search for a goal, for God, for love, for truth. Which means, really, that without giving significance to life, our life has no meaning for us at all. Living isn't good enough for us, so we want to give a significance to life. I do not know if you see that.

What is the significance of our life, yours and mine, apart from the philosophers? Has it any significance, or are we giving it a significance through belief, like the intellectual who becomes a Catholic, this or that, and thereby finds shelter? His intellect has torn everything to pieces; he cannot stand being alone, lonely, and all the rest of it, so he has to have a belief in Catholicism, in communism, or in something else which nourishes him, which for him gives significance to life.

Now, I am asking myself: Why do we want a significance? And what does it mean to live without significance at all? Do you understand? Our own life being empty, harried, lonely, we want to give a significance to life. And is it possible to be aware of our own emptiness, loneliness, sorrow, of all the travail and conflict in our life, without trying to get out of it, without artificially giving a significance to life? Can we be aware of this extraordinary thing which we call life, which is the earning of a livelihood, the envy, the ambition, the frustration—just be aware of all that without condemnation or justification, and go beyond? It seems to me that as long as we are seeking or giving a significance to life, we are missing something extraordinarily vital. It is like the man who wants to find the significance of death, who is everlastingly rationalizing it, explaining it—he never experiences what is death. We shall go into that in another talk.

So, aren't we all trying to find a reason for our existence? When we love, do we have a reason? Or is love the only state in which there is no reason at all, no explanation, no endeavor, no trying to be something? Perhaps we do not know that state. Not knowing that state, we try to imagine it, give significance to life; and because our minds are conditioned, limited, petty, the significance we give to life, our gods, our rituals, our endeavors, is also petty.

Isn't it important, then, to find out for ourselves what significance we give to life, if we do? Surely, the purposes, the goals, the Masters, the gods, the beliefs, the ends through which we are seeking fulfillment are all invented by the mind; they are all the outcome of our conditioning, and realizing that, is it not important to uncondition the mind? When the mind is unconditioned and is therefore not giving significance to life, then life is an extraordinary thing, something totally different from the framework of the mind. But first we must know our own conditioning, must we not? And is it possible to know our conditioning, our limitations, our background, without forcing, without analyzing, without trying to sublimate or suppress it? Because that whole process involves the entity who observes and separates himself from the observed, does it not? As long as there is the observer and the observed, conditioning must continue. However much the observer, the thinker, the censor, may try to get rid of his conditioning, he is still caught in that conditioning because the very division between the thinker and the thought, the experiencer and the experience, is the perpetuation of conditioning; and it is extremely difficult to let this division disappear because it involves the whole problem of will.

Our culture is based on will—the will to be, to become, to achieve, to fulfill—therefore, in each one of us there is always the entity who is trying to change, control, alter that which he observes. But is there a difference between that which he observes and himself, or are they one? This is a thing that cannot be merely accepted. It must be thought of, gone into with tremendous patience, gentleness, hesitancy, so that the mind is no longer separated from that which it thinks, so that the observer and the observed are psychologically one. As long as I am psychologically separate from that which I perceive in myself as envy, I try to overcome envy; but is that 'I', the maker of effort to overcome envy, different from envy? Or are they both the same, only the 'I' has separated himself from envy in order to overcome it because he feels envy is painful, and for various other reasons? But that very separation is the cause of envy.

Perhaps you are not used to this way of thinking, and it is a little bit too abstract. But a mind that is envious can never be tranquil because it is always comparing, always trying to become something which it is not; and if one really goes into this problem of envy radically, profoundly, deeply, one must inevitably come upon this problem—whether the entity that wishes to be rid of envy is not envy itself. When one realizes that it is envy itself that wants to get rid of envy, then the mind is aware of that feeling called envy without any sense of condemning or trying to get rid of it. Then from that the problem arises: Is there a feeling if there is no verbalization? Because the very word *envy* is condemnatory, is it not? Am I saying too much all at once?

Is there a feeling of envy if I don't name that feeling? By the very naming of it, am I not maintaining that feeling? The feeling and the naming are almost simultaneous, are they not? And is it possible to separate them so that there is only a sense of reaction without naming? If you really go into it, you will find that when there is no naming of that feeling, envy totally ceases—not just the envy you feel because somebody is more beautiful or has a better car, and all that stupid stuff, but the tremendous depth of envy, the root of envy. All of us are envious; there isn't one who is not envious in different ways. But envy isn't just the superficial thing; it is the whole sense of comparing which goes very deep and occupies our minds so vastly, and to be radically free of envy, there must be no censor, no observer of the envy who is trying to get rid of envy. We shall go into that another time.

Question: To be without condemnation, justification, or comparison is to be in a higher state of consciousness. I am not in that state, so how am I to get there?

KRISHNAMURTI: You see, the very question, "How am I to get there?" is envious. (Laughter) No, sirs, please pay attention. You want to get something, so you have methods, disciplines, religions, churches, this whole superstructure which is built on envy, comparison, justification, condemnation. Our culture is based on this hierarchical division between those who have more and those who have less, those who know and those who don't know, those who are ignorant and those who are full of wisdom, so our approach to the problem is totally wrong. The questioner says, "To be without condemnation, justification, or comparison is to be in a higher state of consciousness." Is it? Or are we simply not aware that we are condemning, comparing? Why do we first assert that it is a higher state of consciousness and then out of that create the problem of how to get there and who is going to help us to get there? Is it not much simpler than all that?

That is, we are not aware of ourselves at all; we do not see that we are condemning, comparing. If we can watch ourselves daily without justifying or condemning anything, just be aware of how we never think without judging, comparing, evaluating, then that very awareness is enough. We are always saying, "This book is not as good as the other," or "This man is better than that man," and so on; there is this constant process of comparison, and we think that through comparison we understand. Do we? Or does understanding come only when one is not comparing but is really paying attention? Is there comparison when you are looking attentively at something? When you are totally attentive, you have no time to compare, have you? The moment you compare, your attention has gone off to something else. When you say, "This sunset is not as beautiful as that of yesterday," you are not really looking at the sunset; your mind has already gone off to yesterday's memory. But if you can look at the sunset completely, totally, with your whole attention, then comparison ceases, surely.

So the problem is not how to get something but why we are not attentive. We are not attentive, obviously, because we are not interested. Don't say, "How am I to be interested?" That's irrelevant, that's not the question. Why should you be interested? If you are not interested in listening to what is being said, why bother? But you are bothered because your life is full of envy, suffering, so you want to find an answer, you want to find a meaning. If you want to find a meaning, give full attention. The difficulty is that we are not really serious about anything, serious in the right sense of that word. When you give complete attention to something, you are not trying to get anything out of it, are you? At that moment of total attention, there is no entity who is trying to change, to modify, to become something; there is no self at all. In the moment of attention the self, the 'me', is absent, and it is that moment of attention that is good, that is love.

August 13, 1955

Fourth Talk in The Oak Grove

One of the most difficult things to understand, it seems to me, is this problem of change. We see that there is progress in different forms, so-called evolution, but is there a fundamental change in progress? I do not know if this problem has struck you at all, or whether you have ever thought about it, but perhaps it will be worthwhile to go into the question this morning.

We see that there is progress in the obvious sense of that word; there are new inventions, better cars, better planes, better refrigerators, the superficial peace of a progressive society, and so on. But does that progress bring about a radical change in man, in you and me? It does superficially alter the conduct of our life, but can it ever fundamentally transform our thinking? And how is this fundamental transformation to be brought about? I think it is a problem worth considering. There is progress in self-improvement—I can be better tomorrow, more kind, more generous, less envious, less ambitious. But does self-improvement bring about a complete change in one's thinking? Or is there no change at all, but only progress? Progress implies time, does it not? I am this today, and I shall be something better tomorrow. That is, in self-improvement or self-denial or self-abnegation, there is progression, the gradualism of moving towards a better life, which means superficially adjusting to environment, conforming to an improved pattern, being conditioned in a nobler way, and so on. We see that process taking place all the time. And you must have wondered, as I

have, whether progress does bring about a fundamental revolution.

To me, the important thing is not progress but revolution. Please don't be horrified by that word *revolution,* as most people are in a very progressive society like this. But it seems to me that unless we understand the extraordinary necessity of bringing about not just a social amelioration but a radical change in our outlook, mere progress is progress in sorrow; it may effect the pacification, the calming of sorrow, but not the cessation of sorrow, which is always latent. After all, progress in the sense of getting better over a period of time is really the process of the self, the 'me', the ego. There is progress in self-improvement, obviously, which is the determined effort to be good, to be more this or less that, and so on. As there is improvement in refrigerators and airplanes, so also there is improvement in the self, but that improvement, that progress, does not free the mind from sorrow.

So, if we want to understand the problem of sorrow and perhaps put an end to it, then we cannot possibly think in terms of progress because a man who thinks in terms of progress, of time, saying that he will be happy tomorrow, is living in sorrow. And to understand this problem, one must go into the whole question of consciousness, must one not? Is this too difficult a subject? I'll go on and we'll see.

If I really want to understand sorrow and the ending of sorrow, I must find out, not only what are the implications of progress, but also what that entity is who wants to improve himself, and I must also know the motive with which he seeks to improve. All this is consciousness. There is the superficial consciousness of everyday activity: the job, the family, the constant adjustment to social environment, either happily, easily, or contradictorily, with a neurosis. And there is also the deeper level of consciousness, which is the vast social inheritance of man through centuries: the will to exist, the will to alter, the will to become. If I would bring about a fundamental revolution in myself, surely I must understand this total progress of consciousness.

One can see that progress obviously does not bring about a revolution. I am not talking of social or economic revolution—that is very superficial, as I think most of us will agree. The overthrow of one economic or social system and the setting up of another does alter certain values, as in the Russian and other historical revolutions. But I am talking of a psychological revolution, which is the only revolution, and a man who is religious must be in that state of revolution, which I shall go into presently.

In grappling with this problem of progress and revolution, there must be an awareness, a comprehension of the total process of consciousness. Do you understand? Until I really comprehend what is consciousness, mere adjustment on the surface, though it may have sociological significance and perhaps bring about a better way of living, more food, less starvation in Asia, fewer wars, it can never solve the fundamental problem of sorrow. Without understanding, resolving, and going beyond the urge that brings about sorrow, mere social adjustment is the continuance of that latent seed of sorrow. So I must understand what is consciousness, not according to any philosophy, psychology, or description, but by directly experiencing the actual state of my consciousness, the whole content of it.

Now, perhaps this morning you and I can experiment with this. I am going to describe what is consciousness; but while I am describing it, don't follow the description, but rather observe the process of your own thinking, and then you will know for yourself what consciousness is without reading any of the contradictory accounts of what the various experts have found. Do you understand? I am describing something. If you merely listen to the description, it will have very little meaning; but if through the description you are experiencing your own consciousness, your own process of thinking, then it will have tremendous importance now, not tomorrow, not some other day when you will have time to think about it, which is absolutely nonsense because it is mere postponement. If through the description you can experience the actual state of your own consciousness as you are quietly sitting here, then you will find that the mind is capable of freeing itself from its vast inheritance of conditioning, all the accumulations and edicts of society, and is able to go beyond self-consciousness. So if you will experiment with this, it will be worthwhile.

We are trying to discover for ourselves what is consciousness, and whether it is possible for the mind to be free of sorrow—not to change the pattern of sorrow, not to decorate the prison of sorrow, but to be completely free from the seed, the root of sorrow. In inquiring into that, we shall see the difference between progress and the psychological revolution which is essential if there is to be freedom from sorrow. We are not trying to alter the conduct of our consciousness; we are not trying to do something about it; we are just looking at it. Surely, if we are at all observant, slightly aware of anything, we know the activities of the superficial consciousness. We can see that on the surface our mind is active, occupied in adjustment, in a job, in earning a livelihood, in expressing certain tendencies, gifts, talents, or acquiring certain technical knowledge; and most of us are satisfied to live on that surface.

Please do not merely follow what I am telling you, but watch yourself, your own way of thinking. I am describing what is superficially taking place in our daily life—distractions, escapes, occasional lapses into fear, adjustment to the wife, to the husband, to the family, to society, to tradition, and so on—and with that superficiality most of us are satisfied.

Now, can we go below that and see the motive of this superficial adjustment? Again, if you are a little aware of this whole process, you know that this adjustment to opinion, to values, this acceptance of authority, and so on, is motivated by self-perpetuation, self-protection. If you can go still below that, you will find there is this vast undercurrent of racial, national, and group instincts, all the accumulations of human struggle, knowledge, endeavor, the dogmas and traditions of the Hindu, the Buddhist, or the Christian, the residue of so-called education through centuries—all of which has conditioned the mind to a certain inherited pattern. And if you can go deeper still, there is the primal desire to be, to succeed, to become, which expresses itself on the surface in various forms of social activity and creates deep-rooted anxieties, fears. Put very succinctly, the whole of that is our consciousness. In other words, our thinking is based on this fundamental urge to be, to become, and on top of that lie the many layers of tradition, of culture, of education, and the superficial conditioning of a given society—all forcing us to conform to a pattern that enables us to survive. There are many details and subtleties, but in essence that is our consciousness.

Now, any progress within that consciousness is self-improvement, and self-improvement is progress in sorrow, not the cessation of sorrow. This is quite obvious if you look at it. And if the mind is concerned with being free of all sorrow, then what is the mind to do? I do not know if you have thought about this problem, but please think about it now.

We suffer, don't we? We suffer, not only from physical illness, disease, but also from loneliness, from the poverty of our being; we suffer because we are not loved. When we love somebody and there is no loving in return, there is sorrow. In every direction, to think is to be full of sorrow; therefore, it seems better not to think, so we accept a belief and stagnate in that belief, which we call religion.

Now, if the mind sees that there is no ending of sorrow through self-improvement, through progress, which is fairly obvious, then what is the mind to do? Can the mind go beyond this consciousness, beyond these various urges and contradictory desires? And is going beyond a matter of time? Please follow this, not merely verbally, but actually. If it is a matter of time, then you are back again in the other thing, which is progress. Do you see that? Within the framework of consciousness, any movement in any direction is self-improvement and therefore the continuance of sorrow. Sorrow may be controlled, disciplined, subjugated, rationalized, superrefined, but the potential quality of sorrow is still there; and to be free from sorrow, there must be freedom from this potentiality, from this seed of the 'I', the self, from the whole process of becoming. To go beyond, there must be the cessation of this process. But if you say, "How am I to go beyond?" then the "how" becomes the method, the practice, which is still progress, therefore there is no going beyond but only the refinement of consciousness in sorrow. I hope you are getting this.

The mind thinks in terms of progress, of improvement, of time; and is it possible for such a mind, seeing that so-called progress is progress in sorrow, to come to an end—not in time, not tomorrow, but immediately? Otherwise you are back again in the whole routine, in the old wheel of sorrow. If the problem is stated clearly and clearly understood, then you will find the absolute answer. I am using that word *absolute* in its right sense. There is no other answer.

That is, our consciousness is all the time struggling to adjust, to modify, to change, to absorb, to reject, to evaluate, to condemn, to justify; but any such movement of consciousness is still within the pattern of sorrow. Any movement within that consciousness as dreams, or as an exertion of will, is the movement of the self; and any movement of the self, whether towards the highest or towards the most mundane, breeds sorrow. When the mind sees that, then what happens to such a mind? Do you understand the question? When the mind sees the truth of that, not merely verbally but totally, then is there a problem? Is there a problem when I am watching a rattler and know it to be poisonous? Similarly, if I can give my total attention to this process of suffering, then is not the mind beyond suffering?

Please follow this. Our minds are now occupied with sorrow and with the avoidance of sorrow, trying to overcome it, to diminish it, to modify it, to refine it, to run away from it in various ways. But if I see, not just superficially, but right through, that this very occupation of the mind with sorrow is the movement of the self which creates sorrow— if I really see the truth of that, then has not the mind gone beyond this thing that we call self-consciousness?

To put it differently, our society is based on envy, on acquisitiveness, not only here in America, but also in Europe, in Asia; and we are the product of that society, which has existed for centuries, millennia. Now, please follow this. I realize that I am envious. I can refine it, I can control it, discipline it, find a substitute for it through charitable activities, social reform, and so on; but envy is always there, latent, ready to spring forward. So, how is the mind to be totally free from envy? Because envy inevitably brings conflict, envy is a state in which there is no creativity, and a man who wishes to find out what is creativity must obviously be free from all envy, from all comparison, from the urges to be, to become.

Envy is a feeling which we identify with a word. We identify the feeling by calling it a name, giving it the term envy. I shall go slowly, and please follow this, for it is the description of our consciousness. There is a state of feeling, and I give it a name, I call it envy. That very word *envy* is condemnatory; it has social, moral, and spiritual significances which are part of the tradition in which I have been educated, so by the very employment of that word, I have condemned the feeling, and this process of condemnation is self-improvement. In condemning envy, I am progressing in the opposite direction, which is nonenvy, but that movement is still from the center which is envious.

So, can the mind put an end to naming? When there is a feeling of jealousy, of lust, or of ambition to be something, can the mind, which is educated in words, in condemnation, in giving it a name, stop that whole process of naming? Experiment with this, and you will see how extraordinarily difficult it is not to name a feeling. The feeling and the naming are almost simultaneous. But if the naming does not take place, then is there the feeling? Does the feeling persist when there is no naming? Are you following all this, or is it too abstract? Don't agree or disagree with me, because this is not my life, it is your life.

This whole problem of naming a feeling, of giving it a term, is part of the problem of consciousness. Take a word like *love*. How immediately your mind rejoices in that word! It has such significance, such beauty, ease, and all the rest of it. And the word *hate* immediately has quite another significance, something to be avoided, to be got rid of, to be shunned, and so on. So words have an extraordinary psychological effect on the mind, whether we are conscious of it or not.

Now, can the mind be free from all that verbalizing? If it can—and it must, otherwise the mind cannot possibly go further—then the problem arises: Is there an experiencer apart from experience? If there is an experiencer apart from experience, then the mind is conditioned because the experiencer is always either accumulating or rejecting experience, translating every experience in terms of his own likes and dislikes, in terms of his background, his conditioning; if he has a vision, he thinks it is Jesus, a Master, or God knows what else, some stupid nonsense. So as long as there is an experiencer, there is progress in suffering, which is the process of self-consciousness.

Now, to go beyond, to transcend all that, requires tremendous attention. This total attention, in which there is no choice, no sense of becoming, of changing, altering, wholly frees the mind from the process of self-consciousness; there is then no experiencer who is accumulating, and it is only then that the mind can be truly said to be free from sorrow. It is accumulation that is the cause of sorrow. We do not die to everything from day to day; we do not die to the innumerable traditions, to the family, to our own experiences, to our own desire to hurt another. One has to die to all that from moment to moment, to that vast accumulative memory, and only then the mind is free from the self, which is the entity of accumulation.

Perhaps in considering this question together, we shall clarify what has already been said.

Question: What is the unconscious, and is it conditioned? If it is conditioned, then how is one to set about being free from that conditioning?

KRISHNAMURTI: First of all, is not our consciousness, the waking consciousness, conditioned? Do you understand what the word *conditioned* means? You are educated in a certain way. Here in this country you are conditioned to be Americans, whatever that may mean, you are educated in the American way of life, and in Russia they are educated in the Russian way of life. In Italy the Catholics educate the children to think in a certain way, which is another form of conditioning, while in India, in Asia, in the Buddhist countries, they are conditioned in still other ways. Throughout the world there is this deliberate process of conditioning the mind through education, through social environment, through fear, through the job, through the family—you know, the innumerable ways of influencing the superficial mind, the waking consciousness.

Then there is the unconscious, that is, the layer of the mind below the superficial, and the questioner wants to know if that is conditioned. Isn't it conditioned—conditioned by all the racial thought, the hidden motives, desires, the instinctual responses of a particular culture? I am supposed to be a Hindu, born in India, educated abroad, and all the rest of it. Until I go into the unconscious and understand it, I am still a Hindu with all the Brahmanic, symbolic, cultural, religious, superstitious responses—it is all there, dormant, to be awakened at any moment, and it gives warning, intimation, through dreams, through moments when the conscious mind is not fully occupied. So the unconscious is also conditioned.

It is quite obvious, then, if you go into it, that the whole of one's consciousness is conditioned. There is no part of you, no higher self, which is not conditioned. Your very thinking is the outcome of memory, conscious or unconscious; therefore, it is the result of conditioning. You think as a communist, as a socialist, as a capitalist, as an

American, as a Hindu, as a Catholic, as a Protestant, or what you will, because you are conditioned that way. You are conditioned to believe in God, if you are, and the communist is not; he laughs at you and says, "You are conditioned," but he himself is conditioned, educated by his society, by the party to which he belongs, by its literature, not to believe. So we are all conditioned, and we never ask, "Is it possible to be totally free from conditioning?" All we know is a process of refinement in conditioning, which is refinement in sorrow.

Now, if I see that, not merely verbally, but with total attention, then there is no conflict. Do you understand what I mean? When you attend to something with your whole being, that is, when you give your mind completely to understand something, there is no conflict. Conflict arises only when you are partly interested and partly looking at something else, and then you want to overcome that conflict, so you begin to concentrate, which is not attention. In attention there is no division, there is no distraction; therefore, there is no effort, no conflict, and it is only through such attention that there can be self-knowledge, which is not accumulative.

Please follow this. Self-knowledge is not a thing to be accumulated; it is to be discovered from moment to moment, and to discover there cannot be accumulation, there cannot be a referent. If you accumulate self-knowledge, then all further understanding is dictated by that accumulation; therefore, there is no understanding.

So the mind can go beyond all conditioning only in awareness in which there is total attention. In that total attention there is no modifier, no censor, no entity who says, "I must change," which means there is a complete cessation of the experiencer. There is no experiencer as the accumulator. Please, this is really important to understand. Be-

cause, after all, when we experience something lovely—a sunset, a single leaf dancing in a tree, moonlight on the water, a smile, a vision, or what you like—the mind immediately wants to grasp it, to hold it, to worship it, which means the repetition of that experience; and where there is the urge to repeat, there must be sorrow.

Is it possible, then, to be in a state of experiencing without the experiencer? Do you understand? Can the mind experience ugliness, beauty, or what you will, without the entity who says, "I have experienced"? Because that which is truth, that which is God, that which is the immeasurable, can never be experienced as long as there is an experiencer. The experiencer is the entity of recognition; and if I am capable of recognizing that which is truth, then I have already experienced it, I already know it; therefore, it is not truth. That is the beauty of truth; it remains timelessly the unknown, and a mind that is the result of the known can never grasp it.

Question: You have said that all urges are in essence the same. Do you mean to say that the urge of the man who pursues God is no different from the urge of the man who pursues women or who loses himself in drink?

KRISHNAMURTI: All urges are not similar, but they are all urges. You may have an urge towards God, and I may have an urge to get drunk, but we are both compelled, urged—you in one direction, I in another. Your direction is respectable, mine is not; on the contrary, I am antisocial. But the hermit, the monk, the so-called religious person whose mind is occupied with virtue, with God, is essentially the same as the man whose mind is occupied with business, with women, or with drink, because both are occupied. Do you understand? The one has sociological value, while the other, the man whose mind is occupied with drink, is socially unfit. So you are judging from the social point of view, are you not? The man who retires into a monastery and prays from morning till night, doing some gardening for a certain period of the day, whose mind is wholly occupied with God, with self-castigation, self-discipline, self-control—him you regard as a very holy person, a most extraordinary man. Whereas, the man who goes after business, who manipulates the stock exchange and is occupied all the time with making money, of him you say, "Well, he is just an ordinary man like the rest of us." But they are both occupied. To me, what the mind is occupied with is not important. A man whose mind is occupied with God will never find God because God is not something to be occupied with; it is the unknown, the immeasurable. You cannot occupy yourself with God. That is a cheap way of thinking of God.

What is significant is not with what the mind is occupied but the fact of its occupation, whether it be with the kitchen, with the children, with amusement, with what kind of food you are going to have, or with virtue, with God. And must the mind be occupied? Do you follow? Can an occupied mind ever see anything new, anything except its own occupation? And what happens to the mind if it is not occupied? Do you understand? Is there a mind if there is no occupation? The scientist is occupied with his technical problems, with his mechanics, with his mathematics, as the housewife is occupied in the kitchen or with the baby. We are all so frightened of not being occupied, frightened of the social implications. If one were not occupied, one might discover oneself as one is, so occupation becomes an escape from what one is.

So, must the mind be everlastingly occupied? And is it possible to have no occupation of the mind? Please, I am putting to you a question to which there is no answer be-

cause you have to find out, and when you do find out, you will see the extraordinary thing happen.

It is very interesting to find out for yourself how your mind is occupied. The artist is occupied with his art, with his name, with his progress, with the mixing of colors, with fame, with notoriety; the man of knowledge is occupied with his knowledge; and a man who is pursuing self-knowledge is occupied with his self-knowledge, trying like a little ant to be aware of every thought, every movement. They are all the same. It is only the mind that is totally unoccupied, completely empty—it is only such a mind that can receive something new, in which there is no occupation. But that new thing cannot come into being as long as the mind is occupied.

Question: You say that an occupied mind cannot receive that which is truth or God. But how can I earn a livelihood unless I am occupied with my work? Are you yourself not occupied with these talks, which is your particular means of earning a livelihood?

KRISHNAMURTI: God forbid that I should be occupied with my talks! I am not. And this is not my means of livelihood. If I were occupied, there would be no interval between thoughts, there would not be that silence which is essential to see something new. Then talking would become utter boredom. I don't want to be bored by my own talks; therefore, I am not talking from memory. It is something totally different. It doesn't matter; we shall go into that some other time.

The questioner asks how he is to earn his livelihood if he is not occupied with his work. Do you occupy yourself with your work? Please listen to this. If you are occupied with your work, then you do not love your work. Do you understand the difference? If I love what I am doing, I am not occupied with it, my work is not apart from me. But we are trained in this country, and unfortunately it is becoming the habit throughout the world to acquire skill in work which we don't love. There may be a few scientists, a few technical experts, a few engineers who really love what they do in the total sense of the word, which I am going to explain presently. But most of us do not love what we are doing and that is why we are occupied with our livelihood. I think there is a difference between the two if you really go into it. How can I love what I am doing if I am all the time driven by ambition, trying through my work to achieve an aim, to become somebody, to have a success? An artist who is concerned with his name, with his greatness, with comparison, with fulfilling his ambition, has ceased to be an artist; he is merely a technician like everybody else. Which means, really, that to love something there must be a total cessation of all ambition, of all desire for the recognition of society, which is rotten anyhow. (Laughter) Sirs, please don't. And we are not trained for that, we are not educated for that; we have to fit into some groove which society or the family has given us. Because my forefathers have been doctors, lawyers, or engineers, I must be a doctor, a lawyer, or an engineer. And now there must be more and more engineers because that is what society demands. So we have lost this love of the thing itself, if we ever had it, which I doubt. And when you love a thing, there is no occupation with it. The mind isn't conniving to achieve something, trying to be better than somebody else; all comparison, competition, all desire for success, for fulfillment, totally ceases. It is only the ambitious mind that is occupied.

Similarly, a mind that is occupied with God, with truth, can never find it because that which the mind is occupied with, it already knows. If you already know the immeasurable, what you know is the outcome of the past; therefore, it is not the immeasurable. Reality cannot be measured; therefore, there is no occupation with it; there is only a stillness of the mind, an emptiness in which there is no movement— and it is only then that the unknown can come into being.

August 14, 1955

Fifth Talk in The Oak Grove

One of the grave problems about which most of us must have thought is the complete control of the mind, because one can see that without a deep, rational, balanced control of the mind, there is not the conservation of energy which is so essential if one is to do anything, and especially in matters that pertain to so-called search—the search of truth, of reality, of God, or what you will. One is aware, I think, that this stability of mind is necessary to penetrate into fundamental problems, which a superficial mind cannot touch. And yet the difficulty lies in how to control the mind, does it not? Many systems of discipline, various religious sects and monastic communities, have always insisted on the absolute control of the mind; and this evening I would like to discuss whether such a thing is possible at all, and how this absolute steadiness of the mind is to be brought about. I am using the word *absolute* in its correct sense, meaning complete, total control of the mind. As I said, it is essential to have such steadiness because in that state there is no conflict, no dissipation, no distraction of any kind; therefore, it brings enormous energy, and such a mind, being completely steady, is capable of deep, radical penetration into reality.

Now, however much it may control, dominate, discipline itself, can a petty mind ever be steady? Most of our minds are narrow, limited, prejudiced, petty, and a petty mind is occupied incessantly with things that are very superficial—with a job, with quarrels, with resentment, with the cultivation of virtues, with trying to understand something, with gossip, with its own evolution and its own problems. And can such a mind, however much it may control, discipline itself, ever be free to be steady? Because without freedom, the mind obviously cannot be steady.

That is, a mind which is striving after success, a result, groping after something which it cannot have, is essentially narrow, conditioned, limited, made petty by that very effort; and however much it may attempt to be steady by controlling itself, can such a mind ever bring about that essential energy which comes with deep, fundamental steadiness, or will it only build another series of limitations, further pettiness? I hope I am making the problem clear.

If my mind is nationalistic, bound by innumerable beliefs, superstitions, fears, caught up in envy, in resentment, in the cruelty of words, of gesture, thought, however much it may try to think of something beyond itself, it is still limited. So the problem is how to break up this pettiness of the mind, is it not? That is one of the fundamental issues, and if it is clear, then we can proceed to find out what it means to have complete control of the mind.

To find out what is truth, what is God, or whatever name you may like to give it, one must obviously have enormous energy, and in search of that energy, we do all kinds of nonsensical things. Either we resort to monasteries or become cranky about food, or we try to control the various passions, lusts, hoping thereby to canalize energy in order to find something beyond the mind. After all, that is what most of us are endeavoring to do in different ways. We are trying to control our thoughts, our desires, cultivate virtue, be watchful of our words, our actions, and so

on, either with the intention of being good, respectable citizens or in the hope of canalizing all this extraordinary vitality of desire in order to find out what lies beyond; but we cannot find that out, however much we may struggle, as long as we do not understand the pettiness of the mind. When a petty mind seeks God, its God will also be petty, obviously; its virtues will be mere respectability. So, is it possible to break up this pettiness? Is the question clear? All right, then let us proceed.

Our minds are petty, envious, acquisitive, fearful, whether we admit it or not. Now, what makes the mind petty? Surely, the mind is narrow, limited, shallow, petty, as long as it is acquisitive. It may give up worldly things and become acquisitive in the pursuit of knowledge, wisdom, but it is still petty because in acquiring, it develops the will to achieve, to gain, and this very will to achieve constitutes pettiness.

May I say something here about attention? Attention is very important, but attention is entirely different from concentration or absorption in something. A child is absorbed in a toy; the toy attracts him, and so he gives his mind to the toy. That is what happens, is it not? The object draws the mind, absorbs the mind, or else the mind absorbs the object. If you are interested in something, the object of that interest is so enticing that it absorbs you; whereas, if you deliberately concentrate on something, which is another form of absorption, then you absorb the object, do you not?

Now, I am talking of something entirely different. I am talking of an attention in which there is no object at all, no strain, no conflict, an attention in which you are neither absorbed nor are you trying to concentrate on something. In listening to what is being said here, you are endeavoring to understand, your listening has an object; therefore, there is an effort, a strain; there is no relaxed attention at all. That is a fact, is it not? If you want to listen to something, there must be no strain, no effort, no object which attracts your attention and absorbs you; otherwise, you are merely hypnotized by what is being said, by a personality, and all the rest of that nonsense. If you observe closely this process of absorption, you will see that in it, there is always a conflict, a sense of strain, an effort to get something; whereas, in attention there is no particular object at all—you are just listening as you would listen to distant music or to the notes of a song. In that state you are relaxed, attentive; there is no strain.

So, if I may suggest, try just being attentive while you are listening to what is being said here. What I am talking about may be difficult and somewhat new and therefore rather disturbing, but if you can listen with this relaxed attention, you won't be mentally agitated though you may be disturbed in a different way, which perhaps is good. What I am saying is something which is essential to understand. I am saying that the mind must be completely steady. But this steadiness cannot come about if the mind tries to make itself steady because the mind, the maker of effort, is in its very nature petty. The mind may be full of encyclopedic knowledge, it may be capable of clever discussions and possess vast accumulations of technique, but it remains essentially petty as long as it is based on the sense of acquisitiveness and therefore on the cultivation of will—that is, as long as there is the 'I', the entity who is acquiring, who is making an effort, who is putting aside and gathering. The mind may think of God, it may discipline itself, try to control its various desires in order to be virtuous, in order to have more energy to seek truth, and so on; but such a mind is narrow, limited—it can never be free and therefore steady.

Our problem, then, is how to break up this pettiness of the mind. Is the question clear?

If it is clear, then what are you to do? One sees the necessity of a very steady, deep, quiet mind, a mind which is completely controlled—but not controlled by a separate entity who says, "I must control it." Do you follow? That is, I see the importance of a steady mind. Now, how is this steadiness to be brought about? If another part of the mind says, "I must have a steady mind," then it develops conflicts, controls, subjugations, does it not? One part of the mind dictates to the other part, trying to prevent it from wandering, controlling it, shaping it, disciplining it, suppressing various forms of desire; so there is conflict all the time, is there not?

Now, a mind in conflict is in its very essence petty because its desire is to acquire something. Desiring to acquire a steady mind, you say, "I must control my mind, I must shape it, I must push away all conflicting desires," but as long as there is this dual process in your thinking, there must be conflict, and that very conflict indicates pettiness because that conflict is the outcome of the desire to gain something. So, can the mind obliterate, forget this whole process of acquisition, of acquiring a very steady mind in order to find God, or whatever it is? That is, as you listen, can you see the truth of what is being said immediately? I am saying that there must be complete and absolute steadiness of the mind, and that any endeavor to achieve that state indicates a mind that is divided, a mind that says, "By Jove, I must have that steadiness, it will be marvelous," and then pursues that state through discipline, through control, through various forms of sanction, and so on. But if the mind is capable of listening to the truth of that statement, if it sees the absolute necessity of complete control, then you will find there is no endeavor to achieve a state.

Is this too difficult? I'm afraid it is because, you see, most of us think in terms of effort; there is always the entity who is making an effort to achieve a result, and hence there is conflict. You hear the statement that the mind must be absolutely steady, controlled, or you have read and thought about it, and you say, "I must have that state," so you pursue it through control, discipline, meditation, and so on. In that process there is effort, there is conformity, the following of a pattern, the establishment of authority, and the various other complications that arise. Now, any effort to achieve a result, any form of desire to acquire a state, makes for a petty mind, and such a mind can never possibly be free to be steady. If one sees the truth of that very clearly, then is there not an absolute steadiness of the mind? Do you understand?

To put it differently, one can see very clearly that energy is needed for any form of action. Even if you want to be a rich man, you must devote your life to it, you must give to it your concentrated energy. And to find that which is beyond the activities, the movements of the mind—which implies a tremendous depth in self-knowledge—concentrated energy is essential. Now, how is this concentrated energy to come into being? Seeing the necessity of it, we say, "I must control my temper, I must eat the right food, I must not be oversexual, I must control my passions, my lusts, my desires"—you know, we go off at tangents. These are all tangents because the center is still petty. As long as the mind thinks in terms of acquiring something, of achieving a result, it is ambitious, and an ambitious mind is in its very nature small, shallow. Such a mind, like that of an ambitious man in this world, obviously has a certain amount of energy, but what we are discussing demands much deeper, wider, more unlimited energy in which the self is totally absent.

So, one has been conditioned through centuries—religiously, socially, and morally—to control, to shape one's mind to a particular pattern, or to follow certain ideals, in order to conserve one's energy; and can such a mind break free from all that without effort and come immediately to that state in which the mind is totally still, completely steady? Then there is no such thing as distraction. Distraction exists only when you want to go in a certain direction. When you say, "I must think about this and nothing else," then everything else is a distraction. But when you are completely attentive with that attention in which there is no object because there is no process of acquiring, no cultivation of the will to achieve a result, then you will find that the mind is extraordinarily steady, inwardly still—and it is only the still mind that is free to discover or let that reality come into being.

Question: How can one stop habits?

KRISHNAMURTI: If we can understand the whole process of habit, then perhaps we shall be able to stop the formation of habits. Merely to stop a particular habit is comparatively easy, but the problem is not then solved. All of us have various habits of which we are either conscious or unconscious, so we have to find out whether the mind is caught in habit, and why the mind creates habits at all.

Is not most of our thinking habitual? From childhood we have been taught to think along a certain line, whether as a Christian, a communist, or a Hindu, and we dare not deviate from that line because the very deviation is fear. So fundamentally our thinking is habitual, conditioned; our minds function along established grooves, and naturally there are also superficial habits which we try to control.

Now, if the mind ceases altogether to think in habits, then we shall approach the problem of a superficial habit entirely differently. Do you understand? If you are investigating, trying to find out whether your mind thinks in habits, if that is what you are really concerned with, then the habit of smoking, for example, will have quite a different meaning. That is, if you are interested in inquiring into the whole process of habit, which is at a deeper level, you will treat the habit of smoking in a totally different manner. Being inwardly very clear that you really want to stop, not only the habit of smoking, but the whole process of thinking in habits, you do not fight the automatic movement of picking up a cigarette, and all the rest of it, because you see that the more you fight that particular habit, the more life you give to it. But if you are attentive, completely aware of the habit without fighting it, then you will see that that habit ceases in its time; therefore, the mind is not occupied with that habit. I do not know if you are following this.

Inwardly I see very clearly that I want to stop smoking, but the habit has been set going for a number of years. Shall I fight that habit? Surely, by fighting a habit, I am giving life to it. Please understand this. Anything I fight, I am giving life to. If I fight an idea, I am giving life to that idea; if I fight you, I am giving you life to fight me. I must see that very clearly, and I can see it very clearly only if I am looking at the whole problem of habit, not just at one specific habit. Then my approach to habit is at a different level altogether.

So the question now is: Why does the mind think in terms of habit, the habit of relationship, the habit of ideas, the habit of beliefs, and so on? Why? Because essentially it is seeking to be secure, to be safe, to be permanent, is it not? The mind hates to be uncertain, so it must have habits as a means of security. A mind that is secure can never be free from habit, but only the mind that is completely insecure—which doesn't mean ending up in an asylum or a mental hospital. The mind that is completely insecure, that is uncertain, inquiring, perpetually finding out, that is dying to every experience, to everything it has acquired, and is therefore in a state of not-knowing—only such a mind can be free of habit, and that is the highest form of thinking.

Question: Is it possible to raise children without conditioning them, and if so, how? If not, is there such a thing as good and bad conditioning? Please answer this question unconditionally. (Laughter)

KRISHNAMURTI: "Is it possible to raise children without conditioning them?" Is it? I don't think so. Please listen, let's go into this together. But first of all, let's dispose of this latter question, whether there is good conditioning and bad conditioning. Surely, there is only conditioning, not good and bad. You may call it a good conditioning to believe that there is God, but in communist Russia they will say, "What nonsense, that is an evil conditioning." What you call good conditioning, somebody else may call bad, which is obvious, so we can dispose of that question very quickly.

The question is, then, can children be brought up without conditioning, without influencing them? Surely, everything about them is influencing them. Climate, food, words, gestures, conversation, the unconscious responses, other children, society, schools, churches, books, magazines, cinemas—all that is influencing the child. And can you stop that influence? It is not possible, is it? You may not want to influence, to condition your child, but unconsciously you are influencing him, are you not? You have your beliefs, your dogmas, your fears, your moralities, your intentions, your ideas of what is good and what is bad, so consciously or unconsciously you are shaping the child. And if you don't, the school does with its history books that say what marvelous heroes you have and the other fellows haven't, and so on. Everything is influencing the child, so let us first recognize that, which is an obvious fact.

Now, the problem is: Can you help the child to grow up to question all these influences intelligently? Do you understand? Knowing that the child is being influenced all around, at home as well as at school, can you help him to question every influence and not be caught in any particular influence? If it is really your intention to help your child to investigate all influences, then that is extremely arduous, is it not? Because it means questioning, not only your authority, but the whole problem of authority, of nationalism, of belief, of war, of the army—you know, investigating the whole thing, which is to cultivate intelligence. And when there is that intelligence so that the mind no longer merely accepts authority or conforms through fear, then every influence is examined and put aside; therefore, such a mind is not conditioned. Surely, that can be done, can it not? And is it not the function of education to cultivate that intelligence which is capable of examining objectively every influence, of investigating the background, the immediate as well as the deep background, so that the mind is not caught in any conditioning?

After all, you are conditioned by your background; you are this background, which is made up of your Christian inheritance, of the extraordinary vitality, energy, progress of America, of innumerable influences—climatic, social, religious, dietetic, and so on. And can you not look at all that intelligently, bring it out, put it on the table and examine it, without going through the absurd process of keeping what you think is good and throwing out what you think is bad? Surely, one has to look objectively at all of this so-called culture. Cultures create religions but not the religious man. The religious man comes into being only when the mind rejects culture, which is the background, and is therefore

free to find out what is true. But that demands an extraordinary alertness of mind, does it not? Such a person is not an American, an Englishman, or a Hindu but a human being; he does not belong to any particular group, race, or culture and is therefore free to find out what is true, what is God. No culture helps man to find out what is true. Cultures only create organizations which bind man. Therefore, it is important to investigate all this, not only the conscious conditioning, but much more the unconscious conditioning of the mind. And the unconscious conditioning cannot be examined superficially by the conscious mind. It is only when the conscious mind is completely quiet that the unconscious conditioning comes out, not at any given moment, but all the time—when you are on a walk, riding in a bus, or talking to somebody. When the intention is to find out, then you will see that the unconscious conditioning comes pouring out, so the doors are open to discovery.

Question: When I first heard you speak and had an interview with you, I was deeply disturbed. Then I began watching my thoughts, not condemning or comparing, and so on, and I somewhat gathered the sense of silence. Many weeks later, I again had an interview with you and again received a shock, for you made it clear to me that my mind was not awake at all, and I realized that I had become somewhat smug in my achievement. Why does the mind settle down after each shock, and how is this process to be broken up?

KRISHNAMURTI: Socially, religiously, and personally, we are constantly avoiding any form of change, are we not? We want things to go on as they are because the mind hates to be disturbed. When it achieves something, there it settles down. But life is a process of challenge and response, and if there is no response adequate to the challenge, there is conflict. In order to avoid that conflict, we settle down in comfortable grooves and so decay. That is a psychological fact.

That is, life is a challenge; everything in life is demanding a response, but because you have your limitations, your worries, your conditioning, your beliefs, your ideals of what you should and should not do, you cannot respond to it fully; therefore, there is conflict. In order to avoid or to overcome that conflict, you settle back, you do something else which gives you comfort. The mind is seeking continuously a state in which there will be no disturbance at all, which you call peace, God, or what you like; but essentially the desire is not to be disturbed. The state of nondisturbance you call peace, but it is really death. Whereas, if you understand that the mind must be in a state of continuous response, and there is therefore no desire for comfort, for security, no mooring, no anchorage, no refuge in belief, in ideas, in property, and all the rest of it, then you will see that you need no shock at all. Then there is not this process of being awakened by a shock only to fall asleep again.

You see, that brings up a question which is really very important. We think we need teachers, gurus, leaders, who will help us to keep awake. Probably that is why most of you are here—you want another to help you to keep awake. When somebody can help you to keep awake, you rely on that person, and then he becomes your teacher, your guide, your leader. He may be awake—I do not know—but if you depend on him, you are asleep. (Laughter) Please don't laugh it away because this is what we all do in our life. If it is not a leader, it's a group or a family or a book or a gramophone record.

So, is it possible to keep awake without any dependence at all, either on a drug, on a guru, on a discipline, on a picture, or on anything else? In experimenting with this, you may make a mistake, but you say, "That doesn't matter, I am going to keep awake." But this is a very difficult thing to do because you depend so much on others. You have to be stimulated by a friend, by a book, by music, by a ritual, by going to a meeting regularly, and that stimulation may keep you temporarily awake, but you might just as well take a drink. The more you depend on stimulation, the duller the mind gets, and the dull mind must then be led, it must follow, it must have an authority or it is lost.

So, seeing this extraordinary psychological phenomenon, is it not possible to be free from all inward dependence on any form of stimulation to keep us awake? In other words, is not the mind capable of never being caught in a habit? Which means, really, goodbye to whatever we have understood, whatever we have learned, goodbye to everything that we have gathered of yesterday so that the mind is again fresh, new. The mind is not new if it hasn't died to all the things of yesterday, to all the experiences, to all the envies, resentments, loves, passions, so that it is again fresh, eager, awake, and therefore capable of attention. Surely, it is only when the mind is free from all sense of inward dependence that it can find that which is immeasurable.

August 20, 1955

Sixth Talk in The Oak Grove

It is an obvious fact that human beings demand something to worship. You and I and many others desire to have something sacred in our lives, and either we go to temples, to mosques, or to churches, or we have other symbols, images, and ideas which we worship. The necessity to worship something seems very urgent because we want to be taken out of ourselves into something greater, wider, more profound, more permanent, so we begin to invent Masters, teachers, divine beings in heaven or on the earth; we devise various symbols—the cross, the crescent, and so on. Or, if none of that is satisfactory, we speculate about what lies beyond the mind, holding that it is something sacred, something to be worshiped. That is what happens in our everyday existence, as I think most of us are well aware. There is always this effort within the field of the known, within the field of the mind, of memory, and we never seem able to break away and find something sacred that is not manufactured by the mind.

So this morning I would like, if I may, to go into this question of whether there is something really sacred, something immeasurable, which cannot be fathomed by the mind. To do that, there must obviously be a revolution in our thinking, in our values. I do not mean an economic or social revolution, which is merely immature; it may superficially affect our lives, but fundamentally it is not a revolution at all. I am talking of the revolution which is brought about through self-knowledge—not through the superficial self-knowledge which is achieved by an examination of thought on the surface of the mind, but through the profound depths of self-knowledge.

Surely, one of our greatest difficulties is this fact that all our effort is within the field of recognition. We seem to function only within the limits of that which we are capable of recognizing—that is, within the field of memory—and is it possible for the mind to go beyond that field? Memory is obviously essential at a certain level. I must know the road from here back to where I live. If you ask me a question about something with which I am very familiar, my response is immediate.

Please, if I may suggest, observe your own mind as I am talking because I want to go into this rather deeply, and if you merely follow the verbal explanation without applying it immediately, the explanation will have no significance whatsoever. If you listen and say, "I will think about it tomorrow or after the meeting," then it is gone, it has no value at all; but if you give complete attention to what is being said and are capable of applying it, which means being aware of your own intellectual and emotional processes, then you will see that what I am saying has significance immediately.

As I was saying, there is an instantaneous response to anything that you know intimately; when a familiar question is asked, you reply easily, the reaction is immediate. And if you are asked a question with which you are not very familiar, then what happens? You begin to search in the cupboards of memory; you try to recall what you have read or thought about it, what your experience has been. That is, you turn back and look at certain memories which you have acquired because what you call knowledge is essentially memory. But if you are asked a question of which you know nothing at all so that you have no referent in memory, and if you are capable of replying honestly that you do not know, then that state of not-knowing is the first step of real inquiry into the unknown.

That is, technologically we are extraordinarily well-developed; we have become very clever in mechanical things. We go to school and learn various techniques, the "know-how" of putting engines together, of mending roads, of building airplanes, and so on, which is but the cultivation of memory. With that same mentality, we wish to find something beyond the mind, so we practice a discipline, follow a system, or belong to some stupid religious organization; and all organizations of that kind are essentially stupid, however satisfactory and gratifying they may temporarily be.

Now, if we can go into this matter together—and I think we can if we give our attention to it—I would like to inquire with you whether the mind is capable of putting aside all memory of technique, all search into the known for that which is hidden. Because, when we seek, that is what we are doing, is it not? We are seeking in the field of the known for that which is not known to us. When we seek happiness, peace, God, love, or what you will, it is always within the field of the known because memory has already given us a hint, an intimation of something, and we have faith in that. So our search is always within the field of the known. And even in science, it is only when the mind completely ceases to look into the known that a new thing comes into being. But the cessation of this search into the known is not a determination; it does not come about by any action of will. To say, "I shall not look into the known but be open to the unknown," is utterly childish, it has no meaning. Then the mind invents, speculates; it experiences something which is absolute nonsense. The freedom of the mind from the known can come about only through self-knowledge, through the revolution that comes into being when every day you understand the meaning of the self. You cannot understand the meaning of the self if there is the accumulation of memory which is helping you to understand the self. Do you understand that?

You see, we think we understand things by accumulating knowledge, by comparing. Surely, we do not understand in that way. If you compare one thing with another, you are merely lost in comparison. You can understand something only when you give it your complete attention, and any form of comparison or evaluation is a distraction.

Self-knowledge, then, is not cumulative, and I think it is very important to understand that. If self-knowledge is cumulative, it is merely mechanical. It is like the knowledge of a doctor who has learned a technique and everlastingly specializes in a certain part of the body. A surgeon may be an excellent

mechanic in his surgery because he has learned the technique, he has the knowledge and the gift for it, and there is the cumulative experience which helps him. But we are not talking of such cumulative experience. On the contrary, any form of cumulative knowledge destroys further discovery, but when one discovers, then perhaps one can use the cumulative technique.

Surely what I am saying is quite simple. If one is capable of studying, watching oneself, one begins to discover how cumulative memory is acting on everything one sees; one is forever evaluating, discarding or accepting, condemning or justifying, so one's experience is always within the field of the known, of the conditioned. But without cumulative memory as a directive, most of us feel lost, we feel frightened, and so we are incapable of observing ourselves as we are. When there is the accumulative process, which is the cultivation of memory, our observation of ourselves becomes very superficial. Memory is helpful in directing, improving oneself, but in self-improvement there can never be a revolution, a radical transformation. It is only when the sense of self-improvement completely ceases, but not by volition, that there is a possibility of something transcendental, something totally new coming into being.

So it seems to me that as long as we do not understand the process of thinking, mere intellection, mentation, will have little value. What is thinking? Please, as I am talking, watch yourselves. What is thinking? Thinking is the response of memory, is it not? I ask you where you live, and your response is immediate because that is something with which you are very familiar; you instantly recognize the house, the name of the street, and all the rest of it. That is one form of thinking. If I ask you a question which is a little more complicated, your mind hesitates; in that hesitation it is searching in the vast collection of memories, in the record of the past, to find the right answer. That is another form of thinking, is it not? If I ask you a still more complicated question, your mind becomes bewildered, disturbed; and as it dislikes disturbance, it tries in various ways to find an answer, which is yet another form of thinking. I hope you are following all this. And if I ask you about something vast, profound, like whether you know what truth is, what God is, what love is, then your mind searches the evidence of others who you think have experienced these things, and you begin to quote, repeat. Finally, if someone points out the futility of repeating what others say, of depending on the evidence of others, which may be nonsense, then you must surely say, "I do not know."

Now, if one can really come to that state of saying, "I do not know," it indicates an extraordinary sense of humility; there is no arrogance of knowledge; there is no self-assertive answer to make an impression. When you can actually say, "I do not know," which very few are capable of saying, then in that state all fear ceases because all sense of recognition, the search into memory, has come to an end; there is no longer inquiry into the field of the known. Then comes the extraordinary thing. If you have so far followed what I am talking about, not just verbally, but if you are actually experiencing it, you will find that when you can say, "I do not know," all conditioning has stopped. And what then is the state of the mind? Do you understand what I am talking about? Am I making myself clear? I think it is important for you to give a little attention to this, if you care to.

You see, we are seeking something permanent—permanent in the sense of time, something enduring, everlasting. We see that everything about us is transient, in flux, being born, withering, and dying, and our search is always to establish something that

will endure within the field of the known. But that which is truly sacred is beyond the measure of time; it is not to be found within the field of the known. The known operates only through thought, which is the response of memory to challenge. If I see that, and I want to find out how to end thinking, what am I to do? Surely, I must through self-knowledge be aware of the whole process of my thinking. I must see that every thought, however subtle, however lofty, or however ignoble, stupid, has its roots in the known, in memory. If I see that very clearly, then the mind, when confronted with an immense problem, is capable of saying, "I do not know," because it has no answer. Then all the answers of the Buddha, of the Christ, of the Masters, the teachers, the gurus, have no meaning because if they have a meaning, that meaning is born of the collection of memories, which is my conditioning.

So, if I see the truth of all that and actually put aside all the answers, which I can do only when there is this immense humility of not-knowing, then what is the state of the mind? What is the state of the mind which says, "I do not know whether there is God, whether there is love," that is, when there is no response of memory? Please don't immediately answer the question to yourselves because if you do, your answer will be merely the recognition of what you think it should or should not be. If you say, "It is a state of negation," you are comparing it with something that you already know; therefore, that state in which you say, "I do not know" is nonexistent.

I am trying to inquire into this problem aloud so that you also can follow it through the observation of your own mind. That state in which the mind says, "I do not know," is not negation. The mind has completely stopped searching; it has ceased making any movement, for it sees that any movement out of the known towards the thing it calls the unknown is only a projection of the known. So the mind that is capable of saying, "I do not know," is in the only state in which anything can be discovered. But the man who says, "I know," the man who has studied infinitely the varieties of human experience and whose mind is burdened with information, with encyclopedic knowledge, can he ever experience something which is not to be accumulated? He will find it extremely hard. When the mind totally puts aside all the knowledge that it has acquired, when for it there are no Buddhas, no Christs, no Masters, no teachers, no religions, no quotations; when the mind is completely alone, uncontaminated, which means that the movement of the known has come to an end—it is only then that there is a possibility of a tremendous revolution, a fundamental change. Such a change is obviously necessary, and it is only the few—you and I, or X, who have brought about in themselves this revolution—that are capable of creating a new world, not the idealists, not the intellectuals, not the people who have immense knowledge or who are doing good works; they are not the people. They are all reformers. The religious man is he who does not belong to any religion, to any nation, to any race, who is inwardly completely alone, in a state of not-knowing, and for him the blessing of the sacred comes into being.

Question: The function of the mind is to think. I have spent a great many years thinking about the things we all know—business, science, philosophy, psychology, the arts, and so on—and now I think a great deal about God. From studying the evidence of many mystics and other religious writers, I am convinced that God exists, and I am able to contribute my own thoughts on the subject. What is wrong with this? Does not thinking about God help to bring about the realization of God?

KRISHNAMURTI: Can you think about God? And can you be convinced about the existence of God because you have read all the evidence? The atheist has also his evidence; he has probably studied as much as you, and he says there is no God. You believe that there is God, and he believes that there is not; both of you have beliefs, both of you spend your time thinking about God. But before you think about something which you do not know, you must find out what thinking is, must you not? How can you think about something which you do not know? You may have read the Bible, the Bhagavad-Gita, or other books in which various erudite scholars have skillfully described what God is, asserting this and contradicting that; but as long as you do not know the process of your own thinking, what you think about God may be stupid and petty, and generally it is. You may collect a lot of evidence for the existence of God and write very clever articles about it, but surely the first question is: How do you know what you think is true? And can thinking ever bring about the experience of that which is unknowable? Which doesn't mean that you must emotionally, sentimentally, accept some rubbish about God.

So, is it not important to find out whether your mind is conditioned rather than to seek that which is unconditioned? Surely, if your mind is conditioned, which it is, however much it may inquire into the reality of God, it can only gather knowledge or information according to its conditioning. So your thinking about God is an utter waste of time; it is a speculation that has no value. It is like my sitting in this grove and wishing to be on the top of that mountain. If I really want to find out what is on the top of the mountain and beyond, I must go to it. It is no good my sitting here speculating, building temples, churches, and getting excited about them. What I have to do is to stand up, walk, struggle, push, get there, and find out; but as most of us are unwilling to do that, we are satisfied to sit here and speculate about something which we do not know. And I say such speculation is a hindrance, it is a deterioration of the mind, it has no value at all; it only brings more confusion, more sorrow to man.

So, God is something that cannot be talked about, that cannot be described, that cannot be put into words because it must ever remain the unknown. The moment the recognizing process takes place, you are back in the field of memory. Do you understand? Say, for instance, you have a momentary experience of something extraordinary. At that precise moment there is no thinker who says, "I must remember it"; there is only the state of experiencing. But when that moment goes by, the process of recognition comes into being. Please follow this. The mind says, "I have had a marvelous experience, and I wish I could have more of it," so the struggle of the 'more' begins. The acquisitive instinct, the possessive pursuit of the 'more' comes into being for various reasons—because it gives you pleasure, prestige, knowledge, you become an authority, and all the rest of that nonsense.

The mind pursues that which it has experienced, but that which it has experienced is already over, dead, gone, and to discover that *which is,* the mind must die to that which it has experienced. This is not something that can be cultivated day after day, that can be gathered, accumulated, held, and then talked and written about. All that we can do is to see that the mind is conditioned and through self-knowledge to understand the process of our own thinking. I must know myself, not as I would ideologically like to be, but as I actually am, however ugly or beautiful, however jealous, envious, acquisitive. But it is very difficult just to see what one is without wishing to change it, and that very desire to change it is another form of conditioning; and so we go on, moving from conditioning to conditioning, never experiencing something beyond that which is limited.

Question: I have listened to you for many years, and I have become quite good at watching my own thoughts and being aware of everything I do, but I have never touched the deep waters or experienced the transformation of which you speak. Why?

KRISHNAMURTI: I think it is fairly clear why none of us do experience something beyond the mere watching. There may be rare moments of an emotional state in which we see, as it were, the clarity of the sky between clouds, but I do not mean anything of that kind. All such experiences are temporary and have very little significance. The questioner wants to know why, after these many years of watching, he hasn't found the deep waters. Why should he find them? Do you understand? You think that by watching your own thoughts, you are going to get a reward—if you do this, you will get that. You are really not watching at all because your mind is concerned with gaining a reward. You think that by watching, by being aware, you will be more loving, you will suffer less, be less irritable, get something beyond; so your watching is a process of buying. With this coin you are buying that, which means that your watching is a process of choice; therefore, it isn't watching, it isn't attention. To watch is to observe without choice, to see yourself as you actually are without any movement of the desire to change, which is an extremely arduous thing to do; but that doesn't mean that you are going to remain in your present state. You do not know what will happen if you see yourself as you are without wishing to bring about a change in that which you see. Do you understand?

I am going to take an example and work it out, and you will see. Let us say I am

Ojai, California, 1955 **115**

violent, as most people are. Our whole culture is violent, but I won't enter into the anatomy of violence now because that is not the problem we are considering. I am violent, and I realize that I am violent. What happens? My immediate response is that I must do something about it, is it not? I say I must become nonviolent. That is what every religious teacher has told us for centuries—that if one is violent one must become nonviolent. So I practice; I do all the ideological things. But now I see how absurd that is because the entity who observes violence and wishes to change it into nonviolence is still violent. So I am concerned, not with the expression of that entity, but with the entity himself. You are following all this, I hope.

Now, what is that entity who says, "I must not be violent"? Is that entity different from the violence he has observed? Are they two different states? Do you understand, sirs, or is this too abstract? It is near the end of the talk, and probably you are a bit tired. Surely, the violence and the entity who says, "I must change violence into nonviolence," are both the same. To recognize that fact is to put an end to all conflict, is it not? There is no longer the conflict of trying to change because I see that the very movement of the mind not to be violent is itself the outcome of violence.

So, the questioner wants to know why it is that he cannot go beyond all these superficial wrangles of the mind. For the simple reason that, consciously or unconsciously, the mind is always seeking something, and that very search brings violence, competition, the sense of utter dissatisfaction. It is only when the mind is completely still that there is a possibility of touching the deep waters.

Question: When we die, are we reborn on this earth, or do we pass on into some other world?

KRISHNAMURTI: This question interests all of us, the young and the old, does it not? So I am going into it rather deeply, and I hope you will be good enough to follow, not just the words, but the actual experience of what I am going to discuss with you.

We all know that death exists, especially the older people, and also the young who observe it. The young say, "Wait until it comes, and we'll deal with it"; and as the old are already near death, they have recourse to various forms of consolation.

Please follow and apply this to yourselves; don't put it off on somebody else. Because you know you are going to die, you have theories about it, don't you? You believe in God, you believe in resurrection, or in karma and reincarnation; you say that you will be reborn here, or in another world. Or you rationalize death, saying that death is inevitable, it happens to everybody; the tree withers away, nourishing the soil, and a new tree comes up. Or else you are too occupied with your daily worries, anxieties, jealousies, envies, with your competition and your wealth, to think about death at all. But it is in your mind; consciously or unconsciously, it is there.

First of all, can you be free of the beliefs, the rationalities, or the indifference that you have cultivated towards death? Can you be free of all that now? Because what is important is to enter the house of death while living, while fully conscious, active, in health, and not wait for the coming of death, which may carry you off instantaneously through an accident, or through a disease that slowly makes you unconscious. When death comes, it must be an extraordinary moment which is as vital as living.

Now, can I, can you, enter the house of death while living? That is the problem—not whether there is reincarnation, or whether there is another world where you will be reborn, which is all so immature, so infantile.

A man who lives never asks, "What is living?" and he has no theories about living. It is only the half-alive who talk about the purpose of life.

So, can you and I while living, conscious, active, with all our capacities, whatever they be, know what death is? And is death then different from living? To most of us, living is a continuation of that which we think is permanent. Our name, our family, our property, the things in which we have a vested interest economically and spiritually, the virtues that we have cultivated, the things that we have acquired emotionally—all of that we want to continue. And the moment which we call death is a moment of the unknown; therefore, we are frightened, so we try to find a consolation, some kind of comfort; we want to know if there is life after death, and a dozen other things. Those are all irrelevant problems; they are problems for the lazy, for those who do not want to find out what death is while living. So, can you and I find out?

What is death? Surely, it is the complete cessation of everything that you have known. If it is not the cessation of everything you have known, it is not death. If you know death already, then you have nothing to be frightened of. But do you know death? That is, can you while living put an end to this everlasting struggle to find in the impermanent something that will continue? Can you know the unknowable, that state which we call death, while living? Can you put aside all the descriptions of what happens after death which you have read in books, or which your unconscious desire for comfort dictates, and taste or experience that state, which must be extraordinary, now? If that state can be experienced now, then living and dying are the same.

So, can I, who have vast education, knowledge, who have had innumerable experiences, struggles, loves, hates—can that 'I' come to an end? The 'I' is the recorded memory of all that, and can that 'I' come to an end? Without being brought to an end by an accident, by a disease, can you and I while sitting here know that end? Then you will find that you will no longer ask foolish questions about death and continuity—whether there is a world hereafter. Then you will know the answer for yourself because that which is unknowable will have come into being. Then you will put aside the whole rigmarole of reincarnation, and the many fears—the fear of living and the fear of dying, the fear of growing old and inflicting on others the trouble of looking after you, the fear of loneliness and dependency—will all have come to an end. These are not vain words. It is only when the mind ceases to think in terms of its own continuity that the unknowable comes into being.

August 21, 1955

Seventh Talk in The Oak Grove

One of our greatest problems, it seems to me, is this question of violence and the desire on our part to find peace. I do not think peace can be found without comprehending the whole anatomy of violence. And peace is not something which is the opposite of violence; it is a totally different state; therefore, it cannot be conceived by a mind that is caught up in violence. As most of our lives are entrenched in violence, and most of our thought is hedged about by violence, it seems to me that it is very important to understand this problem, which is very complex and needs a great deal of penetration, insight; and this afternoon I would like, if I can, to go into it.

Strangely, no organized religions, except perhaps Buddhism and Hinduism, have ever stopped wars and put an end to this astonishing antagonism between man and man. On the contrary, some so-called religions have instigated wars and have been responsible for an enormous slaughter of human beings. Our lives, as we examine them daily, are fraught with violence, and why is it that we are violent? From where does violence spring, and can we really put an end to it? It seems to me that one can come to the end of violence—drastically, radically put a stop to it—only when one understands from what source this violence springs. And I would beg of you not merely to listen to my description of violence but rather, in the very process of my talking, to observe the ways of your own thinking and, through the description, perhaps experience directly the issue that lies behind this word *violence*.

Why is it that we are violent, not only as a race, but also as individuals? I do not know if you have ever asked yourself that question. And what is our approach to violence when we look at it, when we are aware of it, when we think about it? Obviously, most of us say it cannot be helped; we are brought up in this particular society which conditions, encourages us to be violent, and so we slur over the problem very briefly and quickly. But let us see if we cannot go below all that and investigate this problem to find out why each one of us has this extraordinary feeling of violence, and whether it is possible to put an end to it, not superficially, but fundamentally, deeply.

Obviously, this culture, this civilization, is based on violence, not only in the Western world, but also in the East; society encourages violence; our whole economic, social, and religious structure is based on it. I am using that word violence, not in the superficial sense of anger or animosity only, but to include this whole problem of acquisition, of competition, the desire on the part of the individual as well as the collective to seek power. Surely, that desire breeds violence, does it not? There must be violence as long as I am competing with another, as long as I am ambitious, acquisitive—acquisi-

tive, not only in the worldly sense of being greedy for many things, but acquisitive in a deeper sense of that word, which is to be driven by the urge to become something, to dominate, to have security, an unassailable position.

So, as long as one is seeking power in any form, surely there must be violence. Please do not say, "In a culture that is based on violence, what shall I as an individual do?" I think that question will be answered if you can listen to what is being said and not ask what is to be done. The doing is not important. The action comes, I think, when we understand this whole complex problem of violence. To be eager to act with regard to violence without understanding the desire to be something, the desire to assert, to dominate, to become, is really quite immature. Whereas, if we can understand the whole process of violence and perceive the truth of it, then I think that very perception will bring about an action which is not premeditated and therefore true. I do not know if you are following this.

We see in the world what is happening. Every politician talks about peace, and everything he does is preparing for division, for antagonism, for war. And it seems to me very important that those of us who are really serious about such matters should understand the truth of the problem and not ask what to do—because if we understand the truth of the problem, that very perception of what is true will precipitate an action which is not yours or mine, and of which we cannot possibly envisage or foresee all the implications.

It is an obvious fact that everything we do in this world—socially, economically, and religiously—is based on violence, that is, on the desire for power, position, prestige, in which is involved ambition, achievement, success. The enormous buildings that we put up, the colossal churches, all indicate that sense of power. I wonder if you have noticed these extraordinary buildings and what your reaction is when you see them? They may have beauty, but to me beauty is something entirely different. For beauty there must be austerity and a total abandonment, and there cannot be abandonment if there is any sense of ambition expressing itself as an achievement. When there is austerity, there is simplicity, and only the mind that is simple can abandon itself, and out of this abandonment comes love. Such a state is beauty. But of that we are totally unaware. Our civilization, our culture is based on arrogance, on the sense of achievement, and in society we are at each other's throats, violently competing to achieve, to acquire, to dominate, to become somebody. These are obvious psychological facts.

Now, why does this state of violence exist? And recognizing this state, can we go beyond it? If we can, then I think we shall be able to penetrate into something entirely different. Let us take, as an example, the desire to dominate. Why do we want to dominate? First of all, are we at all aware, in our relationships and in our attitude towards life, of this sense of domination, this sense of wanting power, position? If we are aware of it, from what does it spring? Do you understand what I am asking? If we can discover from what the sense of domination springs, that discovery may answer the question of why we are violent. We are all violent in the sense that we all in different ways want to be somebody; we are competitive, ambitious, acquisitive; we want to dominate. Those are the outward symptoms of an inward state, and we are trying to find out what that inward state is which makes us do these things. And are we aware of that state at all, or are we merely adjusting to a moral pattern, being ideologically nonviolent, unambitious, without really tackling the source, the root, which makes us do all these things? If we can go

into that, then perhaps our approach to the problem of violence will be entirely different. So please listen to what is being said, not with an attitude of, "Oh, is that all?" but rather let it be a self-discovery. If through my talking about it you can discover, actually experience the thing for yourself, then it will have an extraordinary effect.

Why am I violent? I want to find out. I see that I am violent because socially, religiously, there is this extraordinary urge to be something. That is a fact. In the business world I want to be richer, to be more capable, to be on top, and in the so-called spiritual world I follow an authority who will help me to be something there. So I see that my activities, my thoughts, my relationships are all based on domination, on dependence. When I depend, I must follow an authority, which breeds violence.

Now, I want to understand the whole process of violence and not merely adjust to a social pattern, which is very superficial and not at all interesting. I want to find out if the mind can be totally free from violence, if this whole process can be radically uprooted from the mind. I am really interested in this; I want to find out. I see that mere adjustment of the superficial urges, demands, and influences to a different pattern does not solve the problem. To substitute one social structure for another, to set up a communist society in place of a capitalist society, will not bring about freedom from domination, freedom from violence. I see that, so I am inquiring into myself to find out what is the source of all these extraordinary urges, demands, pursuits, which breed animosity, violence.

Why am I violent, competitive, ambitious, acquisitive? Why is there in me this constant struggle to be, to become? Obviously, I am running away, taking flight from something through ambition, through acquisitiveness, through wanting to be a success. I am afraid of something, which is making me do all these things. Fear is a state of escape. So I am inquiring into what it is that I am really afraid of. I am not for the moment concerned with the fear of darkness, of public opinion, of what somebody may or may not say of me, because all that is very superficial; I am trying to find out what it is that is fundamentally making me afraid, which in turn drives me to be ambitious, competitive, acquisitive, envious, thereby creating animosity and all the rest of it.

Please think with me. First of all, it seems to me that we are very lonely people. I am very lonely, inwardly empty, and I don't like that state; I am afraid of it, so I shun it, I run away from it. The very running away creates fear, and to avoid that fear, I indulge in various kinds of action. There is obviously this emptiness in me, in you, from which the mind is escaping through action, through ambition, through the urge to be somebody, to acquire more knowledge—you know, the whole business of violence. And without running away, can the mind look at this emptiness, this extraordinary sense of loneliness, which is the ultimate expression of the self?—the self being the entity, the self-consciousness which is empty when it doesn't run. Do you understand what I am explaining? If it is not clear, I shall talk about it in a different manner.

After all, the self, the ego, the 'I' is expressing itself through ambition, through acquisitiveness, through envy, through being violent and trying to be nonviolent, and so on. These are all expressions of the 'me'. I see all that, and going behind it, I also see that that very activity of the self arises from this extraordinary sense of emptiness. I do not know if you have noticed that when you have traced the 'I' in all its movements, you come to this point where the mind is totally aware of the self as being completely empty; but the mind has never really looked at this

emptiness—it has always run away, taken flight.

Now, if I can understand what this emptiness is, then perhaps I shall be able to solve the problem of violence, but to understand what emptiness is, I must look at it, and I cannot look at it as long as I am running away. It is the very running away which causes fear and precipitates the action of envy, competitiveness, ruthlessness, enmity, and all the rest of it. So, can the mind look at the thing from which it has always run away into action? I hope I am making myself clear.

Aren't you aware that you are lonely, empty? We are not considering what you should do about it. The "what you should do about it" has produced this stupid, chaotic world. I am asking what is back of the desire to do something—which is extremely difficult to discover because the mind has always avoided that central issue. But if the mind can be totally aware of itself as being empty, lonely, which means a complete discovery of the ways of the self which have brought it to that state, then you will find that any action, any action without that understanding must precipitate violence in different forms. Being a mere pacifist or an ideologist who is pro-this and anti-that does not solve the problem. The man who practices nonviolence hasn't solved the problem of violence at all; he is merely practicing an idea, and he has never tackled this deep, fundamental issue from which all action springs.

Now, please watch yourself; do not just follow my description. Can your mind be aware of this emptiness without running away from it? It is because you are empty, lonely, that you want a companion, you want somebody on whom to depend, and that dependence breeds authority, which you follow; so the very following of authority is an indication of violence. Can the mind, seeing the truth of all that, stop running away and look at this emptiness? Do you understand what it means to look? You cannot look at this emptiness if you are frightened of it, if you want to avoid it; you can be fully aware of it only when there is no sense of condemnation. Please follow this closely. I am going into it slowly, deliberately, so that our communication and understanding can be equal.

I am aware that I am lonely, empty, and I am watching that emptiness, but I cannot watch it if I condemn it. The very condemnation is a distraction from watching. Now, can I watch, be aware of it, without giving it a name? Do you understand? And when I do not give it a name, is the observer who watches it different from that which he watches? It is only when the watcher gives it a name that there is a division, isn't it? Do you follow? Goodness! I'll make it simpler.

When I say, "I am angry," the very naming of that sensation, that reaction, brings about a duality, does it not? But if I do not name it, then that very thing is myself. Do you understand? Look, I name a feeling because the mind is trained to recognize, to give a label; but if the mind doesn't give a label, then the separation, the division between the observer and the observed disappears. In other words, when naming ceases there is only a state, and in that state there is no separate entity to do something about it. The mind is no longer operating upon that which it wishes to understand; therefore, there is a cessation of the activity of the mind, which in its very nature is violent.

Please, this is not intellectual. Don't say it is too high-flown, too abstract, it is absurd, and all that. I am inquiring, step by step, into the anatomy of violence. Our social structure is based on violence; not only is there violence between nations, but individually we are at each other's throats; we are competitive, ruthless. Now, if I want to understand that whole problem, I must understand the activities of the mind in relation to this thing which I call emptiness, and the moment there is that understanding, I no longer want to be anything. Do you follow? It is the desire to be something that breeds enmity and violence. The idealist who wants to create a perfect utopia is in his very nature violent. The man who is practicing nonviolence is a violent human being because he hasn't really understood the problem; he is dealing with it superficially.

So, I see that as long as the mind is operating in terms of ambition or nonambition, it must create chaos, struggle, misery for itself and for others. And if the mind, going more deeply into the problem, understands the whole process of this urge to be something, then it must inevitably come to the point where it sees that it is seeking an escape from not being anything, which is a state of emptiness. And can I understand that emptiness? Can the mind go into it, taste of it, feel it out? Surely, the mind cannot experience and understand that extraordinary thing that we call emptiness, loneliness, as long as it is in any way condemning it, as long as it wants to reject, dominate, or go beyond it. The mind will reject, dominate that state as long as it is giving it a name; and recognizing, naming, is the very process of the mind.

After all, you cannot think without symbols, without ideas, without words. And can the mind cease to verbalize? Can it let that process come to an end and look at what it has called emptiness without giving it a name or creating an imaginative symbol? And when it does, then is the state which it has called emptiness different from itself? Surely it is not. Then there is only a state in which there is no verbalization, no naming, and therefore the whole activity of the mind which separates, which competes, which breeds antagonism, has come to an end. In that state there is quite a different movement taking place. It is no longer violent. There is a gentleness that cannot be understood by the mind which says, "I must be gentle." All volition has totally ceased, for will is also the outcome of violence.

Question: What you say seems so foreign and Oriental. Is such a teaching as yours applicable to our Western civilization which is based on efficiency and progress, and which is raising the standard of living throughout the world?

KRISHNAMURTI: Do you think thought is Oriental and Occidental? Manners may vary. I may eat with my hands in India, another with chopsticks in China, and here you eat in still a different way; but what makes the Oriental outlook different from the Western outlook? Is there a difference? If I were born in America and said the same things that I am saying now, would you say it is Oriental? Perhaps you would say it is mystical, impractical, or eccentric. But the problems are the same, whether in India, in Japan, or here. We are human beings, not Asiatics and Americans, Russians and Germans, communists and capitalists. We all have the same human problems.

Now, what I am saying is applicable, surely, both here and in India. Violence is as much your problem as it is a problem in India. The problem of relationship, of love, of beauty, the problem of bringing about a state of mind in which there will be peace, of creating a society which will not be destructive of itself as well as of others—all that is obviously the concern of each one of us, whether we live in the East or in the West. Here you have the problem of the building up of an army, which is an indication of the deterioration of any society because the very basis of the army is authority, nationalism, security; and it is exactly the same problem in India, in Japan, in Asia. So this arbitrary division of thought as Oriental and Occidental

does not exist for one who is really inquiring. The man who is conditioned by an Asiatic outlook or philosophy, and who tells you how to live according to that conditioning, is obviously dividing thought as Oriental and Occidental. But we are talking of something entirely different, which is to free the mind from all conditioning, not shape it according to an Oriental philosophy, which is too childish.

What we are trying to do is to investigate together the extraordinary complexity of our lives and to find out if we can really look at these complex problems very simply, but one cannot look at these problems very simply unless one understands oneself. The self is an extraordinarily complex being with innumerable contradictory desires. We are everlastingly at war within ourselves, and this inner conflict precipitates itself into outer activities. To understand the self—the conscious as well as the unconscious—is an enormous task, and one can only understand it from day to day, from moment to moment. It is a book that never ends; therefore, it is not something to be concluded.

So, if one can listen to what is being said, not as an American, a European, or an Oriental, but as a human being who is directly concerned with all these problems, then together we shall create a different world; then we shall be really religious people. Religion is the search for truth, and for the religious person there is no nationality, no country, no philosophy; he does not follow anybody; therefore, he is really a revolutionary in the most profound sense of the word.

Question: Is the release we experience in various forms of self-expression an illusion, or is this sense of fulfillment related to the creativeness of which you speak?

KRISHNAMURTI: Is there such a thing as self-fulfillment at all? We have accepted that there is, have we not? If I am an artist, I must fulfill; if you are a writer, you must fulfill. We are all trying to fulfill ourselves in different ways, through family, through children, through husband or wife, through property, through ideas. If you are ambitious, you must fulfill your ambition; otherwise, you are thwarted, and in that very thwarting there is misery. We are all trying to fulfill ourselves, but we have never asked if there is such a thing as self-fulfillment at all. Surely, the man who is seeking fulfillment is hounded by frustration. That is simple enough, is it not? If I am all the time trying to fulfill through my son, through my wife, through an idea, through action, there is always the shadow of frustration and fear behind it. So if I want to understand fear, frustration, the agony of psychosomatic complexities, and all the rest of it, I must question this whole idea that there is such a thing as fulfilling myself, which is the 'me' trying to become something. May not the 'me' be an illusion, though a reality in the sense that it is operative in action? To the man who is ambitious, competitive, acquisitive, envious, the 'me' is not illusory; it is a very real thing. But to a man who begins to inquire into this whole problem, who really wants to understand what is peace—not the peace of terror, the peace of politicians, nor the peace of self-satisfaction after gathering something which one has longed for, but the peace in which there is no contention, no struggle to be anything—to such a man there comes the experience of being totally nothing, and in that state there is a creativity which is timeless. What we call creativeness is a process of learning a technique and expressing it, but I am talking of something entirely different, of a mind in which the self is totally absent.

Question: Does the creativeness of which you speak confine itself to the ecstasy of personal atonement, or might it also liberate one's power to make use of one's own and other men's scientific achievements for the helping of man?

KRISHNAMURTI: Such questions—if this happens, then what will follow?—are obviously put by people who are listening very superficially. As I said, the action of a man who is seeking, and for whom reality comes into being, will be different from that of the man who has had a glimpse of this state and tries to express it. After all, most of us are educated in some kind of technique: painting, engineering, medicine, and so on. That is obviously necessary, but merely learning the mechanics of a particular profession is not going to release this creative thing. Creative reality—call it God, truth, or what you like—comes into being, not through a technique, but only when the mind has understood itself. And do you know how difficult it is to understand oneself? It is difficult because we are dilettantes; we are not really interested. But if you are really aware, if you give your whole attention to understanding yourself, then you will find an indestructible treasure. You don't have to read a single book about philosophy, psychology, analysis, and all the rest of it because you are the total content of all humanity, and without understanding yourself, you will go on creating innumerable problems, endless miseries. To understand oneself requires, not impetuous urges, conclusions, but great patience. One must go slowly, millimeter by millimeter, never missing a step—which doesn't mean that you must everlastingly keep awake. You can't. It does imply that you must watch and drop what you have watched, let it go and pick it up again, so that the mind does not become a mere accumulation of what it has learned but is capable of watching each thing anew. When the mind is capable of looking at itself and understanding itself, then there is that creativeness of reality, and such a mind can use technique without causing misery.

Question: What is the significance of dreams, and how can one interpret them for oneself?

KRISHNAMURTI: I would like to go into this question rather deeply and not just deal with it superficially, and I hope you are sufficiently interested to follow it step by step.

Most of us dream. There are nightmares from overeating or from eating the wrong things, but I am not talking of such dreams. I am talking of dreams that have a psychological significance. There are various states in dreaming, are there not? You dream, wake up, and then you try to find the meaning of what you have dreamed—you interpret it. The interpretation depends on your knowledge, on your conditioning, on what you have learned from various philosophers, psychologists, and so on. And if you misinterpret, your whole conclusion will be wrong. Then one may dream, and as one is dreaming, the interpretation is going on at the same time so that one wakes up with clarity; one has understood the dream, and it is no longer influencing one. I do not know if that has happened to you.

So the problem is not how to interpret dreams but why we dream at all. Do you understand? If you interpret your dreams according to any psychologist, then the interpretation depends on his particular conditioning, and if you try to interpret them for yourself, your interpretation is shaped by your own conditioning. In either case the interpretation may be wrong, and any conclusion or action based upon it may therefore prove to be entirely false. So the problem is not how to interpret dreams but why do you dream at all? If you could solve that problem, then interpretation would not be necessary. If you could really understand the whole process of dreaming, then it would become a very simple issue.

Why do we dream? Please, let us think it out together, not according to some authority who has written a book about it. Leave all those things completely aside if you can, and let us think it out together very simply. Why do we dream? What do we mean by dreaming? You go to bed, fall asleep, and while you are asleep, action is going on, taking the form of various symbols or scenes; and on waking you say, "Yes, that is the dream I have had."

Now, what has happened? Please follow this, it is very simple. When you are awake during the day, the superficial mind is occupied with many things—with your job, with quarrels, with children, with money, with going to the market, with washing dishes—you know, it is occupied with dozens of things. But the superficial mind is not the whole mind; there is also the unconscious, is there not? You don't have to read a book to find out that there is an unconscious. Our hidden motives, our instinctual responses, our racial urges, our inherited contradictions, beliefs—they are all there in the unconscious. The unconscious obviously wants to tell the superficial mind something, and as the superficial mind is quiet when it is asleep, the unconscious tries to tell it. The unconscious is also in movement all the time, only it has no opportunity to express anything during the day, so it projects various symbols when the conscious mind is asleep, and then we say, "I have had a dream." It is not complex if you can go into it.

Now, I do not want to occupy myself everlastingly with the interpretation of dreams, which is like being occupied with the kitchen, with God, with drink, with women, or what you will. I want to find out why I dream and whether it is possible not to dream at all. The psychologists may say it is impossible not to dream, but leave the experts to their expertness, and let us find out. (Laughter) No, no, please don't laugh it off.

Why are there dreams? And is it possible for dreams to come to an end without suppressing, or trying to go beyond dreaming, so that in sleep the mind is totally still? I want to find out, so that is my first inquiry.

Why do I dream? I dream because my conscious mind is occupied during the day with so many things. But can the conscious mind be open during the day to all the unconscious intimations and promptings? Do you understand? Can the superficial mind be so alert during the day that it is aware of the unconscious motives, the glimpses of the things that are hidden, without trying to suppress them, change them, do something about them? If you can be merely aware, not critically, but choicelessly, of this whole conflict; if you can be open so that the unconscious gives its hints from moment to moment during the day, while you are on the bus or riding in a car, while you are sitting at the table or talking to friends; if you can just watch how you look at somebody, the manner of your speech, the way you treat people who are not of your own quality—then you will find, as you observe deeper, more profoundly, that there is the cessation of dreaming altogether. Then there is no need for intimations, hints, from the unconscious during sleep to tell you what you should or should not do because the whole thing is being revealed as you are living from day to day.

So, we have come to a very interesting point, which is this: During the daytime, the mind is extraordinarily alert, watching without judging, without condemning; and when the whole process of consciousness has been uncovered, examined, and understood, then you will find that in sleep there is a total quietness, and that, being totally quiet, the mind can go to depths which it is not possible for the waking consciousness to touch at any time. Do you understand? I am afraid not. I shall explain again, and I hope you don't mind being a little late.

You see, our search is for happiness, for peace, for God, for truth, and so on; there is a constant struggle to adjust, to love, to be kind, to be generous, to put away this and acquire that. If we are at all aware, we know that to be a fact; there is this total activity of turmoil, of struggle, of adjustment, going on all the time, and a mind in that state can obviously never find anything new. But if I am aware during the day of the various thoughts and motives that arise, if I am aware that I am ambitious, condemning, judging, criticizing, and see the whole of that activity, then what happens? My mind is no longer struggling, it is no longer pushing, there is not that turmoil created by the urge to find. So the mind is completely quiet, not only the superficial mind, but the whole content of consciousness; and in that state of complete quietness in which there is no movement to find, no effort to be or not to be, the mind can touch depths which it can never possibly touch when it is trying to find something. That is why it is very important to be aware without condemnation, to look without criticism, without judgment. And you can do this all day long, off and on, so that the mind is no longer an instrument of struggle when it sleeps, is no longer catching intimations from the unconscious through symbols and trying to interpret them, is no longer inventing the astral plane and all that nonsense. Being free from all conditioning, the mind in sleep is then capable of penetrating into depths which the waking consciousness can never reach, and when you awake, you will find there is a newness totally unexperienced before. It is like shedding the past and being born anew.

August 27, 1955

Eighth Talk in The Oak Grove

It is quite difficult, I think, to differentiate between the collective and the individual, and to discover where the collective ends and the individual begins, also, to see the significance of the collective, and to find out whether it is at all possible ever to be free from the collective so as to bring about the totality of the individual. I do not know if you have thought about this problem at all, but it seems to me that it is one of the fundamental issues confronting the world, especially at the present time when so much emphasis is being laid on the collective. Not only in the communistic countries, but also in the capitalistic world where welfare states are being created, as in England, more and more significance is being given to the collective; there are collective farms and co-operatives in various forms, and looking at all this, one wonders where the individual comes into the picture and whether there is an individual at all.

Are you an individual? You have a particular name, a private bank account, a separate house, certain facial and psychological differentiations, but are you an individual? I think it is very important to go into this because it is only when there is the incorruptibility of the individual, which I shall discuss presently, that there is a possibility of something totally new taking place. That implies finding out for oneself where the collective ends, if it ends at all, and where the individual begins, which involves the whole problem of time. This is quite a complex subject, and being complex, one must attack it simply, directly, not in a roundabout way; and if I may, I would like to go into it this morning.

Please, if I may suggest, observe your own thinking as I am talking, and do not merely listen with approval or disapproval to what is being said. If you are merely listening with approval or disapproval, with a su-

perficial, intellectual outlook, then this talk and the talks that have taken place will be utterly useless. Whereas, if one is capable of observing the functioning of one's own mind as I am describing it, then that very observation does bring about an astonishing action which is not imposed or compelled.

I think it is very important for each one of us to find out where the collective ends and where the individual begins. Or, though modified by temperament, personal idiosyncrasies, and so on, is the whole of our thinking, our being, the collective? The collective is the conglomeration of various conditionings brought about by social action and reaction, by the influences of education, by religious beliefs, dogmas, tenets, and all the rest of it. This whole heterogeneous process is the collective, and if you examine, look at yourself, you will see that everything you think, your beliefs or nonbelief, your ideals or opposition to ideals, your efforts, your envies, your urges, your sense of social responsibility—all that is the result of the collective. If you are a pacifist, your pacificism is the result of a particular conditioning.

So, if we look at ourselves, it is astonishing to see how completely we are the collective. After all, in the Western world, where Christianity has existed for so many centuries, you are brought up in that particular conditioning. You are educated either as a Catholic or a Protestant, with all the divisions of Protestantism. And once you are educated as a Christian, as a Hindu, or whatever it be, believing in all kinds of stuff—hell, damnation, purgatory, the only Savior, original sin, and innumerable other beliefs—by that you are conditioned, and though you may deviate, the residue of that conditioning is there in the unconscious. You are forever afraid of hell, or of not believing in a particular savior, and so on.

So, as one looks at this extraordinary phenomenon, it seems rather absurd to call oneself an individual. You may have individual tastes, your name and your face may be quite different from those of another, but the very process of your thinking is entirely the result of the collective. The racial instincts, the traditions, the moral values, the extraordinary worship of success, the desire for power, position, wealth, which breeds violence—surely, all that is the result of the collective, inherited through centuries. And from all this conglomeration is it possible to extricate the individual? Or is it utterly impossible? If we are at all serious in the matter of bringing about a radical change, a revolution, isn't it very important to consider this point fundamentally? Because it is only for the man who is an individual in the sense in which I am using that word, who is not contaminated by the collective, who is entirely alone, not lonely, but completely alone inwardly—it is only for such an individual that reality comes into being.

To put it differently, we start our lives with assumptions, with postulates: that there is or there is not God, that there is heaven, hell, that there must be a certain form of relationship, morality, that a particular ideology must prevail, and so on. With these assumptions, which are the product of the collective, we build a structure which we call education, which we call religion, and we create a society in which rugged individualism is either rampant or controlled. This society is based on the assumption that it is inevitable and necessary to have competition, that there must be ambition, envy. And is it possible not to build on any assumption but to build as we inquire, as we discover? If the discovery is that of somebody else, then we immediately enter the field of the collective, which is the field of authority; but if each one of us starts with freedom from assumptions, from all postulates, then you and I will build a totally different society, and it seems to me that this is one of the most fundamental issues at the present time.

Now, seeing this whole process, not only at the conscious level, but at the unconscious level as well—the unconscious being also the residue of the collective—is it possible to extricate from it the individual? Which means, is it possible to think at all if thinking is stripped of the collective? Is not all your thinking collective? If you are educated as a Catholic, a Methodist, a Baptist, or what you will, your thinking is the result of the collective, conscious or unconscious; your thinking is the result of memory, and memory is the collective. This is rather complex, and one must go into it rather slowly, neither agreeing nor disagreeing; we are trying to find out.

When we say there is freedom of thought, it seems to me such utter nonsense because, as you and I think, thinking is the reaction of memory, and memory is the outcome of the collective—the collective being Christian, Hindu, and all the rest of it. So, there can never be freedom of thought as long as thinking is based on memory. Please, this is not mere logic. Don't brush it aside that way, saying, "Oh well, this is just intellectual logic." It isn't. It happens to be logical, but I am describing a fact. As long as thought is the reaction of memory, which is the residue of the collective, the mind must function in the field of time—time being the continuation of memory as yesterday, today, and tomorrow. For such a mind there is always death, corruptibility, and fear, and however much it may seek something incorruptible, beyond time, it can never find it because its thought is the result of time, of memory, of the collective.

So, can a mind whose thought is the result of the collective, whose thought is the collective, extricate itself from all that? Which means, can the mind know the timeless, the incorruptible, that which is alone, which is not influenced by any society? Don't assert or deny; don't say, "I have had an experience of it"—all that has no meaning because this is really an extraordinarily complex question. We can see that there will always be corruption as long as the mind is functioning in the collective. It may invent a better code of morality, bring about more social reforms, but all that is within the collective influence and therefore corruptible. Surely, to find out if there is a state which is not corruptible, which is timeless, which is immortal, the mind must be totally free from the collective; and if there is total freedom from the collective, will the individual be anticollective? Or will he not be anticollective but will function at a totally different level which the collective may reject? Are you following all this?

The problem is: Can the mind ever go beyond the collective? If there is no possibility of going beyond the collective, then we must be content with decorating the collective, opening up windows in the prison, installing better lights, more bathrooms, and so on. That is what the world is concerned with, which it calls progress, a higher standard of living. I am not against a higher standard of living; that would be silly, especially if one comes from India where one sees starvation as it is never seen in any other part of the world except perhaps in China, where people have half a meal a day and not even that, where there is sorrow, suffering, disease, and the incapacity to revolt because they are starved. So, no intelligent man can be against a higher standard of living, but if that is all, then life is merely materialistic. Then suffering is inevitable; then ambition, competition, antagonism, ruthless efficiency, war, and the whole structure of the modern world, with occasional witchhunting and social reform, is perfectly all right. But if one begins to inquire into the problem of sorrow—sorrow as death, sorrow as frustration, sorrow as the darkness of ignorance—then one must question this whole structure, not just parts of it, not just the army or the government, in order to bring about a particular reform. Either one must accept this society in its entirety, or one must reject it completely—reject it, not in the sense of running away from it, but finding out its significance.

So, if there is no possibility for the mind to extricate itself from this prison of the collective, then the mind can only go back and reform the prison. But to me, there is such a possibility because to struggle everlastingly in the prison would be too stupid. And how is the mind to extricate itself from this heterogeneous mass of values and contradictions, pursuits, and urges? Until you do that, there is no individuality. You may call yourself an individual, you may say you have a soul, a higher self, but those are all inventions of the mind which is still part of the collective.

One can see what is happening in the world. A new group of the collective is denying that there is a soul, that there is immortality, permanency, that Jesus is the only Savior, and all the rest of it. Seeing this whole conglomeration of assertions and counterassertions, the inevitable question arises: Is it possible for the mind to disentangle itself from it? That is, can there be freedom from time—time as memory, the memory which is the product of any particular culture, civilization, or conditioning? Can the mind be free from all this memory? Not the memory of how to build a bridge, or the structure of the atom, or the way to one's house; that is factual memory, and without it, one would be insane or in a state of amnesia. But can the mind be free from psychological memory? Surely, it can be free only when it is not seeking security. After all, as I was saying yesterday afternoon, as long as the mind is seeking security, whether in a bank account, in a religion, or in various forms of social action and relationship, there must be violence. The man who has much breeds violence, but the man who sees the much and becomes a hermit, he also breeds violence because he is seeking security, not in the world, but in ideas.

The problem is, then: Can the mind be free from memory—not the memory of information, of knowledge, of facts, but the collective memory which has accrued through centuries of belief? If you put that question to yourself with full attention and do not wait for me to answer, because there is no answer, then you will see that as long as your mind is seeking security in any form, you belong to the collective, to the memory of many centuries. And not to seek security is astonishingly difficult because one may reject the collective but develop a collective of one's own experience. Do you understand? I may reject society with all its corruption, with its collective ambition, greed, competitiveness; but having rejected it, I have experiences, and every experience leaves a residue. That residue also becomes the collective because I have collected it; it becomes my security, which I give to my son, to my neighbor, so I again create the collective in a different pattern.

Is it possible for the mind to be totally free from the memory of the collective? That means being free from envy, from competitiveness, from ambition, from dependence, from this everlasting search for the permanent as a means to be secure; and when there is that freedom, only then is there the individual. Then a totally different state of mind and being exists. Then there is no possibility of corruption, of time, and for such a mind, which may be called individual or some other name, reality comes into being. You cannot go after reality; if you do, it becomes your security; therefore, it is utterly false, meaningless, like your pursuing money,

ambition, fulfillment. Reality must come to you, and it cannot come to you as long as there is the corruption of the collective. That is why the mind must be completely alone, uninfluenced, uncontaminated, therefore free of time—and only then that which is measureless, timeless, comes into being.

Many questions have been sent in, and unfortunately they cannot all be answered. But what we have done is to select the more representative ones, and I am going to try to answer as many of them as possible this morning.

I hope that you are not being mesmerized by me. Please, what I am saying has meaning; I am not saying it casually. You listen with silence. If that silence is merely the result of being overpowered by another personality, or by ideas, then it is utterly valueless. But if your silence is the natural outcome of your attention in observing your own thoughts, your own mind, then you are not being mesmerized, you are not being hypnotized. Then you do not create a new collective, a new following, a new leader—which is a horror; it has no meaning and is most destructive. If you are really alert, inwardly observant, you will find that these talks will have been worthwhile because they will have revealed the functioning of your own mind. Then you have nothing to learn from another; therefore, there is no teacher, no disciple, no following. The totality of all this is in your own consciousness, and one who describes that consciousness does not constitute a leader. You don't worship a map or the telephone, or the blackboard on which something is written. So this is not the creation of a new group, a new leader, a new following, at least not for me. If you create it, it is your own misery. But if you observe your own mind, which is what the blackboard says, then such observation leads to an extraordinary discovery, and that discovery brings its own action.

Question: Many people who have been through the shattering experience of war seem unable to find their place in the modern world. Tossed about by the waves of this chaotic society, they drift from one occupation to another and lead a miserable life. I am such a person. What am I to do?

KRISHNAMURTI: If you are in revolt against society, what generally happens? Through compulsion, through necessity, you conform to a particular social pattern, and so you have an everlasting battle within yourself and with society. Society has made you what you are; it has brought about wars, destruction. This culture is based on envy, turmoil; its religions do not make a religious man. On the contrary, they destroy the religious man. Then what is an individual to do? Having been shattered by war, either you become a neurotic, or you go to somebody who will help you to be nonneurotic and fit into the social pattern, thereby continuing a society that breeds insanity, wars, and corruption. Or else—which is really very difficult—you observe this whole structure of society and are free of it. Being free of society implies not being ambitious, not being covetous, not being competitive; it implies being nothing in relation to that society which is striving to be something. But you see, it is very difficult to accept that because you may be trodden on, you may be pushed aside; you will have nothing. In that nothingness there is sanity, not in the other. The moment you see that, the moment you are as nothing, then life looks after you. It does. Something happens. But that requires immense insight into the whole structure of society. As long as one wants to be part of this society, one must breed insanity, wars, destruction, and misery; but to free oneself from this society—the society of violence, of wealth, of position, of success—requires patience, inquiry, discovery,

not the reading of books, the chasing after teachers, psychologists, and all the rest of it.

Question: I am puzzled by the phrase you used in last week's talk, "a completely controlled mind." Does not a controlled mind involve will or an entity who controls?

KRISHNAMURTI: I did use that expression "a controlled mind," and I thought I had explained what I meant by it. I see it has not been understood, so I shall explain again.

Isn't it necessary to have, not a controlled mind, but a very steady mind, a mind that has no distractions? Please follow this. A mind that has no distractions is a mind for which there is no central interest. If there is a central interest, then there are distractions. But a mind that is completely attentive, not towards a particular object, is a steady mind.

Now, let us examine briefly this whole question of control. When there is control, there is an entity who controls, who dominates, who sublimates or finds a substitute. So in control there is always a dual process going on—the one who controls, and the thing that is controlled. In other words, there is conflict. Surely, you are aware of this. There is the controller, the evaluator, the judge, the experiencer, the thinker, and opposed to him there is the thing which he examines, controls, suppresses, sublimates, and all the rest of it. So there is always a battle going on between these two—the one that is, and the one that says, "I must be." This contradiction, this conflict is a waste of energy. And is it possible to have only the fact and not the controller? Is it possible to see the fact that I am envious without saying that it is wrong to be envious, that it is antisocial, antispiritual, and must be changed? Can the entity who evaluates totally disappear and only the fact remain? Can the mind look at the fact without evaluation, that is, without opinion? When there is an opinion about a fact, then there is confusion, conflict. I hope you are following all this.

So, confusion is a waste of energy, and the mind must be confused as long as it approaches the fact with a conclusion, with an idea, with an opinion, with a judgment, with condemnation. But when the mind sees the fact as true without opinion, then there is only the perception of the fact, and out of that comes an extraordinary steadiness and subtlety of mind because there is then no deviation, no escape, no judgment, no conflict in which the mind wastes itself. So there is only thinking, not a thinker, but the experiencing of that is very difficult.

Look what happens. You see a lovely sunset. At the precise moment of seeing it, there is no experiencer, is there? There is only the sense of great beauty. Then the mind says, "How beautiful that was. I would like to have more of it," so the conflict begins of the experiencer wanting more. Now, can the mind be in a state of experiencing without the experiencer? The experiencer is memory, the collective. Oh, do you see it? And can I look at the sunset without comparing, without saying, "How beautiful that is. I wish I could have more of it"? The 'more' is the creation of time, in which there is the fear of ending, the fear of death.

Question: Is there a duality between the mind and the self? If there is not, how is one to free the mind from the self?

KRISHNAMURTI: Is there a duality between the 'me', the self, the ego, and the mind? Surely not. The mind is the self, the ego. The ego, the self, is this urge of envy, of brutality, of violence, this lack of love, this everlasting seeking of prestige, position, power, trying to be something—which is what the mind is also doing, is it not? The mind is thinking all the time how to advance itself, how to have more security, how to

have a better position, more comfort, greater wealth, increased power, all of which is the self. So the mind is the self; the self is not a separate thing, though we like to think it is because then the mind can control the self; it can play this game of back and forth, subjugating, trying to do something about the self—which is the immature play of an educated mind, educated in the wrong sense of that word.

So, the mind is the self; it is this whole structure of acquisitiveness, and the problem is: How is the mind to be free of itself? Please follow this. If it makes any movement to free itself, it is still the self, is it not?

Look, I and my mind are the same; there is no division between myself and my mind. The self that is envious, ambitious, is exactly the same as the mind that says, "I must not be envious, I must be noble," only the mind has divided itself. Now, when I see that, what am I to do? If the mind is the product of environment, of envy, greed, conditioning, then what is it to do? Surely, any movement it makes to free itself is still part of that conditioning. All right? Do you understand? Any movement on the part of the mind to free itself from conditioning is an action of the self which wants to be free in order to be more happy, more at peace, nearer the right hand of God. So I see the whole of this, the ways and trickeries of the mind. Therefore the mind is quiet, it is completely still, there is no movement; and it is in that silence, in that stillness, that there is freedom from the self, from the mind itself. Surely, the self exists only in the movement of the mind to gain something or to avoid something. If there is no movement of gaining or avoiding, the mind is completely quiet. Then only is there a possibility of being free from the totality of consciousness as the collective and as opposed to the collective.

Question: Having seriously experimented with your teachings for a number of years, I have become fully aware of the parasitic nature of self-consciousness and see its tentacles touching my every thought, word, and deed. As a result, I have lost all self-confidence as well as all motivation. Work has become drudgery and leisure, drabness. I am in almost constant psychological pain, yet I see even this pain as a device of the self. I have reached an impasse in every department of my life, and I ask you as I have been asking myself: What now?

KRISHNAMURTI: Are you experimenting with my teachings, or are you experimenting with yourself? I hope you see the difference. If you are experimenting with what I am saying, then you must come to, "What now?" because then you are trying to achieve a result which you think I have. You think I have something which you do not have, and that if you experiment with what I am saying, you also will get it—which is what most of us do. We approach these things with a commercial mentality—I will do this in order to get that. I will worship, meditate, sacrifice in order to get something.

Now, you are not practicing my teachings. I have nothing to say. Or rather, all that I am saying is: Observe your own mind, see to what depths the mind can go; therefore, you are important, not the teachings. It is important for you to find out your own ways of thinking and what that thinking implies, as I have been trying to point out this morning. And if you are really observing your own thinking, if you are watching, experimenting, discovering, letting go, dying each day to everything that you have gathered, then you will never put that question "What now?"

You see, confidence is entirely different from self-confidence. The confidence that comes into being when you are discovering from moment to moment is entirely different

from the self-confidence arising from the accumulation of discoveries, which becomes knowledge and gives you importance. Do you see the difference? Therefore the problem of self-confidence completely disappears. There is only the constant movement of discovery, the constant reading and understanding, not of a book, but of your own mind—the whole, vast structure of consciousness. Then you are not seeking a result at all. It is only when you are seeking a result that you say, "I have done all these things, but I have got nothing, and I have lost confidence. What now?" Whereas, if you are examining, understanding the ways of your own mind without seeking a reward, an end, without the motivation of gain, then there is self-knowledge, and you will see an astonishing thing come out of it.

Question: How can one prevent awareness from becoming a new technique, the latest fashion in meditation?

KRISHNAMURTI: As this is a very serious question, I am going into it rather deeply, and I hope you are not too tired to follow with relaxed alertness the workings of your own mind.

It is important to meditate, but what is still more important is to understand what is meditation; otherwise, the mind gets caught in mere technique. Learning a new trick of breathing, sitting in a certain posture, holding your back straight, practicing one of the various systems for silencing the mind—none of that is important. What is important is for you and me to find out what is meditation. In the very finding out of what is meditation, I am meditating. Do you understand? Take it easy, sirs, don't agree or disagree.

It is enormously important to meditate. If you do not know what meditation is, it is like having a flower without scent. You may have a marvelous capacity to talk or to paint or to enjoy life; you may have encyclopedic information and correlate all knowledge, but those things will have no meaning at all if you do not know what meditation is. Meditation is the perfume of life; it has immense beauty. It opens doors that the mind can never open; it goes to depths that the merely cultured mind can never touch. So meditation is very important. But we always put the wrong question and therefore get a wrong answer. We say, "How am I to meditate?" so we go to some swami, some foolish person, or we pick up a book, or follow a system, hoping to learn how to meditate. Now, if we can brush all that aside, the swamis, the yogis, the interpreters, the breathers, the "sitting-stillers," and all the rest of it, then we must inevitably come to this question: What is meditation?

So, please listen carefully. We are now asking, not how to meditate, or what the technique of awareness is, but what is meditation?—which is the right question. If you put a wrong question, you will receive a wrong answer, but if you put the right question, then that very question will reveal the right answer. So, what is meditation? Do you know what meditation is? Don't repeat what you have heard another say, even if you know somebody, as I do, who has devoted twenty-five years to meditation. Do you know what meditation is? Obviously you don't, do you? You may have read what various priests, saints, or hermits have said about contemplation and prayer, but I am not talking of that at all. I am talking of meditation—not the dictionary meaning of the word, which you can look up afterwards. What is meditation? You don't know. And that is the basis on which to meditate. (Laughter) Please listen, don't laugh it off. "I don't know." Do you understand the beauty of that? It means that my mind is stripped of all technique, of all information about meditation, of everything others have said about it. My mind does not know. We can proceed with finding out what is meditation only when you can honestly say that you do not know; and you cannot say, "I do not know," if there is in your mind the glimmer of secondhand information, of what the Gita or the Bible or Saint Francis has said about contemplation or the results of prayer—which is the latest fashion; in every magazine they are talking about it. You must put all that aside because if you copy, if you follow, you revert to the collective.

So, can the mind be in a state in which it says, "I do not know"? That state is the beginning and the end of meditation because in that state every experience—every experience—is understood and not accumulated. Do you understand? You see, you want to control your thinking, and when you control your thinking, hold it from distraction, your energy has gone into the control and not into thinking. Do you follow? There can be the gathering of energy only when energy is not wasted in control, in subjugation, in fighting distractions, in suppositions, in pursuits, in motivations; and this enormous gathering of energy, of thought, is without motion. Do you understand? When you say, "I do not know," then there is no movement of thought, is there? There is a movement of thought only when you begin to inquire, to find out, and your inquiry is from the known to the known. If you don't follow this, perhaps you will think it out afterwards.

Meditation is a process of purgation of the mind. There can be purgation of the mind only when there is no controller; in controlling, the controller dissipates energy. Dissipation of energy arises from the friction between the controller and the object he wishes to control. Now, when you say, "I do not know," there is no movement of thought in any direction to find an answer; the mind is completely still. And for the mind to be still, there must be extraordinary energy. The mind cannot be still without energy—not the energy that is dissipated through conflict, suppression, domination, or through prayer, seeking, begging, which implies a movement, but the energy that is complete attention. Any movement of thought in any direction is a dissipation of energy, and for the mind to be completely still, there must be the energy of complete attention. Only then is there the coming into being of that which is not to be invited, that which is not to be sought after, that for which there is no respectability, which cannot be pursued through virtue or sacrifice. That state is creativity—that is the timeless, the real.

August 28, 1955

Sydney, Australia, 1955

---- ✳ ----

First Talk in Sydney

As there are many misconceptions, fantastic ideas, and a great many hopes which have no fundamental basis, I think it is important that we should understand each other and establish the right kind of relationship between the speaker and the individual person who is here.

First of all, what I am going to speak about during these several talks is not based on any Indian religion, nor am I representing any particular philosophy. Thought has neither nationality nor frontier, and what we are trying to do this evening is to find out for ourselves what it is that most of us are seeking. You may have come here with various ideas, with certain hopes, seeking something from the speaker, and I think we ought to begin by clearing up any misconceptions; so I would like to suggest that you listen to find out what I want to convey, which is not merely to hear but really to understand what is being said. It is very difficult to listen rightly because most of us have opinions, judgments, conclusions, values, and so we never really listen at all; we are only comparing, evaluating, translating, or opposing one idea with another. But if you can listen, not with a so-called open mind, but with the intention to understand, then perhaps you and I together will find out how to approach the many problems which we have.

We can understand our problems only if we have the capacity to listen, to pay full attention, and such attention is not possible if we are seeking an end, an answer. There is attention only when the mind is really quiet, and then it is able to receive, to comprehend; but a mind that is occupied with its own answers, that is caught up in the search for a result, is never quiet, and such a mind is incapable of full attention. So I think it is important to listen with full attention, not just to what is being said, but to everything in life, for only then is the mind free to discover what is true and find out if there is something beyond its own inventions.

That is what I would like to talk about this evening and throughout these talks. Is it possible to free the mind, not to accept, but to investigate, to inquire profoundly and find out if there is or there is not reality, God? Surely, the mind is incapable of such inquiry as long as it is merely concerned with finding solutions for its own petty problems, that is, as long as it is only concerned with escapes. The mind cannot be free unless it has understood the problem in which it is caught, and this implies self-knowledge, a full awareness of its own activities.

All our problems are really individual problems because the individual is society. There is no society without the individual, and as long as the individual does not totally understand himself, his conscious as well as his unconscious self, whatever reforms he may devise, whatever gods he may invent, whatever truths he may seek will have very little significance. So the individual problem is the world problem, which is fairly obvious; and the world problem can come to an end only when the individual understands himself, the activities of his own mind, the workings of his own consciousness. Then there is a possibility of creating a different world, a world in which there are no nationalities, no frontiers of belief, no political or religious dogmas.

So it seems to me very important to find out what it is we are seeking. This is not a rhetorical question but a question that each one of us must inevitably put to himself; and the more mature, intelligent, and alert we are, the greater and more urgent our demand to find out what it is that we are seeking. Unfortunately most of us put this question superficially, and when we receive a superficial answer, we are satisfied with it. But if you care to go into the matter, you will find that the mind is merely seeking some kind of satisfaction, some kind of pleasant invention which will gratify it; and once having found or created for itself a shelter of opinion and conclusion, therein it stays, so our search seemingly comes to an end. Or if we are dissatisfied, we go from one philosophy to another, from one dogma to another, from one church, from one sect, from one book to another, always trying to find a permanent security, inwardly as well as outwardly, a permanent happiness, a permanent peace. Our search starts with a mind that has already been made petty and superficial by so-called education, so it finds answers which are equally petty and superficial.

Before we begin to seek, then, is it not important to understand the process of the mind itself? Because what we are seeking now is fairly obvious. We are discontented

with so many things, and we want contentment. Being unhappy, in conflict with each other and with society, we want to be led to some kind of haven, and we generally do find a leader or a dogma that satisfies us. But surely all such effort is very superficial, and that is why it seems to me important to understand the ways of the mind and not try to find something. To understand oneself needs enormous patience because the self is a very complex process, and if one does not understand oneself, whatever one seeks will have very little significance. When we do not understand our own urges and compulsions, conscious as well as unconscious, they produce certain activities which create conflict in ourselves; and what we are seeking is to avoid or escape from this conflict, is it not? So, as long as we do not understand the process of ourselves, of our own thinking, our search is extremely superficial, narrow, and petty. To ask if there is God, if there is truth, or what lies beyond death, or whether there is reincarnation—all such questioning is infantile, if I may say so, because the questioner has not understood himself, the whole process of his thinking; and without self-knowledge such inquiry only leads one to assertions which have no basis.

So, if we really want to create a different world, a different relationship between human beings, a different attitude towards life, it is essential that we should first understand ourselves, is it not? This does not mean self-centered concentration, which leads to utter misery. What I am suggesting is that without self-knowledge, without deeply knowing oneself, all inquiry, all thought, all conclusions, opinions, and values have very little meaning. Most of us are conditioned—conditioned as Christians, as socialists, as communists, as Buddhists, as Muslims, or what you will, and within that narrow area we have our being. Our minds are conditioned by society, by education, by the culture about us, and without understanding the total process of that conditioning, our search, our knowledge, our inquiry can only lead to further mischief, to greater misery, which is what is actually happening.

Self-knowledge is not according to any formula. You may go to a psychologist or a psychoanalyst to find out about yourself, but that is not self-knowledge. Self-knowledge comes into being when we are aware of ourselves in relationship, which shows what we are from moment to moment. Relationship is a mirror in which to see ourselves as we actually are. But most of us are incapable of looking at ourselves as we are in relationship because we immediately begin to condemn or justify what we see. We judge, we evaluate, we compare, we deny or accept, but we never observe actually *what is,* and for most people this seems to be the most difficult thing to do; yet this alone is the beginning of self-knowledge. If one is able to see oneself as one is in this extraordinary mirror of relationship which does not distort, if one can just look into this mirror with full attention and see actually *what is,* be aware of it without condemnation, without judgment, without evaluation—and one does this when there is earnest interest—then one will find that the mind is capable of freeing itself from all conditioning; and it is only then that the mind is free to discover that which lies beyond the field of thought. After all, however learned or however petty the mind may be, it is consciously or unconsciously limited, conditioned, and any extension of this conditioning is still within the field of thought. So freedom is something entirely different.

What is important, then, is self-knowledge—seeing oneself as one is in the mirror of relationship. It is very difficult to observe oneself without distortion because we are educated to distort, to condemn, to compare, to judge; but if the mind is capable—which it is—of observing itself without distortion, then you will find, if you will experiment with it, that the mind can uncondition itself.

Most of us are concerned, not with unconditioning the mind, but with conditioning it better, making it nobler, making it less this and more that. We have never inquired into the possibility of the mind's unconditioning itself completely. And it is only the totally unconditioned mind that can discover reality, not the mind that seeks and finds a gratifying answer, not the mind that is Christian, Hindu, communist, socialist, or capitalist; such a mind only creates more misery, more conflict, more problems. Through self-knowledge the mind can free itself from all conditioning, and this is not a matter of time. Freedom from conditioning comes into being only when we see the necessity of a mind that is unconditioned. But we have never thought about it, we have never inquired; we have merely accepted authority, and there are whole groups of people who say that the mind cannot be unconditioned and must therefore be conditioned better.

Now, I am suggesting that the mind can be unconditioned. It is not for you to accept what I say because that would be too stupid, but if one is really interested, one can find out for oneself whether it is possible for the mind to be unconditioned. Surely, that possibility exists only if one is aware that one is conditioned and does not accept that conditioning as something noble, a worthwhile part of social culture. The unconditioned mind is the only truly religious mind, and only the religious mind can create a fundamental revolution, which is essential, and which is not an economic revolution, nor the revolution of the communists or the socialists. To find out what is true, the mind must be aware of itself; it must have self-knowledge, which means being alert to all its conscious and unconscious urges and compulsions; but a mind which is the residue of traditions, of values, of so-called culture and education, such a mind is incapable of finding out what is true. It may say it believes in God, but its God has no reality, for it is only the projection of its own conditioning.

So our search within the field of conditioning is no search at all, and I think it is important to understand this. A petty mind can never find that which is beyond the mind, and a conditioned mind is a petty mind whether it believes in God or not. That is why all the beliefs and dogmas that we hold, all the authorities, especially the spiritual authorities, have to be put aside, and only then is there a possibility of finding that which is everlasting, timeless.

There are some questions here, but before we consider them together, I think it is important to understand that serious questions have no assertive answers, either positive or negative. There is no yes or no to the questions of life. What is important is to understand the question, for the answer is in the question and not away from it. But for most of us this seems an impossibility because we are so eager to find an immediate answer, a palliative for our suffering and confusion; and when we seek an immediate answer, we are bound to be led into illusions, into further misery. It is extremely difficult for us to understand the problem because our minds are already seeking an answer and are therefore not giving full attention to the problem. We think of the problem as an impediment, as something to be got rid of, something to be pushed away, avoided. But if the mind can look at the problem without seeking an answer, without translating the problem in terms of its own comfort, then the problem undergoes a fundamental change.

Question: You have said that one can discover oneself only in relationship. Is the self an isolated reality, or is there no self at all without relationship?

KRISHNAMURTI: This is really a very interesting question, and I hope you and I can think it out together. We are thinking it out together; you are not awaiting an answer from me. It is your problem, and if through my verbalization we can go into it seriously, I think we shall directly or indirectly discover a great many things and not have to be told.

I have said that one can discover oneself only in relationship. That is so, is it not? One cannot know oneself, what one actually is, except in relationship. Anger, jealousy, envy, lust—all such reactions exist only in one's relationship with people, with things, and with ideas. If there is no relationship at all, if there is complete isolation, one cannot know oneself. The mind can isolate itself, thinking that it is somebody, which is a state of lunacy, unbalance, and in that state it cannot know itself. It merely has ideas about itself, like the idealist who is isolating himself from the fact of what he is by pursuing what he should be. That is what most of us are doing. Because relationship is painful, we want to isolate ourselves from this pain, and in the isolating process we create the ideal of what we should be, which is imaginary, an invention of the mind. So we can know ourselves as we actually are, consciously as well as unconsciously, only in relationship, and that is fairly obvious.

I hope you are interested in all this because it is part of our daily activity; it is our very life, and if we do not understand it, merely going to a series of meetings or acquiring knowledge from books will have very little meaning.

The second part of the question is this: "Is the self an isolated reality, or is there no self at all without relationship?" In other words, do I exist only in relationship, or do I exist as an isolated reality beyond relationship? I think the latter is what most of us would like because relationship is painful. In the very fulfillment of relationship, there is fear, anxiety; and knowing this, the mind seeks to isolate itself with its gods, its higher self, and so on. The very nature of the self, the 'me', is a process of isolation, is it not? The self and the concerns of the self—my family, my property, my love, my desire—is a process of isolation, and this process is a reality in the sense that it is actually taking place. And can such a self-enclosed mind ever find something beyond itself? Obviously not. It may stretch its walls, its boundaries; it may expand its area, but it is still the consciousness of the 'me'.

Now, when do you know you are related? Are you conscious of being related when there is complete unanimity, when there is love? Or does the consciousness of being related arise only when there is friction, when there is conflict, when you are demanding something, when there is frustration, fear, contention between the 'me' and the other who is related to the 'me'? Does the sense of self in relationship exist if you are not in pain? Let us look at it much more simply.

If you are not in pain, do you know that you exist? Say, for instance, you are happy for a moment. At the precise moment of experiencing happiness, are you aware that you are happy? Surely, it is only a second afterwards that you become conscious that you are happy. And is it not possible for the mind to be free from all self-enclosing demands and pursuits so that the self is not? Then perhaps relationship can have quite a different meaning. Relationship now is used as a means of security, as a means of self-perpetuation, self-expansion, self-aggrandizement. All these qualities make up the self, and if they cease, then there may be another state in which relationship has a different significance altogether. After all, most relationship is now based on envy because envy is the basis of our present culture, and therefore in our relationship with each other,

which is society, there is contention, violence, a constant battle. But if there is no envy at all, neither conscious nor unconscious, neither superficial nor deep-rooted, if all envy has totally ceased, then is not our relationship entirely different?

So there is a state of mind which is not bound by the idea of the self. Please, this is not a theory; it is not some philosophy to be practiced, but if you are really listening to what is being said, you are bound to experience the truth of it. These meetings will be utterly futile, they will have no meaning at all, if you are treating what is being said as a lecture to be listened to, talked over, and forgotten. They will have meaning only if you are listening and directly experiencing these things as they are being said.

Question: What do you mean by awareness? Is it just being conscious, or something more?

KRISHNAMURTI: May I again suggest that you listen not merely to my words but to the significance of the words, which is really to follow experimentally, through my description, the actual functioning of your own mind as you are sitting here.

I think it is important to find out what awareness is because it is an extraordinarily real process. It is not a thing to be practiced, to be meditated upon daily in order to be aware. That has no meaning at all.

What do we mean by awareness? To be aware is to know that I am standing here and that you are sitting there. We are aware of trees, of people, of noise, of the swift flight of a bird, and most of us are satisfied with this superficial experience. But if we go a little deeper, we become conscious that the mind is recognizing, registering, associating, verbalizing, giving names; it is constantly judging, condemning, accepting, rejecting, and to see this whole process in operation is also part of awareness. If we go still deeper, we begin to see the hidden motives, the cultural conditioning, the urges, the compulsions, the beliefs, the envy, the fear, the racial prejudices that lie hidden in the unconscious and of which most of us are unaware. All this is the process of consciousness, is it not? So, awareness is to see this process in operation, both the outward consciousness and the consciousness which is hidden, and one can be aware of it in relationship, while one sits at the table, while one eats, while one is traveling on a bus.

Now, is there something other than this? Is awareness something more than merely the awareness of the process of consciousness? The something more cannot be discovered if you have not understood the whole content of your consciousness because any desire to find something more will be a mere projection of that consciousness. So you must first understand your own consciousness; you must understand what you are, and you can understand what you are only by being aware, which is to see yourself in the mirror of relationship, and you cannot see yourself as you are if you condemn what you see. That is fairly simple. If you condemn a child, obviously you do not understand him, and you condemn because that is the easiest way to get rid of the problem.

So, to be aware is to see the total process of the mind, not only of the conscious mind, but also of the mind which is hidden and which reveals itself through dreams; but we won't go into that now.

If the mind can be aware of all its own activities, both conscious and unconscious, then there is a possibility of going beyond. To go beyond, the mind must be completely still, but a still mind is not one that is disciplined. A mind that is held in control is not a still mind; it is a stale mind. The mind is still, tranquil, only when it understands the whole process of its own thinking, and then there is a possibility of going beyond.

November 9, 1955

Second Talk in Sydney

One of our great problems, it seems to me, is how to free the mind from its own shallowness, because most of our lives are very superficial, narrow, and petty. Our thinking is also very shallow, and I feel that if we could free the mind from its pettiness, its self-centered activity, then perhaps there would be a possibility of wider, deeper experience and happiness.

If we are aware that we are petty and that all our thinking is shallow, we try to free the mind from this shallowness through various forms of effort. We dig deeply into ourselves, analyzing, imitating, forcing, disciplining, hoping thereby to enlarge the mind and have wider experiences. But is it possible through thought to break down the self-enclosing walls of experience? Is thought the way to free the mind?

Before I go further, may I suggest that you neither accept nor reject what is being said. Let us investigate the problem together so that you do not merely repeat what is being said but rather directly experience the truth or the falseness of it for yourself. To do that, it seems to me very important to know how to listen, how to pay attention. A mind that is occupied cannot pay attention, and most minds are occupied with some kind of idea, opinion, judgment. When anything new is presented to such a mind, there is an immediate reaction either of acceptance or rejection, which actually prevents understanding, does it not? And what we are trying to do this evening is to see if the mind, which in most people is very shallow, petty, can be freed through any form of thinking, which is really the cultivation of memory.

We have enormous problems before us, and a petty mind—however cunning, however clever, however scholarly—can never tackle these problems fully, completely, and hence breeds further misery. So, is it possible to free the mind through the process of thinking?

One is aware that one's thinking is petty shallow, limited in every direction; and is it possible for such a mind to break down the walls of its own limitation through the process of thinking? That is what we are trying to do, is it not?

Now, does thinking free the mind? What is thinking? The mind, both the conscious and the unconscious, is the result of time, of memory; it is the residue of centuries of knowing, and the totality of this consciousness is the process of thinking. All thinking, surely, springs from a background of various cultures, of innumerable experiences, individual as well as collective, and this background is obviously conditioned.

If one observes oneself and is aware of one's own consciousness, one sees that it is the outcome of many influences: climate, diet, various forms of authority, the society about one, with its taboos, its do's and don't's, the religion in which one has been brought up, the books one has read, the reactions and experiences one has had, and so on. All these influences condition and shape the mind, and from this background our thinking comes. This is an actual fact, and I do not think we need to discuss it at very great length.

So, thinking is obviously the result of memory, and this result has produced the chaos, the misery, the strife that exists within and without. The mind is the outcome of time, of many influences, of so-called culture and education, and how can such a mind free itself from its own destructive activities? I hope I am making myself clear.

We see there is chaos and misery in the world, a passing happiness. We have developed various forms of technique in order to earn a livelihood, and we have cultivated memory to a vast extent. All our education leads to the cultivation of memory, which is the process of time, and when the mind is functioning wholly within this area, it is very superficial, narrow, limited. So, is it possible through thinking, which is the process of time, to reach or to discover something which is beyond time, where true creativeness is?

Most of us spend our energy in the most uncreative thinking; our lives are guided by respectability, by the edicts of society, by various forms of discipline, suppression, resistance, so there is always conformity and fear. Very few know this extraordinary sense of creativity which is obviously beyond time. It is not the creativity of writing a poem or of painting a picture, but a sense of being creative without necessarily expressing it in any form. This creativity may be reality; it may be the highest, the sublime, and until the mind is aware of this creative state, whatever thinking it does can only produce further misery.

So, is it possible for the mind to be aware of the whole process of influence: the influence of society, of culture, of relationship, of food, of education, of the books we read, the religions and the dogmas we follow? Can it be aware of all this and not create thought out of its awareness but allow thought to come to an end? This is really the complete cessation of all movement of the mind, which is the result of the past. Thinking can never discover anything new because thinking is the result of time, of the past.

All verbalization of thought is the outcome of time, of memory, and through this process the mind can never discover anything new. Surely, that which you call God, truth, reality, or whatever name you like to give it, must be something totally new, unexperienced before. It must be discovered from moment to moment, and that can happen only when the mind is dead to the past, to all accumulated influences. When the mind, which is the product of time, of memory, is able to die from day to day to everything that it has accumulated, only then is it possible to experience something which is totally new—and this new thing is reality.

So, the mind which knows continuity, which is the product of time, of memory, can never discover the new. When the mind is totally still, not made still through desire, through any form of compulsion, repression, or imitation, when there is that stillness which comes with the deep understanding of this whole process of thinking—it is only then that one can experience the new. Until that happens, all thinking is obviously petty. We may be very clever, erudite, capable of keen analysis and discovery, but such analysis and discovery only lead to further misery, as has been shown in the world. That is why it seems to me important for those who think differently, who are really seeking to go beyond the limitations of the mind, to understand themselves and the whole content of their consciousness, for only then is it possible to have an extraordinarily still mind; and perhaps in that stillness reality comes into being.

There are several questions, or problems. And what is a problem? Surely, the mind creates a problem when it is occupied in analyzing, examining, worrying about something. Life is a series of challenges, and is it possible to meet these challenges without creating problems, that is, without giving soil in the mind for problems to take root and become corroding, destructive? To put it differently, can the mind be unoccupied so as to meet each challenge anew? After all, it is an occupied mind that creates problems, not an unoccupied mind. I think we shall discuss this in different ways during the coming talks.

Question: Some people say that there are actually two paths to the highest attainment—the occult and the mystic. Is this a reality, or a purposeful invention?

KRISHNAMURTI: Most of us, I think, have an idea that reality, God, or whatever name you like to give it, is something fixed, permanent, and that there are various paths to that reality. Now, is there anything permanent? Or is it that the mind desires something permanent, something enduring, as it does in all relationship? Surely, the mind is seeking permanency, a permanent stillness, a permanent happiness, a reality which is secure, unchanging; and as long as the mind is seeking a permanent state, it must create paths to that state.

But is there a permanency, anything that is everlasting, enduring? Or is there no permanency but a constant movement, not the movement that we know in time, but a movement beyond time? If it is believed that there is something permanent, fixed, unchangeable, in the sense in which we use those words within the area of time, then people will think that there are various paths to it, and the occult and the mystic become the purposeful invention of those who have a vested interest in both. So, what is important is to find out directly for ourselves whether there is anything permanent.

Though the mind may wish to have a permanent tranquillity, a permanent peace, bliss, or what you will, is there such a permanent state? If there is, then there must be a path to it, and practice, discipline, a system of meditation are necessary to achieve that state. But if we look at it a little more closely and deeply, we find that there is nothing permanent. But the mind rejects that fact because it is seeking some form of security, and out of its own desire it projects the idea of truth as being something permanent, absolute, and then proceeds to invent paths leading to it. This purposeful invention has very little significance to the man who really wishes to find out what is true.

So there is no path to truth because truth must be discovered from moment to moment. It is not a thing that is the outcome of accumulated experience. One must die to all experience because that which is accumulating, gathering, is the self, the 'me', which is everlastingly seeking its own security, its own permanency and continuity. Any mind, whose thought springs from this desire for self-perpetuation, the desire to attain, to succeed, whether in this world or in the next, is bound to be caught in illusion and, therefore, in suffering. Whereas, if the mind begins to understand itself by being aware of its own activities, watching its own movements, its own reactions, if it is capable of dying psychologically to the desire to be secure so that it is free from the past—the past which is the accumulation of its own desires and experiences, the past which is the perpetuation of the 'me', the self, the ego—then you will see that there are no paths to truth at all, but a constant discovery from moment to moment.

After all, that which gathers, which hoards, which has continuity, is the 'me', the self that knows suffering and is the outcome of time. It is this self-centered memory of the 'me' and the 'mine'—my possessions, my virtues, my qualities, my beliefs—which seeks security and desires to continue. Such a mind invents all these paths, which have no reality at all. Unfortunately, people who have power, position, exploit others by saying that there are different paths—the occult, the mystic, and so on—but the moment one realizes all this, one discovers for oneself that there is no path to truth. When the mind can die psychologically to all the things it has gathered for its own security, it is only then that reality comes into being.

Question: What, according to you, is freedom?

KRISHNAMURTI: This is really quite a complex question, and if you have the patience, let us go into it.

Is freedom something to be attained, or must it be from the very beginning? Is freedom to be achieved through discipline of the mind, through control, through suppression, through conformity, or must it come into being in the very moment of thinking, of feeling? Which does not mean that one must give way to one's desires.

Can freedom be discovered through conforming to the pattern of any particular society, or must freedom be encouraged from the very beginning? Society as we know it now is based on envy, greed, ambition, revenge, on the economic competition for success, on the desire to be something; and in conforming to this pattern, is there freedom? Or does freedom lie outside of this society? Surely, there is freedom only when the mind is no longer acquiring, possessing, when it has ceased to be greedy, envious. There is freedom only when the mind is not occupied with itself, with its own success, with its own concerns and problems. And does this freedom exist at the end or at the beginning? Everyone says, "Discipline yourself, conform, imitate in order to be free." We are all talking of freedom and at the same time exercising authority, so I think it is important to go into this question very deeply.

Does freedom lie within the field of time, within the field of consciousness—consciousness being the reactions and responses of a particular culture or society, the urges and compulsions of man, collective as well as personal? All that is your consciousness, is it not? The 'you' is made up of this consciousness. You are the collective; you are not the individual. You may have a name, a bank account, a separate house, certain capacities, but essentially you are the collective, which is fairly obvious. Being Christian, Australian, Indian, Buddhist, or whatever it is, you have certain superstitions, prejudices, beliefs; therefore, you are the result of the collective. One is really not an individual, and it is only when one understands the whole collective influence that there is freedom, and then perhaps the individual comes into being.

We can see that as long as we are conforming to the pattern of society and are merely the product of the collective, there can be no freedom but only greed and conflict, the conflict between groups and between the so-called individuals within the group. Conflict, discipline, the desire for expansion, and so on, are all within the pattern of society, and surely there is freedom only when there is no sense of acquisitiveness, when there is no demand to be psychologically secure, safe, when there is no envy. When we understand this pattern and are therefore free from all the beliefs that society has imposed, whether communist or capitalist, Christian or Hindu, then perhaps there is the true individual, one who is completely alone, not one who is lonely. The man who is lonely is caught up in his self-enclosing activity, completely cut off in his selfishness, his self-centered concern. But I am talking of something entirely different, of the aloneness which is incorruptible, and with that aloneness there is freedom.

Question: You said that it is possible to be unconditioned. Living in this world, how can we come to this unconditioned state, and in what way will it transform our lives here?

KRISHNAMURTI: I wonder if we are aware that we are conditioned? That is the first question, is it not? Do you and I know that we are conditioned as Christians or as Hin-

dus, conditioned to a certain way of thinking, to a certain pattern of action, conditioned to the routine of an everyday job and to all the fears and the boredom involved in it? Do we know that we are the product of the innumerable influences of society? The churches, the ceremonies, the beliefs and dogmas, the very words we use have an extraordinary influence on us neurologically as well as psychologically.

Are we aware of all this? If we are, then do we not also want to improve, to become better? There is no noble and honorable conditioning; there is only conditioning, yet most of us are seeking a better way of being conditioned. And is it possible for the mind to uncondition itself? I know some people will say it is not possible and will advance various arguments to prove that it is not. But what we are first trying to do is to experience, not theoretically or in any illusory sense, but actually to experience the fact that we are conditioned, and then to see how the mind seeks a better form of conditioning.

The next thing to find out for ourselves, and not depend on some authority to tell us, is whether it is possible for the mind to be unconditioned. Obviously, if we accept any form of belief with regard to conditioning we are like the man who believes or does not believe in God. Neither the believer nor the nonbeliever can ever find out what is true. It is only when we free ourselves from both belief and nonbelief that we are in a position to find out, to discover.

So, first we must be clear that we are conditioned, which is quite obvious. And if the mind is not capable of unconditioning itself, surely any form of thinking, any reform, any activity will only produce further conflict, further misery.

Now, being aware that it is conditioned, what is the mind to do? As long as there is a separate entity who observes that his thought is conditioned, there can never be freedom from conditioning because both the observer and the observed, the thinker and the thought, are conditioned. There is no separate thinker who is unconditioned, for the thinker is the result of thought, and thought is the outcome of conditioning; therefore, the thinker cannot uncondition the mind by any practice. When the thinker is aware that he is the thought, that the observer is the observed—which is extremely arduous, it requires a great deal of penetration, insight, understanding—only then is it possible for the mind to be unconditioned.

The questioner wants to know in what way an unconditioned mind will transform the life, the daily activities, of the individual. Will it be utilitarian? If the mind is unconditioned, in what way will it be useful to living in this world? Will such a mind help to change or reform the world? What relationship will it have with the society in which it must live? It may have no relationship at all with society—society being the activity of greed, envy, fear, acquisitiveness, and all the moral values based on this activity. A man who is unconditioned may affect society, but that is not his principal concern.

So, our problem is whether the mind can be unconditioned, is it not? If you really and honestly put this question to yourself, not temporarily, not just while you are sitting here, but if you actually let the seed of this question operate, rather than you operating on the question, then you will find out directly for yourself whether the mind can be liberated from all the influences of society, from the innumerable memories and traditional values which lie in the unconscious; and having unconditioned itself, whether this transformation has any significance in relation to society.

Most of us, unfortunately, never put serious questions to ourselves. We are afraid of putting a serious question to ourselves because it may result in serious action, it may

create a revolution in our lives—and I assure you that it does. When you really put a serious question to yourself, it brings about an extraordinary response, which you may not desire or wish to be aware of. But you are confronted with a serious question, whether you like it or not, because as the world is being conducted, it is divided by nationalities, plagued by wars, misery, and starvation, and a totally different approach must be made to find the right answer. The old answers, the old arguments, the beliefs, traditions, and dogmas are utterly useless. Whether you are a Christian or a Hindu, a communist or a capitalist is completely irrelevant. It is belief which is dividing the world, belief in nationalism, in patriotism, in the so-called superiority of this race or that; it is belief which divides people into Protestants and Catholics, mystics and occultists, which is all utter nonsense. So a different mind is required, a truly religious mind. Only the mind that loves is truly religious, and it is the religious mind that is revolutionary, not the mind that is weighed down by beliefs and dogmas. When the mind is choicelessly aware that it is conditioned, in this awareness there comes a state which is not conditioned.

November 12, 1955

Third Talk in Sydney

Most of us, I think, want some authority to mold our lives, our whole being. Because in ourselves we are very uncertain, confused, we turn to others for guidance and try to find the right person or leader to look up to in the conduct of our lives. We think that others know better or know more, and so in our desire to find out if there is a reality, a permanent happiness, a state of bliss, we gradually create authority.

Now, it seems to me that this process is totally wrong, if I may use that word, because if we could find the light in ourselves, then there would be no necessity for any authority whatsoever, for any savior or Master, for any teacher, and that is what I would like to discuss this evening.

This is one of the most fundamental issues in our lives, is it not? We invariably look for a teacher, for a guide, to shape the conduct of our lives; and the moment we look to another for a mode of action, for a way of living, we create authority and are bound by that authority. We attribute to that person great wisdom, great knowledge; our attitude is, "I am ignorant but you know, you are more experienced; therefore, tell me what to do." This attitude invariably breeds the sense of fear, does it not? And does it not also bring about the disciplining of oneself according to the authority of an idea or a person?

So, where there is authority created by oneself, there must also be the desire to achieve what that authority offers, or what one wants from that authority. Therefore one begins to discipline oneself in order to achieve, through a gradual process of the mind, what one thinks is true. To me, this whole process is totally false because that which is true, whatever name you may like to give it, cannot come into being through any control of the mind, through any form of discipline, or through following any authority. What we are seeking in this process is essentially self-perpetuation, which is not the search for truth at all. It is merely the continuation of one's own gratification in a more subtle form.

Surely, as long as we follow, imitate, have an authority, the mind can never be free, for freedom is at the beginning, not at the end. This extraordinary thing which may be called truth, love, or what you will, cannot come into being through any form of obedience to authority, and there are different types of authority. There is the authority of another

who is supposed to know, and whose authority the so-called individual may reject, but there is also the authority of experience, of memory, which is much more subtle.

Being confused, out of my confusion I look to another, to a teacher, to a book, to an organization, to bring me peace or to help me find out what is true; but when I am confused, my search will also be confused, and my action will be the outcome of this confusion. So what is important, surely, is to free the mind from all sense of authority, from all giving of value to someone else's experience and therefore imitating, following.

Now, is it possible to find this light within oneself and not look to another? I think it is possible and that it is the only way. There is no other way, and it requires considerable insight, arduous investigation into oneself. The disciplining of the mind, the following of various teachers, the practice of yoga—all these things are empty, utterly futile to a man who is really serious, because there is self-knowledge, the real thing, only through oneself; it cannot be found through another.

But most of us are unwilling to undertake the arduous task of looking into ourselves, so we turn to somebody else who will help us out of our confusion, out of our misery, thereby further increasing our confusion and misery. This love, this truth, or what name you will, obviously cannot be found through another. So, can we as individual human beings discover directly for ourselves what is true and what is false? I think it is very important to ask ourselves this question.

To find out for ourselves what is true, must we not put aside all authority? Must we not discard the authority of the book, the authority of the priest, the authority of the Masters, of the saviors, of the various religious teachers, of those who practice yoga, and all the rest of it? Which means, really, that we must be able to stand alone, without support, without looking to another for any kind of encouragement. It is like taking a journey where there is no guide. Where there is no guide, the mind must be extraordinarily alert to every form of deception, and it is only when one has totally put aside all sense of authority, all desire for guidance, that one is capable of looking into oneself without fear. It is fear that makes us turn to others for guidance.

We deeply want to be secure, do we not? We want to be certain that we shall arrive, that we shall gain this state of immortality, of truth, of love, of peace. Because we are uncertain of ourselves and of our capacity to find, we look to another to guide us, and in the very process of looking to another, we create authority, which brings into being the practice of discipline, and all the rest of it.

So, can we undertake by ourselves the journey to find out? In the very asking of this question there is the beginning of freedom, and it is only the free mind that can discover, not the mind that is bound by tradition, by authority, by discipline and control. The mind that is free is capable of facing itself completely as it is, and it is only such a mind that can find out what is true, not the mind that is frightened and therefore follows, imitates.

This evening, instead of answering questions, I would like, if I may, to suggest that we discuss what I have just said. In discussing together, you and I must stick to the point and not deviate or make long speeches. We are trying to find out through discussion, not whether you are right or I am right, or whether we should or should not follow, but the truth of this whole problem of following, and to do this we must not just make statements. We must together investigate the problem, which is very complex, because our whole life is a process of imitation from childhood until we die. Society, tradition, the established values all make us conform, copy. To function in society, you must ob-

viously conform to the pattern of society; you have to adjust yourself to its values. But the truly religious man is free of society— society being the values of greed, envy, ambition, success, fear.

Now, this evening can we discuss or verbally exchange what each one of us thinks about this particular matter of following, disciplining, imitating? I think it would be worthwhile if we could discuss it easily, spontaneously, freely, so that you yourself experience the truth of the fact that the mind invents stages as the one who knows and the one who does not know, as the master and the disciple, the leader and the follower. As long as we think in terms of stages, time, achievement, there must be this illusory idea of following somebody. Where there is love, reality, there is obviously not the teacher and the follower; and in talking it over together, can we directly experience this state? I do not think it is very difficult. It is difficult only when we dogmatically or obstinately assert that we must follow, that there must be a compulsion to hold us to a particular pattern of behavior; otherwise, we shall be lost. Any person who makes such an assertion is obviously not inquiring; he is merely accepting a certain tradition and is afraid to face himself as he is.

So, let us see if we can discuss this matter, and if I may, I shall stop those who are not really sticking to the point. We are trying to find out if the mind can actually free itself now, as we are discussing, from this fear of not achieving truth or happiness, which drives it to follow somebody, to set up another as the savior, whom it must obey. This is the whole point which we are discussing.

Question: Yes, sir, it can be done if we have the proper authority to help us, just as we have medical authority to tell us what to do and what not to do when we are ill.

KRISHNAMURTI: Just a minute. You have medical authority, but you do not put the doctor on a pedestal, you do not worship him, you do not mold your mind according to his dictates. This is a difficult problem. We are trying to find out how your mind or my mind functions, and whether it can be free from the fear of not achieving an end.

Question: Must one lead a solitary life?

KRISHNAMURTI: I am not suggesting that you should lead a solitary life. You cannot live in isolation. But for most of us, all relationship is conflict, and as we do not know how to deal with it, we look to somebody to help us.

Question: If I am stupid, what then?

KRISHNAMURTI: What actually takes place when I am stupid? Do I ever discover that I am stupid, or am I told I am stupid? And what is the immediate reaction? I want to be clever, so I make an effort to be more clever, more intelligent than I am; and the moment I demand the 'more', I have already set a goal which inculcates fear in me. Whereas, if I am capable of looking at what I am, at the fact that I am stupid, surely that very looking at *what is* brings about a transformation of *what is*. A stupid mind can never be intelligent through trying to be, but the very recognition that it is stupid has already brought a transformation in itself. That is an obvious fact, is it not, sir?

Comment: It merely means that the mind has a knowledge that it never had before.

KRISHNAMURTI: What do you mean, sir?

Comment: Previously it thought it was stupid; now it knows it is stupid.

KRISHNAMURTI: Please watch your own reactions. If I realize that I am stupid, the immediate reaction is that I must do something about it, so I strive, I make an effort. Whereas, if I acknowledge I am stupid without trying to do something about it, that very acknowledgment or awareness of my stupidity actually brings a change within, does it not?

Comment: May I say that it does not entail fear to find joy, peace, and security in following the Savior.

KRISHNAMURTI: All right, why do we follow at all? This is complex; it is a deep psychological problem, so let us go into it simply. Do we follow anybody? If we do, why do we follow?

Comment: Because the other is much more clever than we are.

Question: Sir, may I, with great respect and deference, ask you please to qualify what you mean by "the mind."

KRISHNAMURTI: That is a question which is not to the point, if I may humbly point it out. We follow, do we not? We are following a book, a savior, a teacher, a guru, an ideal, a standard. Or is this not so?

Question: You say, sir, that if we seek truth, we may not seek outside authority. What, then, is the first step?

KRISHNAMURTI: I am going to come to that soon, but first let us see what we actually do. We follow, do we not? Why?

Comment: Because we are afraid. It seems that there is a certain gratification involved in following.

KRISHNAMURTI: We are not yet discussing the process of following. The fact is that we follow. Why? Please do not answer me. I am asking in order for you to find out for yourself, not to verbalize and tell me. Please, what we are doing here is very important. If we can do this really intelligently, it will lead us to great depths because we are finding out how our minds operate, what our thinking process is.

The fact is that we follow. Why do we follow? Please do not answer me immediately. Investigate, go into it. Why does one follow? There are different types of following. You follow what the doctors say, what your boss in the office says, or you are being dominated by your wife, by your husband, by the neighbor. You follow tradition, the edicts of society, the opinion of another. You follow the beliefs and dogmas of a religious organization, or you follow what the priests say, what the sacred books say. This is what we are actually doing, and we never question why we do it. Now, I am asking myself, and I hope you are asking yourself, why does one follow?

Comment: If through introspection I realize why I follow, then maybe I shall cease to follow and shall act in a way which I feel is correct and free. Yet the freedom which I practice may be harmful to somebody else.

KRISHNAMURTI: Let us go into this slowly, if you do not mind. The fact is that I follow, and I want to know why I follow—the inward nature of it. I want to unearth, open up, the psychological factor that makes me follow. One follows in a worldly sense for obvious reasons. Having a job, I know I must do what the boss says. This much is fairly clear. But what we are discussing is: *Why* do I psychologically follow another?

Question: Do you feel that you have experienced this freedom?

KRISHNAMURTI: I can answer that question, but it is irrelevant, is it not? If I say yes or no, what value will it have? How can you judge? You can only judge according to your standards, according to your psychological inclination or disinclination. But please, this is irrelevant, it is unimportant. What we are trying to find out directly, each one of us, is why we follow psychologically. If we go slowly, step by step, we shall begin to see the process of our own thinking—what is taking place in our minds, in our hearts—of which we are now unconscious.

Question: Are you suggesting that by analyzing his experiences, the individual can find freedom of expression?

KRISHNAMURTI: No, sir, I am not suggesting that at all. I question the whole accumulation of what we call experience—whether it has any validity at all—because experience is merely a conditioned response. But I don't want to go into that for the moment.

We are asking ourselves why we follow. Is it habit?

Comment: I do not follow. I lead the way.

KRISHNAMURTI: Then you are a leader. If you are a leader psychologically, there must be a follower for you to lead, and he who is a leader is also a follower.

Question: Sir, don't you realize that to follow a person is not necessarily to be his follower? One is not his follower if one just treats him as a milestone.

KRISHNAMURTI: I am trying to find out why you or I follow psychologically.

Question: Are we not seeking personal proof?

KRISHNAMURTI: You are jumping so far ahead.

Question: When the intuition is aroused we do not follow, we obey what the intuition says.

KRISHNAMURTI: Please, when we talk about intuition, the inner voice, what do we mean by that? The inner voice may be entirely false. Please, I am not trying to destroy your intuition. I am trying to find out whether intuition is true or false. Surely, until you understand the whole process of desire, conscious as well as unconscious, you cannot rely on intuition because desire may bring you to certain "facts" which are not facts at all. The unconscious desire to be or not to be something makes you accept or reject; therefore, you must first understand the whole process of your desire and not say, "Intuition tells me this is true."

Let me take a very simple example, and you will see it. We all die, fortunately or unfortunately, and my desire for continuity is very strong, as it is in most people. When I hear the word *reincarnation,* my intuition says, "Yes, that is true." But is it my intuition, or my desire? My desire to continue is so embedded, so strong, that it takes the form of so-called intuition, which has no meaning at all. Whereas, if I can understand this extraordinary thing called desire, then death will have quite a different significance.

Well, let us come back. Why do you or I psychologically follow another? Are we aware that we are following, not only a person, but a teaching or an ideal? I have set up an ideal of the perfect man, the perfect life, the perfect goal, and I follow that. Why? Please do not merely listen to me, but look at the operation of your own mind. You see, you are probably disinclined to put this question to yourself because the moment you inquire why you follow, many things in your daily life—your Masters, your teachers, guides, philosophers, your books and ideals—can no longer be accepted; they have to be investigated, which means that there must be the freedom to investigate, to find out.

So, why do you have an ideal? Why do you follow? Obviously, you follow in order to reach something. You have guides, have you not? Being confused, you have some teacher—he may be in India or standing on the platform now, or it may be somebody you know around the corner—who tells you what to do. Please see this. One is confused, miserable, in conflict within oneself, so one goes to somebody.

Question: It may be that one has an inferiority complex.

KRISHNAMURTI: It is not a question of inferiority or superiority complexes. I am looking at the fact that I am confused. I am confused, and you are not confused; at least I think you are not confused, so in my confusion I follow you—you being the Master, the savior, the leader. My choice is made in confusion; therefore, whoever I choose is also confused, including the politicians. So, being confused, what am I to do? Surely, I have to understand my confusion and not look to somebody else to help me out of it.

Question: But one can follow and still not be confused.

KRISHNAMURTI: Will I follow if I am not confused?

Comment: One can follow in the sense that one agrees with the other's philosophy.

KRISHNAMURTI: Sorry, you are missing my point.

Comment: I am not confused.

KRISHNAMURTI: Then you are out of the picture. Sir, this is not a debate. Please take this seriously; it is not a laughing matter. If I am not confused, then I do not need to follow anybody, then I am my own light—something has happened to me which puts me out of this chaos. But most of us are not in that position. We are confused; we have great sorrow, insoluble problems, and we look to somebody to help us out of our confusion; but that very choice is the product of confusion, so the result is greater confusion. This is fairly obvious, is it not?

Now, if I do not follow, if I do not go to another but say, "Let me understand this confusion," then what happens? What happens when I simply acknowledge that I am confused? I don't rush about looking for someone to help me. I see there is confusion, and I remain with it. I know I have created this confusion and that no one else can resolve it—which does not mean that I am cut off, isolated, but I am fundamentally alone, and my whole attitude is that I am willing to discuss with another. I do not follow any authority because I want to solve this problem of confusion, so I begin to tackle it, to find out what confusion is.

So the problem is: Why do we follow? Is it that we are afraid? The Master, the teacher, the priest, or the sacred book says there is a state of bliss, and we want to achieve it; therefore, we follow, we practice a system of yoga, and all the rest of it. So, as long as one has an urgent demand to be something psychologically, as long as one wants to arrive at a state in which one will be unconfused, happy, secure, one must obviously follow. Is that not clear?

Please, you are not merely listening to what I am saying; you are being aware of your own confusion, of your own desire to be something.

Question: We follow somebody who we think knows more than we do.

KRISHNAMURTI: You see, that is just it. You follow somebody because he is supposed to be more perfect, which means there is a distance, a gap between you and the other. Is this so, or is it a false creation of the mind? When there is love, do you say, "He loves more and I less"? There is only this state of being, is there not? You say you follow somebody because you think he knows more than you do. Does he? And what does he know? Do not answer, but please think it out with me. What does he know? If he is really a true person, he knows only a very few things; he knows love, which is not to be envious, not to be greedy, not to be ambitious, to do without the 'me'. He may or may not be in that state, and you come along and seek something from him. You see a glitter in his eyes, a smile, and you want to be like this man, so your greed is operating. Because you are confused, you go to him and say, "Please tell me how you got into that state," and if he also is confused, he will tell you because such a man thinks he has achieved. It is the man who dies every day to everything he has known, experienced—it is only such a man who can have a really still mind and an uncorrupted heart. But let us come back.

Is it not important for all of us, if we are at all serious about these matters, to be aware of our own activities and investigate, inquire, into their validity? We follow out of habit, do we not? It is the tradition of centuries. Every religious book tells us to seek and follow, but they may all be wrong and probably are, so I cannot depend on any of them. I must find out for myself, which does not mean I am greater than somebody else, or that I am self-centered, egotistic, proud. I must find out; I must know that I am confused. So I begin, not by following the ideal, the tradition, the Master, the book, the priest, or my wife or husband, but by seeing the fact of what I am.

In myself I am uncertain, I am miserable, confused, unhappy, and I want to find a way out of all this chaos, so I turn to symbols, to examples, to the teachings of certain persons because through them I hope to get what I want. It is a very simple psychological process if I am at all alert, aware. And if I am also aware that nobody can help, that help lies everywhere, not in any one particular direction, then as I walk down the street and look at a person, a dancing leaf, a smile, there may be a spontaneous hint which will uncover a great many things. But this is not possible as long as the mind says, "My leader, my teacher, will help me," as long as it obstinately clings to a particular book or follows a chosen path, and to be aware of this whole process in oneself is the beginning of freedom, of wisdom.

You do not learn wisdom from books, from teachers. Wisdom is the uncovering of the mind, of the heart, which is self-knowledge. That is why it is very important not to accept anything but to understand the extraordinary process of your own thinking. You require great subtlety to find out the ways of the self, and the mind cannot be sub-

tle when it is merely following, disciplining, controlling, suppressing—which does not mean that you must go to the other extreme, to the opposite.

You see, the difficulty in all this is that we do not look at anything simply. The problem is complex, and in approaching a complex problem there must be simplicity; otherwise, you cannot solve it. To be simple you must understand yourself, which you cannot do through what a priest or someone else says. You can only understand yourself directly, and it is not a difficult process; it is not a God-given gift reserved for the few, which is all nonsense. If one has the intention to find out what one is thinking, if one is constantly watching every invention of the mind—looking at it, playing with it, being open to every spontaneous reaction—out of this comes self-knowledge, and this is meditation.

But wisdom does not come to a human being who follows, because he is merely an imitator; he disciplines himself out of greed. A mind which is imitative, fearful, which is merely copying, following, can never have self-knowledge, and without self-knowledge everything becomes a prison, does it not? It is the mind that creates the division of the high and the low. In reality there is neither high nor low; there is only a state of being, and to come to that state, there must be freedom at the very beginning, not just at the end.

November 16, 1955

Fourth Talk in Sydney

This evening I would like to talk about a very complex problem, and I think the understanding of it will depend a great deal on what kind of attention one gives to it. I want to talk about the problem of fundamental change, and whether such a change can be brought about through effort, through discipline, through an ideation. It is fairly obvious that there must be a fundamental, radical change in each one of us, and how is this change to be brought about? Can it be brought about through the action of will, through deliberate thought, through any form of compulsion? And at what level of consciousness does this change come into being? Does it occur at the superficial or at the deeper levels of consciousness? Or does the change come about beyond all the levels of consciousness?

Before we go into this problem, I think it is important to understand what it means to pay the right kind of attention. If one is merely thinking in terms of exclusive experience, that is, listening to and accepting what is being said as a method by which to attain a certain result, then this method can be opposed by another method, and so exclusiveness comes into being; and all exclusiveness is obviously evil. Whereas, if one can put aside all such ways of thinking— your method as opposed to my method, or your particular line as opposed to mine—and listen to find out the truth of the matter, then that truth is neither yours nor mine and there will be no exclusiveness. Then you do not have to read a single book or follow a single teacher to find out what is true, and I think it is important to understand this. Basically, fundamentally, there is no path to truth, no method, neither your way nor my way. In religious experience, surely, there is no exclusiveness; it is neither Christian, Hindu, nor Buddhist. The moment there is any sense of exclusiveness, out of this comes evil. So I would suggest that you listen to find out rather than merely to oppose one argument, one ideation, or way of thinking with another.

It is obvious, I think, that there must be some kind of radical change, a profound transformation within oneself. How is this change to be brought about? There must be a change in each one of us that will bring with it a totally different outlook, a way of life that is true, not according to any particular person, but true at all times and in every place; and how is this change to be brought about? Will an ideal bring about such a change? The ideal has been established through experience either by oneself or by someone else, and will an ideal of any sort bring about this change, this radical transformation? I think ideals are fictitious, unreal; they are inventions of the mind and have no reality in themselves at all. We hope that through following an ideal the mind will change itself. That is why we all have ideals: the ideal of goodness, the ideal of nonviolence, and so on. We hope that by persistently practicing, pursuing, submitting to the ideal, we shall bring about a radical change, or at least a change for the better.

Now, do ideals bring about this change or are they merely a convenient projection of the mind to postpone action? Please, may I ask you not to reject this but to listen to what I am saying. Most of us are idealists; we have some form of ideal which we have established through habit, through custom, through tradition, through our own volition, and we hope that by conforming to this ideal, we shall radically change. But after all, the ideal is merely a projection of the opposite of *what is*. Being violent, I project the ideal of nonviolence and try to transform my violence according to that ideal, which creates a constant conflict within me between *what is* and what should be.

We think conflict, effort, is necessary to bring about this change. Such effort obviously implies discipline, control, constant practice, adjusting oneself to 'what should be'. Most of us are accustomed to this way of thinking, and our activities, our outlook, and our values are based on it; the 'what should be', the ideal, has become extraordinarily dominant in our lives. To me, this way of thinking is completely erroneous, and since you are here to find out what the speaker has to say, please listen to it, do not reject it.

I feel that a radical change can come only when there is no effort, when the mind is not trying to become something, not trying to be virtuous—which does not mean that the mind must be nonvirtuous. As long as there is effort to achieve virtue, there is a continuation of the self, of the 'me', who is trying to be virtuous, which is merely another form of conditioning, a modification of *what is*. In this process is involved the question of who is the maker of effort and what he is striving after, which is obviously self-improvement; and as long as there is effort to improve oneself, there is no virtue. That is, as long as there are ideals of any sort, there must be effort to conform, to adjust to the ideal, or to become this ideal. If I am violent and I have the ideal of nonviolence, there is a conflict, a struggle going on between *what is* and 'what should be'. This struggle, this conflict, is the state of violence; it is not freedom from violence.

Now, can I look at *what is,* the state of violence, without making an ideal of the opposite? Surely, I am only concerned with violence, and not with how to become nonviolent, because the very process of becoming nonviolent is a form of violence. So, can I look at violence without any desire to transform it into another state? Please follow patiently to the end what is being said. Can I look at the state which I call violence or greed or envy or whatever it is without trying to modify or change it? Can I look at it without any reaction, without evaluating or giving it a name?

Are you following all this? Please experiment with what I am saying, and you will see it directly, now, not when you go home.

Being violent, can one look at this state which one has called violence without condemning it? Not to condemn is an extremely complex process because the very verbalization of this feeling, the very word *violence* is condemnatory. And can one look at this feeling, at this state which one has called violence, without giving it a name? When one does not give it a name, what is happening? The mind is made up of words, is it not? All thinking is a process of verbalization. And when one does not give this feeling a name, when one does not term it as violence, is there not a profound revolution taking place in the attention one gives to this feeling?

Let us look at it differently. The mind divides itself as violence and nonviolence, so there are supposedly two states: the state which it wants to attain, and the state which is. There is a dualistic process going on, and I feel there can be a radical change only when this dualistic process has altogether ceased, that is, when the totality of consciousness, of the mind, can give complete attention to *what is.* And the mind cannot give complete attention if there is any sense of condemnation, any desire to change *what is,* any form of distraction as verbalization, naming. When attention is complete, then you will find that such attention is in itself the good, and that the good is not this effort to transform *what is* into something else.

I think this is perhaps a very difficult explanation of a very simple fact. As long as the mind wishes to change, any change is merely a modified continuity of *what is,* because the mind cannot think of total change. There can be total change only when the mind pays complete attention to *what is,* and attention cannot be complete if there is any form of verbalization, condemnation, justification, or evaluation.

You know, when a question is put, most of us expect a gratifying answer; we want to be told how to get there or what to do. I am afraid I have no such answer, but what we can do is to look at the problem, go into it together and discover the truth of the matter; and in considering some of these questions, let us bear this in mind. To look for an answer which will be gratifying, to want to be told how to get there or what to do, is really an immature way of thinking. But if we can examine the problem, go into it together, in the very unfolding of the problem we shall discover what is true, and then it will be the truth which operates, not you or I who operate on the truth.

Question: Being both a parent and a teacher, and seeing the truth of the freedom of which you speak, how am I to regard and help my children?

KRISHNAMURTI: I think the first question is whether one really comprehends deeply that freedom is at the beginning and not at the end. If as a parent and a teacher I really understand this truth, then my whole relationship with the child changes, does it not? Then there is no attachment. Where there is attachment, there is no love. But if I see the truth that freedom is at the beginning, not at the end, then the child is no longer the guarantee, the way of my fulfillment, which means that I do not seek the continuation of myself through the child. Then my whole attitude has undergone a tremendous revolution.

The child is the repository of influence, is he not? He is being influenced, not only by you and me, but by his environment, by his school, by the climate, by the food he eats, by the books he reads. If his parents are Catholics or communists, he is deliberately shaped, conditioned, and this is what every parent, every teacher does in different ways. And can we be aware of these multiplying influences and help the child to be aware of them, so that as he grows up he will not be caught in any one of them? So what is important, surely, is to help the child as he ma-

tures not to be conditioned as a Christian, as a Hindu, or as an Australian, but to be a totally intelligent human being, and this can take place only if you as the teacher or the parent see the truth that there must be freedom from the very beginning.

Freedom is not the outcome of discipline. Freedom does not come after conditioning the mind or while conditioning is going on. There can be freedom only if you and I are aware of all the influences that condition the mind and help the child to be equally aware, so that he does not become entangled in any of them. But most parents and teachers feel that the child must conform to society. What will he do if he does not conform? To most people conformity is imperative, essential, is it not? We have accepted the idea that the child must adjust himself to the civilization, the culture, the society about him. We take this for granted, and through education we help the child to conform, to adjust himself to society.

But is it necessary that the child should adjust himself to society? If the parent or the teacher feels that freedom is the imperative, the essential thing, and not mere conformity to society, then as the child grows up, he will be aware of the influences that condition the mind and will not conform to the present society with its greed, its corruption, its force, its dogmas and authoritarian outlook; and such people will create a totally different kind of society.

We say that some day there is going to be a utopia. Theoretically it is very nice, but it does not come into existence, and I am afraid the educator needs educating, as the parent does. If we are only concerned with conditioning the child to conform to a particular culture or pattern of society, then we shall perpetuate the present state with its everlasting battle between ourselves and others and continue in the same misery. But if there is an understanding of this problem of right attention, which begins not with the child but with the parent and the teacher, then perhaps we shall help to bring about an unconditioning of the mind, which is not a hopeless task. It is a hopeless task only if you as the parent or the teacher feel that it is impossible. But if you perceive the necessity, the urgency, the truth of all this, then that very perception does bring about a revolution within yourself, and therefore you will help the child to grow into an intelligent human being who will put an end to all this misery, strife, and sorrow.

Question: All life is a form of ceremony, and the ritual in a church is a divine form of the ceremony of life. Surely you cannot condemn this totally. Or are you condemning, not the ritual itself, but only the corruption that arises from the rigidity of the mind?

KRISHNAMURTI: Whether they are divine or not divine, I wonder why we are so fond of ceremonies, rituals, why they are so important to us? To me the whole ceremonial approach to life, the church and its ceremonies included, is totally immature and absurd. Ceremonies have no significance; they are vain repetitions, though you may give divine significance to the ceremonies of the church. To say, "Ceremonies are my way and not your way" is to breed evil, so let us look at it dispassionately to find out the truth of the matter.

There is the daily repetition of going to bed, getting up, going to the office, doing certain things, but would you call it a ceremony? Do we give extraordinary meaning to all this, a divine significance? Do we regard it as something from which to get inspiration? Obviously not. There are various daily actions which may become habitual, but perhaps we have thought them out intelligently and are not caught in them. But when we perform ceremonies, the rituals of the church, and so on, do we not look to them

for inspiration? We feel good when the ceremony is going on; we feel a certain sense of beauty, and we are quiet. The repetition dulls our minds. The ritual absorbs us; it temporarily takes us away from ourselves, and we like that feeling, so we give extraordinary meaning to all this. These are simple, obvious facts. Ceremonies are also used for exploitation, to control people, to bring them to a sense of unity which they do not feel. The present society is a society of disunion, but in the church, in rituals, through vain repetition, people are temporarily. . . (Interruption)

Please, would you mind sitting down? This is not a discussion. I am talking, I am not attacking, so please do not defend. I am showing you *what is.* You can take it or leave it. It does not matter to me.

Question: What you are saying is not the truth.

KRISHNAMURTI: Please, if you think ceremonies are necessary, perform them. But if you are willing to examine the whole issue, let us go into it, and you will see how the mind is caught in habits, in vain repetitions, in sensations, in obedience to some authority. A mind that is caught in habit is obviously not free, and such a mind cannot find out what is true.

Through habit—I am not for the moment talking about physical habit—the mind seeks a sensation; it becomes psychologically attached to a particular form of ceremony from which it derives a certain satisfaction, a sense of security. Such a mind is obviously not free, and it cannot discover what is true. It is only a free mind that can discover, not the mind that is clogged with beliefs, dogmas, fear, with the constant demand for security.

Throughout the centuries, every religion has had some kind of ceremony, some kind of ritual to hold the people together, and in ceremonies the people themselves find a certain ease, a forgetfulness of their tiresome daily existence. Their everyday life is boring, and religious rituals, like the processions of kings and queens, offer an escape. But the mind that is seeking escape cannot find that which is timeless, immortal.

It does not matter which church says that ceremonies are divine; they are still the inventions of the mind, of the human mind that is conditioned. It is not a matter of my path as opposed to your path, nor are there people who are going to arrive at the truth through ceremonies while others will arrive by a different way. There is only truth, not your way and my way. To think in terms of your way and my way is false because it tends to exclusiveness, and what is exclusive is evil.

Question: We have been taught to believe in personal immortality and in the continuation of the individual life after death. Is this real to you also?

KRISHNAMURTI: Is there personal immortality after death? Is there continuity of the 'me' with its accumulation of experiences, knowledge, qualities, and relationships? Does all that continue when I die? And if it does not continue, then what is the value of this whole process? If the cultivation of character, with its struggles, joys, and miseries merely comes to an end at death, then what significance has life?

Now, let us look into it. It is not a matter of what I believe and what you believe because beliefs have nothing to do with the discovery of truth. A mind that is caught in belief, whether it is belief in reincarnation or in God, is incapable of discovering or experiencing what is true. I think it is really important to understand this, if you will bear the repetition, because the mind is taught, conditioned, either to believe or not to believe, which is obviously what is happening in the world. The communist does not believe in immortality; he says it is all nonsense because he has been taught, conditioned, not to believe, so he fulfills himself in the state, which for him is the only good. Others believe in the hereafter, and they are hoping for some form of resurrection or reincarnation. So when you ask me, "Do you also believe?" I am afraid that is not the question at all because if you will pay attention, we are going to find out the truth of the matter.

Does the 'I', the personal 'me', continue? What is the 'me'? Various tendencies, traits of character, beliefs, the accumulation of knowledge, experience, the memory of pain, of joy and suffering, the sense of my love, my hate—all this is the 'me' of the moment; and realizing that it is a very transient 'me', we say that beyond it there is the permanent soul, something which is divine. But if that thing is permanent, real, divine, it is beyond time and therefore does not think in terms of dying or having continuity. If there is the soul, or whatever other word you may give to it, it is something beyond time, and you and I cannot think about it because our thinking is conditioned. Our thinking is the outcome of time; therefore, we cannot possibly think of that which is beyond time. So all our fear is the product of time, is it not?

Again, this is not a matter of my way and your way. We are examining, trying to find out what actually *is*. And can we look at *what is* without introducing the belief in something beyond, something which we all want, something super-permanent, a so-called spiritual entity which is timeless? We want to know if we shall survive, and we ask this question primarily because we are frightened of death. So what do we do? We try to have immortality here in our property, do we not? Our whole society is based on this. Property is yours and mine to be handed on to our children, which is a form of immortality through our children. We seek immortality through name, through achievement, through success; we want the perpetuation of ourselves, the endless fulfillment of ourselves. Knowing that we are going to die, that death is inevitable, we say, "What is beyond?" We want a guarantee that there is continuity, so we believe in the hereafter, in reincarnation, in resurrection, in anything to avoid that extraordinary state which we call death. We invent innumerable escapes because none of us wants to die, and all our questions concerning personal immortality are put in the hope of finding a way to avoid that which we fear. But if we can understand death, there will be no fear, and then we shall not seek personal immortality either here or in the hereafter. Then our perception, our whole outlook will have undergone a complete revolution. So belief has nothing to do with the discovery of what is true, and we are now going to find out what is true with regard to death.

What is death? Can one experience it while living? Can you and I experience what death is—not at the moment when through disease or accident there is a cessation of all thinking, but while we are living, vital, clearly and fully conscious? Can you and I find out what it means to die; can we enter the house of death while we are sitting here looking at the whole problem?

What is it to die? Obviously, it is to die to everything that one has accumulated, to every experience, to every memory, to all attachments. To die is to cease to be the self, the 'I', is it not? It is to have no sense of continuity as the 'me' with all its memories, its hurts, its feeling of vengeance, its desire to fulfill, to become. And can there be the experiencing of this moment when the self is not? Then surely we shall know what death is. The mind is the known, the result of the known—the known being all the experiences of countless yesterdays—and it is only when the mind frees itself from the known, and so

is part of the unknown, that there is no fear of death. Then there is no death at all. Then the mind is not seeking personal immortality. Then there is the state of the unknown, which has its own being. But to find that out, the mind has to free itself from the known. You may have innumerable beliefs which give you comfort, a sense of security, but until there is freedom from the known, there will always be the gnawing of fear. That which continues can never be creative. Only that which is unknown is creative, and the unknown comes into being only when the mind is free from the idea of the perpetuation of the known.

You see, the difficulty with most of us is that we want some kind of continuity, and so we invent illusory beliefs. After all, beliefs are merely explanations, and we are satisfied with explanations. But explanations have very little meaning except to a man who wants some form of security, and to find out what is true, the mind must reject all explanations, whether of the church, of the priests, of the books, or of those who want to believe.

When the mind is free of all explanations, free of the known, you will find the unknown is death, and then there is no fear. That state is totally different, and it cannot possibly be conceived of by a mind that is conditioned in the known. When the mind is free from the known, the unknown is.

November 19, 1955

Fifth Talk in Sydney

This evening I would like to discuss what is perhaps rather a complex problem, but I think we can make it quite simple. You see, our minds are full of conclusions, knowledge, experiences; they are crowded with the things that we know. And is it possible to free the mind from the known? The known is made up of the facts, the struggles, the sorrows, the greed of everyday living, as well as the accumulated experience of man through centuries; and is it possible for the mind to recognize these facts that make up the known, and yet be free of them so that some other state may come into being?

When one's mind is full of conclusions, assumptions, experiences, filled with the happiness, the travail, the sorrows that have pursued one all through life, there is then no freedom to look at anything new. If, for instance, in listening to what I am saying, you have assumed certain things about me—that you know and I do not, or that I know and you do not—or your mind is shaped, conditioned by what you have read so that you listen with a preconception, a conclusion, a background, then your mind is not simple; and it seems to me that one needs great simplicity to find out if there is something which is not a mere product of the mind.

If the mind is functioning all the time only within the field of the known, as it does with most of us, we find this area so limited, so narrow and petty that the mind begins to invent ideals, imaginations, delusions through which it escapes from the actual. Most religions offer such an escape, and the so-called religious person is full of fantastic ideas, beliefs, and dogmas.

So the mind functions all the time within the field of the known, does it not? That is an actual fact which we are not seeking to deny or put aside. And the question is whether such a mind is capable of investigating or receiving something which is not merely an experience or a conclusion of the known. One cannot forget the road by which one travels, the name of the street on which one lives, and so on—that would be too absurd. But the mind gets used to the known and develops habits; it gets caught in certain conclusions, assumptions, postulates, and so

we think in this area all the time; therefore, the mind is never free to be really simple, and we think that the more we learn, read, pray, or practice a particular kind of meditation, the better we shall be able to find something beyond.

So the question is: Can the mind—being the residue, the result of the known, of knowledge, of experience—free itself from the known and find something beyond? I would like to discuss this with you, if you will, because I think it is an important question. When we talk about religious experience, we mean going beyond the self, the 'me', the known, do we not? Or perhaps most of us do not think in those terms at all. But it seems to me that the more thoughtful, alert, and aware we are, and the more deeply we go into this question, the more obvious it is that any real revolution can come into being only through the religious person; and the religious person is not one who believes, who follows certain dogmas or practices a particular form of meditation. To me, the religious person is one who is aware of the known and does not allow the known to interfere with his search into the unknown.

This is what I would like to discuss with you this evening, and I hope the problem is clear.

Question: Why is it more important or more vital to be concerned with the unknown, however real, than with the known, which is both real and present?

KRISHNAMURTI: I have insisted in all my talks that the mind must be free from the known to find something which may be called the unknown. If I have preconceived ideas, assumptions about you, surely I do not understand you. Now, can the mind be freed of all these assumptions, beliefs, dogmas, habits of thought? To put it differently, can the mind be made simple so that it is capable of a completely new experience, not an experience based on the old, an experience which is projected? Can the mind be open to the unknown, whatever that is, and yet be aware of the known, of the present fact? Is the problem clear? If it is, then let us discuss it. I think this is an important problem to understand because if we do not understand this problem, we shall be going around in circles thinking we are experiencing something very real when it is merely a projection of our own desire—and therefore living in an illusory world of our own imagination. So, a religious man is one who is inwardly free from the known, is he not?

Does all this mean anything to you? After all, we have been brought up as Christians, Hindus, Muslims, Buddhists, or what you will, with certain dogmas, traditions, and beliefs; and the mind is so conditioned by its background that all its experiences are consciously or unconsciously the outcome of this conditioning. As a Hindu I may have visions of the various gods which the Hindu culture has imprinted on me, just as you who have been brought up as Christians may have visions of Christ, and so on. Such a vision we call a religious experience, but actually, psychologically, what is taking place? The mind is merely projecting, in the form of an image, a symbol, the quality of the background it has inherited, is it not? Therefore the experience is not real at all, but the conditioning is a fact.

Now, can a mind on which have been imprinted the culture, the traditions, the dogmas of Christianity, of Hinduism, or of Buddhism, know its conditioning? Can it be aware of and free itself from this conditioning so that it is able to find out if there is something more than the mere activity of the mind, which is always functioning within the field of the known?

I think the question is clear by now, so let us discuss it.

Question: Whatever may be one's conditioning, there is experience going on which is real, and that experience is not related to one's conditioning. Such experience gives one proof that certain things are true.

KRISHNAMURTI: Please go slowly. Do not assume that you are right and I am wrong, or that you are wrong and I am right. This requires thorough going into, investigating.

Is there experience—apart from my conditioning—which gives me proof that something which others have said is true? That is, I see my conditioning, but besides this conditioning, I experience something which proves to me that my conditioning is right. Now, is there experience apart from and unconnected with my conditioning? If I am a Buddhist, for example, and I experience a vision of the Buddha or of the Buddhistic state, is that experience unconnected with my conditioning as a Buddhist? Yet such an experience convinces many people that their conditioning is right, that what they believe is true. If I happen to be a communist and do not believe in gods and all the rest of the nonsense, obviously I do not have that experience at all. I may have visions of a wondrous utopian state, but not of the Buddha or the Christ. It is the background or conditioning that creates the image, the vision, and this experience only convinces me further that what I believe is true. So when we dissociate experience from the background of our thinking, surely that division is without validity; it has no meaning.

Question: What would be the nature of an experience which was not resulting from the background of the mind?

KRISHNAMURTI: That is right, sir, surely that is the question. What kind of experience is it that is free of the background? And can there be such an experience? We cannot assume anything. If we are going to find out the truth of the matter, there must be no assumption, no sense of obedience to any authority.

The question has been asked: What kind of experience is it that is not dictated by the background, that is not the outcome of the background? Now, can one describe this experience? I am not trying to avoid the question. Can you or I communicate to another this experience which is not the outcome of the background? Obviously not. First we must see the truth of the fact that all our experiences are dictated by the background, and not imagine that we are experiencing something dissociated from the background.

May I here suggest that those of you who are taking notes should not do so. You and I are trying to experience directly, now, the thing we are discussing, and if you take notes, you are not really listening to what is being said. If you take notes, you are doing so in order to think about it tomorrow. But thinking about it directly, now, will have much greater significance than thinking about it tomorrow, so may I suggest that you do not distract others and yourself by taking notes.

If one is to find out whether there is an experience which does not arise from the conditioning of the mind, must one not first see the truth of the fact that all experience is at present either the outcome of one's background, one's conditioning, or the reaction of that background to challenge? Do you see this fact? Are you conscious of the fact that your mind is conditioned as a Christian, as a socialist, a communist, or what you will, and that all your experiences and reactions spring from this conditioning? That is so, is it not?

Comment: Whether one is a Christian or belongs to some other religion is largely a matter of destiny.

KRISHNAMURTI: Please do not introduce words like destiny. That is off the main subject; it is not what we are discussing for the time being. Not that we cannot discuss it another time, but we must restrict ourselves to the point.

Question: By the word experience *do you not really mean understanding or knowledge?*

KRISHNAMURTI: Those three words—*experience, knowledge* and *understanding*—are related to each other, are they not?

Comment: But they are not the same.

KRISHNAMURTI: No, of course not, sir. They are related to each other. If I want to understand not only what you are saying but the totality of you, I must not have a preconception about you; I must not have a prejudice or retain in memory either the injuries you may have caused me or your pleasant flatteries. I must be free of all that in order to understand you, must I not? Understanding comes only when I can meet you anew, not through the screen of experience.

This is a sufficiently complicated question, so do not let us make it more complicated. If it is clear what we mean by understanding, and what we mean by experience and knowledge, let us go on.

I cannot understand if my mind reacts according to the limitation of my conditioning. Surely, this much is fairly simple. And is one aware that one reacts according to one's conditioning? Are you aware of the fact that as a Christian, a communist, a socialist, or whatever you may happen to be, you defend certain beliefs, religious or nonreligious? Are you aware that your mind, being the residue of the past, is limited, and that whatever it may choose or experience is also limited?

Question: Is spontaneous love or affection dependent on the background?

KRISHNAMURTI: Sir, do we know what spontaneous love is? Do you and I know love which is not the outcome of a conditioning, of a motive, of a social morality, of a sense of duty or responsibility? Do we know love in which there is no attachment? Or is it that we have read of such a state and we want to be in that state?

Coming back to the point: Are we aware, you and I, that our minds are so complex, so conditioned, that there is in us nothing original—if I may use this word without being misunderstood? Are we capable of original understanding, of experiencing something uncontaminated, untouched, pristine, or are we mere gramophone records repeating what we have read, or what our background instigates? Are not fear and desire dictating some fancy, some imagination or hope? And can one be free of all this? One can be free, surely, only when one is aware that one's visions, hopes, beliefs are the outcome of one's own desire and are based on one's particular conditioning.

Is it clear up to this point?

Audience: Yes.

KRISHNAMURTI: Now, what do you mean by yes? Please do not be impatient or laugh it off. Have you merely accepted an explanation or are you directly aware of the fact that you are conditioned, apart from the explanation? Do you see the difference between the two?

Audience: Yes.

KRISHNAMURTI: Please go slowly.

Question: Would it be that as we become more aware of present things, it creates the incoming of a new force?

KRISHNAMURTI: Sir, I am not talking about the incoming or outgoing of a new force. What I am talking about is very simple. Do you know that you are conditioned? And when you say yes, does this statement reflect merely the verbal understanding of a verbal explanation, or are you aware that you are conditioned? Now, which is it?

Comment: I am aware that I am conditioned.

KRISHNAMURTI: Please be patient. This is important.

Question: If I am conditioned, can I be aware that I am conditioned?

KRISHNAMURTI: Can I be aware that I am nationalistic, that I have certain beliefs, dogmas, prejudices? Can I know this? Surely I can, can I not? So, do I know that I have assumptions, prejudices, certain experiences, which are the outcome of my conditioning, and that my mind is therefore very limited? Am I aware of this, not theoretically, but actually? Am I directly experiencing the fact that my mind is conditioned?

Comment: One can only say that one was conditioned.

KRISHNAMURTI: Do you mean that before you came to this meeting, you were conditioned, and now you are not conditioned?

Question: We can know that we had an original experience only after we have had it, when the mind is again full of the known.

KRISHNAMURTI: Please, this is a very complex problem, but if you will go slowly into it, you will see for yourself the whole significance of what we are talking about. As human beings we are not creative; our minds are burdened with memories, sorrows, greed, dogmas, the nationalistic spirit, and so on. And is it possible for the mind to see all this and extricate itself? Surely, the mind can be free only when it knows that it is not free, that it is conditioned. Do I know this, am I directly experiencing this conditioning? Do I really see that I am prejudiced, that I have many assumptions? We have assumed that there is or is not God, that there is immortality or annihilation, that there is resurrection or reincarnation, and many other things; and can the mind be aware of all these assumptions, or at least of some of them?

Question: When you say "we," do you mean that your mind as well as ours is conditioned by these traditions and greeds which have molded us? What do you mean by "we"?

KRISHNAMURTI: It is a way of speaking. We are looking at the mind, yours and mine. Let us stick to this for the moment.

Question: As long as we are satisfied, what is the problem?

KRISHNAMURTI: As long as you are satisfied, as long as you say it is perfectly all right to be a Christian, a Hindu, or a communist, it is not a problem.

Comment: Then we have to be dissatisfied.

KRISHNAMURTI: No, it is not that you have to be dissatisfied. But you are dissatisfied, are you not?

Audience: Yes.

KRISHNAMURTI: You see, the problem of dissatisfaction or discontent is quite different. If I am not satisfied, I want to find some way to be satisfied, so I do not accept the present state, the present condition.

Question: Do you imply that verbalization is a bar to understanding, to direct experience?

KRISHNAMURTI: Obviously, because the whole process of the mind is verbalization. I may not use a word; I may have instead an image or a symbol. If I have a symbol in my mind, the Hindu or the Christian idea of reality, of God, or what you will, even though I do not verbalize or put it into words, that symbol prevents the understanding of the real.

Please, let us not go into these various points even though they are related, but let us stick to one thing. Can you and I know, while sitting here, that we are conditioned? Can we be conscious, fully aware of that fact?

Audience: Yes.

Question: What has all this got to do with the primary need of every human being, which is food, clothing, and shelter?

KRISHNAMURTI: Sir, we all need sufficient food, clothing, and shelter, each one of us, but there are millions, practically the whole of Asia, who have not got them. An equitable distribution of the physical necessities is prevented by our psychological greed, our nationalism, our religious differences. Psychologically we use these necessities to aggrandize our own selves, and if we go slowly into this thing we are discussing, you will yourself answer this question instead of asking me. What we are trying to do here is to liberate ourselves from each other so that you and I are original individuals, real human beings, not the mass of the collective.

So, if that is understood, can we say, "I know I am conditioned"?

Question: Yes, I know I am conditioned, and I must do something about it. Now, how do I free myself?

KRISHNAMURTI: The lady says that she knows she is conditioned, conditioned in the known. She knows her prejudices, her assumptions, her conscious and unconscious desires, urges, compulsions, and knowing all that, she asks, "What can I do, how am I to break through it?" Is that what most of you are asking too?

Audience: Yes.

KRISHNAMURTI: All right. Let us go step by step, and please follow this a little patiently. I am aware that I am conditioned, and my immediate reaction to that awareness is that I must be free from conditioning, so I say, "How am I to be free? What is the method, the system, the process by which to be free?" But if I practice a method, I become a slave to the method, which then forms another conditioning.

Comment: Not necessarily.

KRISHNAMURTI: Sir, let this idea float around a little bit. Being aware that I am conditioned, that I am greedy, I want to know how to get rid of it. The question of how to get rid of it is prompted by another form of greed, is it not? I may practice non-greed day after day, but the motive, the desire to be free from greed, is still greed. Go slowly, please. So the "how" cannot solve the problem; it has only complicated the problem. But the question can be answered totally, as you will presently see for yourself.

If I am fully aware that I am greedy, does not that very awareness free the mind from greed? If I know a snake is poisonous, that is enough, is it not? I do not go near the snake. But we do not see that greed is poison. We like the pleasant sensation of it; we like the comfortable feeling of being conditioned. If we were trying to free the mind from conditioning, we might be antisocial, we might lose our job, we might go against the whole tradition of society; so unconsciously we take warning, and then the mind asks, "How am I to get rid of it?" So the "how" is merely a postponement of the realization of the fact. Is this point clear?

What is important, then, is why the mind asks for a method. You will find that there are innumerable methods which say, "Do these things every day, and you will get there." But in following the method, you have created a habit and to that you are a slave—you are not free. Whereas, if you see that you are conditioned, conditioned to the known, and are therefore afraid of the unknown, if you are fully aware of this fact, then you will find that that very awareness is operating, is already bringing about a measure of freedom which you have not deliberately tried to achieve. When you are aware of your conditioning, actually, not theoretically, all effort ceases. Any effort to be something is the beginning of another conditioning.

So it is important to understand the problem and not find an answer to the problem.

The problem is this: The mind, being the result of time, of centuries of conditioning, moves and has its being in the area of the known. This is the actual fact; it is what is happening in our daily lives. All our thinking, our memories, our experiences, our visions, our inner voices, our intuitions, are essentially the outcome of the known.

Now, can the mind be aware of its own conditioning and not try to battle against it? When the mind is aware that it is conditioned and does not battle against it, only then is the mind free to give its complete attention to this conditioning. The difficulty is to be aware of conditioning without the distraction of trying to do something about it. But if the mind is constantly aware of the known, that is, of the prejudices, the assumptions, the beliefs, the desires, the illusory thinking of our daily life—if it is aware of all this without trying to be free, then that very awareness brings its own freedom. Then perhaps it is possible for the mind to be really still, not just still at a certain level of consciousness and frightfully agitated below. There can be total stillness of the mind only when the mind understands the whole problem of conditioning—how it is conditioned— which means watching, off and on, every movement of thought, being aware of the assumptions, the beliefs, the fears. Then perhaps there is a total stillness of the mind in which something beyond the mind can come into being.

November 23, 1955

Sixth Talk in Sydney

I would like this evening to discuss the problem of time, for if we could really understand this problem, I think it would answer many of our questions and probably put a stop totally to this endless desire to find, this urge to discover what is true. To me the search for truth through time has no meaning, and if we could understand the desire, the drive to find, then perhaps we should be able to look at the problem of time in a different way altogether.

We think that there is a gap or an interval between *what is* and 'what should be', between the ugly and the beautiful, and that time is necessary to achieve that which is beautiful, that which is true; so our endeavor, our everlasting search is to find a way to bridge this gap. We pursue gurus, teachers, we control ourselves, we accept the most fantastic ideas, all in the hope of bridging the gap, and we think that a system of meditation or the practice of discipline is necessary in order to arrive at that which is the absolute, the real, the true. This is what I would like to go into, and I hope you will discuss it with me after I have talked a little.

Now, we accept this process, do we not? All the religious teachers and the sacred books prescribe it, and all religious endeavor is based on it: I am this, and I must become that. But this process may be entirely false. There may be no gap at all; it may be purely a mental one, a totally unreal division created by the mind in its desire to arrive somewhere, and I think it is very important to understand this. We assume that truth must be achieved through time, through various forms of effort, but this assumption may be utterly illusory, and I think it is. It may be that all we have to do is to perceive the illusion of it, to see, not as a philosophical idea, but as a factual reality, that there is no arriving through time, that there is no becoming but only being, and that we cannot be if there is any attempt to achieve an end. To understand, to perceive that whatever that other state is, it cannot be found or realized through time, we must be capable of thinking very simply and directly; and it seems to me, for most of us, this is the difficulty. We are so used to making effort to achieve through practice, through discipline, through a process of time, that it has never occurred to us that this effort may be an illusion.

Now, this evening can we think of this problem entirely differently, and not be concerned with the "how"? Can we look at it as though there were no gurus, no teachers, no disciplines, no systems of yoga, and all the rest of it? Can we wipe away all these things and perhaps see directly that which may be called truth, God, or love?

One of our difficulties is that we have accepted this idea that we must make effort through time to achieve, to become, to arrive. Has this idea any reality, or is it merely an illusion? I know that the teachers, the swamis, the yogis, the various philosophers and preachers have maintained that effort is necessary—the right kind of effort, the right kind of discipline—because they all have an idea, as we also have, that there is a gap between ourselves and reality; or they have said reality is in us, and having accepted it, we ask, "How am I to get to that reality?"

So, can we put aside all assumption, all conception of an end to be achieved through effort, through time? If that whole process is seen to be false, then is there not a state of being, a direct, instantaneous perception without any intermediary? This is not to hypnotize oneself; it is not to say, "I am in that state"—which has no meaning at all and is merely the outcome of assumptions and traditions.

Can we go into this problem together?

Question: Is physical effort also illusory?

KRISHNAMURTI: What do you think, sir?

Question: What do you mean by time?

KRISHNAMURTI: Please, just a minute. May I suggest that we listen to each other

and not merely be occupied with our own particular question. This gentleman asked if physical effort is also illusory. Need he ask that question? If we did not make an effort physically, what would happen? It is obvious, is it not? So, either he was asking the question sarcastically or he was really inquiring where physical effort ceases and the other thing begins in which there is no effort at all.

Psychologically we are making effort, are we not? Our whole desire is to be something psychologically. We want to be virtuous, inwardly peaceful; we want a mind that is silent, a richness of life. That being our psychological urge, we consider it essential to make tremendous inward effort, so we become very serious about this effort. If a person makes such an effort and maintains it constantly, if he conforms to an ideal, to a goal, to the so-called purpose of life, and so on, we call him virtuous; but I wonder if such a person is virtuous at all or is merely pursuing a glorified projection of his own desire?

Now, if one could understand this psychological urge to become, then perhaps physical effort would have quite a different meaning. At present there is conflict between the psychological urge in one direction and physical effort in another. Many of us go to the office every day and are perfectly bored with the whole thing because psychologically we want to be something else. If there were no psychological urge to be something, then perhaps there would be an integration, a totally different approach to physical activity.

What were you saying, sir?

Question: I was interested to find out what you mean by time.

KRISHNAMURTI: Chronological time is obvious; it exists, it is a fact. But I am using this word *time* in the psychological sense, the time which is necessary to close the gap between me and that which I want to be, to cover the distance which the mind has created between me and that which is God, truth, or what you will. Though the mind has invented this psychological time and insists that it is necessary in order to practice various forms of discipline, in order to achieve bliss, heaven, and all the rest of it, I am questioning—and I hope you are also questioning—its validity; I am asking whether or not it is an illusion.

If there were not effort to arrive, to achieve, to become, we are afraid that we would stagnate, vegetate, are we not? But would we? Are we not deteriorating now in making this effort to become something? The actual fact is that through effort, through time we are trying to bridge the gap between *what is* and 'what should be', which creates a constant battle within ourselves, and this whole process is based on fear, on imitation, not on direct perception or understanding.

So, one of our difficulties is that the mind, which is obviously the result of time, has invented this gap which perpetuates desire, the will to be something; and seeing that desire is part of the process, we try to be desireless, so again there is this effort to be, to become.

Now, I am questioning this whole issue, which we have accepted and according to which we live. To me this way of living has no meaning. There is a state in which there is direct perception without effort, and it is effort that is preventing the coming into being of that state. But if you say, "How am I to live without psychological effort?" then you have not understood the problem at all. The "how" again introduces the problem of time. You may perhaps feel that it is necessary to live without effort, that it is the true way to live, and the mind immediately asks, "How am I to achieve that state?" So you are again caught in the process of time.

I do not know if it has happened to you, but there are moments of complete cessation of all effort to be something, and in that state

one finds an extraordinary richness of life, a fullness of love. It is not some faraway illusory ideal but an actuality which is perceived directly, not through time.

You see, this opens up another issue: Is knowledge necessary to that perception? To build a bridge, I must have the "know-how"; I must be able properly to evaluate certain facts, and so on. If I know how to read, I can turn to any book which gives the required facts, but what we do is to accumulate knowledge psychologically. We pursue the various teachers, the wise people, the sages, the saints, the swamis and yogis, hoping that by accumulating knowledge, by gathering virtue, we shall be able to bridge this gap. But is there not a different kind of release, a freedom, not from anything or towards anything, but a freedom in which to be?

Is this all too abstract?

Audience: No.

Comment: We are already free if we realize that we are one with God.

KRISHNAMURTI: Please, sir, that is an assumption, is it not? The mind assumes in order to arrive. A conclusion helps one to struggle towards that conclusion. Whether we say, "I am one with God," or "I am merely the product of environment," it is an assumption according to which we try to live. You see, that is what I mean by knowledge. You may say, "I am one with life," but what significance has it? This whole layer of assumptions, gathered through one's own effort or from the effort of others, may be totally wrong, so why should one assume anything? Which does not mean that one must have an empty mind.

Question: Is there not in all this a certain fear of desire itself?

KRISHNAMURTI: Is there fear of having desire? Let us go into this a little bit. What is fear? Surely, fear comes only in the movement away from *what is*. I am this and I do not like it, or I do not want you to find out about it, so I am moving away from it. The moving away from it is fear. There is desire, the desire to be rich and a hundred other desires. In fulfilling or in not fulfilling desire there is conflict, there is fear, there is frustration, agony, so we want to avoid the pain which desire brings but hold on to the things of desire which are pleasurable. This is what we are trying to do, is it not? We want to hold the pleasure which desire brings and avoid the pain which desire also brings. So our conflict is in accepting or clutching the one while avoiding the other, and when we ask, "How am I to be free of sorrow, how am I to be perpetually happy and at peace?" it is essentially the same problem.

Question: Sir, will you tell us what is a better method to attain oneness beyond the mind.

KRISHNAMURTI: Please, you are not listening to what I am saying. This desire to be one with everything is the same problem as wanting to be successful in the world, is it not? Instead of saying, "I want to have money and how am I to get it?" you say, "I want to realize God or truth or oneness, and how am I to do it?" Now, both are on the same level; one is not superior to or more spiritual than the other because both have the same motive. Do please listen to this. One thing you call worldly, the other you call unworldly, spiritual, but if you examine the motive, it is essentially the same. The man who pursues money may look up to the man who says, "I want to be spiritual, I want to achieve God," because wanting to be spiritual is considered virtuous, but if you go into this matter seriously, you will see that the two pursuits are intrinsically the same. The man who wants a drink and the man who wants God are essentially the same because they both want something. One goes to the pub and gets a drink immediately while the other has this time interval, but there is no fundamental difference between them.

This is very serious; it is not a laughing matter. We are all caught in the same struggle. And is it possible to have this extraordinary sense of completeness, of reality, this fullness of love, not tomorrow, not through time, but now? Can there be direct perception, which means awakening to all the false thinking, to the pursuit of the "how" and seeing it as false?

Question: Sir, is not time necessary to this perception?

KRISHNAMURTI: Is not time necessary to perceive *what is*? You see, we all assume this; it is the accepted thing, and this is what I have been questioning. Sirs, this is not a matter of yes or no, of saying, "You go your way and I go mine." It is not at all like that. We are trying to understand the problem; we are trying to go into it very deeply. We are not making any assumption, any dogmatic or authoritarian assertion, but are trying to feel out this problem, and we can feel it out only when the heart is not obstinate. You may investigate, but if you are obstinate, that obstinacy prejudices your investigation.

The lady says she feels time is necessary. Why? Do you understand what we mean by time? Not chronological time, but the time created by desire, by our psychological intentions and pursuits. You say that time is necessary to realize truth, and you have accepted it as the inevitable process. But someone comes along and says this process may be unnecessary, it may be utterly false, illusory, so let us find out why you think it is necessary.

Comment: I think time is necessary for the realization of freedom.

KRISHNAMURTI: Sir, please go into it slowly, deeply, and you will see. Why do we think time is necessary? Is it not because we regard truth as being over there while we are here, so we say this distance, this gap, must be covered through time? That is one of the reasons, is it not? The ideal, the 'what should be' is over there, and to arrive at that I must have time— time being the process which will bridge the gap. Are you following all this?

Comment: No, sir, not quite.

KRISHNAMURTI: Let me put it differently. Where there is the desire to become, psychologically, there must be time. As long as I have an ambition, either for worldly things or for the so-called spiritual things, to fulfill that ambition I must have time, must I not? If I want to be rich, I must have time. If I want to be good, if I want to realize truth, God, or what you will, I must also have time. Is this a fact or not? It seems such an obvious thing. Surely that is what we are all doing; it is what is actually taking place.

Comment: Nothing happens without time.

KRISHNAMURTI: Sir, this is really a very complex problem; it needs deep investigation, not mere assertions which we reject or accept. That has no value.

Question: The mind is free of time altogether, is it not?

KRISHNAMURTI: Is it? Is that not an assumption?

Sirs, what is it we are talking about? What are we trying to find out? You see, we are all suffering; we are living in relationship, which is pain, an endless conflict with society or with another. There is confusion, and a vast conditioning of the mind is going on through so-called education, through the inculcation of various religious and political doctrines; communism, like Catholicism, completely binds the mind, and the other religions are doing the same thing in a minor form. Seeing the extraordinary discontent of man, his unfathomable loneliness, his sorrow, his struggle—being aware of all this, not just theoretically but actually, one wants to find out if there is not a different way of living altogether. Have you ever asked yourself this question? Have you asked yourself whether a savior, a teacher, a guru, or a discipline is necessary? Will these things rid man of all sorrow, not ten years later, but now?

Comment: Time is the crux of the problem, and to me time seems inevitable.

KRISHNAMURTI: It is not a matter of how it seems to you or to me. A hungry man does not think in terms of time, does he? He says, "I am hungry, feed me." But I am afraid most of us are not hungry, so we have invented this thing called time—time in which to arrive. We see this whole process of human misery, conflict, degradation, travail, and we want to find a way out of it, or a method to change it, which again implies time. But there may be a totally different state of being which will resolve all this turmoil, and which is not a theoretical abstraction, a mere verbalization or imitation.

Question: Why does love appear to be a burden?

KRISHNAMURTI: Is that what we are discussing? Sirs, please, if we can understand at least this one thing, then all these talks will have been worthwhile, and you will not have wasted your time coming here in spite of the rain. Can we really see that there is no teacher, no guru, no discipline, that the guru, the discipline, the method exist only because of the division between *what is* and 'what should be'? If the mind can perceive the illusion of this whole process, then there is freedom; not freedom to be something or freedom from something, but just freedom.

Comment: We are not ideal beings. We must learn to love.

KRISHNAMURTI: Sir, is love, goodness, or beauty something to be achieved through effort? Let us think about it simply, shall we? If I am violent, if I hate, how am I to have love in my heart? Will one have love through effort, through time, through saying, "I must practice love, I must be kind to people"? If you have not got love today, through practice will you get it next week or next year? Will this bring about love? Or does love come into being only when the maker of effort ceases, that is, when there is no longer the entity who says, "I am evil and I must become good"? The very cognition that "I am evil" and the desire to be good are similar because they spring from the same source, which is the 'me'. And can this 'me' who says, "I am evil and must be good" come to an end immediately, not through time? This means not being anything, not trying to become something or nothing. If one can really see this, which is a simple fact, have direct perception of it, then everything else is delusion. Then one will find that the desire to make this state permanent is also an illusion because effort is involved in that desire. If one understands deeply the whole desire for permanency, the urge to continue, sees the illusion of it, then there is quite a different state which is not the opposite.

So, can we have direct perception without introducing time? Surely, this is the only revolution. There is no revolution through time, through this misery of perpetually wanting to be something. That is what every seeker is doing. He is caught in the prison of sorrow, and he keeps on pushing, widening and decorating that prison; but he is still in prison because psychologically he is pursuing the desire to be, to become something. And is it not possible to see the truth of this and so be nothing? It is not a matter of saying, "I must be nothing," and then asking how to be nothing—which is all so grotesque, childish, and immature—but of seeing the fact directly, not through time.

Comment: There is a famous saying: "Be still and know God."

KRISHNAMURTI: You see, that is one of the extraordinary things in life—you have read so much that you are full of other people's knowledge. Someone has said, "Be still and know God," and then the problem arises: How am I to be still? So you are back again in the old game. Be still—full stop. And you can be really still, not verbally but totally, completely, only when you understand this whole process of becoming, when you see as illusion that which now is a reality to you because you have been brought up on it, you have accepted it, and all your endeavor goes towards it. When you see this process of becoming as illusion, the 'other' is, but not as the opposite. It is something entirely different.

Surely, this is not a matter of acceptance. You cannot possibly accept what I am saying. If you do, it has no meaning at all. This demands a direct perception, independent of everybody, a complete breaking away from all the traditions, the gurus, the teachers, the systems of yoga, from all the complications of trying to be, to become something. Only then will you find freedom, not to be or to become, which is all self-fulfillment and therefore sorrow, but freedom in which there is love, reality, something which cannot be measured by the mind.

November 26, 1955

Banaras, India, 1955

---- ✳ ----

First Talk at Rajghat

If we could go into the question of what is teaching and learning, I think it might be of significance because, after all, you have gathered here to learn something, have you not? When you attend a talk, it is generally to gather information, to learn something of which you may not yet be aware. So I think it is important to discuss what it is that we are learning and what it is that is being taught, and I hope at the end of this little talk that we can go into the matter together, so that it becomes clear to each one of us what it is that we are trying to do when we attend a meeting of this kind.

Are you here to learn something from the speaker? You may come with the idea that you are going to learn something which is being taught, but if that is not the intention of the speaker at all, then there is no direct communication between the speaker and the audience, and therefore you will go away feeling rather disappointed and asking yourself what you have got from it.

In order to prevent that entirely, we must discuss this question of learning and teaching, and I hope you will go into it with me. It is important to unravel this idea that we are learning something, for I think a great deal of mischief lies in this conception of learning.

Through learning, does one perceive directly something which may be true, real, something other than the formulations of the mind? Do you follow what I mean? Is there direct perception through learning, through knowledge, or do we perceive directly only when there is no barrier of learning, when there is no knowledge?

What do you mean by learning? You want to find happiness, reality, serenity, freedom— that is what most of you are groping after. Being discontented, dissatisfied with things, with relationships, with ideas, you are seeking something beyond, and you go to a swami, a guru, or X, who you think has this quality you are seeking. You want to learn how to arrive at this extraordinary integration of the totality of human consciousness, so you come here, as you go to any religious teacher, with the intention to learn. After all, that is the intention of the majority of the people who are here, and if you will kindly pay attention to what is being said, I am sure it will be worthwhile.

Now, can you be taught to have direct perception? Can there be this totality of integration, this clarity of perception, through knowledge, through learning, through a method? Will the learning of a technique or the following of a particular system lead to it? With the majority of us, learning is the acquiring of a new technique, substituting the new for the old. I hope I am making myself clear in this matter.

There are various methods with which you are quite familiar, one or other of which you practice in the hope of directly perceiving something which may be called reality, that state which has no becoming but is only being. Similarly, you have come here to learn, have you not? You want to find out what method the speaker will offer to reveal this extraordinary state. You want to learn how to approach this state, step by step, through the practice of certain forms of meditation, through the cultivation of virtue, self-discipline, and so on. But I do not think that any method will bring about clear perception—on the contrary.

Method implies time, does it not? When you practice a method, you must have time to bridge the gap between *what is* and 'what should be'. Time is necessary to travel the distance created by the mind between the fact and the dissolution of the fact, which is the end to be achieved. Our whole ideology is based on this sense of achievement through time, so we begin to acquire, to learn, and therefore we rely on the Master, the guru, the teacher, because he is going to help us to get there.

So, is perception or direct experience of that reality a matter of time? Is there a gap that must be bridged over by the process of knowledge? If there is, then knowledge becomes extraordinarily important. Then the more you know, the more you practice, the more you discipline yourself, and so on, the greater your capacity to build this bridge to reach reality. We have taken it for granted that time is necessary. That is, if I am violent, I say time is necessary for me to be in a state of nonviolence; I must have time to practice nonviolence, to control, discipline the mind. We have accepted this idea and it may be an illusion, it may be totally false. Perception may be immediate, not in time. I think it is

not a matter of time at all—if I may use the phrase "I think," not to convey an opinion, but an actual fact. Either one perceives, or one does not perceive. There is no gradual process of learning to perceive. It is the absence of experience, which is based on knowledge, that gives perception.

Is this all too difficult or too abstract? Let me put the problem differently.

Our activities, our pursuits, are self-centered. To use an ordinary word, our action, our thought, is selfish; it is concerned with the 'me', and we read or hear that the self is a barrier and that it is therefore necessary for the self to cease—not the higher or the lower self, but the self, the mind which is ambitious, which is afraid, which is cunning in the devious pursuits of its own greed and dependence, the mind which is the result of time. That mind is self-concerned; and can that self-concern be washed away immediately, or must it be peeled off, layer after layer, through a gradual process of knowledge, experience, and the continuation of time? Do you understand the problem, sirs?

Please, we are going to discuss this matter when I have talked a little while longer, if I may; because, after all, we are here to experience, not to learn, and I want to differentiate between learning and experiencing. You can experience what you learn, but such experience is conditioned by what you have learned. You can learn something and then experience it, which is fairly obvious. I can read about the life of the Christ and get very emotional, very thrilled by it all, and then experience what I have read. I can read the Gita, conjure up all kinds of ideas, and experience them. Both conscious reading and unconscious learning bring about certain forms of experience. You may not have read a single book, but because you are a Hindu, conditioned by centuries of Hinduism, consciously or unconsciously, the mind has become the repository of certain traditions and beliefs which may produce experiences to which you attach tremendous importance; but actually, when you examine these experiences, they are nothing but the reaction of a conditioned mind.

Now, what we are trying to find out in this talk, and in the coming talks that are to be held here, is whether there can be direct experience, stripped of all knowledge, of all learning, so that it is true and not merely the reaction of one's conditioning as a Hindu, a Buddhist, a Christian, or as a member of some other silly sect. Perception cannot be true as long as it is based on a method because the method obviously produces its own experience. If I believe in Christianity or in some other religion, and I practice a method which will lead me to truth according to that belief, surely the experience it produces has no validity at all. It is an experience based on my own conviction, on my own pettiness, on my conditioned mind. What is experienced is merely the outcome of that particular method, whereas what I am talking about is something entirely different.

If we see that the method is false, an illusion, the product of time, and that time cannot lead to direct experience, then that very perception is the liberation from time. Our relationship is then entirely different. Do you follow, sirs? We are not here to learn a new method or technique, a new approach to life, and all that business. We are here to strip the mind of all illusion and perceive directly, and that requires astonishing attention to what is being said, not a casual communication with each other as if you were attending just another talk. What matters is to free the mind from knowledge and from the method, the practice based on that knowledge, which can lead only to the thing we crave for. That is why it is very important to understand what I am saying, to see the illusion the mind has created as time through which to acquire, to learn, to arrive, to gain.

Don't immediately say that reality, God, the atma, is within us, and all the rest of it. It is not. That is your idea, your superstition, your conditioned way of thinking. You say that God is within us, and the communist, who has been differently trained from childhood, says that there is no God at all, that what you are saying is nonsense. You are conditioned to believe in one way, and he in another, so you are both the same. Whereas, the whole concern of this talk is to find out if the mind can strip itself immediately of this belief, this knowledge, this conditioning, so that there is direct perception. One may live a thousand lives and practice self-discipline, one may sacrifice, subjugate, meditate, but this will never lead to direct perception, which can take place only in freedom, not through control, subjugation, discipline; and there can be freedom only when the mind is immediately aware of its conditioning, which brings about the cessation of that conditioning.

Now, can we discuss this?

Comment: We are normally so closely identified with our conditioning that we are not aware of our conditioning at all.

Question: There is a ceaseless movement with which we are totally identified and from which we are constantly trying to run away, and the nervous exhaustion born of this conflict brings about dullness of body and mind. Would it be right to say that a certain alertness of both body and mind is absolutely essential if we are to pursue the investigation which you have laid before us?

KRISHNAMURTI: Obviously, sir. If I want to run a race, I must have the proper diet; if I want to do anything very efficiently, I must eat the right food, not overload the stomach, get the proper amount of exercise, and so on.

My mind and body must be extraordinarily alert.

Comment: This alertness does not come to us unless we have lived thoughtfully the previous day. The moment we sit down in serious thought, it is necessary that we should sit properly; otherwise, the mind will wander and we shall not be able to think strenuously. When you say that direct perception cannot come through any form of discipline but only when there is the utmost freedom, our minds immediately tend to slouch into a kind of slothfulness. I see it happening to myself. While it is obvious that such things as discipline, correct posture, and regulated breathing are not going to give us direct experience, they do bring about a certain alertness of body in which the mind is neither slothful nor is it chasing about without knowing what it is running after. Unless one is able to live in this state of alertness, which is a normal condition of the mind, anything that you are talking about is Greek.

KRISHNAMURTI: I understand, sir, but I think the problem is somewhat different. One may acquire the correct posture of body, breathe rightly, and all the rest of it, but that has relatively little significance in regard to what we are talking about.

Let me put it differently. If I see that I hate, is it possible for me to love immediately, or must hate be gradually washed away so that I can love eventually? That is the problem. Do you follow, sir? Is it possible for the mind to transform itself immediately and be in a state of love?

Question: If I may refer to your previous talk about memory, it is conceded that a great deal of our mentation is a purely mechanical response of memory, and through identification most of us are constantly get-

ting lost in our loves and hates without being aware of it. Even when we are aware of it, is that awareness not also mechanical, the result of effort? Is this relevant to what you are saying, or not?

KRISHNAMURTI: I am not sure it is relevant. The problem is this: One is aware that one is ambitious, and being sufficiently alert, intelligent, or watchful, one sees how absurd, how destructive it is. Ambition, spiritual ambition included, obviously implies a state in which there is no love. Wanting to be somebody spiritually, wanting to be nonviolent, is still ambition. Perceiving all that, is it possible for one to wipe away ambition instantly and not go through this everlasting struggle of investigation, analysis, discipline, idealization, and all the rest of it? Can the mind wipe away ambition instantly and be in the other state? Is this possible? Don't agree, sirs; it is not a matter of agreement or disagreement. Have you thought about it?

Comment: Our minds are always trying to modify our conditioning.

KRISHNAMURTI: Just stick to my point if it is a problem to you. Or am I making it a problem to you, and therefore it is not really your problem? What is your response?

Question: We should like to know how to do it.

KRISHNAMURTI: The gentleman here asks how to do it, and that is the whole thing. First please look at the question itself, the "how." I am ambitious, and I want to be in a state of love; therefore, I must wipe away ambition, and how am I to do it? Please follow this. The very question involves time, does it not? The moment you ask how, you have introduced the problem of time—time to bridge the gap, time to arrive at that state called love—and therefore you can never arrive at it. Do you understand, sirs?

Question: You have talked about the state of direct perception. Is it not legitimate to inquire into that state? Perception involves three factors: the seer, the seeing, and the object seen. That is how we apprehend perception. Are you talking of a faculty apart from this?

KRISHNAMURTI: I also am quite good at all this kind of stuff! What is the perceiver, and is the perceiver separate from the object of his perception? Is the thinker apart from the thought? That is what you are saying, is it not? But that is not our problem for the moment. Don't misunderstand me, I am not trying to. . .

Question: You used the words direct perception.

KRISHNAMURTI: We can change the words; they are not important. Let me put it differently.

I am aware that I am ambitious, cruel, stupid, what you will; and it is generally accepted and supported by the sacred books, the rituals, the belief in Masters, in evolution, and all the rest of it, that through a slow, gradual process of effort, I shall transcend what I am and come to something beyond. I see what is involved in that: the maker of effort, the effort, and the object towards which he is making the effort, which is all a process of mentation. Seeing this, I say to myself, "Is it possible for me to drop ambition completely and be in that state which may be called love?" I am not going to describe what that state is. My problem is: I am violent, and is it possible for me to drop my violence completely, instantly?

Question: Is the possibility a matter of chance or of effort?

KRISHNAMURTI: Just look at it, sir. If there is effort, you are back in the old field of gradualness. If it is merely chance, a matter of good luck, then it has no meaning. If I may say so, I don't think you are really putting the question to yourself.

I am aggressive, ambitious, and I see that the whole rotten society around me is also ambitious and aggressive in different degrees. It is all very tawdry, stupid, vain, and yet I am caught in it; and is it possible to drop ambition completely, to leave it and never touch it again? Do you follow my question, sir? But this is not my question; it is your question if you have ever tackled this problem. Or do you say, "I am ambitious and I will get rid of ambition slowly, tomorrow or in my next life, through discipline, through using the right mantra, practicing right awakening, and the whole rigmarole of it?" Is this your problem, sir? If it is not, I am not going to foist it on you. But if it is your problem, what will you do with it?

Sir, look. Most of us have no love, whatever that quality is. We may have a temporary feeling which we call love, but which is almost akin to hate; it is not that extraordinary thing. Perhaps some of us may have this flowering, this nourishing, creative thing, but most of us are in a state of confusion and sorrow. Now, can one simply drop all this and be the other without going through the tremendous complications of trying to become something, without arguing about whether the perceiver is apart from the object perceived, and so on?

Comment: Again it will involve time.

KRISHNAMURTI: What will you do, sir?

Comment: Nothing.

KRISHNAMURTI: Sir, what is actually happening to you now? Either we talk theoretically, abstractly, in order to pass an afternoon discussing together, or else we really want to find out, to experience, and not just keep on everlastingly verbalizing. What is the actual response to this problem on the part of each one of us? If we can discuss, verbalize what is actually taking place in response to the problem, it will have significance, but merely to spin a lot of words, theories, is of no value.

Comment: This whole discussion is nothing but a verbal one.

KRISHNAMURTI: What does it mean to you? Leave the others alone. Please, sir, I am not attacking you; I am not pushing you into a corner, but when this problem is put to you, what is your response?

Comment: Being is being. It cannot be described by any words.

KRISHNAMURTI: I understand that, sir. But here is a very grave problem involving a complete revolution in thinking; it means scrapping all leaders, all gurus, all methods, does it not? And what happens when a problem of this kind is put to one?

That is, when we are aware that we hate, and we want to be free from hate, what do we generally do? We try to find a method of getting rid of it from a book, from a guru, and so on. Now, does one see that the practice of a method is an illusion, or does one say that a method is necessary? That is the first question, obviously. What do you feel, sir? Not that you are being compelled by me to say there must be no method; that would be another illusion, a mere repetition of

words, or a pose, which would have no meaning at all. But if you actually see that any practice of a method to get rid of hate is an illusion and therefore has no validity at all, then your looking at hate will have undergone a total transformation, will it not?

When we look at hate now, we say, "How am I to get rid of it?" But if we can look at hate without the "how," then we shall have quite a different reaction to that which we perceive. So we must know what our response is to this question. Do you understand, sir?

Please, would you kindly listen to find out first, and not ask how to get rid of hate. I am not concerned with how to get rid of it. That is a very trivial matter. The problem is this: Being aware that we hate, we now say, "How am I to get rid of it; what am I to do to be free of this venom?" The moment that reaction arises in us—how to be free—we have introduced several factors which have no validity at all. One of those factors is the process of gradually wearing down hate over a period of time; another is the making of effort to achieve a result; and still another is depending on somebody to tell us how to do it. These are all self-centered activities which are also a form of hate. I don't know if you are following all this.

So, does one still think in terms of how to get rid of hate? That is the issue—not how to be free, or what happens when one is free, but does one still think in terms of "how"?

Comment: Then the "how" is not so important.

KRISHNAMURTI: What is actually happening to you, sir? What really takes place when you are confronted with this question? If you are very honest with yourself, you will see that you are still thinking in terms of "how," which reveals that the mind still wants to achieve a state, does it not? And achievement is the process of time. A scientist who is experimenting to find something, for example, obviously needs time, but is hate to be dissolved through time? The yogis, the swamis, the Gita, the mahatmas—all of them say that hate is to be dissolved through time, but they may all be wrong, and probably they are. Why should they not be? And I want to find out if there is a different way of looking at this problem instead of accepting the traditional approach, which, I see, invariably degenerates into mediocrity. Merely to accept tradition is stupid. Even if ten thousand people say that something is true, it does not mean they are right. So my problem is: Is it possible to be free of hate now, not in the future?

Question: If one may ask a direct question, what is the purpose of your talks?

KRISHNAMURTI: What is the purpose of talking? To communicate, is it not? Otherwise one would not talk. Now, what is it that I am trying to communicate to you? I am trying to communicate to you the fact that a certain widely accepted way of thinking is illusory and has no basis at all. But to communicate, there must be someone to listen, someone who says, "I am really listening to you." Are you, sir, listening to me? Yes? And what do you mean by listening? I am not trying to corner you. Do you really ever listen to anything, or do you listen only partially? If your mind is still concerned with the "how," you are not listening. You can listen only when you give complete attention, and you are not giving complete attention as long as you are thinking that there must be a method because then your mind is not free to look at what is being said. There is complete attention only when one says, "He may be totally wrong, he may be talking nonsense, but at least I am going to find out what it is he is trying to convey." And are you doing

that? That is a very difficult thing in itself, is it not? Because to give complete attention is to know love; it is to have the total feeling that one is going to find out what another is saying, without acceptance or rejection—which does not mean that I am going to become your authority. Do you give attention in that way?

Question: Is it possible, sir?

KRISHNAMURTI: If it is not possible, there is no communication. That is the difficulty. Sir, look. If you are telling me something, and I want to find out what it is you are trying to convey, I must listen to you, must I not? I cannot be thinking to myself that you are talking the same old stuff, that you are this or that, or that it is time to go. I must pay complete attention to what you are saying and have no verbal or other barrier in my mind. Do we listen in that way?

Question: Is complete attention a state of mind different from the ordinary state of attention?

KRISHNAMURTI: You see, you are not listening at all to what I am talking about. You want to know what complete attention is. I can describe it, but what does that matter? The thing of first importance is, are you listening? You see how difficult it is for most of us really to inquire, to find out, to listen. Not that you must listen especially to me, because whether you listen to me or not does not matter to me; but since you have taken the trouble to come here, I say: For God's sake listen, not only to me, but to the working of the machinery of your own mind, which is now confronted with a problem. The problem is: Can hate be dissolved immediately? To find out how you respond to that question has validity. If you say, "Yes, I am listening," but your intention is to find a method to get rid of hate, then you are not looking at the problem because you are concerned only with the "how." But in psychological matters, is there ever a "how"? Do you follow, sirs? This is a very complex problem, so don't just say yes or no. In technical processes, in building, cooking, putting together the jet plane, washing dishes efficiently, and so on, there is a "how," and the more alert you are, the more efficient the "how" becomes; but in psychological matters, is there a "how" at all? Is there a gradual process of evolution, change, or only immediate transformation?

Question: Then what is to be done with the psychological problem?

KRISHNAMURTI: Sir, look at the problem. I shall have to stop now. You cannot absorb more than an hour of this kind of talk.

There is the problem of dying. We are all dying, and can the mind be in a state in which there is no death? It is essentially the same problem, only I am using a different set of words. The mind is aware that it is going to die, so it turns to various doctrines, to knowledge, to experiment; it believes in reincarnation, it reads the Upanishads, and so on, all of which is based on the desire to continue. And can I find out directly for myself if there is a state in which there is no death, and not depend on some bearded gentleman to tell me what there is after death? This is the same problem as being ambitious, violent, greedy, envious, and whether it is possible to drop all that completely—which means, really, finding out if one is pursuing a method.

Are you pursuing a method to help you to dissolve hate? Most of you have accepted as a fact that a method is necessary, and as I am now questioning the factual nature of that which you have accepted, you are resisting what I am saying. But if through questioning, through looking at the problem, you yourself are aware that the practice of a method is a total illusion, then your way of looking at hate will have undergone a tremendous change, and this perception of illusion obviously does not come about through effort.

Sirs, please, we are going to meet, I don't know how often, and instead of my lecturing, can't we for a change go into this matter as two human beings, as friends who are really listening to the problem and trying to find out what is true? We are not opposing each other, nor are you accepting what I say, because in this search there is no authority, there is no Master and *sishya,* no guru and all that nonsense. Here we are all equal because in trying to find out what is true there is real equality. Please, sirs, listen to what I am telling you. It is only when you are not seeking reality that there is this phony division of the Master and the disciple. Surely, where there is love, there is no inequality. There must be love when we seek, and we are not seeking when we treat another as a disciple or as a guru. For the inquiry into truth, there must be the cessation of all knowledge. Where there is love, there is equality, not the man who is high and the man who is low.

December 11, 1955

Second Talk at Rajghat

I would like, if I may, to discuss with you the problem of search, and what it is to be serious. What do we mean when we say we are seeking? So-called religious people are supposed to be seeking truth, God. What does that word signify? Not the dictionary meaning, but what is the inward nature of seeking, the psychological process of it? I think it would be significant if we could go into this matter very deeply; and may I again remind those who are here that through the description or verbal explanation they should actually experience what is being discussed; otherwise, it will have very little meaning. If you regard these talks merely as something to be taken down, just a new set of ideas to be added to your old set of ideas, they will have no value.

So, let us see if together we can go into this real problem of what it is to seek. Can anything new be found through search? Why do we seek, and what do we seek? What is the motive, the psychological process that makes us seek? On that depends what we find, surely. Why do I seek truth, happiness, peace, or something beyond all mentation? What is the impetus, the urge, that compels one to seek? Without understanding that urge, mere search will have very little meaning because what one is really seeking may be some kind of satisfaction, unrelated to reality. But if we can uncover the whole mechanism of this process of seeking, then perhaps we shall come to a point where there is no search at all, and it may be that that is the necessary state for anything new to take place.

As long as the mind is seeking, there must be endeavor, effort, which is invariably based on the action of will, and however refined, will is the outcome of desire. Will may be the outcome of many integrated desires, or of a single desire, and that will expresses itself through action, does it not? When you say you are seeking truth, behind all the meditation, the devotion, the discipline entailed in that search, there is surely this action of will, which is desire; and in pursuing the fulfillment of desire, in trying to arrive at a peaceful state of mind, to find God, truth, or to have this extraordinary state of creativity, seriousness comes in.

One may seek, but if there is no seriousness, one's search will be dissipated, sporadic, disconnected. Seriousness invariab-

ly goes with search, and it is apparently because you are serious that most of you are here. Sunday afternoon is a pleasant time to go boating, but instead you have gone to the trouble of coming here to listen, perhaps because you are serious. Being dissatisfied with traditional ideas and the accustomed point of view, you are seeking, and you hope by listening to find something new. If you were completely satisfied with what you have, you would not be here, so your presence at these talks indicates that you are dissatisfied; you are seeking something, and your search is obviously based on the desire to be satisfied at a deeper level. The satisfaction which you are seeking is nobler, more refined, but your search is still the pursuit of satisfaction.

That is, we want to find the total integration of our whole being because we have read or heard or imagined that that is the only state in which there is undisturbed happiness, lasting peace. So we become very serious; we read, search out philosophers, analysts, psychologists, yogis, in the hope of finding this integrated state; but the impetus, the drive, is still the desire to fulfill, to find some kind of satisfaction, a state of mind which will never be disturbed.

Now, if we are really to inquire into this matter, our inquiry must surely be based on negative thinking, which is the supreme form of thinking. We cannot inquire if our minds are tethered to any positive directive or formula. If we accept or assume anything, then all inquiry is useless. We can inquire, search, only when there is negative thinking, not thinking along any positive line. Most of us are convinced that positive thinking is necessary in order to find out what is true. By positive thinking I mean accepting the experience of others, or of oneself, without understanding the conditioned mind which thinks. After all, all our thinking is at present based on the background, on tradition, on experience, on the knowledge which we have accumulated. I think that is fairly clear. Knowledge gives a positive direction to our thinking, and in pursuing this positive direction, we hope to find that which is truth, God, or what you will; but what we actually find is based on experience and the process of recognition.

Surely, that which is new cannot be recognized. Recognition can only take place from memory, the accumulated experience which we call knowledge. If we recognize something, it is not new, and as long as our search is based on recognition, whatever we find has already been experienced; therefore, it comes from the background of memory. I recognize you because I have met you before. Something totally new cannot be recognized. God, truth, or whatever it is that results from the total integration of one's whole consciousness is not recognizable; it must be something totally new, and the very search for that state implies a process of recognition, does it not?

I don't think what I am talking about is as difficult as it sounds. It is really fairly simple. Most of us wish to find something— let us for the moment call it God or truth, whatever that may mean. How do we know what truth or God is? We know what it is either because we have read about it or experienced it, and when that experience comes, we are able to recognize it as truth or God. The recognizing of it can arise only from the background of previous knowledge, which means that what is recognized is not new; therefore, it is not truth, it is not God. It is what we think it is.

So, I am asking myself, and I hope you are asking yourself, what is this thing which we call search? I have explained what is implied in this whole problem of seeking. When we go from guru to guru, when we practice various disciplines, when we sacrifice, meditate, or train the mind in some way, the impetus behind all this effort is the urge to

find something, and what is found must be recognizable; otherwise, it cannot be found. So what the mind finds can only be the outcome of its own background, of its own conditioning; and if once the mind understands this fact, then search may not have this meaning at all; it may have a totally different significance. The mind may then stop seeking altogether—which does not mean that it accepts its conditioning, its travails, its miseries. After all, it is the mind itself that has created all the misery, and when the mind begins to understand its own process, then perhaps it is possible for that other state, whatever it be, to come into being without this everlasting effort to find.

Now, sirs, let us discuss this. Is this a problem to you, or am I imposing this problem on you? You must have observed how millions of people are seeking, each one following a particular guru or practicing a particular system of meditation; or else they go from teacher to teacher, joining one society, dropping it and going on to another, everlastingly seeking, seeking, seeking, which of course can also become a game. So perhaps you have asked yourself what it all means. You read the Upanishads or the Gita, or listen to a talk in which certain explanations are given, certain states described, and they all say, "Do this, abandon that, and you will discover the eternal." All of us are seeking in some degree, intensively or in a weak way, and I think it is important to find out what this search means. Can we very simply and directly ask ourselves, each one of us, whether we are seeking, and if we are seeking, what is the drive behind this search?

Comment: Dissatisfaction.

KRISHNAMURTI: Are you sure this is your own experience and not somebody else's? If it is your own experience that your search is based on the urge of dissatisfaction, then what do you do, sir?

Comment: We go from guru to guru until we find satisfaction. But even then we don't know what will happen in the future. Dissatisfaction is compelling us; it is the state in which we pass our lives.

KRISHNAMURTI: And as you grow older, you become more and more serious in this search, but you have never inquired if there is such a thing as satisfaction at all.

Comment: Man is always thirsty, and he wants to satisfy his thirst.

KRISHNAMURTI: Sir, if you were always thirsty after drinking, would you not find out whether thirst can ever be quenched? And if satisfaction is only momentary, then why give this enormous significance to gurus, sacrifices, disciplines, *sadhanas,* and all the rest of it? Why break yourselves up into sects and create conflict with your neighbors and in society for the sake of a passing comfort? Why get caught in Hinduism or Christianity if it is merely a temporary relief? You may say, ''I know all this gives only temporary relief, and I do not attach much significance to it.'' But do you really go to your guru and say that you have just come for a temporary relief? Must you not inquire into this? And can there be inquiry if one's heart is obstinate? The obstinacy of the heart prevents inquiry, does it not?

Let us begin with that. If I am obstinate in my way of thinking, which is called being positive, if my mind is committed to some form of conclusion, opinion, or judgment, can I inquire at all? You say no. We all agree, but are not our minds caught in some conclusion, in some experience? Therefore, inquiry is not only biased but impossible.

Sirs, can we really talk a little bit definitely about this, searching deeply in our own minds and thereby awakening self-knowledge? Can we find out if we are committed to some formula, to some conclusion or experience, to which the mind clings?

Comment: There is always a hope of finding the ultimate satisfaction.

KRISHNAMURTI: First let us see if our minds are committed to some experience, to some conclusion or belief, which makes us obstinate, unyielding, in the deep sense. I just want to begin with that because how can there be inquiry as long as the mind is incapable of yielding? We have read the Gita, the Bible, the Upanishads, this or that book, which has given a bias to the mind, a certain conclusion to which the mind is tethered. Can such a mind inquire? Is not that the case with most of us, and must not our minds be free of all commitments—as Hindus, Theosophists, Catholics, or whatever it be—before we can inquire? And why are we not free of all that? When we have commitments and then inquire, it is not inquiry; it is merely a repetition of opinions, judgments, conclusions. So, in talking this evening, can we drop these conclusions?

Surely, even the greatest scientists must drop all their knowledge before they can discover something new; and if you are serious, this dropping of knowledge, of belief, of experience, must actually take place. Most of us are somewhat serious in terms of our particular conclusions, but I don't consider that to be seriousness at all. It has no value. The serious man, surely, is he who is capable of dropping all his conclusions because he sees that, only then, is he in a position to inquire.

Comment: We may say we have dropped our conclusions, but they come up again.

KRISHNAMURTI: Do we know that our minds are anchored to a conclusion? Is the mind aware that it is held in a particular belief? Sir, let me put it very simply. My son dies and I am in sorrow, and I come across the belief in reincarnation. There is great hope and promise in that belief, so my mind holds on to it. Now, is such a mind capable of inquiring into the whole problem of death, and not just into the question of whether there is a hereafter? Can my mind drop that conclusion? And must not the mind drop it if it is to find out what is true—drop it, not through any form of compulsion or reward, but because the very inquiry demands that it be dropped? If one doesn't drop it, one is not serious.

Sirs and ladies, please don't feel frustrated by my questions, which seem so obvious. If my mind is tethered to the peg of belief, experience, or knowledge, it cannot go very far, and inquiry implies freedom from that peg, does it not? If I am really seeking, then this state of being tethered to a peg must end; there must be a breaking away, I must cut the rope. There is, then, never a question of how to cut the rope. When there is perception of the fact that inquiry is possible only when there is freedom from obstinacy, or from attachment to a belief, then that very perception liberates the mind.

Now, why does this not happen to each one of us?

Comment: One feels safer with the rope.

KRISHNAMURTI: That is so, is it not? You feel safer when the mind is conditioned, so there is no adventure, no daring, and the whole social structure is that way. I know all these answers, but why don't you drop your belief? If you don't, you are not serious. If you are really inquiring, you do not say, "I am seeking along a particular line, and I must be tolerant of any line which is different," be-

cause that whole way of thinking comes to an end. Then there is not this division of "your path" and "my path," the mystic and the occult, and all the stupid explanations of the man who wants to exploit are brushed aside.

Question: Is search itself brushed aside? Search for what?

KRISHNAMURTI: That is not our problem for the moment. I am saying that there is no inquiry when the mind is attached. Most of us say we are seeking, and to seek is really to inquire; and I am asking: Can you inquire as long as your mind is attached to any conclusion? Obviously, when the question is put to you, you say, "Of course not."

Question: Do you visualize the day when there will be no churches or temples of any kind? And as long as there are churches and temples, can people keep their minds untethered?

KRISHNAMURTI: The people are always you and I. We are talking about ourselves, not the people.

Question: But can we keep our minds untethered as long as there are churches?

KRISHNAMURTI: Why not, sir? May I say something? Forget the people, churches, and temples. I am asking: Is your mind bound? Is your mind obstinate, attached to some experience, to some form of knowledge or belief? If it is, then such a mind is incapable of inquiry. You may say, "I am seeking," but you are obviously not seeking, are you sir? How can the mind have freedom of movement if it is held? We say we are seeking, but there is really no seeking at all. Seeking implies freedom from attachment to any formula, to any experience, to any form of knowledge, for only then is the mind capable of moving extensively. This is a fact, is it not? If I want to go to Banaras, I can't be tied, held in a room; I must leave the room and go. Similarly, your mind is now held, and you say you are seeking; but I say you cannot seek or inquire as long as your mind is held—which is a fact which you all acknowledge. Then why does not the mind break away? If it does not, how can you and I inquire together? And that is our difficulty, is it not, sirs?

Comment: As long as the churches and temples are there, it is difficult to break away.

KRISHNAMURTI: Sir, who has created the churches and temples? Men like you and me.

Comment: They were unlike me, unlike us.

KRISHNAMURTI: You and I may not have created an outward temple, but we have our inward temples.

Comment: That is a very high conception. It is not possible for every ordinary human being to seek the inward self.

KRISHNAMURTI: We are not meeting each other, I am afraid. It is not a question of seeking the inward self. I am saying that there is no seeking at all when there is attachment to any formula, to any experience, to knowledge in any form. That is so obvious. If you think in terms of Catholicism, Protestantism, Buddhism, or Hinduism, your mind is obviously incapable of inquiry. When you see a fact of this kind, why is it so difficult for the mind to drop its attachment and begin to inquire? You are sitting

here listening, trying to find out, trying to inquire, and I say you cannot inquire if there is any form of attachment, that is, if the mind is in bondage to any conclusion, to any formula, to any kind of knowledge or experience. You agree that this is perfectly true, and yet you don't say, "I am going to drop all attachment"—which really indicates that you are not serious, does it not? You may talk of being serious, but I say that word has no value, no meaning, as long as your mind is tethered. You may get up at four o'clock and meditate, control your words, your gestures, do all the disciplinary things, thinking that you are very serious; but I say these are mere superficial observances. A serious mind is one which, being aware of its bondage, drops it and begins to inquire.

Question: What is the means of breaking one's attachment to a conclusion?

KRISHNAMURTI: Sir, is there a means? If there is, then you are attached to the means. (Laughter) I know, you laugh it away, but that is not merely a clever statement. Sirs, is not freedom implicit in inquiry? And that is why freedom is at the beginning, not at the end. When you say, "I must go through all this discipline in order to be free," it is like saying, "I will know sobriety through drunkenness." Surely, there can be inquiry only when there is freedom. So freedom must be at the beginning, and as long as it is not, though what you do may be socially and conventionally satisfying, it has no meaning. It has a certain value for people who are after a sense of security, but it has not the value of discovery. Though these people get up early and go through all the rigors of discipline, I say they are not serious. Seriousness lies in being aware that the mind is tethered to an experience, or a belief, and breaking away from it—which is what you don't want to do. So is it not important for you to inquire into this? Otherwise, you will come here day after day, year after year, and listen merely to words, which will have very little meaning.

Comment: You say freedom precedes inquiry, but we wish to inquire into freedom.

KRISHNAMURTI: Sir, how can you inquire if your mind is held? This is just ordinary reason, common sense. If your guru says, "This is the way," and you are held by that, how can you look beyond it? You go to the guru in order to inquire, and you get caught in his words; you are mesmerized by his personality; you become involved in all the things which he stands for. Your original impetus is to inquire, but that impetus is based on your desire for some kind of hope, satisfaction, and all the rest of it. So I say: To inquire there must first be freedom. You don't have to search for freedom. I am reversing your whole process of thinking, which is obviously false, even though the sacred books say otherwise.

Question: What will come after the inquiry?

KRISHNAMURTI: That is merely an intellectual question, if I may say so. Don't you see? You want to know what will happen "after," which is theoretical. The mind likes to spin words, to speculate. I say you will find out. It is like a prisoner saying, "What will it be like after I leave the prison?" To find out, he must leave the prison.

Question: Sir, we who are sitting in this hall are people of various cults, creeds, and beliefs, and we are listening to what you are saying, even though we do not really understand it. What you are saying is new to most of us; we have never heard it before, and while it sounds very nice to the ear, we cannot comprehend it. What is it that makes people sit quietly for an hour and listen earnestly to something which they cannot grapple with? Is this not in itself a form of inquiry, which means that the mind is not really tethered to a conclusion? If the mind were tethered to a conclusion, there would not be this wanting to find a different way of life, and these people would not come here, or they would just close their ears; yet they come and listen very intently. Does this not indicate a certain freedom to inquire?

KRISHNAMURTI: What is making you listen, sirs? What is making you listen to someone who says things which are entirely contrary to all that you believe and hold? Is it his personality, his reputation, the ballyhoo, the noise that is made around him? Is that what makes you listen? If it is, then your listening has very little meaning. So, what is it that is making you listen? Perhaps it is the fact that you are confronted with something which happens to be true, and in spite of your being tethered, you cannot help listening; yet you will go back to the conditioned state. Is that what is making you listen? Or are you really listening? Do you follow? Are you really listening, or is it that you have got into the habit of sitting quietly when somebody is talking because you like being lectured to?

These are not vain questions. I am really trying to find out why it is that when something true is said, there is no immediate response. That is the real question I am asking. You say, or I say, "There can be no inquiry without freedom," which is obviously true; it is a fact, regardless of who says it. Now, why does not that fact produce an immediate, trenchant action? Or has that fact a mysterious operation of its own which cannot be immediately expressed? Someone has stated the fact that for inquiry there must be freedom, freedom from being tethered, and you listen to that fact. However partially you listen, that fact has taken root in the mind because it has vitality; the seed is going to blossom, not within a certain period, but it is going to blossom, and that may be why it is important to listen to facts, whether you are listening willingly, consciously, or are only half-listening. But after all, that is the way of propaganda. They keep on repeating, "Buy such and such a soap," and eventually you buy it. Is that what is happening here? If you hear a certain fact being constantly repeated, and you presently act according to that fact, such action is entirely different from the action of the fact itself.

Sirs, we shall have to stop. I won't ask you to think it over because merely thinking it over has no meaning, but if you would really inquire into this whole problem of seeking and what it is to be serious, then the mind must find out how to inquire and what inquiry is. Any assumption, any conclusion, any attachment to knowledge or experience is an impediment to inquiry. As long as the mind is tethered to some conclusion, inquiry is an immense struggle, a process of effort, striving, breaking through; but if the mind sees the truth that there can be inquiry only when there is freedom, then inquiry has quite a different meaning altogether. If one realizes this, one is never a slave to any guru, to any formula, to any belief. Then you and I can pool our inquiry, and out of that we can co-operate, act, live. But as long as one's mind is tethered, there is "your way" and "my way," "your opinion" and "my opinion," "your path" and "my path," and all the many divisions and subdivisions which come between man and man.

December 18, 1955

Third Talk at Rajghat

I think it would be interesting and worthwhile if we could, this evening, go into the question of what makes the mind deteriorate. When we are young, we are full of zeal, we have so many enthusiastic and revolutionary ideas, but generally we get caught in some kind of activity and slowly peter out. We see this happening all around us and in ourselves; and is it possible to stop this process of deterioration, which is surely one of our major problems? Whether socialism or capitalism, the left or the right, should organize the world's welfare now that there is such immense production—I don't think that is the problem. I think the problem is much deeper, and it is this: Can the mind be freed so that it remains free all the time and is therefore not subject to deterioration?

I don't know if you have thought about this problem, or whether you have observed how the vitality, the vigor, the zest of our own minds slowly ebbs away, and the mind gradually becomes merely an instrument of mechanical habits and beliefs, a whole complex of routine and repetition. If we have thought about it at all, I think this must be a problem to most of us. As one grows older, the weight of the past, the burden of things remembered, the hopes, the frustrations, the fears—all this seems to enclose the mind, and there is never anything new out of it, but only a repetition, a sense of anxiety, a constant escape from itself and, ultimately, the desire to find some kind of release, some kind of peace, a God that will be completely satisfactory.

Now, if we could go into this matter, I think it might be worthwhile. Can the mind be freed from this whole process of deterioration and go beyond itself, not mysteriously or by some miracle, not tomorrow or at some future date, but immediately, instantly? To find that out may be the way of meditation. So why is it that our minds deteriorate? Why is it that there is in us nothing original, that all we know is mere repetition, that there is never a constancy of creativity? These are facts, are they not? What causes this deterioration, and can the mind put a stop to it? We shall discuss this presently, and I hope you will take part in the discussion.

To me, it is evident that there must be deterioration as long as there is effort, and one observes that our whole life is based on effort—effort to learn, to acquire, to hold, to be something, or to push aside what we are and become something else. There is always this struggle to be or to become, either conscious or unconscious, either voluntary or compelled by unknown desires; and is not this struggle the major cause of the mind's deterioration?

As I said, we are going to discuss all this after I have talked a little, so please don't just listen to words. We are trying to find out together why the wave of deterioration is always following us. I know there is the immediate problem of food, clothing, and shelter, but I think we must look at this problem from a different angle if we are to resolve it; and even those of us who have enough food, clothing, and shelter have another problem which is much deeper. One sees that there is in the world both complete tyranny and relative freedom; and if we were concerned only with the universal distribution of food and other products, then perhaps absolute tyranny might help. But in that process, the creative development of man would be destroyed, and if we are concerned with the whole of man, and not merely with the social or economic problem, then I think a far more basic question must inevitably arise. Why is there this process of deterioration, this incapacity to discover the new, not in the scientific realm, but within ourselves? Why is it that we are not creative?

If you observe what is happening, either here, in Europe, or America, I think you will see that most of us are imitating; we are complying with the past, with tradition, and as individuals we have never deeply, fundamentally discovered anything for ourselves. We live like machines, which brings a sense of unhappiness, does it not? I don't know if you have looked into it at all, but it seems to me that one of the major causes of this conformity is the desire to feel inwardly secure. To be psychologically secure, there must be exclusiveness, and to be exclusive, there must be effort, the effort to be something; and this may be one of the factors which is preventing the discovery of anything new on the part of each one of us. Can we discuss this? (Pause)

All right, sirs, let us put the problem differently. One can see that meditation is necessary because through meditation one discovers a great many things. Meditation opens the door to extraordinary experiences, both fanciful and real, and we are always inquiring how to meditate, are we not? Most of us read books which prescribe a system of meditation, or we look to some teacher to tell us how to meditate. Whereas, we are now trying to find out, not how to meditate, but what is meditation; and the very inquiry into what is meditation, is meditation. But our minds desire to know how to meditate, and therefore we invite deterioration.

If thought can inquire very deeply and expose itself to itself, never correcting but always watching to find out, never condemning but always probing, then that state of mind may be called meditation; and such a mind, because it is free, can discover. For such a mind there is no deterioration because there is no accumulation. But the mind that says, "Tell me how to be peaceful, tell me how to get there and I will try to follow it," is obviously imitative, without daring, and therefore it is inviting its own deterioration.

Most of us are concerned with the "how," which is a means of security, safety. However noble, however exacting, however disciplinary the "how" may be, and whatever it may promise, it can only lead to conformity. A conforming mind, through its own efforts, enslaves itself to a method, and therefore it loses this extraordinary capacity for discovery; and without the discovery in yourself of something original, new, uncontaminated, though you may have the most perfect organization to produce and distribute the physical necessities, you will still be like a machine. So this is your problem, is it not? Can the mind, which is so mechanical, habit-ridden, full of the past, free itself from the past and discover the new, call it God or what you will? Can we discuss this? (Pause)

Sirs, is this problem new to you, or is it that you have not thought about these things in this way? Let me again put the problem differently.

You are all well-versed in the Upanishads, the Gita, the Bible; you are familiar with the philosophy of Hinduism, of Christianity, of communism, and so on. These philosophies, these religions have obviously not solved man's problem. If you say, ''Man's problem is not solved because we have not strictly followed the injunctions of the Gita,'' the obvious answer is that any following of authority, however noble or tyrannical, makes the mind mechanical, unoriginal, like a gramophone record that repeats over and over again; and you cannot be happy in that state.

Now, being aware of that fact, how would you set about discovering the real for yourself? Do you understand, sirs? God, truth, or whatever it is, must be totally new, something outside of time, outside of memory, must it not? It cannot be something remembered from the past, something of which you have been told, or which the mind has conjectured, created. And how will you find it? It can be found, surely, only when the mind is free from the past, when the mind ceases to formulate any image, any symbol. When the mind formulates images, symbols, is that

not a factor of real deterioration? And that may be what is happening in India as well as in the rest of the world.

Am I explaining the problem? Or is it not a problem to you?

Comment: The mind cannot go beyond its own past experiences.

Comment: When the mind is conditioned . . .

KRISHNAMURTI: *Sir, this gentleman has asked a question.*

Question: Was it a question or a statement?

KRISHNAMURTI: He probably meant it as a question. Unfortunately, most of us are so occupied with the formulation of a question, or with our own way of looking at things, that we never really listen to each other. This gentleman has said that it is not possible for the mind to be free of the past. Is that not our problem as well as his?

Comment: If he wants to know how to be detached from the past, that is a question and not a statement.

KRISHNAMURTI: Sir, please, we are not here verbally to show off or to prove who is right and who is wrong. We are really trying to find out why the mind never discovers anything new. We are not for the moment referring to specialists like the scientists, the physicists, and so on, but to ourselves as common human beings. Why is it that we never discover in ourselves anything new?

Question: With regard to the question raised by that gentleman as to whether the mind can do away with the past, I would like to ask, what is meant by the past?

KRISHNAMURTI: The past is experience, memory, knowledge, the influence of tradition, the impression left by insult and praise, by the books you have read, by laughter and the sight of death. All that is the past, which is time.

Question: You say that the mind is conditioned by the past. But is the mind so rigidly conditioned by the past that it cannot make further inquiry?

KRISHNAMURTI: Sir, what is the mind? Please do not answer this question theoretically or according to what you have read in books. Can you and I here this evening find out what the mind is?

Comment: The mind is the result of the past.

KRISHNAMURTI: Is your mind the result of the past? What do you mean by the past?

Comment: Whatever is in my mind at present is all from the past.

KRISHNAMURTI: Can you separate the past from the mind? Please, let us examine the mind, not a theoretical mind, but the mind of each one of us. Your mind is the result of many influences, both collective and individual, is it not? Your mind is the outcome of education, of food, of climate, of many centuries of tradition; it is made up of your beliefs, desires, memories, the things that you have read, and so on. That is the mind, is it not, sir? The conscious mind which operates every day, and the mind which is deeper, hidden, are both the result of the past. As far as one can see, the whole area of the mind is the result of the past. You may believe that there is God, or that there is no God; you may think there is a higher and a lower self, and so on; but all that is the outcome of your education, conditioning, which means that your mind is the result of the past, does it not? And that same mind is trying to find something new; it says, "I must know what is God, what is truth." Is not that what you are doing, sirs and ladies? And I say it is impossible, it is a contradiction.

Comment: I think most people don't bother about God. We are concerned with life's problems.

KRISHNAMURTI: Which means that there is antagonism, bitterness, frustration, wanting power, position, prestige—because somebody else has what you want, you feel jealous, and so on. These are life's problems, are they not? Wanting to be loved, wanting more money, wanting to improve the village through this system or that system, having a belief or an ideal which is in contradiction with everyday existence and trying to bridge the gap between the fact and the ideal—all this is life.

Comment: Life is something more also. If I am a teacher, I want to teach better.

KRISHNAMURTI: Which is the same thing. These are all life's problems, and in tackling any one of them, you come to the main issue. You say that you want to teach better, to think better, to live a more integrated life, and so on. What do you mean by thinking better? Is it a process of acquiring more information? How do you find out what is better?

Comment: By thinking deeply.

KRISHNAMURTI: What does it mean to think deeply? And what do you mean by thinking? If you don't know what thinking is, you cannot think deeply. What is thinking? You, please, tell me what thinking is.

Comment: *Thinking is a process of bringing in more and more associations.*

KRISHNAMURTI: I am asking you what thinking is, and if you observe your own minds, you will find out how you are reacting to that question—which is thinking, is it not? Are you following what I am saying?

Comment: *This is too technical.*

KRISHNAMURTI: Just watch yourself and you will see. I am asking you a question. What is thinking?

Comment: *Whether you ask what is the mind or what is thinking, it comes to the same thing.*

KRISHNAMURTI: I want to find out what thinking is. Now, what is the process that is set going within you by this question?

Comment: *When we begin to look at thinking, the mind stops. There is no answer.*

Comment: *Thinking is so spontaneous that we don't know what it is.*

KRISHNAMURTI: I am asking you a question: What is thinking? Now, what does your mind do when this question is put to you? Don't you want to know how your mind operates? What happens when the mind is confronted with a question of this kind? For a moment the mind hesitates because it has probably never thought about it before; then it looks into the chamber of memory and says, "Let me see, the Upanishads say this, the Bible says that, Bertrand Russell says something else. And what do I think?" So you are looking for an answer from the past, are you not?

Comment: *We don't think of Bertrand Russell.*

KRISHNAMURTI: Perhaps not, but this is the actual operation of your mind when a question is put to you. If a question is put to you with which your mind is familiar, there is an immediate answer. If someone asks you where you live, you respond instantly because you are familiar with that; your association with it is constant. Whereas, if an unfamiliar question is put to you, your mind hesitates, and that hesitation indicates that you are looking for an answer, does it not? And where do you look for an answer? In your memory, obviously. So your thinking is the response of memory. No?

Question: *Does it mean that a person who has lost his memory cannot think?*

KRISHNAMURTI: Complete forgetfulness is called amnesia, and a person in that state has to learn the whole business over again.

Question: *Is having memory a good thing or a bad thing?*

KRISHNAMURTI: If you did not know where you live, what would you do? If you did not know the name of the street by which to go to your house, would that be good or bad? We are trying to find out, sir, what thinking is. For most of us, thinking is the response of memory, is it not? Because I know where I live, I respond quickly when asked, and when a more subtle question is put to me, I look in my memory to find an answer. But memory is the experience of centuries, so my response must inevitably be conditioned. Surely, this is fairly obvious.

Sir, if you are a Hindu, and I ask you whether there is such a thing as reincarnation, your instinctive response is to say that there is, and this response is based on the influence of your parents, your sacred books, and the general environment around you. You respond according to what you have been told; your thinking is the result of influence; therefore, it is obviously conditioned. Now we are asking ourselves: Can the mind dissociate itself from the past and find out what is true?

Question: You seem to describe the mind as a collection of past experiences, and I think we all agree; but now you are asking if it is possible for the mind to dissociate itself from all that. What does it mean?

KRISHNAMURTI: Are you asking me, or are you asking yourself?

Comment: I am asking myself as well as you.

KRISHNAMURTI: That is better. You are asking yourself, not me. The mind is the result of time, and can such a mind ever discover anything new, which must be timeless? Do you understand my question, sir? I see that my mind is made up of the past, yet it is the only instrument that can observe and discover. Then what is it to do? There is no other instrument of discovery, yet that instrument is the result of the past—which is a fact, and no amount of discussion or denial will have any influence on that fact. And can such a mind ever discover anything new? Or

will the known, which is the past, though I may be unconscious of it, always continue, so there can only be a continuity of the known in different forms? If the mind can never experience the unknown, whatever the unknown may be, then let us modify the known, let us embellish it, polish it up, accumulate more information, but keeping always within the area of the mind, of the known. Do you follow, sir? This assumption that the mind is in a helpless position, that it can never be out of its own area because it is the result of the known, may be the deteriorating factor. Do you follow what I mean? If you accept that, then obviously you must constantly polish the mind, put it in order, discipline it, stuff it with more information, and so on. Then you have no problem because you are living within the area of the known. But the moment you begin to inquire into the unknown, you have a problem, have you not, sir?

Comment: You started by asking what is thinking. It seems to me that thinking is always in relation to something; there is no such thing as pure thinking.

KRISHNAMURTI: Thinking is the response to challenge, is it not? There is no isolated thinking. It is only when there is a challenge that you respond. Even when you think in your bedroom, where there is no outward challenge, thinking is still the response to a challenge within yourself. There is this constant relationship of challenge and response, and because you respond according to your beliefs, your upbringing, and all the rest of it, your response is always restricted, narrow, petty.

Now, we are trying to find out where thinking ceases and something new, which is not thinking, takes place.

Comment: You are asking where thinking ends and meditation begins.

KRISHNAMURTI: All right, sir. Where does thinking end? Wait a minute. I am inquiring into what is thinking, and I say this very inquiry itself is meditation. It is not that there is first the ending of thinking, and then meditation begins. Please go with me, sirs and ladies, step by step. If I can find out what thinking is, then I will never ask how to meditate because in the very process of finding out what thinking is, there is meditation. But this means that I must give complete attention to the problem, and not merely concentrate on it, which is a form of distraction. I don't know if I am explaining myself.

In trying to find out what thinking is, I must give complete attention, in which there can be no effort, no friction, because in effort, friction, there is distraction. If I am really intent on finding out what thinking is, that very question brings an attention in which there is no deviation, no conflict, no feeling that I must pay attention.

So, what is thinking? Thinking, I see, is the response of memory, at whatever level, conscious or unconscious; it is always the reaction of that area of the mind which is the known, the past. The mind sees this as a fact. Then the mind asks itself if all thinking is merely verbal, symbolic, a reaction of the past; or is there thinking without words, without the past?

Now, is it possible to find out if there is any activity of the mind which is not contaminated by the past? Do you follow, sirs? I am inquiring; I am not assuming anything. The mind sees that it is the result of the past, and it is asking itself whether it is possible to be free of the past. If the mind answers one way or the other, if it says it is possible, or is not possible, then that assumption is the result of the past, is it not? Please go step by step with me, and you will see. The mind is aware that it is the result of the past; it is asking if it can free itself from the past, and it sees that any assumption that it can, or cannot, is the outcome of the past. So what is the state of the mind which has no association, which does not assume anything?

Comment: It is no longer the mind, the limited mind that we know.

KRISHNAMURTI: We have not come to that yet. I want to go slowly.

Question: The question is: Who is it that thinks?

KRISHNAMURTI: We know who thinks, sir. The mind has divided itself as the thinker and the thought, but it is still the mind, obviously. The whole process of the separation of the thinker from the thought is still within that area of the mind, which is the result of time, of the past; and the mind is now asking itself whether it can be free of the past.

Comment: Sir, if we who are listening to you doubt the truth of what you are saying, our old conditioning will continue. On the other hand, if we have faith in what you say, then our minds will again be conditioned by that.

KRISHNAMURTI: I am not asking you to have faith. I am just watching the operation of my own mind, and I hope you are doing the same thing. We are watching the operation of the mind and discovering its processes. That is all we are doing, which does not mean that you should or should not have faith. We are trying to find out how our minds operate, which is meditation.

Question: How does a scientist discover a new thing?

KRISHNAMURTI: If you and I were scientists, we could discuss that question; but we are not scientists, we are ordinary people, and we are trying to find out if the mind can ever discover something new. What is the process of it, sir?

We shall have to stop. May I just go into it a little bit?

I am watching the operation of my mind. That is all. There is challenge and response. The response is invariably according to the culture, the values, the tradition in which the mind has been brought up, and which for the moment we shall call its conditioning. The mind realizes this and is asking itself: Is all response the outcome of this conditioning, or is it possible for there to be a response beyond it? I don't say it is or is not possible. The mind is just asking itself. Any assumption on the part of the mind that it is possible or impossible is still a response of the back-ground. That is clear, is it not? So the mind can say only, "I don't know." That is the only right answer to this question as to whether the mind can free itself from the past.

Now, when you say, "I don't know," at what level, at what depth do you say it? Is it merely a verbal statement, or is it the totality of your being which says, "I don't know"? If your whole being genuinely says, "I don't know," it means that you are no longer referring to memory to find an answer. Is not the mind then free from the past? And is not this whole process of inquiry, meditation? Meditation is not a process of learning how to meditate; it is the very inquiry into what is meditation. To inquire into what is meditation, the mind must free itself from what it has learned about meditation, and the freeing of the mind from what it has learned is the beginning of meditation.

December 25, 1955

Madras, India, 1956

First Talk in Madras

It must be fairly obvious to each one of us when we look at the world, and especially at the conditions in this country, that there must be some kind of fundamental revolution. I am using that word to convey not a superficial, patchwork reformation, nor a revolution instigated as a calculated risk according to a particular pattern of thought, but the revolution that can come about only at the highest level, when we begin to understand the whole significance of the mind. Without understanding this fundamental issue, it seems to me that any reformation at any level, however beneficial temporarily, is bound to lead to further misery and chaos.

I think this point must be very clearly understood if there is to be any kind of relationship between the speaker and yourselves, because most of us are concerned with some kind of social reformation. There is an enormous amount of poverty, ignorance, fear, superstition, idolatry; there is the vain repetition of words, which is called prayer, and at the same time a vast accumulation of scientific knowledge as well as the so-called knowledge gathered from sacred books. One has not to go to many countries to see all this; it can be observed as one walks along the streets here or in Europe or America. The physical necessities may be plentiful in America, where materialism is

rampant and one can buy anything, but when one comes to this country, one sees this ruthless poverty. One sees also the class struggle—and I am not using that term "class struggle" in the communistic sense but merely to convey the observation of a fact without interpreting it in any way. One sees the division of religions—the Christian, the Hindu, the Muslim, the Buddhist—with their various sub-divisions, all clamoring to convert or to show a different way, a different path. The machine has made possible miracles of production, especially in America, but here in India everything is limited, short. In this country, though we mouth the word *God*, though we pray, perform rituals, and all the rest of it, we are just as materialistic as the West, only we have made poverty into a virtue, an inevitable necessity, and tolerate it.

Seeing this extraordinarily complex pattern of wealth and poverty, of sovereign governments, of armies and the latest instruments of mass destruction, one asks oneself what is going to come out of all this chaos, and where it is all going to lead. What is the answer? If one is at all serious, I think one must have asked oneself this question. How are we, as individuals and as groups, to tackle this problem? Being confused, most of us turn to some kind of pattern, religious or social; we look to some leader to guide us out of this chaos, or we insist on returning to the ancient traditions. We say, "Let us go back to what the *rishis* have taught us, which is all in the Upanishads, in the Gita; let us have more prayers, more rituals, more gurus, more Masters." This is actually what is happening, is it not?

There is in the world both extraordinary tyranny and relative freedom. Now, looking at this whole chaotic picture—not philosophically, not merely as an observer watching the events go by, but as one whose sympathies are stirred and who has a germ of compassion, which I am sure most of us have—how do you respond to it all? What is your responsibility to society? Or are you merely caught in the wheels of society, following the traditional pattern set by a particular culture, Western or Eastern, and are therefore blind to the whole issue? And if you do open your eyes, are you merely concerned with social reform, political action, economic adjustment? Does the solution to this enormously complex problem lie anywhere there, or does it lie in a totally different direction? Is the problem merely economic and social? Or is there chaos and the constant threat of war because most of us are not concerned at all with the deeper issues of life, with the total development of man? Is it our education that is at fault? Superficially, we are educated to have certain kinds of technique, which brings its own culture, and we seem to be satisfied with that.

Now, seeing this state of things—of which I am sure you are very much aware unless you are insensitive or are trying to block it off—what is your answer? Please do not answer theoretically, according to the communist, the capitalist, the Hindu, or some other pattern, which is merely an imposition and therefore not true, but instead strip the mind of all its immediate reactions, the so-called educated reactions, and find out what is your reaction as individuals. How would you solve this problem?

If you ask the communist this question, he has a very definite answer, and so has the Catholic or the orthodox Hindu or Muslim, but their answers are obviously conditioned. They have been educated to think along certain lines, narrow or wide, by a society or culture which is not at all concerned with the total development of the mind; and because they are responding from their conditioned thinking, their answers are inevitably in contradiction and must therefore always create enmity, which I think is again fairly obvious. If you are a Hindu, a Christian, or what you will, your response is bound to be according to your conditioned background, the culture in which you have been brought up. The problem is beyond all cultures, beyond any particular pattern, yet we are seeking an answer in terms of a particular pattern, and hence there is mounting confusion, greater misery. So unless there is a fundamental breaking away from all conditioning, a total cleavage, we shall obviously create more chaos, however well intentioned or so-called religious we may be.

It seems to me that the problem lies at a different level altogether, and in understanding it, I think, we shall bring about an action entirely different from that of the socialistic, the capitalistic, or the communistic pattern. To me, the problem is to understand the ways of the mind because unless one is able to observe and understand the process of thought in oneself, there is no freedom, and hence one cannot go very far. With most of us, the mind is not free; it is consciously or unconsciously tethered to some form of knowledge, to innumerable beliefs, experiences, dogmas; and how can such a mind be capable of discovery, of searching out something new?

To every challenge there must obviously be a new response because today the problem is entirely different from what it was yesterday. Any problem is always new; it is undergoing transformation all the time. Each challenge demands a new response, and there can be no new response if the mind is not free. So freedom is at the beginning, not just at the end. Revolution must begin, surely, not at the social, cultural, or economic level, but at the highest level; and the discovery of the highest level is the problem—the discovery of it, not the acceptance of what is said to be the highest level. I don't know if I am explaining myself clearly on this point. One can be told what is the highest level by some guru, some clever individual, and one can repeat what one has heard, but that process is not discovery; it is merely the acceptance of authority, and most of us accept authority because we are lazy. It has all been thought out, and we merely repeat it like a gramophone record.

Now, I see the necessity of discovery because it is obvious that we have to create a totally different kind of culture—a culture not based on authority but on the discovery by each individual of what is true, and that discovery demands complete freedom. If a mind is held, however long its tether, it can only function within a fixed radius, and therefore it is not free. So what is important is to discover the highest level at which revolution can take place, and that demands great clarity of thought; it demands a good mind—not a phony mind which is repetitive, but a mind that is capable of hard thinking, of reasoning to the end, clearly, logically, sanely. One must have such a mind, and only then is it possible to go beyond.

So revolution, it seems to me, can take place only at the highest level, which must be discovered; and you can discover it only through self-knowledge, not through the knowledge gathered from your ancient books or from the books of modern analysts. You must discover it in relationship—discover it, and not merely repeat something that you have read or heard. Then you will find that

the mind becomes extraordinarily clear. After all, the mind is the only instrument we have. If that mind is clogged, petty, fearful, as most of our minds are, its belief in God, its worship, its search for truth has no meaning at all. It is only the mind that is capable of clear perception, and therefore of being very quiet, that can discover whether there is truth or not, and it is only such a mind that can bring about revolution at the highest level. Only the religious mind is truly revolutionary, and the religious mind is not the mind that repeats, that goes to church or to the temple, that does puja every morning, that follows some kind of guru or worships an idol. Such a mind is not religious; it is really a silly, limited mind; therefore, it can never freely respond to challenge.

This self-knowledge is not to be learned from another. I cannot tell you what it is. But one can see how the mind operates, not just the mind that is active every day, but the totality of the mind, the mind that is conscious as well as hidden. All the many layers of the mind have to be perceived, investigated—which does not mean introspection. Self-analysis does not reveal the totality of the mind because there is always the division between the analyzer and the analyzed. But if you can observe the operation of your own mind without any sense of judgment, evaluation, without condemnation or comparison— just observe it as you would observe a star, dispassionately, quietly, without any sense of anxiety—then you will see that self-knowledge is not a matter of time, that it is not a process of delving into the unconscious to remove all the motives, or to understand the various impulses and compulsions. What creates time is comparison, surely, and because our minds are the result of time, they are always thinking in terms of the 'more', which we call progress.

So, being the result of time, the mind is always thinking in terms of growth, of achievement; and can the mind free itself from the 'more', which is really to dissociate itself completely from society? Society insists on the 'more'. After all, our culture is based on envy and acquisitiveness, it is not? Our acquisitiveness is not only in material things but also in the realm of so-called spirituality, where we want to have more virtue, to be nearer the Master, the guru. So the whole structure of our thinking is based on the 'more', and when one completely understands the demand for the 'more', with all its results, there is surely a complete dissociation from society; and only the individual who is completely dissociated from society can act upon society. The man who puts on a loincloth or a sannyasi's robe, who merely becomes a monk, is not dissociated from society; he is still part of society, only his demand for the 'more' is at another level. He is still conditioned by, and therefore caught within, the limits of a particular culture.

I think this is the real issue, and not how to produce more things and distribute what is produced. They now have the machines and the technique to produce all that is required by man, and soon there will probably be an equitable distribution of the physical necessities and a cessation of the class struggle, but the basic problem will still remain. The basic problem is that man is not creative; he has not discovered for himself this extraordinary source of creativity which is not an invention of the mind, and it is only when one discovers this timeless creativity that there is bliss.

Question: I have come here to learn and to be instructed. Can you teach me?

KRISHNAMURTI: It is really quite an interesting question, if we can go into it. What do we mean by learning? We learn a technique, we learn to be efficient in earning a livelihood or in performing some physical or mental task. We learn to calculate, to read, to speak a language, to build a bridge, and so on. Learning is finding out how to do things and developing the capacity to do them. Apart from that, is there any other kind of learning? Please do think this out with me.

When we talk about learning, we mean accumulation, do we not? And when there is any form of accumulation, can the mind learn? Learning is a necessity only in order to have capacity. I could not communicate if I did not speak a language, and to speak a language, I have to learn it, I have to store up in my mind the words and the meaning of those words, which is the cultivation of memory. Similarly, one learns how to build a road, to work a machine, to drive a motorcar, and so on.

Now, the questioner does not mean that; he is not here to find out how to drive a motorcar, or anything of that sort. He wants to be instructed, to learn how to discover that which may be called truth or God, does he not? When you go to a guru, to a religious teacher, in order to learn, what is it you are learning? He can teach you only a system, a pattern of what to think. And that is what you want from me. You want to learn a new pattern of behavior, conduct, or a new way of living, which is again the cultivation of memory in another form; and if you observe this process very clearly and closely, you will see that it actually prevents you from learning. It is really very simple.

You are all Hindus, or whatever it is you are, and when something new is put before you, what happens? Either you translate the new in terms of the old, and therefore it is no longer the new, or you reject it—and that is what is actually happening. So a mind that is accumulating, thinking in patterns, a mind that is full of so-called knowledge, that is out to learn a new way of thought or behavior—surely, such a mind can never learn.

And what is there to learn? Please follow this. What is there to learn? Are you going to learn about reincarnation, about God, about what truth is? When you say, "Instruct me, teach me, I am here to learn," what does it all mean? Is it possible to teach? Teach what? How to be aware? You know very well how to be aware. When you are interested, you are aware completely. When you want to make money as a lawyer, you are jolly well aware at the time. When you want to do something with deep, vital interest, your complete attention is there.

Attention is not something to be taught. You can be taught how to concentrate, but attention is not concentration. You see, the mind is always thinking in patterns: how to meditate, how to build a bridge, how to play cards, how to read faster, how to drive a motorcar, how to walk properly, or to have the right kind of diet. Similarly, you want to learn what is the way to God, to truth; you want somebody to show you the path which leads to that extraordinary state. Obviously, there is no path to that state because that state is not static, and any man who says there is a path to it is deceiving you. A path can exist only to that which is static, dead. There are not many paths to truth, nor is there only one path; there are no paths at all, and that is the beauty of it. But the mind rejects this fact because it wants to be secure, and it thinks of truth as the ultimate security; so it seeks a path by which to arrive at that security.

Now, if you see this whole process, then what is there to learn? And can you be free through learning? Please think it out with me, don't accept or reject it. This is your problem. Can a mind that is learning, accumulating, storing up, ever be free? And if the mind is never free, how can it find out, discover? And surely it is essential to discover because to discover, to find out, is the creative potential in man. So the mind must be free of all authority—the poisonous authority of so-called religion and the religious leaders—for only then is it capable of finding out what is truth, what is God, what is bliss.

Sirs, if you are really paying attention to what is being said and are not comparing it with what you have learned or worrying about how it will affect your commitments, your vested interests, your position in society, and all the rest of the silly nonsense, then you will see that there is freedom and discovery immediately.

Learning will not bring truth nearer. It is only the mind that is on a journey of everlasting discovery that is no longer accumulating, that is dead to everything it accumulated yesterday and is therefore fresh, innocent, free—it is only such a mind that can find out what is true and bring about a revolution in this world. It is only such a mind that is capable of love and compassion—not the mind that is practicing love and compassion, cultivating virtue according to a pattern, which is all self-concern.

I am afraid it is too late to answer another question.

If we understand what it is to pay attention, then perhaps this deep revolution will take place in spite of us. If each one of us can be purely attentive without wanting to bring about a result or to transform ourselves, then we shall see that the mind is not a thing of time. Time comes into being only when there is comparison, and the mind that is comparing is not attentive. Have you ever noticed how difficult it is to watch something, just to observe a quality, a person, an idea, a feeling, without any sense of denying, condemning, or justifying it? When the mind is capable of so observing, you will find that reaction has no meaning at all, and in that state of complete attention, the whole content of consciousness can be wiped away.

After all, the totality of our consciousness is the result of many influences: the influence of climate, of diet, of education, of race and religion, of what we read, of society, and the influence of our own intentions and desires. I hope you are listening to me with attention, not merely with memory, and are actually experiencing the fact that your consciousness is the result of many influences. These influences are man-made, and can the consciousness which is conditioned by them find something beyond itself, however much it may try? Obviously it cannot. It can project only its own state in a different form. So consciousness is conditioned, and anything that springs from that consciousness can never be free, and yet it is only the free mind that can discover.

Now, when you are aware that the process of thinking at any level, however deep or shallow, is conditioned, you realize that thinking is not the liberating factor, but you must think very clearly to see the limitation of thinking. Any thought springing from the conditioned mind is still conditioned. When the conditioned mind thinks about God, its God is itself. If the mind is totally aware of this and gives complete attention to it, then you will see there is freedom. Then the mind is no longer the plaything of society; it is no longer put together by man, and only then is it capable of experiencing something that is beyond itself.

January 11, 1956

Second Talk in Madras

If one observes the events of every day, I think it is fairly apparent that in the very attempt to solve the many problems with which we are beset, we only produce more problems; and it seems to me that as long as we do not understand the processes of thought, and are therefore unable to cleanse the mind, our problems will inevitably soar and multiply. Though each one may express it differently, every intelligent person is aware that the mind must be cleansed; and putting it very simply, the implication is that until the instrument with which man acts, which is the mind, is clear, dispassionate, free of the self with its innumerable prejudices and fears, both conscious and unconscious—until the mind is purged of all that, our problems will increase. We all know this, and every religion that is worth its salt asserts it in different ways, yet why is it that we never seem able to cleanse our minds? Is it that there are not enough systems, or that the true system has yet to be invented and applied? Or is it that no method or system can ever bring about this purification? Surely, all systems and methods breed tradition, which brings mediocrity of mind; and a mediocre mind, facing a great problem, will inevitably translate that problem in terms of its own conditioning.

That is, to tackle any main issue in human affairs, we see the necessity of a mind that is clear, purged of all its prejudices, and in order to cleanse the mind, we say we must have a system, a method, a practice; but if one is at all alert, one sees that in the very practicing of a system, the mind gets caught in the system, and therefore it is not free, it is not purged, it is not cleansed. Being caught in a system, the mind translates or responds to the challenge according to that conditioning. This is again fairly obvious if you go into it.

We have many problems at all levels of our existence, and to respond to these problems, the mind must be fresh, eager, alert. In order to produce that clear, fresh, innocent mind, we say the practice of a system is necessary; but we see that in the very practice of a system, the mind gets warped, limited, twisted. So it is very clear that systems do not free the mind, and I think this fact must be thoroughly understood before we can go further into what I want to discuss this evening.

Most of us think that a method, a system, a practice, is going to free the mind or help the mind to think clearly. But does a system of any kind help the mind to think very clearly, without bias, without the center of the 'me', the self? Does not the practice of a system encourage the self? Though the system is supposed to help you to get rid of the self, the 'me', the ego, or whatever term one may use for that self-centered activity of the mind, does not the very practice of a system accentuate self-centeredness, only along a different line?

So the mind can never be made free by a system. Yet most minds are caught in a system, which is the way of tradition, and it invariably breeds mediocrity. That is what has happened to almost all of us, is it not? Functioning in habits, in tradition, ancient or modern, which we call knowledge, the mind is confronted with an immense problem, a problem which is always changing. Whether it is personal or impersonal, collective or individual, no problem is static. But the mind is static because it is caught in a groove of tradition, of habits; it is addicted to a certain way of thinking, so there is always a contradiction between the static condition of the mind and the problem which is constantly changing, moving. Such a mind is incapable of meeting and resolving the problem—which I think is fairly obvious.

After all, you are meeting problems as a Hindu, that is, with the tradition of Hindu culture, just as the Catholic or the communist meets any issue according to his particular conditioning. Yet most of us agree that the mind must be cleansed, purified, in order to meet life, to find God, truth, or what you will.

Now, desiring to meet that challenge, to discover that new thing, we say the mind must be purified through the practice of a

system; and yet when we look at it very closely, we see that a system cripples the mind—it does not set the mind free. So what is one to do? This is a problem we are all facing, is it not? The challenge, which is the world as it is today, is totally new, with new demands, and we cannot possibly respond to the new with the deteriorating traditions, ideas, memories, and knowledge of the old. One sees that in the very practice of a method, the mind is crippled, that in the very process of cultivating virtue, the self becomes strengthened. There must be virtue because virtue brings order, yet virtue that is cultivated, practiced day after day, ceases to be virtue. Seeing this, what is the mind to do?

One can see very well that to meet the challenge, to meet this extraordinary world with its multiplying sorrows, with its vast contradictions and frustrations, the mind must be made new, fresh, pure, innocent; and how is this state of the mind to be brought about? Can time do it? That is, by pursuing the ideal of purity, innocence, clarity, can the mind which is dull, stupid, mediocre, achieve that other state through time? Can *what is* be transformed into 'what should be' through the pursuit of the ideal? When the mind says, "I am here, and it will take time to reach the ideal state, which is over there," what has the mind done? It has invented the ideal apart from the fact, and then time is necessary to bridge the distance between them—at least that is what we say. So we have convenient theories concerning the inevitability of time: evolution, development through growth, and so on. But if you look very closely into the notion that time is a means of achieving the ideal, you will find that it is born of an extremely lazy and subtle attitude of postponement.

From childhood we are raised on this concept of the ideal, the example, the ultimate perfection, for the achievement of which we say time is necessary. But will time dissolve the self-centered activity of the 'me', of the self, which is the cause of all mischief, of all misery? Time implies practice, progress towards something which should be, but that something is the projection of a mind caught in its own misery, in its own conditioning. So the ideal, the 'what should be', is the outcome of a conditioned mind; it is the projection of a mind which is in sorrow, which is ignorant, which is full of self-centered activity; therefore, the ideal contains the seed of the present, and if you look into it very carefully, consider it deeply, you will see that time does not bring about the purgation of the self. Then what is the mind to do?

Do you understand? No system will solve this problem. Even if you were to practice a system for a thousand years, the self would remain because the very practice of a system strengthens the self. Nor will the ideal ever solve this problem because the ideal demands time in which to progress from *what is,* which is the fact, to 'what should be'; and this pursuit of 'what should be' interferes with the understanding of *what is.* The *what is* can be understood only when the mind is completely free from the ideal, from the idea of progress through time. Yet these are the only two means you have, are they not? You use the ideal as a lever to get rid of *what is,* or you practice a system, which inevitably breeds mediocrity; and the mediocre mind cannot possibly respond to a challenge that is extraordinarily dynamic, that demands your complete attention. So what is the mind to do?

I don't know if you have thought of this matter at all. We have problems at every level of our existence, economic, social, emotional, intellectual, and we have always approached these problems with a traditional or idealistic point of view. We meet facts with theories, and one can see very well that a mind which is caught in formulations, in

conclusions, which spins a theory about a fact, cannot possibly understand the fact. There is always conflict between the fact and the theory; and our meditation, our sacrifice, our practice, which is the cultivation of virtue, can never solve the problem because to cultivate virtue is to strengthen the 'me'. The 'me' becomes respectable, that is all. Seeing this, what is the mind to do?

Perhaps this evening we should experiment with something. So far you have followed what I have said, which is fairly clear, and I don't think you will disagree. There is nothing with which to agree or disagree because these are facts. If you disagree, you are merely denying a fact, and however much you may deny a fact, the fact exists. The difficulty is that most of us are caught in tradition—tradition as inherited or acquired knowledge, experience—and with such a mind we are approaching a fact, denying or translating it according to our conditioning. That is what is actually taking place within each one of us, at different levels and with different degrees of intensity.

As I was saying, can we try something this evening, which is to listen, not with memory, not with tradition, not with the intention of getting something through listening, but with complete attention? If one is capable of listening in that way, there is immediate transformation—whether for a long or a short time is unimportant. The duration is unimportant, but what is important is the capacity to listen with complete attention. If the mind can remove all the traditions, the opinions, the evaluations, the comparisons, and just listen to what is being said, out of that complete attention you will find that you will be able to tackle any problem because in that attention there is no problem. The problem is created by inattention. Attention is the good, but the good cannot be cultivated by the mind—the mind that is conditioned by tradition, by environment, by every kind of influence. What matters is to have the capacity of attention without interpretation or evaluation, but you cannot possibly practice this attention. If you do, you reduce it again to mediocrity; it becomes mere tradition. But if the mind can face the problem with complete attention, then you will find that the problem has ceased because then the mind is a totally different entity; it is no longer the product of time, and such a mind is capable of receiving that which is eternal.

The difficulty with most of us is that we never give our complete attention to anything, even when we are interested. When we are interested in something, it absorbs us, as the toy absorbs the child, and absorption is not attention. But if you can listen completely without interpretation, without comparison, without evaluation, which is to give your whole attention, then all tradition is transcended and the mind is extraordinarily clear, innocent, pure; and such a mind is capable of resolving the problems of life.

Question: Gandhiji had recourse to fasting as a means of changing the hearts of others. His example is being followed by some leaders in India who look upon fasting as a means of purifying themselves and also the society around them. Can self-invited suffering be purifying, and is there vicarious purification?

KRISHNAMURTI: Without accepting or denying anything, let us investigate the matter. It is said that suffering is necessary as a means of purifying the mind. Whole philosophies and religions are built on this idea that someone suffers for you and purifies you. Can that be done? And what do we mean by suffering? There is the suffering caused by starvation, decay, disease, physical deterioration. A society based on acquisitiveness and envy must inevitably create physical suffering: those who have, and those who

have not. That is all very clear. Then there is psychological suffering. If I love you, and you don't love me, I suffer. If I am ambitious, if I want to fulfill myself through having a prominent position, and something happens which prevents me, I am frustrated and I suffer. We say suffering is an inevitable process, and we accept it; we never question it, we never ask if it is necessary to suffer psychologically.

And can I suffer for the good of another? Can I change society through my example? When there is an example, what happens? Authority is established; the following of authority breeds fear, and fear breeds the mediocrity of a shallow mind. We are brought up on this idea that the example, the hero, the saint, the leader, the guru, is necessary; so we become followers without any initiative, gramophone records repeating the same old pattern. When we merely follow, we lose all sense of individuality, the fullness of understanding as individuals, and obviously that does not solve our problems.

Besides, if you must fast, why must you fast in public? Why this ballyhoo, this noise, this publicity, this beating of the drum? Because you want to impress people, and people are easily impressed. And then what? Have they changed? Is your intention in fasting to impress people, or to discover your own state of mind? If you are trying to impress people, then it has very little meaning; it is merely political, and therein lies exploitation.

But if your intention is to bring about self-purification and understanding, then is fasting necessary? What is necessary is an acuteness, a clarity of mind, not at certain periods of the year, but at every moment, which is to be fully aware in your relationships; and it is this awareness that reveals to you what you are. A heavy stomach obviously makes a dull mind, but a dull mind is also a mind which practices a system in order to be clear. The mind is obviously made dull through the practice of virtue, and yet we think suffering, fasting, examples, are necessary to bring a change in society. Surely, example breeds authority, however noble, stupid, or historical it may be; and when there is the tyranny of example, the mind is merely conforming to a pattern. The pattern may be wide or narrow, but it is still a pattern, a frame, and the mind that follows a pattern is inevitably very shallow.

Conformity is obviously a curse. Through conformity can the mind be free? Must the mind be made slavish in order to be free, or must freedom exist from the very beginning? Freedom is not a thing to be gained as a reward at the end of life; it is not the goal of life because a mind that is incapable of being free now can never discover what is true.

Society is not changed by example. Society may reform itself; it may bring about certain changes through political or economic revolution, but only the religious man can create a fundamental transformation in society, and the religious man is not he who practices starvation as an example to impress society. The religious man is not concerned with society at all because society is based on acquisitiveness, envy, greed, ambition, fear. That is, mere reformation of the pattern of society only alters the surface; it brings about a more respectable form of ambition. Whereas, the truly religious man is totally outside of society because he is not ambitious, he has no envy, he is not following any ritual, dogma, or belief; and it is only such a man who can fundamentally transform society, not the reformer. The man who sets out to be an example merely breeds conflict, strengthens fear, and brings about various forms of tyranny.

It is very strange how we worship examples, idols. We don't want that which is pure, true in itself; we want interpreters, ex-

amples, Masters, gurus, as a medium through which to attain something—which is all sheer nonsense and is used to exploit people. If each one of us could think clearly from the very beginning, or reeducate ourselves to think clearly, then all these examples, Masters, gurus, systems would be absolutely unnecessary, which they are anyhow.

You see, the world is unfortunately too much for most of us; our circumstances are too heavy; our families, our country, our leaders, our jobs pin us down, hold us on the wheel, and we hope vaguely somehow to find happiness. But this happiness does not come vaguely; it does not come if you are pinned down by society, if you are a slave to environment. It comes only when there is freedom of the mind—which is not freedom of thought. Thought is never free, but the mind can be free, and that freedom comes, not through going into the many layers of the unconscious, analyzing the memory of incidents and experiences, but only when there is complete attention. In the process of self-analysis, there must always be the analyzer; but the analyzer is part of the analyzed, as the thinker is part of the thought, and if you don't understand the central issue, you will only increase the problems and bring about further misery.

The mind cannot be made clear, pure, innocent, through any method, through any discipline, through the practice of any virtue. Virtue is essential, but a cultivated virtue is not virtue. Suffering obviously has to be understood. As long as there is the self, the 'me', the ego, there must be suffering. Man avoids that suffering, but in the very avoidance of it he strengthens the ego, and all his social activities, his reforms, only create further mischief, further sorrow. Again, this is obvious if you are at all thoughtful.

So, there must be an action totally dissociated from society, a way of thinking that is not contaminated by society, and only then is there a possibility of real revolution—which is not this superficial revolution at merely one level, economic, social, or any other. A total revolution must take place in man himself, and it is only such a mind that can resolve the mounting problems of society.

Now, you have listened to all this, either agreeing or disagreeing, but as I said, there is nothing with which to agree or disagree. These are facts, and knowing these facts, what are you going to do? Surely, that is very important to find out. Will you return to the society of which you are a prisoner, or have you listened with complete attention? If you listen with complete attention, then that very attention brings its own action; you don't have to do anything. It is like love. Love, and it will act; but without love, do what you will—practice, discipline, reform—the heart can never be clear. And that is what is happening in the world. We have examples, disciplines, marvelous techniques, yet our hearts are empty because they are filled with the things of the mind; and when our hearts are empty, our solutions to the many problems are also empty. Only the mind that is capable of complete attention knows how to love, because that attention is the absence of the self.

January 15, 1956

Third Talk in Madras

One of our great problems, I should think, is what to do, what kind of action to take in this civilization which is so confused, so contradictory, so demanding. Most of us are educated for one thing and really want to do something else. The governments want efficient soldiers and bureaucrats, and parents desire that their children should fit into society and earn a livelihood, and that is more or less the pattern followed throughout the world. The individual's occupation is very largely determined by his education and the demands of the society about him.

If you don't mind, I am going to discuss a rather complicated problem this evening, and if you will be good enough to pay a little attention, I think you will find that an action comes into being which is not cultivated or shaped by a particular culture; and that action may be the solution to the complicated problem of our existence.

Naturally we are all concerned with action, with what to do, and the "what to do" is generally dictated by the world about us. That is, we know that we have to earn a livelihood in some capacity, either as an engineer, a scientist, a lawyer, a clerk, or what you will; and our superficial culture, our education, is restricted to that. Our minds are occupied most of the day with how to earn a livelihood, how to conform to the pattern of a particular society. Our so-called education is limited to the cultivation of skills and the memorizing of a series of facts which will help us to pass some examination and get a particular job, so our action settles at that level; it is shaped according to the necessities of a particular society, a society that is preparing for war. Industrialization demands more scientists, more physicists, more engineers, so this particular layer of the mind is cultivated, and that is what society is chiefly concerned with.

Actually, if you examine it, that is what most of us are concerned with: to adapt ourselves to the demands of society. So there is a contradiction in our life between the so-called educated layer of the mind and the deep, unconscious occupation, a contradiction of which very few of us are aware; and if we are aware of this contradiction, we are merely seeking some kind of satisfaction, some kind of easy solution for the misery of having to earn a livelihood in a particular profession while inwardly wanting to be or to do something else. This is what is actually happening in our life, whether we are aware of it or not. Any action born of the superficial, educated layer of the mind is obviously an incomplete action, and such a partial action is always in contradiction with the total action of man. I think this is fairly clear.

That is, one is educated as a clerk, as a lawyer, or for some other profession, and society is concerned only with that. The government and industry demand scientists, physicists, engineers, to prepare for war, to increase production, and so on. So one is educated for a profession, but the totality of one's being is undiscovered, unrevealed, and hence man is always in conflict within himself. I think this is very clear if we observe the social and political activities and the religious pursuits of man. Most of us do something in daily life which is contradictory to everything that we feel we really want to do. We have responsibilities which bind us and from which we want to escape, and the escape takes the form of speculation, theories about God, religious rites, and so on. There are innumerable forms of escape, including drink, but none of them resolve this inner conflict. So what is one to do?

I do not know if you have ever put that question to yourself. Any action born of this inner contradiction is bound to create more mischief and misery. That is what the politicians are doing in the world. However wise a politician may be, he must inevitably create mischief unless he understands the total occupation of the mind and brings about an action out of the comprehension of that totality. And this is what I want to discuss: whether an action can come into being which is not the action of mere influence and motive.

Please follow this a little bit. Action born of influence is restricted. Our minds are the result of innumerable and contradictory influences, and any action born of that con-

tradictory state must also be contradictory; and a culture, a society which is based on this contradiction must create endless conflict and misery. This again is fairly obvious; it is a historical fact whether you like it or not. We can see that while the mind is occupied on the surface with daily living, below that, there are innumerable motives of satisfaction, of greed, of envy, the compulsions of passion, fear, and so on, with which the mind is also occupied, though one may not be conscious of it. And can the mind go still below that?

To put it differently, with what is the mind occupied? Please, not my mind, but your mind. Do you know what your mind is occupied with? It is obviously occupied during the day, when you are busy at the office, with the routine of your work. Below that superficial occupation of the mind, there is another kind of occupation going on, which may be self-protection, security, ambition, and so on, and which is generally in contradiction with the other occupation.

To make this talk worthwhile and significant, may I suggest that you listen to observe and discover how your own mind is occupied. I want to go into the problem of occupation because I feel if we can understand this whole question of the mind's occupation, out of that understanding an action will come which is true action, an action which is not born of will, of discipline, and is therefore not contradictory. Am I making myself clear?

That is, unless you understand the totality of your occupation, there cannot be an integrated action. Your mind is superficially occupied during the day with the pursuit of your job and similar activities, but it is also occupied at other levels, in other directions. So there is a contradiction between these two layers of the mind, and we try to overcome the contradiction through discipline, through conformity, through various forms of adjustment based on fear; therefore, action always remains contradictory, which is what is happening with all of us. What to do is not the problem at all because when you ask what to do, the answer is inevitably according to the layers of your occupation and will only create further contradiction.

Now, what is your mind occupied with? Please follow this. Do you know what your mind is occupied with every day? You know very well that it is occupied with daily activities. Below that, what else is it occupied with? Are you aware of that deeper occupation? If you are, then you will see that it is in contradiction with the daily pursuits, and either the mind manages somehow to conform, to adjust itself to the daily pursuits or the contradiction is so total that there is a perpetual conflict going on, which leads to all kinds of diseases.

Now, sirs, from where should action take place? I want to do things in the world; I have to earn a livelihood, and I must work hard, or I want to paint, to write, to think, or be a religious entity. I want to work in some way, and there must be action. From what source, from what center, should this action spring? That is the problem. I see that action springing from any layer of occupation is bound to create contradiction, misery. There is no difference between the action of a housewife, the action of a lawyer, and the action of the mind which is pursuing God. Socially they may be different, but in reality there is no difference because the housewife, the lawyer, and the man who pursues God are all occupied. One occupation may be socially better than another, but fundamentally all occupation is more or less the same; there is no "better" occupation.

So, from where should action take place? From what center will action not be contradictory, not lead to mischief, misery, and corruption? Can there be action from a true source, which is not the action of occupation? Am I making my point clear? Probably not. As I said, it is a very complex problem, and I hope I am not making it too complicated.

Let me put the issue differently. Your minds are occupied, are they not? That is fairly obvious. Now, why is the mind occupied? And what would happen if the mind were not occupied? What would happen to a woman if she were not occupied with the kitchen, or to a man if he were not occupied with business? What would happen to you if your mind were not occupied with these things? The immediate response is to say with what one would be occupied if one were not occupied with one's present activities—which indicates the demand for occupation. A mind which is not occupied feels lost, so the mind is always seeking occupation. Its occupation is invariably contradictory, which creates mischief, and after creating the mischief, we are concerned with how to remove the mischief; we are never concerned with the occupation of the mind. But if we can understand the occupation of the mind at different levels, then we shall discover the action which comes when the mind is not occupied, and which does not create mischief.

Have you ever tried to find out why the mind is occupied? Try it now, sirs, if only for the fun of it. But first you must be aware that your mind is occupied—which is obvious. You are occupied with your business, with your promotion or failure, with how your wife quarrels with you, or you quarrel with her, and so on; and there is the occupation of a sannyasi, of the so-called religious man, who is always reading, muttering words, chanting, who is caught in the repetition of rituals, who keeps busy disciplining himself, conforming to the pattern of an ideal. All that is occupation.

We are all occupied, are we not? Why? Why is the mind occupied? Is it the nature of the mind to be occupied? If it is the nature of the mind to be occupied, whether with the high or with the low, which are relative, then such a mind can never find true action. The mind can observe, attend, discover, not when it is constantly busy, but only when it is capable of not being occupied. As long as the mind is occupied, any action born of that occupation must be restrictive, limiting, confusing. Try it and you will see how extraordinarily subtle and difficult it is to have a mind which is not everlastingly full, yet if there is the urgency to find out what is right action in this mad, confused, and suffering world, you have to come to this point.

Our problem is, then: From what source, from what center must action arise if it is not to be contradictory and confusing? The social reformer does not ask this question because he wants to act, to reform—and in the very process of reformation, he is creating mischief. All politicians and religious leaders are doing this. No amount of reading scriptures, of conforming, adjusting to society, has ever solved our problems; on the contrary, they are multiplying. Seeing all this, we have to understand why this confused and sorrowful state has come into being. It has come into being because we all want immediate action, and immediate action can be found only in the superficial layers of our consciousness; it comes out of occupation, out of the so-called educated mind.

Now, is there an action which is not the result of effort, which is not the action of will? The action of will is the action of desire, and desire, whether educated or uneducated, restrained or free, is limited to the contradictory layers of consciousness. Have you not noticed, sirs, that when you want to do one particular thing, immediately there is a contradiction in the form of restrictive fears, demands, examples, a sense of discipline which says, "Don't do that"? And so you are caught in conflict. Right through life we are caught in this way; from childhood

until we die there is this everlasting contradiction and conformity. Seeing this, can the mind discover an action which is not contradictory, which is not mere conformity, which is not the product of influence? I think that is the fundamental issue, the right question, and one can find such action only when one is aware of and understands the total occupation of the mind.

Do you know what your mind is occupied with? Go layer by layer, and you will discover that there is no space anywhere in the mind which is not occupied. And when you do inquire into the unconscious to discover what its occupation is, even then the superficial mind, which is examining the unconscious, has its own occupation. So what is one to do? One wants to find out the total occupation of the mind because one sees that without being aware of the total occupation of the mind, any action is bound to create contradiction and therefore greater misery.

Now, what is the mind, your mind, occupied with? And if it were not occupied, what would happen? Would you not be frightened to discover that your mind is not occupied at all? Therefore, there would be an immediate urge to be occupied with something. Try it, and you will find out that there is never a moment when the mind is not occupied; and if you do experience a rare moment when the mind is not occupied, which is an extraordinary state, then how to get back to or to retain that state becomes your new occupation.

So, I am suggesting that true action can come only when the mind has understood the totality of its occupation, conscious as well as unconscious, and knows the moment of not being occupied. You will find that action from those moments when the mind is not occupied is the only integrated action. When it is not occupied, the mind is uncontaminated by society; it is not the product of innumerable influences; it is neither Hindu nor Christian, neither communist nor capitalist; therefore, it is itself a totality of action which you do not have to be occupied with or think about.

Now, if you have been good enough to listen to all this attentively, if you have not been asleep but have listened with complete attention, then you will have experienced immediately the state of not being occupied. As one speaks or listens, one is aware of the various layers of occupation and of how contradictory they are, and being aware of the total contradictory nature of consciousness, the mind discovers a state in which it is not occupied. This brings a totally different sense of action. Then you have to do nothing, for the mind itself will act.

Question: There is deep discontent in me, and I am in search of something to allay this discontent. Teachers like Shankara and Ramanuja have recommended surrender to God. They have also recommended the cultivation of virtue and following the example of our teachers. You seem to consider this futile. Will you kindly explain.

KRISHNAMURTI: Why are we discontented, and what is wrong with discontent? Obviously we are discontented because, to put it very simply, we want to be something. If I am a good painter, I paint in order to be better known; if I write a poem, I am dissatisfied because it is not good enough, so I struggle to improve. If I am a so-called religious person, there too I want to be something. I follow the example of the various saints, and I want to have as good a reputation as they have. From childhood I have been told I must be as good as or better than somebody else. I have been brought up in comparison, competition, ambition, so my whole life is burdened with discontent. After all, discontent is envy, and our culture, religious and social, is based on envy. We are encouraged to be something for the sake of God. On the one hand, discontent is stimulated, and on the other, we try to find ways and means to overcome that discontent. Being discontented economically, socially, we turn to religious examples to find satisfaction; we meditate, practice disciplines in order to have no discontentment and to be at peace. This is what is happening with all of you, and I say it is a futile business—it has no meaning at all. To follow, to imitate, to have authority in religious matters is evil, just as it is evil to have tyranny in government because then the individual is completely lost.

At present you are not individuals; you are merely imitative machines, the product of a particular culture, of a particular education. You are the collective, not the individual—which is again fairly obvious. You are all Hindus or Christians, this or that, with certain dogmas, beliefs, which means that you are the product of the mass; therefore, you are not individuals. You must be totally discontented to find out, but society does not want you to be discontented because then you would be vital, you would begin to inquire, to search, to discover, and therefore you would be dangerous.

Unfortunately, discontent with most of you is based on the demand for satisfaction, and the moment you are satisfied, your discontent goes. Then you wither and decay. Have you not observed how people who are discontented when they are young lose their discontent the moment they have a good job? Give the communist a good job, and it is all over. It is the same with religious people. Don't laugh, it is the same with you. You want to find the right Master, guru, the right discipline—which is a cage that will smother you, destroy you, and this destruction is called the search for truth. That is, you want to be permanently satisfied so that you will have no disturbance, no discontent, no sense of inquiry. That is what has actually happened, and the more ancient the culture, the more destructive it is because tradition invariably breeds mediocrity.

So we see that discontent, as we know it now, is merely the desire to find permanent satisfaction. And is there such a thing as permanent satisfaction, a permanent state of peace? Or is there only a state in which nothing is permanent? Only the mind that is totally impermanent, that is totally uncertain, can discover what is true because truth is not static. Truth is always new, and it can be understood only by a mind which is dying to all accumulation, to all experience, and is therefore fresh, young, innocent.

Now, is there a discontent which has no object, no motive? Do you understand? A mind whose discontent has a motive will find a conclusion that will satisfy it and destroy its discontent; and such a mind decays, withers. All our discontent is based on a motive, is it not? But now we are asking quite a different question. Is there a discontent which has no motive, which is not the product of a cause? Must you not inquire into this and find out? Surely, such a discontent is necessary—or let us use a different word, it does not matter; let us call it a movement which has no cause, no motive. I think there is such a movement, and it is not mere speculation or a hopeful idea. When the mind understands the discontent that has a motive, the discontent that is born of the demand for satisfaction, for permanency—when the truth of that discontent is really seen—then the other is. But the other cannot be understood or experienced if there is discontent with a motive, and at present all our discontent has a motive: I cannot get what I want; my wife does not love me; I am no good as I am, so I must be different, and so on. There is this endless multiplication of cause and effect, out of which comes the thing we call discontent.

Now, if the mind is aware of that whole process and understands it totally, sees the truth of it, then you will find there is a movement which has no motive at all. It is a movement, an action; it is not static, and it may be called God, truth, or what you will. In that movement there is enormous beauty, and that movement may be called love because, after all, love is without motive. If I love you and want something from you, it is not love—though I may call it by that name—because there is a motive behind it. Social or religious activity based on a motive, though it is called service, is not service at all; it is self-fulfillment.

So, can one find out what it is to love without motive? It must be discovered; it cannot be practiced. If you say, "How am I to get that love?" you are asking a question which has no meaning because in wanting to get it, you have a motive. When you use a method in order to get that love, the method only strengthens the motive, which is the 'you'. Then 'you' are important, not love.

If you will go into this very deeply—which is quite hard work, and which in itself is meditation—I think you will find that there is a movement without motive, a movement which has no cause; and it is such a movement that brings peace to the world, not your discontented movement with a cause. The man in whom there is this movement without a cause is a religious man; he is a man who loves; therefore, he can do what he will. But the politician, the social reformer, the man who cultivates virtue in order to be happy or to know God, whose efforts are the result of a motive at whatever level—the activities of such a man only breed hatred, antagonism, and misery.

That is why it is very important for each one of us to find out for ourselves, and not follow Shankara, Ramanuja, Buddha, or Christ. To find out for ourselves, to discover something, we must be free, and we are not free if we merely quote Shankara or some other authority. If we follow, we shall never find. So freedom is at the beginning, not at the end. Liberation is now, not in the future. Liberation means freedom from authority, from ambition, from greed, from envy, and from this smothering of real discontent by the discontent which has a motive and demands an end.

It is essential for a revolution to take place which is not within the pattern of society but within each one of us so that we become total individuals, and not little Shankaras, little Buddhas, little Christs. We must undertake the journey by ourselves, completely alone, without support, without influence, without encouragement or discouragement—because that way there is no motive. The journey itself is the motive, and only those who undertake that journey will bring something new, something uncorrupted to this world—not the social reformers, the do-gooders, not the Masters and their pupils, nor the preachers of brotherhood. Such people will never bring peace to the world. They are mischief-makers. The man of peace is the man who puts aside all authority, who understands the ways of ambition, of envy, who cuts himself off totally from the structure of this acquisitive society, and from all the things that are involved in tradition. Only then is the mind fresh, and you need a fresh mind to find God, truth, or what you will, not a mind that is put together by culture, by influence.

January 18, 1956

Fourth Talk in Madras

It seems to me that one of the most difficult things for us to do is to find out for ourselves what it is that we are seeking, whether collectively or individually. Some of us may want to improve society, to bring about an economic equality of opportunity for all according to the socialist, the communist, or some other pattern, hoping thereby to foster the well-being of man. Or perhaps we are trying to find out, as individuals, what this life means, why we suffer, why we have only rare moments of joy. There is the inevitable end, which we call death, and the fear of complete annihilation; so our minds are always hoping to find a remedy, an economic or religious system that will, for the time being at least, solve our many difficult problems. Others are trying to find a better way of bringing up or educating their children so that the human being will not have to go through all this battle of competition, comparison, the struggle of greed, envy, and lustful desires.

So it seems to me very important to find out what it is we are after, individually as well as collectively. When you sit here and listen, what is it that you are listening to? And what is the motive, the intention, the compelling urge that is not only making you listen now but which drives you everlastingly to seek, to strive? Is the search individual, or is it collective?

That is, we all want something; we are all groping after some end. Some of us think we have found an economic system which would solve the problems of the world if people would only listen and could be organized. Others are not concerned with the many but are individually seeking to bring about a better world through understanding themselves, or through the realization of God, truth, or what you will.

So it is important, is it not, to be conscious of what we are seeking and why we seek. Until we deliberately make ourselves conscious of what the mind is striving after, why we join various organizations, follow a particular guru, or live according to some pattern which promises a well-ordered society—until we are aware of the significance of that whole process, I think what we struggle after, and what we find, will have very little meaning.

Most of us want a well-organized society which is not based on the values of ambition, on acquisitiveness, greed, and envy. Any intelligent man wants to bring about a society of that kind, and he also wants to find out if there is something more than physical survival, something beyond the action and reaction of the mind—call it love, God, truth, or what you will. I think the majority of us want a sane, orderly, and balanced world, where poverty and degradation are nonexistent, and where there are not the wealthy few, or the few who become extraordinarily powerful and tyrannical in the name of the proletariat, and all the rest of it. We want to bring about a different world. Surely, that is what the intelligent, the sensitive, the people who have sympathy want and are struggling to create. And we also feel that life is not merely a matter of production and consumption, do we not? Life must be something more vital, more significant, more worthwhile.

Now, this is what most of us want, and where shall we begin? If I feel this is essential for human beings everywhere—at what end shall I work? Shall I dedicate my life, my energies, my activities, to bringing about a sane, orderly, and balanced world, a world in which there will be no tyranny, no poverty, a world in which the few will not direct the lives of the many through violence, through concentration camps, and so on? Shall I begin by being concerned with the improvement of the world and the economic welfare of man? Or shall I start at the psychological end, which eventually dominates the other? Even if we were to create a well-organized and equitable world, would not the man who is seeking power, whose psychological urge is to have position, prestige, again bring about chaos and misery? So, where shall we begin? Shall we lay emphasis on the psychological or on the physical, the economic?

This is a problem with which we are all confronted; I am not foisting it on you. Obviously there must be some kind of revolution. Shall the revolution be economic or religious? That is really the question. Considering the extraordinary state of the world—the violence, the misery, the confusion, the clamor of the various experts—is it not your problem, if you are at all earnest, actively inquiring, to discover for yourself whether you as an individual can contribute to a fundamental revolution? If the revolution is merely economic, I do not think it will have much significance; I feel the revolution should be religious, that is, psychological. To me, the primary thing is to have the capacity to bring about a different way of thinking, a total revolution of the mind, because, after all, it is the mind that we are concerned with, for the mind can use any system to gain profit for itself. Whatever legislation, whatever sanctions you may introduce, the mind will continue to work for its own benefit. We have seen this historically, revolution after revolution.

So, for those of us who feel it is imperative that the mind should undergo a revolution, how is this religious revolution to take place? By religious I do not mean the dogmatic, the traditional, the acceptance of this or that doctrine, belief; to me, these things are not religious. The people who practice certain forms of ceremony, who wear the sacred thread, who put whatever it is on their foreheads or meditate for a certain number of hours each day are not religious at all. They are merely accepting authority and following it without thought. Religion, surely, is something entirely different.

Now, how is this revolution in the mind to take place? I think it can take place only when we understand the totality of consciousness, which is a very complicated affair, as almost everything else in life is. If the mind can understand entirely its own workings, then there is a possibility of its ridding itself of the collective and bringing about this inward revolution.

At present you are not an individual, are you? You may have a separate house, a distinctive name, a bank account of your own, and certain qualities, idiosyncrasies, capacities; but is that what makes individuality? Or does individuality come into being only when we understand the collective process of the mind? The mind, after all, is the result of the collective; it is shaped by society and is the outcome of innumerable conditionings. Whether you are a Hindu, a Muslim, a Christian, or a communist, you are the result of conditioning, of education, of social, economic, and religious influences which make you think in a certain way. So you are the product of the collective, and can the mind free itself from the collective? Surely, it is only then that there is a possibility of thinking totally anew, and not in terms of any religion or ism, whether of the West or of the East. Our problems demand a response which is not traditional, which is not according to some pattern or system of thought. So the question is: Can the mind free itself from the past, from all the influences it has inherited, and discover something totally new, something not experienced before, which may be called reality, God, or what you will? Am I making this clear?

We have an extraordinary series of challenges to face, have we not? The challenge is always new, and as long as the mind is conditioned by belief, caught in tradition, shaped according to a certain pattern, can it respond adequately to the new? Obviously it cannot. And yet most of us are in that position. The politicians, the experts, the so-called religious people are all responding from a conditioned background, which means that their response is always inadequate, and

therefore it creates more and more problems. We accept these problems as inevitable, as part of the process of living, and put up with them, but perhaps there is a different way of tackling this whole issue.

That is, can the mind uncondition itself? Please listen. Don't say yes or no, but let us find out together whether the totality of the mind, not only the conscious mind that is occupied with everyday events, but also the deeper layers of the mind, the mind which is conditioned to think in terms of the tradition in which it has been brought up—whether this total mind can free itself from all conditioning. And is that freedom a matter of time, or is it immediate? A conditioned mind may assert that the unconditioning of itself must be done gradually, over a period of time, but that very assertion may be another response of its conditioning.

Please follow the process of your own mind, not just what I am saying. To laugh this off or to accept or deny it would obviously be absurd because this question must continue to arise. Most of us have accepted as part of our conditioning the idea that the unconditioning of the mind is a gradual process extending over several lives and demanding the practice of discipline and so on. Now, that may be the most erroneous way of thinking, and the unconditioning of the mind may be, on the contrary, an immediate thing. I think it is immediate—which is not a matter of opinion. If you examine the whole process of your mind, you will see that the mind is the result of time, of accumulative experience, knowledge, and that its response is always from this background; so when you assert that the unconditioning of the mind can only be done gradually and is a matter of time, you are merely responding according to your conditioning. Whereas, if you don't respond at all but merely listen because you don't know—you actually don't know whether the mind can be unconditioned immediately or not—then there is a possibility of discovering the truth of the matter.

There are those who say that the mind can never be unconditioned; therefore, let us condition it better. Formerly it was conditioned to worship God, which is a fantasy, a myth, an unreality, and now we shall condition it in a better way, which is to worship the state—the state being the few, the experts of this or that ideology. For such people, the problem is very simple. They assert that the mind cannot be unconditioned, and therefore they are only concerned with bettering its conditioning, but their assertion is again mere dogmatism, and there is no inquiry to find out what is true. Surely, to find out what is true, the mind cannot assert anything; it can neither accept nor reject.

Now, what is the state of the mind—and I hope you are in that state—which neither accepts nor rejects? Surely, your mind is then free to inquire, and when the mind is free to inquire, is it not already unconditioned? When the mind is inquiring, not superficially, inquisitively, curiously, but with persistency, with its total capacity to find out, such a mind is obviously free from all religious and political dogmas, it does not belong to any religion, it is not caught in the net of any belief or ideology, it has no authority. Where there is inquiry, there can be no authority. It is only the mind that is free to inquire, to discover—it is only such a mind that can bring about the religious revolution which is so essential. A free mind is truly religious because it is fresh, innocent, new; and then, perhaps, that very mind itself is the real.

Question: You say the way of tradition invariably breeds mediocrity. But will one not feel lost without tradition?

KRISHNAMURTI: What do we mean by tradition? It is the handing down, either in writing or through verbal expression, of a belief, of a custom, of experience, of knowledge, whether scientific, musical, artistic, religious, or moral. Surely, that is what we mean by tradition. And when I vainly repeat the traditions which have been handed down, that repetition makes my mind dull, mediocre. Knowledge is necessary in certain occupations. To build a bridge, to split the atom, to run a motor, to produce the many things that are necessary in modern life, knowledge is necessary; but the moment that knowledge becomes traditional, the mind ceases to create and merely functions mechanically. There are machines which can calculate faster than man, and if religiously, and in other ways, we merely accept tradition, obviously we are just like machines. Tradition gives us a certain security in society, and we are afraid to step out of that groove. We are afraid of what the neighbors might say; we have a daughter to marry off, and therefore we have to be careful. Our minds function traditionally, so we become mediocre and perpetuate misery, which is fairly obvious. Verbally we acknowledge this fact, but inwardly and in action, we do not because we all want to be secure. And security is a very strange thing. The moment we seek to be secure, invariably we create circumstances and values that bring about insecurity—which is exactly what is happening in the world at the present time. All of us are seeking security in every direction, economic, social, national, and yet that very desire to be secure is creating chaos and bringing about insecurity.

So, the mind functions in the groove of tradition because it hopes to be secure, and a mind that is seeking security is never free to discover. You cannot put away tradition; but if you understand the whole process, the psychological implications of it, you will find that tradition no longer has any meaning, and then you don't have to put it away—it drops off like a withered leaf. Then life has quite a different significance.

Question: There are various systems of meditation for the realization of one's divinity, but you don't seem to believe in any of them. What do you think is meditation?

KRISHNAMURTI: It does not matter very much what one thinks meditation is because thought is always conditioned, and surely it is very important to find out that thought is conditioned. There is no free thinking because thought is the response of memory, and if you had no memory, you would be unable to think. The reaction of memory, which is conditioned, is what we call thinking, so it is not a matter of what we think about meditation but of finding out what meditation is.

A mind that is incapable of complete attention—not concentration, but complete attention—can never discover anything new. So meditation is necessary, but most of us are concerned with the system, the method, the practice, the posture, the manner of breathing, and all the rest of it. We are concerned, not with the discovery of what is meditation, but with how to meditate, and I think there is a vast difference between the two. To me, meditation is the very process of discovering what is meditation; it is not the following of a system, however ancient, and regardless of who has taught it to you. When the mind follows a particular system or discipline, however beneficial, however productive of a desired result, it is conditioned by that system—which is obvious; therefore, it can never be free to discover what is real. So we are trying to find out what is meditation, not how to meditate; and if you will listen to this, not merely verbally, but actually, you will discover for yourself what it is.

Do you know what meditation is? You can know only in terms of a system because

you want a result out of meditation. You want to be happy, to achieve this or that state, so your meditation is already premeditated. Please don't laugh it away, but watch it. Your meditation is merely repetition because you want a result which is already established in your mind: to be happy, to be good, to discover God, truth, peace, or what you will. You have projected what you desire and have found a method to attain it—and that is what you call meditation. After all, that projection is the result, the opposite, of what you have, of what you are. Being violent, you want peace, so you find a system, a method to achieve it, but in the very process of achieving that peace, you condition your mind so that it is incapable of discovering what is peace. The mind has only projected the idea of peace out of its own violence.

Most of us think that learning to concentrate is meditation, but is it? Every child concentrates when you give him a new toy. When you do your job, if you are at all interested in it, you are concentrating, or you concentrate because your livelihood depends on it. But nothing very vital depends on your so-called meditation, so you have to force yourself to concentrate; your mind wanders off, and you keep struggling to bring it back again—which is obviously not meditation. That is merely learning a trick, how to concentrate on something in which you are not vitally interested. And one can see that a virtue that is practiced is no longer virtue. Virtue is something that has no motive. Goodness has no incentive; if it has an incentive, it is no longer good. If I am good because I am rewarded for it, surely it ceases to be good; and to be free of reward, incentive, my mind has to undergo a complete revolution through the right kind of education. All this is meditation; it helps the mind to discover what is meditation.

Surely, meditation cannot come into being without self-knowledge; and self-knowledge is to see how the mind seeks incentives, how it uses systems and disciplines itself in order to achieve what it is after, what it hopes to gain. To be aware of all this is meditation, and not merely trying to produce stillness of mind. Stillness of mind can be produced very easily by taking a drug or by repeating certain phrases, but in that state, the mind is not still. The mind can be still only when there is the understanding of what is meditation. A still mind is not asleep; it is extraordinarily alert, but a mind that is made still is stagnant, and a stagnant mind can never understand what is beyond itself. The mind can discover or experience something beyond itself only when it understands the total process of itself, and that understanding requires complete attention, being fully awake to the significance of its own activities. You don't have to practice a system of discipline. For the mind to watch itself without distortion is in itself an astonishing discipline. Not to distort what it sees, the mind must be free of all comparison, judgment, condemnation—not eventually, but free at the very beginning, and that requires a great deal of attention. Then you will find that the mind becomes totally quiet without being urged, not just at the superficial level, but deep down. At rare moments one may have an experience of stillness, but that very experience becomes a hindrance because it becomes a memory, a dead thing.

So, for the mind to be still, one must die to every experience, and when the mind is really still, then in that very stillness there is something which cannot be put into words because there is no possibility of recognition. Anything that is recognizable has already been known, and when the mind is still, there is a total freedom from the known.

January 29, 1956

Fifth Talk in Madras

It seems to me that one of the most difficult and arduous things in life is to look at something as a whole, to have a feeling for the totality of things; and I think it is very important to understand why the mind so invariably breaks up the immediate action into patterns, into details, why it is seemingly incapable of grasping the total significance of existence at one glance. I don't know if you have thought about it at all from this point of view. Most of us approach all the complexities, the problems, the miseries and struggles of life with a detailed outlook, with a mind that is very small, a mind that is conditioned, shaped by the culture, the society, in which we live. We never seem able to grasp immediately the full significance of anything. Instead of seeing the whole tree at once, it is as if we looked at only one leaf and from there gradually began to see the whole tree. So I think it is important to find out why the mind is apparently not capable of seeing the truth of something immediately and letting that truth operate instead of itself operating on the truth. After all, reality, God, or what you will, is not to be approached little by little; it cannot be put together piece by piece, as a wheel is; it must be seen immediately, or one does not see it at all.

Most of us have been trained, I think, to approach this problem through the accumulation of knowledge, through analysis, or the cultivation of virtue. If one observes the everyday activities of one's own mind, all the ways of its operation, one sees how it is always gathering, learning, acquiring, putting things together little by little, hoping thereby to capture something which is beyond this process of accumulation; and this may be the gravest mistake.

What is it that most of us are seeking? Whether we are Hindus, Christians, or what you will, we are trying to find something beyond the mere process of the mind, are we not? It is this search that we call religion. We practice various disciplines; we meditate according to certain systems, always in the hope of coming upon that which is not merely the result of a cultivated mind. But surely, to understand or to experience what is beyond the mind, there must be not a carefully-nurtured letting go of the self, of the 'me' and the 'mine', but the complete abandonment of it without cultivation. I don't know if I am making myself clear on this point. Though we see it is important that the self, the 'me', the ego, should go, yet all our activities, our thoughts, our practices, our religious disciplines are actually encouraging the self. And seeing the futility of the analyzer and the analyzed, perceiving that the various forms of substitution, the various disciplines, are only strengthening the 'me' in a subtle way and are therefore an impediment, can the mind abandon the whole of that process?

To put it differently, our minds are conditioned, are they not? The culture, the society in which we are brought up, and various other influences shape our minds from childhood as Hindus, as communists, and so on. And can the totality of the mind, the unconscious as well as the conscious, be unconditioned, not by degrees, not little by little, but immediately? Surely, that is one of our problems. Our minds are shaped, conditioned, held within a frame; and however much the mind may try to break the frame in which it is held, that very effort is the outcome of its conditioning because the thinker is not separate from the thought; the maker of the effort to escape from the prison of the self, is also part of the self, is he not? And when we see that, when we realize the truth of it, can the mind abandon completely this conditioned way of thinking?

I think we should consider here the problem of what it means to listen to something. When we listen to what is being said, how do we listen? If we listen with the intention or the desire to find something, to discover, to learn, then obviously there is no listening at all because we are concerned with acquiring. Listening then becomes merely a superficial hearing without much significance. But if we can listen with that attention which has no object of attainment, then I think something revolutionary, the unexpected, the unpremeditated, takes place.

You know, sirs, as I was saying the other day, all of us are in search of something, and most of us don't know what it is we are really seeking. To seek, to inquire, there must first be freedom, but we are obviously not free; therefore, our search has no meaning at all. Our search is only for greater comfort, greater security, and so we are prisoners of our own desire. What we seek is the fulfillment of our own longing, and so our search is no longer true search. If we observe ourselves, we will see that there is this constant desire to find some peace, to have a permanent state of comfort, complete security; and this desire makes us prisoners at the very beginning.

So it seems to me that what is important is not whether there is a reality, God, this or that, but to understand the process of one's own mind. Without self-knowledge, without knowing oneself, all search is obviously vain. And is it very difficult to know oneself? The self is made up of one's desires, greeds, ambitions, motives, envies, and the beliefs that the mind clings to; and to know that whole process, the conscious as well as the unconscious, is surely essential before one can discover anything new. And yet we are not concerned with that. We are not concerned with self-knowledge, with knowing the ways of our own minds. On the contrary, we are always escaping from that and imposing on the mind certain patterns according to which we try to live.

Surely the beginning of wisdom is self-knowledge. Without knowing oneself, which is a very complex entity, all thinking has very little meaning. If the mind does not know its own prejudices, vanities, fears, ambitions, greeds, how can it be capable of discovering what is true? All it can do is to speculate about what is true, have beliefs, dogmas, put restrictions on itself, think mechanically, follow tradition, and thereby create more and more problems. So what is important is to understand the ways of the self; and to understand the self is not to alter it, not to deny or control it, but to observe it. If I want to understand something, I cannot condemn it, can I? If I want to understand a child, I must neither condemn nor compare him with another child; I must study, watch him, be aware of all his ways. Similarly, if I want to understand the total process of my mind, I must be observant, watchful, passively aware of the way I talk, of my gestures, of the underlying motives; and that is not possible if I condemn or compare. I think that to understand the totality of one's own mind is really the most important thing in life, and one can watch the operations of the mind only in relationship because nothing exists in isolation. We exist only in relationship, and relationship is the mirror in which to observe the mind's activities.

So, the mind is conditioned; it is the result of the past; all our thinking is the process of the past, and the problem is: Can such a mind comprehend that which is timeless, beyond itself? As I was pointing out the other day, what is necessary is a religious revolution, and a religious revolution can come about only when each one of us frees himself from all dogmas, beliefs, and rituals. Surely, it is only then that the mind is capable of understanding itself and thereby coming to that state in which there is no thinking—thinking being the movement of the past.

We now try to solve our problems through thought—and it is thought that has created the problems because thought is the result, the process of the past. All thinking is conditioned. If you observe, you will see that there is no free thinking because thinking is the movement of the past; it is the reaction of memory, and we have used thought as a means of discovering what is true. But what is true can be discovered only when the mind is completely still, not made still, not disciplined, coerced. Stillness comes into being only when through self-knowledge the totality of the mind is understood. Self-knowledge comes through awareness, through watchfulness of thought, in which there is no entity who is observing thought. The observer of thought arises only when there is condemnation, when there is a desire to direct thought. After all, the thinker is part of thought, is he not? There is no thinker if there is no thought, but we have divided the thinker from the thought for reasons of our own security. We have created this division out of our desire to have a permanent entity, which we call the spiritual, but if you observe very closely, you will see that there is no permanency at all. There is only thinking, and thinking is a movement of the past, of experience, of knowledge.

Now, as long as there is the thinker separate from thought, there must be conflict, the process of duality, there must be this gap between action and idea. But cannot the mind actually experience that extraordinary state when there is only thinking, and not the thinker, when there is only an awareness in which there is no condemnation or comparison? The condemnatory and comparative process is the way of the thinker separate from thought. There is only thinking, and thinking is impermanent. Realizing the impermanency of thinking, the mind creates the permanent as the atma, the higher self, and all the rest of it, but it is still the process of thinking. Thinking is conditioned; it is the result of the past, of accumulated experience, knowledge, so it can never lead to the unknown, the timeless. After all, the self, the 'me', is nothing but a bundle of memories, and even though you give it a spiritual quality, a permanent value, it is still within the area of thought and, therefore, impermanent.

The difficulty for most people is to let go of this "permanent" quality of the mind, which is its own invention. Most of us want permanency in one form or another, and so the mind has given a quality of permanency to what it calls reality, God. Surely, there is nothing permanent. Reality is not continuous, not permanent, but something to be discovered from moment to moment. When the mind has a momentary experience of something real, it desires to make that reality permanent, and the permanent becomes the past; it is held within the field of time, but the new can exist only when the past is dead. That is why one must die to every experience. It is only when the mind is simple, fresh, innocent, unburdened with knowledge, that it is capable of immediate perception.

Every form of experience becomes the means of further recognition, does it not? Having met you yesterday, I recognize you today. The mind is a process of recognition, and with that process of recognition we try to experience the real, but the real cannot be so experienced, for it cannot be recognized. If you can recognize it, it is out of the past, it is held in memory, it has already been known; therefore, it is not the real. So the mind must be in that state when there is no experiencer at all, which means that the process of recognition must cease. You will find that this is not as fantastic as it sounds. When you see a beautiful sunset, what happens? There is an immediate reaction to that beauty, and then you begin to compare—the sunset which you saw a week ago was much

more beautiful. So you have established a connection; the new experience is already related to the past. This process of comparison is the action of recognition which prevents the mind from constantly experiencing something new.

After all, the mind is the result of the known, and it is always trying to capture the unknown in terms of the known. The coming into being of the unknown is possible only when there is freedom from the known. The known is the 'me', and whether you place it at the highest or the lowest level, it is still the 'me', which is accumulated experience, the process of recognition. The 'me' is incapable of seeing the totality of this extraordinary thing that we call life, and that is why we have broken up the worlds as Christian and Hindu, Buddhist and Muslim, and why we are breaking up India into little linguistic pieces. All that is the process of the petty mind held within the field of the known.

There must be freedom from the known for the unknown to be. That is a fact; it is obviously so because reality, God, or what you will, cannot be known, cannot be recognized. Knowledge, recognition, is the result of the past, and a mind that is looking for the unknown through the known can never find it. It is only when the mind is free from the known that the other is.

Now, when you listen to that statement, which is an obvious fact, what happens? If you give your whole attention to it, you do not ask how to be free from the known. The mind can never make itself free from the known; if it does, it merely creates another known. But if you give your whole attention to that fact, then you will see that the very fact itself begins to operate, just like the life in the seed begins to push up through the soil. Then the mind has to do nothing. If the mind operates on the fact, it can only operate in detail, putting many little parts together to find the whole, but the putting together of many parts does not make the whole. The whole must be perceived instantaneously. That is why it is important to understand the ways of the mind, not through books, not through reading the Gita or the Upanishads, but by watching yourself in relationship with your wife, with your children, with your neighbor, with your boss, by observing the way you talk to your servant, to the busman. Then you will begin to discover to what depths the mind is conditioned, and in that very discovery of the mind's conditioning, there is freedom. What is important is to discover, not merely to repeat. Through this constant discovery of the ways of the self, the mind becomes very quiet without suppression, without restriction, without being put in a frame; and for such a mind, because it is free from the known, there is a possibility of the coming into being of the unknown.

Question: In India we have been told for centuries to be spiritual, and our daily life is an endless round of rituals and ceremonies. Is this spirituality? If not, then what is it to be spiritual?

KRISHNAMURTI: Sir, let us find out what it means to be spiritual—not the definition of that word, which you can look up in a dictionary, but as we are sitting here together, let us really experience that state, if there is such a state at all.

A mind which is crippled by authority, whether it be the authority of a book, of a guru, of a belief, or of an experience, is obviously incapable of discovering what is true, is it not? And can the mind be free from all authority? That is, can the mind stop seeking security in authority? Surely, only a mind that is not afraid of being insecure, uncertain, is capable of finding out what it is to be spiritual. The man who merely accepts a belief, a dogma, who performs rituals and

ceremonies, is not capable of discovering what is true, or what it is to be spiritual, because his mind is held within the pattern of tradition, of fear, of greed.

Now, can the mind which has been held in ceremonies drop them immediately? Surely that is the only test because in dropping them, you will discover all the implications involved; the fears, the antagonisms, the quarrels, all the things which the mind has been unwilling to face will come out. But we never do that. We merely talk about being spiritual. We read the Upanishads, the Gita, repeat some mantras, play around with ceremonies, and call this religion.

Surely, that which is spiritual must be timeless. But the mind is the result of time, of innumerable influences, ideas, impositions; it is the product of the past, which is time. And can such a mind ever perceive that which is timeless? Obviously not. It can speculate, it can vainly grope after or repeat some experiences which others may have had, but being the result of the past, the mind can never find that which is beyond time. So all that the mind can do is to be completely quiet, without any movement of thought, and only then is there a possibility of the coming into being of that state which is timeless; then the mind itself is timeless.

So ceremonies are not spiritual, nor are dogmas, nor beliefs, nor the practicing of a particular system of meditation; for all these things are the outcome of a mind which is seeking security. The state of spirituality can be experienced only by a mind that has no motive, a mind that is no longer seeking, for all search is based on motive. The mind that is capable of not asking, of not seeking, of being completely nothing—only such a mind can understand that which is timeless.

Question: I have attended the recent morning discussions. Do you want us not to think at all? And if we have to think, how are we to think?

KRISHNAMURTI: Sir, not to think at all would be a state of amnesia, a state of idiocy. If you did not know where you lived, if you could not remember the way to your home, something would be wrong, would it not? We have to think. We have to think clearly, sanely, purposefully, and directly. The mind is the only instrument we possess, and we have to think in order to learn a technique, which will enable us to get a job and earn a livelihood; but beyond that, our thinking becomes ambition, greed, envy, and our society is built on these things. In our education we are everlastingly concerned with helping those who are being educated to fit into society, so our thinking, and the thinking of the generation to come, is concerned with fitting into a society which is based on greed, envy, and acquisitiveness. But the function of education, surely, is not to help the young to conform to this rotten society, but to be free of its influences, so that they may create a new society, a different world.

Thinking is essential, but when the mind is occupied with greed, with envy, with the whole process of the 'me', then thinking is obviously corrupt, and any society based on that thinking inevitably degenerates. Thinking in which the self is cultivated as virtue, as respectability, as conformity, becomes an impediment to the discovery of what is real. That is why it is important that a revolution should take place in the mind, a religious revolution; and that can come about only when you and I no longer belong to society. This does not mean putting on a loincloth and having little or no shelter, it means cutting oneself away completely, inwardly, from all acquisitiveness. It means not being greedy, not being ambitious, not pursuing power, so that there is no 'me' becoming something, either worldly or spiritual. The only revolution is this religious revolution, which has nothing to do with any church, with any organization, with any dogma or belief. It must take place in each one of us, and only then is there a possibility of creating a new world.

February 1, 1956

Madanapalle, India, 1956

--- ✳ ---

First Talk in Madanapalle

When we are confronted with so many problems, when the world is at war or preparing for war, when there is so much production and at the same time starvation, I think the most important thing in all this human struggle is to understand the mind. Surely, the mind is the only instrument which can find the right answer to the many problems that exist, yet we very rarely give thought to or examine the process of the mind. We think that ready-made answers, or certain patterns of thinking, will solve our problems. As Hindus we have a certain way of thinking which we hope will resolve our complex problems, and if we are communists, Christians, or Buddhists, we have other ready-made answers. Very few of us give real consideration to the process of thinking, to the ways of the mind itself; and it seems to me that the solution lies there, not in approaching the problem with a mind that is already shaped or conditioned.

So, this evening I would like, if I may, to consider this question of what is the mind because it is obvious that without going very deeply into this whole problem, without understanding the composition and state of the mind, mere speculative thinking, or identification with a particular belief, is utterly futile. And in trying to understand the process of the mind, I think it is important to listen rightly. Most of us listen with a mind already made up or burdened with preconceptions, or we listen to find an opposing argument, and very few listen intently, with freedom; but it is only when we are inquiring freely, not tethered to any particular belief, that the mind can find the truth of any problem. So this talk will be of significance only if we can listen rightly, which is quite arduous, and not merely treat it as a lecture to be casually listened to of an evening and set aside.

As I was saying, unless we understand the ways of the mind, we cannot possibly understand the complex problem of living. Now, what is the mind? We are trying to find out, not merely assert or accept. And to find out, you have to observe your own mind in operation as you are listening to the description of what the mind is. That is, though I am talking, describing the mind, be aware of the process of your own thinking, and thereby find out for yourself what the mind is.

Let us be very clear why it is important to understand the mind. The mind is the only instrument we have, the instrument of perception, of understanding, of thought; and without clarification of the mind, our endeavor to find out what is reality, truth, God, or what you will, can have very little significance. So we are trying to inquire into the actual process of the mind; we are not merely accepting or rejecting what is said.

Surely, the mind is the conscious as well as the unconscious; it is a totality which includes both the open and the hidden processes of thought. Most of us are occupied exclusively with the conscious, with the everyday events, ambitions, struggles, greeds; and we are completely unaware of the content of the unconscious, that is, of the mind which lies below the daily activities of the conscious mind; and until we understand the totality, including what is in the unconscious, mere occupation with the conscious will have very little meaning.

We know that the conscious mind is occupied with daily events, with a job, earning a livelihood, with its reactions and constant adjustments to immediate problems. It is the conscious mind that is educated in a certain technique, that accumulates knowledge and so-called culture. Below that superficial mind there are the many layers of the unconscious, in which are rooted the racial, cultural, and social urges, the religious beliefs and traditions, the instinctive responses based on the values of the particular society in which we have been brought up. Without going into many details, that is the totality of the mind, is it not? So, the totality of the mind is conditioned, shaped, limited by many influences—by our diet, by the climate and the culture in which we live, by social and economic values.

Now, with that conditioned mind, with which we are dissatisfied, we are trying to find something beyond the mind. We see that the mind is very small, confused, contradictory, and with that mind we are trying to understand the unknowable. After all, our minds are the result of time—time being the known, the past, the accumulation of knowledge—and with this instrument, which is still within the field of time, the so-called religious people are trying to find something which is beyond time. So the question inevitably arises: Can the conditioned mind understand or experience that which is not of its own fabrication? That is one of our great problems, is it not? And surely we shall never be able to solve our problems as long as we are thinking as Hindus, Christians, or communists because it is by thinking in these very terms that we have created the problems. It is only when the mind is free from all traditions, values, beliefs, superstitions, acceptances, that there is a possibility of solving our many human problems.

The question is, then: Can the mind which has been brought up, educated in a certain pattern, free itself from that pattern? That is, can the mind let go of the beliefs, traditions, and values which are based on authority, on mere acceptance? Can all this be set aside so that the mind is free to investigate, to find out? That is our problem, is it not? Which means, really, is it possible for the mind to free itself from the securities to which it is tethered? Because, after all, what most of us are seeking, outwardly or inwardly, is some form of security. If I have the outward security of position, prestige, money, temporarily I may be satisfied, but a time comes when I begin to demand an inward security; I take psychological refuge in belief, in dogma, in tradition, in a certain patterned way of thinking. And can the mind which is seeking security, which demands to be safe, undisturbed, ever find reality, God, or whatever name you like to give it? Obviously not. The mind that desires to be secure will find what it is seeking, but not that which is true.

So, can the mind free itself from this urge to be secure? And surely, a mind which demands security inwardly, psychologically, will invariably create outward insecurity in the social structure. Nationalism, for example, is an idea to which the mind clings as a means of psychological security, and this worship of nationalism must inevitably create insecurity outwardly—which is precisely what is happening in the world.

Now, if you observe it very closely, you will see that the mind is constantly trying to find something permanent which it calls peace, reality, or what you will. And is there anything permanent? Yet the mind creates values which it assumes to be permanent and then believes in them; it establishes certain habits of thought which become permanent, and such a mind is never free to inquire. I think it is important to understand the significance of this because, after all, freedom is at the beginning, not at the end. It is only the free mind that can inquire, not a tethered mind, not a mind that is held by belief, dogma, tradition; yet all our education is based on these things, not only at school, but as we go through life—which is also part of education. We never inquire into the possibility of having freedom first because inquiry of such a nature demands a thinking process which does not start with an assumption, or with accumulated experience, either its own or that of others.

So it seems to me that to find reality, the unknowable, which is not to be premeditated, or speculated upon, the mind must be free from everything it has known; it must die to all its many yesterdays. Only then is the mind innocent and therefore able to find out what is real.

There are some questions here, and I wonder why we ask questions. Is it with the intention of receiving an answer? And is there an answer or only a probing into the problem without looking for an answer? If I am looking for an answer, then my mind is entirely concentrated on the discovery of the answer, and not on the understanding of the problem. Most of us are concerned with the solution, with the answer, so we give divided attention to the problem; therefore, the problem is never understood, and so there is no answer. To inquire into the problem requires a mind that is not looking for an answer, but one that is capable of investigating without

judging or condemning. Can we look at anything without comparing, judging, condemning? If you will experiment with it, you will see how extraordinarily difficult it is because the whole process of our thinking is based on comparison, judgment, condemnation. But if we can inquire into the problem and not wait for an answer, then the problem itself is resolved without our looking for an answer.

Question: Can there be world peace without a world government to establish and maintain it? And how can that be brought about?

KRISHNAMURTI: Is peace external or inward? Can any government bring peace, even though it be one government for the whole world? It may establish outward order without the constant threat of war, but even that can take place only when there is no nationalism, when there are no frontiers, either political or religious. So we must be clear as to what we mean by peace.

Is peace a thing to be created by the authority of any government, whether communist, imperialist, capitalist, or what you will? Is peace to come about through legislation? One can see that a world government could bring about a certain type of peace. It could perhaps abolish sovereign governments with their armed forces, which are one of the causes of war, but surely that is not the entire meaning of peace. Peace is of the mind. And can the mind be at peace as long as it is ambitious, greedy, envious? It is the greedy, envious, acquisitive mind that has created this warring society in which we live, is it not? Our society is based on acquisitiveness, envy, greed, the driving ambition to be something; and so within our society there is constant battle, conflict.

So, peace is of the mind; it cannot be brought about through mere legislation.

Tyranny may establish some sort of order in a confused and contradictory society, and order can also be brought about through the parliamentary action of a democratic government; but as long as there is the spirit of nationalism, which creates sovereign governments with their armed forces, as long as there are frontiers and racial divisions, there are bound to be wars. So the man who would be peaceful cannot belong to any country, nor can he belong to any religion, for religion at present is merely organized dogmatism.

This thing that we call peace is something that has to be understood inwardly, and not merely sought through legislation or through the coming together of many opinions. If you observe, you will see how we worship nationalism and uphold the flag of a particular country. We identify ourselves with the whole of what we call India because, being petty, inwardly empty, and living in a little place like Madanapalle, it gives us a certain pride, it flatters our vanity, to call ourselves Indians; and for that pride and vanity we are willing to kill, or be killed. This very complex psychological process, which goes on in every country, has to be understood by each one of us, and not merely legislated against. That is why the truly religious man is one who does not belong to any religion or to any particular country.

Question: You are an Indian and an Andhra, born here in Madanapalle. We are proud of you and your good work in the world. Why don't you spend more time in your native country instead of living in America? You are needed here.

KRISHNAMURTI: You know, it is a peculiar process that is going on in the world, this identification of oneself with a particular piece of land or with a so-called religion. Does it matter very much where you were born, or what language you speak, or what particular culture you were raised in? Look at what is happening in this country. We are breaking up into parts, calling ourselves Tamils, Telugus, Maharashtrians, and all the rest of it. This breaking-up process is maintained in Europe too, with the Germans, the English, the French, the Italians, and so on. When a man worships and identifies himself with the particular, his struggles become much greater, his misery increases. As long as I remain an Andhra, belonging to a particular class and to a particular religion, my mind is very petty, small, narrow. It is surely the function of the mind to break through all these limitations and find the whole, but the whole is not made up of parts. By putting many parts together, the whole is not to be found. It is only by not being entangled in the part that there is a possibility of seeing the whole immediately.

Question: I have a son who is very dear to me, and I see that he is being subjected to many bad influences both at home and at school. What am I to do about it?

KRISHNAMURTI: We are all the product, not of one particular influence, but of many contradictory influences, are we not? And the questioner wants to know how he is to prevent his son from being subjected to the bad influences, both at home and at school. But surely the problem is much more complex than merely to find a way of resisting bad influences. What we have to consider is the whole process of influence, is it not? After all, the student is inevitably exposed to many influences, both good and bad. There is not only the home influence and the influence of the school, but there is also the influence of what he reads, of the things he hears, of the climate, of the kind of food he eats, of the religion and the culture in which he is brought up. He is the sum total of these many influences, as you and I are, and we cannot reject some and hold on to others. All that we can do is to observe all these influences and find out if the mind can be free of them. But unfortunately, as it is now, our education is a process of imposing on the student the so called good influences. That is one part of it, and the other part is a process of cramming his mind with certain information so that he can pass some examination, put a few letters after his name and get a job. That is all we are concerned with in what we now call education.

But right education is something entirely different, is it not? It is not merely a matter of giving the student technical knowledge which will enable him to hold a job, but it is to help him to be aware of all these influences and not be caught in any one of them. To do this he must have a good mind, and a good mind is one that is learning, not one that has learned, because the mind that accumulates has ceased to learn. Learning then becomes something out of the past, and so there is no further inquiry.

So, what is right education? Is it merely a definition gathered from some book, or is it a constant process of understanding the many influences that impinge on the mind so that the mind is set free at the very beginning and is therefore capable of inquiry? Surely, a mind that is capable of real inquiry is always learning; it is not merely a repository of information. Anybody who knows how to read can look up information in an encyclopedia. While it is obviously necessary in education to impart technical knowledge so that the student can have a job, at present that is all most parents are concerned with. They want their child to be trained for a good position in the present social structure, to be helped to adjust himself to this society, which is based on greed, envy, and ambition. You want your child to fit into that framework; you don't want him to be a revolutionary, so you have

this so-called education which merely helps him to conform, to imitate, to follow. But is it not possible for those who really love their children to help them to understand the many influences of society, of the culture in which they were born so that when they grow up, they will not conform to the pattern of a particular culture but will perhaps create their own society, free of envy, ambition, and greed? Surely, such people are the only truly religious people. Revolution is religious, not merely economic. Religion is not the acceptance of some dogma, tradition, or so-called sacred book. Religion is the inquiry to find the unknown.

February 12, 1956

Second Talk in Madanapalle

I am sure most of us feel that a fundamental revolution is necessary in a world where there is so much chaos, misery, starvation, and the constant threat of war. We feel there must be some kind of change, and each group has its own particular panacea or method for coping with the miseries of the world. The communists have one pattern, the capitalists another, and the so-called religious people still another. Being eager to bring about a change, which is so obviously necessary, we join one or another of these various groups, and I think it is important to find out what we mean by change—not the change of mere outward, legislative action, but a much more fundamental, more radical change. We can see that any change according to a preconceived plan involves an executive body to carry out that plan, and that the authority which must be vested in such a body invariably becomes tyrannical—which is what is actually happening in the world. There is the tyranny of well-organized authority in the hands of a few, or the tyranny of a particular religion, or the tyranny of authority vested in a particular section of society. Seeing all this, you and I, the ordinary people, are desirous to bring about a change for the better so that mankind everywhere will have adequate food, clothing, and shelter, a wider education, and so on.

Now, as I said, it is important to find out what we mean by change. For most of us, change implies a modified continuity of what has been, does it not? Though the so-called revolutionaries desire to bring about a radical transformation of society, their attitude, their values, their concepts and formulas are all based on the past, on the reaction of what they have known, and any change arising from that source is merely a continuity of what has been, however modified. They may not begin that way, but eventually it comes to that, and to me that is no change at all. Change implies something entirely different, and I would like, if I may, to go into this whole issue.

We realize that there must be a fundamental change in our way of thinking, a radical transformation of the human mind and heart, but this extraordinary change cannot be brought about by merely continuing what has been in a modified form. Nor can this radical revolution in the mind be brought about through education as it now exists, for what we now call education is merely the learning of a technique in order to earn a livelihood and conform to the pattern imposed by society.

So, seeing all this, where are we to begin? Where does one begin to bring about this fundamental change which is so obviously essential in the social order? Surely, the individual problem is the world problem. Society is what we have made it. There are those who have, and those who have not, those who know, and those who are ignorant, those who are fulfilling their ambition, and those who are frustrated; there are the various religions, with their ceremonies and dogmatic beliefs, and the ceaseless battle within society, this everlasting competition with each other to achieve, to become. All this is what you and I have created. Social reforms may be brought about through legislation or through tyranny, but unless the individual radically changes, he will always overcome the new pattern to suit his psychological demands—which is again what is happening in the world.

It seems to me very important, then, to understand the total process of individuality, because it is only when the individual changes radically that there can be a fundamental revolution in society. It is always the individual, never the group or the collective, that brings about a radical change in the world, and this again is historically so.

Now, can the individual, that is, you and I, change radically? This transformation of the individual—but not according to a pattern—is what we are concerned with, and to me it is the highest form of education. It is this transformation of the individual that constitutes religion, not the mere acceptance of a dogma, a belief, which is not religion at all. The mind that is conditioned to a particular pattern which it calls religion, whether Hindu, Christian, Buddhist, or what you will, is not a religious mind, however much it may practice all the so-called religious ideals.

So, can you and I bring about a radical transformation in ourselves without compulsion, without motive? Any form of compulsion is an egocentric activity—it distorts the mind—and motive is always based on the process of the self, the 'me', the ego. And can there be a fundamental change in each one of us without motive, without compulsion? I think this is an issue which requires a great deal of thought, inquiry; it is not to be easily dismissed by saying that there can or cannot be such a change. A man who is really earnest must go deeply into this problem of bringing about a transformation within himself. Surely, this inward change is not according to a pattern or a religious concept, but it comes about only through self-knowledge. That is, without knowing the totality of my consciousness, the whole of my being, any ideal, formula, concept, or belief I may have is merely a wish, an idea; it has no basis, and therefore it is not a reality at all. Unless there is self-knowledge, that is, unless I am beginning to know myself completely, whatever activity I may enter will be destructive and only cause more mischief. So, if one is at all serious, if one is really concerned about the chaos and the misery in the world, is it not vitally important to understand the process of oneself?

Now, what is self-knowledge? Self-knowledge is not according to any book; it cannot be had through the authority of any person. The ways of my thought must be discovered, and I can discover them only in relationship because relationship is a mirror in which I can see myself, not theoretically, but as I actually am. Surely, it is in relationship with my wife, my children, my neighbor, my servants, my boss, with the whole of society, that I discover myself as I am; for in that mirror of relationship I can see my superstitions, my judgments, my habits of thought, the traditions which I follow, the comparative values which I give to experiences and to things.

What generally happens is that we like or dislike what we see in the mirror of relationship, and therefore we either accept or condemn it. But it is possible to discover the ways of thought, the hidden motives and pursuits, the reactions of a mind conditioned by a particular society, only when we look into that mirror without any sense of condemnation or comparison, without judgment. Only then is the mind, the conscious as well as the unconscious, freed from its own bondage and so perhaps able to go beyond the limitation of itself. After all, that is meditation, is it not?

True religion is for the mind to understand its own processes—that is, its ambition, envy, greed, hatred—because the very understanding of those things puts an end to them without compulsion, and therefore the mind is free to explore. Then there is a possibility of finding that which is reality, truth, God, or what name you will. But without self-knowledge, merely to assert or deny that God or reality exists has no significance at all.

We can see that one part of the world is conditioned to accept the idea of God while another part is being conditioned not to believe in God but to believe in and sacrifice itself for the state. And is it possible for the mind to free itself from all conditioning? Surely, it is only the mind that is unconditioning itself and is therefore able to act—it is only such a mind that brings about a radical revolution. That is why it is very important for you and me individually to free ourselves from the collective; because, if one is not free, there is no possibility of exploring to find out what is true.

So the earnest must obviously inquire into this issue and not merely conform to a pattern of thought. Only the individual who is religious in the true sense of the word can bring about a new state, a new way of looking at life; and the truly religious individual is he who is freeing himself from the conditioning of a particular society and is therefore truly revolutionary.

Question: Without believing in a planner of this universe, I feel that life is meaningless. What is wrong with this belief?

KRISHNAMURTI: Surely, by "planner of this universe," you mean God, only you use a different name. Now, what is belief? What do we mean by that word, not just the dictionary meaning, but what is its psychological content?

And what is the process of the mind that necessitates a belief? What makes you say, "I believe in God" or "I don't believe in God"? What is the psychological urge that makes the mind accept or reject belief in God, in a planner of the universe? Until we discover that, mere believing or disbelieving has very little meaning.

Obviously, if from childhood you are told to believe in God, you grow up believing, just as another child, who is told not to believe, grows up disbelieving. One is called a believer and the other an atheist, but both are conditioned. When you believe in a planner of the universe, it is because you have been encouraged to believe from childhood, and your mind has been impregnated with this idea; or else you feel this life is so uncertain, in such a state of flux, that your mind clings to something as permanent, and that permanency you call God, or by some other name, giving it certain attributes, qualities. This is neither right nor wrong; it is the actual process of the mind. Because we see about us so much misery, chaos, such transiency, an utter lack of peace within and without, the mind creates and clings to something timeless, something everlastingly beautiful, peaceful. So in its uncertainty, the mind creates its own certainty. But a mind that believes or disbelieves, that accepts or rejects, can never find out what is God. God must be found, discovered, not believed in. To find, the mind must be free from both belief and disbelief. Surely, that state which we call God, that timeless reality, must be something totally new, unimagined, never experienced before; and only a free mind can discover it, not a mind that is tethered to a dogma, to a belief.

After all, if you observe, if you think about it at all, you will see that the mind is the result of time—time being memory, ex-perience, knowledge. That is, the mind is the result of the known, of the past, of many thousands of years. Now, with that mind we are trying to find the unknown, that something which may be called God, truth, or what you will. But such a mind cannot find the unknown; it can only project what is known into the future. Any belief held by the mind is the result of its own conditioning; any speculative formula or concept is the result of the known; any movement of the mind to inquire into the unknown is utterly useless and vain because the mind can only think in terms of the known. When it understands this total process and is therefore free of the known, the mind becomes very quiet, completely still; and only then is it possible for the unknown to be. Surely, this is meditation—not the projection of the known into the future and the worshiping of that projection.

Question: In this world, goodness does not pay. How can we create a society which will encourage goodness?

KRISHNAMURTI: To the intellectuals, "goodness" is a terrible word, and they generally want to avoid it, but now it is becoming the fashion even among the intellectuals to use that word. And is there goodness when there is a motive behind it? If I have a motive to be good, does that bring about goodness? Or is goodness something entirely devoid of this urge to be good, which is ever based on a motive? Is good the opposite of bad, the opposite of evil? Every opposite contains the seed of its own opposite, does it not? There is greed, and there is the ideal of nongreed. When the mind pursues nongreed, when it tries to be nongreedy, it is still greedy because it wants to be something. Greed implies desiring, acquiring, expanding; and when the mind sees that it does not pay to be greedy, it wants to be nongreedy, so the motive is still the same, which is to be or to acquire something. When the mind wants not to want, the root of want, of desire, is still there. So goodness is not the opposite of evil; it is a totally different state. And what is that state?

Obviously, goodness has no motive because all motive is based on the self; it is the egocentric movement of the mind. So what do we mean by goodness? Surely, there is goodness only when there is total attention. Attention has no motive. When there is a motive for attention, is there attention? If I pay attention in order to acquire something, the acquisition, whether it be called good or bad, is not attention—it is a distraction, a division. There can be goodness only when there is a totality of attention in which there is no effort to be or not to be. Probably you are not used to all this.

To me, making effort to be good is a process which in itself brings about evil. A man who tries to be humble, who practices humility, breeds evil—because the moment you are conscious that you are humble, you are no longer humble, you are arrogant. Sirs, don't laugh it away. Humility is not to be practiced, and a man who practices humility is fostering arrogance. Virtue is not a thing to be cultivated, because a man who cultivates virtue, cultivates the ego, the 'me', only in more respectable clothing. As humility is not to be practiced, so goodness is not to be practiced; it comes into being only when there is the complete attention which comes with the total understanding of yourself.

Think about it, and you will see that the very practice of nonviolence creates violence. To be free of violence, you have to understand all the implications of violence, and for that you must give your whole attention, which you cannot do if you are pursuing the so-called ideal. When the mind is able to give its undivided attention to *what is*, which

is greed, then you will see that the mind is totally free from greed. It does not become nongreedy—it is free from greed, which is an entirely different state. You see, we use the ideal of nongreed as a means of getting rid of greed, but we can never get rid of greed through an ideal. We have practiced that ideal for centuries, and we are still greedy. But a man who really sees the necessity of being free from greed has no ideal; he is concerned only with greed, which means he is giving his whole attention to it. And when you give your whole attention to something, in that attention there is no comparison, no condemnation, no judgment. A mind that is comparing, condemning greed is incapable of giving full attention because it is concerned with comparison and condemnation.

So goodness is not an opposite; it is not a virtue; it is a state of being without motive which comes through self-knowledge.

Question: Do you accept the view that communism is the greatest menace to human progress? If not, what do you think about it?

KRISHNAMURTI: Surely, any form of tyranny is evil. Any form of power over others is evil, whether it be the little power exercised by a bureaucrat in this town, or the widespread tyranny of a group of people who are planning the future of man according to an ideology and forcing everybody to conform for the so-called benefit of the whole. Such power is evil, but let us look at it very simply and see the difficulty involved in this issue.

A society must obviously be planned. But what happens in planning a society, and in executing that plan? There must be an administrative body vested with the authority to carry it out, which means that the few have power; and that very power becomes evil when exercised in the name of God, in the name of society, or in the name of a future utopia. And yet we need planning; otherwise, society becomes chaotic. There is, then, this problem of power vested in the few who become tyrannical, ruthless, who say, "We know the future and you don't. We are planning for the welfare of man, so you must conform; otherwise, we will liquidate you." So, can we plan a society without tyrannizing over man? That is the whole issue.

Communism is only a new word for a game that has been going on for centuries. The Roman Catholic Church has done it with its inquisition, excommunication, and torture to save souls; and various forms of tyranny exist in the history of every religion. It is nothing new; it has only a new name, with a new group of people who claim to know the future. Organized tyranny, torture, destruction, were perpetrated in the past by priests in the name of God; and now it is done by dictators and commissars in the name of the state or the party. So our problem is not the word *communism* but the whole question of whether man lives for the sake of society, or whether society exists for the well-being of man. Do religion and government exist to educate man to be free and find out for himself what is true, to help him to be good and to have the vision of greatness? Or do they exist to tyrannize over man, to brutalize and liquidate him because a few have the power to destroy?

So it is really a very complex question. What is important is not what you or I think about communism but to find out why society, whether communistic or democratic, compels the mind to conform, and why the individual submits himself to conformity. Surely, it is only the free mind that can explore—not a mind that is tethered to a book, to an organized religion, or to an ideology. A society that conditions the mind to worship the state and a society that conditions the

mind to worship the idea called God are equally tyrannous.

Now, can there be a society which does help man, the individual, to be good, to be nongreedy, to be free from envy, from ambition? Surely, that is our concern. Man can be good only when he is free, not to do what he likes, but free to understand the whole movement of life. That requires a different kind of school, a different kind of education; it demands parents and teachers who understand all the implications of freedom. Otherwise, we shall have more tyranny, not less, because the state demands efficiency. You must be efficient to have an industrialized nation; you must be efficient to fight, to kill, to destroy, and that is the whole pursuit of governments as they exist now. And governments are further separated by the so-called religions. No organized religion dares to break away and say to the government, "You are wrong"; on the contrary, they bless the cannons and the battleships. During the last war, a book called *God Is My Co-Pilot* was written by a man who dropped bombs that killed thousands of people. Of course, here in Madanapalle you are not directly concerned with all that, but surely war is merely an exaggerated expression of our daily life. We are in constant battle with ourselves and with our neighbor; we are ambitious, we want more power, more prestige, the best position; and this acquisitiveness expresses itself through the group, through the nation. We want to be powerful to defend ourselves, or to be aggressive, and so it goes on.

What is important, then, is not what you or I think of communism or democracy but to find out how to set the mind free, for it is only the free mind that can realize what is truth, what is God; and without that realization, life has very little meaning. It is the realization of truth, or God—the actual experience of it, not the belief in it—that is of the highest importance, especially now when the world is in such chaos and misery.

February 19, 1956

Third Talk in Madanapalle

I think most of us find life very dull. To earn a livelihood we have to do a certain job, and it becomes very monotonous; a routine is set going which we follow year after year almost until our death. Whether we are rich or poor, and though we may be very erudite, have a philosophical bent, our lives are for the most part rather shallow, empty. There is obviously an insufficiency in ourselves, and being aware of this emptiness, we try to enrich it through knowledge or through some kind of social activity, or we escape through various kinds of amusement or cling to a religious belief. Even if we have a certain capacity and are very efficient, our lives are still pretty dull, and to get away from this dullness, this weary monotony of life, we seek some form of religious enrichment; we try to capture that unworldly state of being which is not routine and which for the moment may be called otherness. In seeking that otherness, we find there are many different systems, different ways or paths which are supposed to lead to it, and by disciplining ourselves, by practicing a particular system of meditation, by performing some ritual or repeating certain phrases, we hope to achieve that state. Because our daily life is an endless round of sorrow and pleasure, a variety of experiences without much significance, or a meaningless repetition of the same experience, living for most of us is a monotonous routine; therefore, the problem of enrichment, of capturing that otherness—call it God, truth, bliss, or what you will—becomes very urgent, does it not? You may be well-off and well-married, you may have children, you may be able to think intelligently and sanely, but without that state of otherness, life becomes extraordinarily empty.

So, what is one to do? How is one to capture that state? Or is it not possible to capture it at all? As they are now, our minds are obviously very small, petty, limited, conditioned, and though a small mind may speculate about that otherness, its speculations will always be small. It may formulate an ideal state, conceive and describe that otherness, but its conception will still be within the limitations of the little mind, and I think that is where the clue lies—in seeing that the mind cannot possibly experience that otherness by living it, formulating it, or speculating about it. Surely, that is a tremendous realization: to see that because it is limited, petty, narrow, superficial, any movement of the mind towards that extraordinary state is a hindrance. To realize that fact, not speculatively, but actually, is the beginning of a different approach to the problem.

After all, our minds are the outcome of time, of many thousands of yesterdays; they are the result of experience based on the known, and such a mind is the continuity of the known. The mind of each one of us is the result of culture, of education, and however extensive its knowledge or its technical training, it is still the product of time; therefore, it is limited, conditioned. With that mind we try to discover the unknowable, and to realize that such a mind can never discover the unknowable is really an extraordinary experience. To realize that however cunning, however subtle, however erudite one's mind may be, it cannot possibly understand that otherness—this realization in itself brings about a certain factual comprehension, and I think it is the beginning of a way of looking at life which may open the door to that otherness.

To put the problem differently, the mind is ceaselessly active, chattering, planning; it is capable of extraordinary subtleties and inventions; and how can such a mind be quiet? One can see that any activity of the mind, any movement in any direction, is a reaction of the past; and how can such a mind be still? And if it is made still through discipline, such stillness is a state in which there is no inquiring, no searching, is it not? Therefore, there is no openness to the unknown, to that state of otherness.

I don't know if you have thought about this problem at all or have merely thought about it in terms of the traditional approach, which is to have an ideal and to move towards the ideal through a formula, through the practice of a certain discipline. Discipline invariably implies suppression and the conflict of duality, all of which is within the area of the mind, and we proceed along this line, hoping to capture that otherness; but we have never intelligently and sanely inquired whether the mind can ever capture it. We have had the hint that the mind must be still, but stillness has always been cultivated through discipline. That is, we have the ideal of a still mind, and we pursue it through control, through struggle, through effort.

Now, if you look at this whole process, you will see that it is all within the field of the known. Being aware of the monotony of its existence, realizing the weariness of its multiplying experiences, the mind is always trying to capture that otherness; but when one sees that the mind is the known, and that whatever movement it makes, it can never capture that otherness, which is the unknown, then our problem is not how to capture the unknown but whether the mind can free itself from the known. I think this problem must be considered by anyone who wants to find out if there is a possibility of the coming into being of that otherness, the unknown. So, how can the mind, which is the result of the past, of the known, free itself from the known? I hope I am making myself clear.

As I said, the present mind, the conscious as well as the unconscious, is the outcome of the past; it is the accumulated result of racial, climatic, dietetic, traditional, and other influences. So the mind is conditioned—conditioned as a Christian, a Buddhist, a Hindu, or a communist—and it obviously projects what it considers to be the real. But whether its projection is that of the communist, who thinks he knows the future and wants to force all mankind into the pattern of his particular utopia, or that of the so-called religious man, who also thinks he knows the future and educates the child to think along his particular line, neither projection is the real. Without the real, life becomes very dull, as it is at present for most people; and our lives being dull, we become romantic, sentimental, about that otherness, the real.

Now, seeing this whole pattern of existence, without going into too many details, is it possible for the mind to free itself from the known—the known being the psychological accumulations of the past? There is also the known of everyday activity, but from this the mind obviously cannot be free, for if one forgot the way to one's house, or the knowledge which enables one to earn a livelihood, one would be bordering on insanity. But can the mind free itself from the psychological factors of the known, which give assurance through association and identification?

To inquire into this matter, we shall have to find out whether there is really a difference between the thinker and the thought, between the one who observes and the thing observed. At present there is a division between them, is there not? We think the 'I', the entity who experiences, is different from the experience, from the thought. There is a gap, a division between the thinker and the thought, and that is why we say, "I must control thought." But is the 'I', the thinker, different from thought? The thinker is always trying to control thought, mold it according to what he considers to be a good pattern, but is there a thinker if there is no thought? Obviously not. There is only thinking, which creates the thinker. You may put the thinker at any level; you may call him the Supreme, the atma, or whatever you like, but he is still the result of thinking. The thinker has not created thought; it is thought that has created the thinker. Realizing its own impermanency, thought creates the thinker as a separate entity in order to give itself permanency—which is after all what we all want. You may say that the entity which you call the atma, the soul, the thinker, is separate from thought, from experience; but you are only aware of a separate entity through thought, and also through your conditioning as a Hindu, a Christian, or whatever it is you happen to be. As long as this duality exists between the thinker and the thought, there must be conflict, effort, which implies will; and a mind that wills to free itself, that says, "I must be free from the past," merely creates another pattern.

So, the mind can free itself—and thereby, perhaps, that otherness can come into being—only when there is the cessation of effort as the 'I' desiring to achieve a result. But you see, all our life is based on effort: the effort to be good, the effort to discipline ourselves, the effort to achieve a result in this world, or in the next. Everything we do is based on striving, ambition, success, achievement; and so we think that the realization of God, or truth, must also come about through effort. But such effort signifies the self-centered activity of achievement, does it not? It is not the abandonment of the self.

Now, if you are aware of this whole process of the mind, the conscious as well as the unconscious, if you really see and understand it, then you will find that the mind becomes extraordinarily quiet without any effort. The stillness which is brought about by discipline, control, suppression, is the stillness of death, but the stillness of which I am speaking comes about effortlessly when one understands this whole process of the mind. Then only is there a possibility of the coming into being of that otherness which may be called truth, or God.

Question: Do you not concede that guidance is necessary? If, as you say, there must be no tradition and no authority, then everybody will have to start laying down a new foundation for himself. As the physical body has had a beginning, is there not also a beginning for our spiritual and mental bodies, and should they not grow from each stage to the next higher stage? Just as our thought is kindled by listening to you, does it not need reawakening by getting into contact with the great minds of the past?

KRISHNAMURTI: Sir, this is an age-old problem. We think that we need a guru, a teacher, to awaken our minds. Now, what is implied in all that? It implies the one who knows, and the other who does not. Let us proceed slowly, not in a prejudiced manner. The one who knows becomes the authority, and the one who does not know becomes the disciple; and the disciple is everlastingly following, hoping to overtake the other, to come up to the level of the Master. Now, please follow this. When the guru says he knows, he ceases to be the guru; the man who says he knows does not know. Please see why. Because truth, reality, or that otherness, has no fixed point; it obviously cannot be approached by a path, but must be discovered from moment to moment. If it has a fixed point, then that point is within the limits of time. To a fixed point there may be a path, as there is a path to your house; but to a thing that is living, that has no abode, that has neither a beginning nor an end, there can be no path.

Surely, a guru who says he will help you to realize can help you to realize only that which you already know, for what you realize, experience, must be recognizable, must it not? If you can recognize it, then you say, "I have experienced," but what you can recognize is not that otherness. The otherness is not recognizable; it is not known; it is not something which you have experienced and are therefore able to recognize. That otherness is a thing that must be uncovered from moment to moment, and to discover it, the mind must be free. Sir, the mind must be free to discover anything, and a mind that is bound by tradition, whether ancient or modern, a mind that is burdened with belief, with dogma, with rituals, is obviously not free. To me, the idea that another can awaken you has no validity. This is not an opinion, it is a fact. If another awakens you, then you are under his influence, you are depending on him; therefore, you are not free, and it is only the free mind that can find.

So the problem is this, is it not?—we want that otherness, and since we don't know how to get it, we invariably depend on someone whom we call the teacher, the guru, or on a book, or on our own experience. So dependence is created, and where there is dependence, there is authority; therefore, the mind becomes a slave to authority, to tradition, and such a mind is obviously not free. It is only the free mind that can find, and to rely on another for the awakening of your mind is like relying on a drug. Of course, you can take a drug that will make you see things very sharply, clearly. There are drugs that can momentarily make life seem much more vital so that everything stands out brilliantly—the colors that you see every day, and pass by, become extraordinarily beautiful, and so on. That may be your "awakening" of the mind, but then you will be depending on the drug, as now you depend on your guru or on some sacred book; and the moment the

mind becomes dependent, it is made dull. Out of dependence, there is fear—fear of not achieving, of not gaining. When you depend on another, whether it be the Savior or anyone else, it means that the mind is seeking success, a gratifying end. You may call it God, truth, or what you like, but it is still a thing to be gained; so the mind is caught, it becomes a slave, and do what it will—sacrifice, discipline, torture itself—such a mind can never find that otherness.

So the problem is not who is the right teacher but whether the mind can keep itself awake, and you will find it can keep itself awake only when all relationship is a mirror in which it sees itself as it is. But the mind cannot see itself as it is if there is condemnation or justification of that which it sees or any form of identification. All these things make the mind dull, and being dull, we want to be awakened, so we look to somebody else to awaken us. But by this very demand to be awakened, a dull mind is made still more dull because it does not see the cause of its dullness. It is only when the mind sees and understands this whole process and does not depend on the explanation of another that it is able to free itself.

But how easily we are satisfied with words, with explanations! Very few of us break through the barrier of explanations, go beyond words, and find out for ourselves what is true. Capacity comes with application, does it not? But we don't apply ourselves because we are satisfied with words, with speculations, with the traditional answers and explanations on which we have been brought up.

Question: In all religions, prayer is advocated as necessary. What do you say about prayer?

KRISHNAMURTI: It is not a matter of what I say about prayer, for then it merely becomes one opinion against another, and opinion has no validity; but what we can do is to find out what the facts are.

What do we mean by prayer? One part of prayer is supplication, petition, demand. Being in trouble, in sorrow, and wanting to be comforted, you pray. You are confused, and you want clarity. Books don't satisfy you, the guru does not give you what you want, so you pray; that is, you either silently supplicate, or you verbally repeat certain phrases.

Now, if you keep on repeating certain words or phrases, you will find that the mind becomes very quiet. It is an obvious psychological fact that quietness of the superficial mind is induced by repetition. And then what happens? The unconscious may have an answer to the problem which is agitating the superficial mind. When the superficial mind becomes quiet, the unconscious is able to intimate its solution, and then we say, "God has answered me." It is really fantastic, when you come to think of it, for the petty little mind, being caught in sorrow which it has brought upon itself, to expect an answer from that otherness, the immeasurable, the unknown. But our petition is answered; we have found a solution, and we are satisfied. That is one form of prayer, is it not?

Now, do you ever pray when you are happy? When you are aware of the smiles and the tears of those about you, when you see the lovely skies, the mountains, the rich fields, and the swift movement of the birds, when there is joy and delight in your heart—do you indulge in what you call prayer? Obviously not. And yet, to see the beauty of the earth, to be cognizant of starvation and misery, to be aware of everything that is happening about us—surely, this is also a form of prayer. Perhaps this has much more significance, a far greater value, for it may sweep away the cobwebs of memory, of

revenge, all the accumulated stupidities of the 'I'. But a mind that is preoccupied with itself and its designs, that is caught up in its beliefs, its dogmas, its fears and jealousies, its ambition, greed, envy—such a mind cannot possibly be aware of this extraordinary thing called life. It is bound by its own self centered activity, and when such a mind prays, whether it be for a refrigerator or to have its problems solved, it is still petty, even though it may receive an answer.

All this brings up the question of what is meditation, does it not? Obviously, there must be meditation. Meditation is an extraordinary thing, but most of us don't know what it means to meditate; we are concerned only with how to meditate, with practicing a method or a system through which we hope to get something, to realize what we call peace, or God. We are never concerned to find out what is meditation and who is the meditator, but if we begin to inquire into what is meditation, then perhaps we shall find out how to meditate. The inquiry into meditation is meditation. But to inquire into meditation, you cannot be tethered to any system because then your inquiry is conditioned by the system. To really probe into this whole problem of what is meditation, all systems must go. Only a free mind can explore, and the very process of freeing the mind to explore is meditation.

Question: The thought of death is bearable to me only if I can believe in a future life, but you say that belief is an obstacle to understanding. Please help me to see the truth of this.

KRISHNAMURTI: Belief in a future life is the result of one's desire for comfort. Whether or not there is a future life in reality can be found out only when the mind is not desirous of being comforted by a belief. If I am in sorrow because my son has died, and to overcome that sorrow I believe in reincarnation, in eternal life, or what you will, then belief becomes a necessity to me; and such a mind can obviously never find out what death is because all it is concerned with is to have a hope, a comfort, a reassurance.

Now, whether or not there is continuity after death is quite a different problem. One sees that the body comes to an end; through constant use, the physical organism wears out. Then what is it that continues? It is the accumulated experience, the knowledge, the name, the memories, the identification of thought as the 'me'. But you are not satisfied with that; you say there must be another form of continuance as the permanent soul, the atma. If there is this atma which continues, it is the creation of thought, and the thought which has created the atma is still part of time; therefore, it is not spiritual. If you really go into this matter, you will see there is only thought, identified as the 'me'— my house, my wife, my family, my virtue, my failure, my success, and all the rest of it—and you want that to continue. You say, ''I want to finish my book before I die,'' or,

''I want to perfect the qualities I have been trying to develop, and what is the point of my having struggled all these years to achieve something if in the end there is annihilation?'' So the mind, which is the product of the known, wants to continue in the future, and because there is the uncertainty which we call death, we are frightened and want reassurance.

Now, I think the problem should be approached differently, which is to find out for oneself whether it is possible, while living, to experience that state of ending which we call death. This does not mean committing suicide, but it is to actually experience that astonishing state, that sacred moment of dying to everything of yesterday. After all, death is the unknown, and no amount of rationalization, no belief or disbelief will ever bring about that extraordinary experience. To have that inward fullness of life, which includes death, the mind must free itself from the known. The known must cease for the unknown to be.

February 26, 1956

Bombay, India, 1956

✳

First Talk in Bombay

I think it is important to understand that freedom is at the beginning and not at the end. We think freedom is something to be achieved, that liberation is an ideal state of mind to be gradually attained through time, through various practices; but to me, this is a totally wrong approach. Freedom is not to be achieved; liberation is not a thing to be gained. Freedom, or liberation, is that state of mind which is essential for the discovery of any truth, any reality; therefore, it cannot be an ideal; it must exist right from the beginning. Without freedom at the beginning, there can be no moments of direct understanding because all thinking is then limited, conditioned. If your mind is tethered to any conclusion, to any experience, to any form of knowledge or belief, it is not free; and such a mind cannot possibly perceive what is truth.

This is something that must be felt and realized immediately, not endlessly argued about, for it is a fact. How can a mind which is crippled, held by a belief, by a dogma, or by its own knowledge and experiences, ever have the capacity to explore and to discover? So freedom is essential to discover what is truth, and it is only the individual who is not merely the result of the collective that can be free. For the mind to be capable of freedom, there must obviously be application—the application which comes through attention; and that is what I would like to discuss this evening. It is essential, I think, to find out how to listen because in the very act of listening there is clarification. There is immediate clarification, not through argumentation or comparative knowledge, but when there is complete listening. It is very difficult to listen completely because our full attention is not there, but it is only when we listen completely to something that there is immediate understanding.

Now, if you observe your own mind as you are sitting here, you will notice that you are listening through various screens—the screen of what you know, of what you have heard or read, the screen of your own experiences—and these screens actually prevent listening. You never really listen; you are always interpreting what you hear according to your background, your prejudices, according to the conclusions you have arrived at; therefore, there is no listening. And there is immediate transformation only when one listens completely, which is not to allow the things that one has learned to come between. To listen completely is not to judge, not to evaluate, so that your whole being is attentive; and when you are listening in that way, you will find there is immediate clarification. Such clarification is timeless freedom, liberation.

It seems to me that we must differentiate between learning and being taught. Most of you, I am pretty sure, are here to listen to somebody who you think will teach you something, so your approach to the speaker is that of an individual who expects to be taught by a teacher. But I do not believe that there is any teaching; there is only learning, and this is very important to understand. When the individual who is listening regards the speaker as one who is teaching him something, such an attitude creates and maintains the division of the pupil and the master, of the one who knows and the one who does not know. But there is only learning, and I think it is very important from the very beginning to understand this and to establish the right relationship between us. The man who says he knows does not know; the man who says he has attained liberation has not realized. If you think you are going to learn something from me which I know and you do not know, then you become a follower—and he who follows will never find out what is truth. That is why it is very important for you to understand this.

A man can have knowledge only about things known; he cannot have knowledge about the unknown. The unknown comes into being from moment to moment; it is not to be gathered, accumulated; being timeless, it cannot be stored up and used. The guru, the so-called teacher, who asserts he knows, can know only the things he has experienced; and what he has experienced is conditioned, is of time; therefore, it is not true. So it is essential, if you and I would understand each other, to establish the right relationship between us from the very beginning. You are not listening in order to be taught by me; you are listening to learn. Life is a process of learning, but there can be no learning as long as the mind is accumulating. How can you learn if the mind is concerned with ac-

cumulating and with using what is newly acquired to further its accumulation?

Please follow this, sirs. When we say, ''I must learn,'' we mean that in the process of learning, we will store up what is learned in order to know more, do we not? Such learning is essential in the acquisition of technical knowledge. If you want to build a bridge, you must accumulate the required knowledge; if you are a scientist, you must know the previous experiments and discoveries of other scientists. That kind of knowledge is essential for the physical well-being of man. But I am not talking of knowledge in that sense. Even in science you don't worship or follow anyone; you follow facts, not individuals. The very process of experimentation in science brings its own discoveries. If you are a great scientist, you have no one to lead you to discovery in experimentation; you are constantly investigating, discarding, exploring, inquiring to find out. But we never do that with regard to the inward, religious life—which is much more important than the mere discovery of scientific facts, because scientific facts can be distorted and used by a mind that is self-centered, that is concerned with itself and its own progress.

What we are concerned with here is the understanding of what is truth, which is the religious life, the good life. If you are merely being taught by a person who asserts he knows, or whom you regard as having achieved something, you are creating a division between yourself and that person; there is always the teacher and the disciple, with the teacher progressing upward and the pupil following. A state of inequality exists, and such inequality in spiritual matters is unspiritual, immoral, because when you become a follower, you destroy yourself.

Please understand this very simple truth: that as long as you are following another, it does not matter who it is, you will never find the eternal, that otherness which is beyond the mind. So there must be freedom right from the beginning—freedom, not to choose your various gurus, which is not freedom, but freedom to investigate, which means there can be no following. Therefore there is no guru, no teacher, no sacred book. To be capable of finding out what is true, the mind must be free, and the mind is not free when it is burdened with accumulated knowledge, with its own experiences. Learning is a process of constantly discarding that which is being accumulated, of discarding in order to discover.

A mind which has committed itself to the Gita, to the Koran, to the Bible, or to some belief, can never learn; it can only follow, and it follows because it wants security. As long as the mind desires to be permanently secure, undisturbed, as long as it is seeking its own perpetuation through a belief, it is obviously incapable of finding out what is God, what is truth.

The mind can learn only when it renounces, that is, when it constantly denudes itself of what it is learning. If learning is merely additive, then there is no learning. Please see this fact. As long as the mind is accumulating, gathering, how can it learn, since what it learns will always be translated according to what it has already gathered? Where there is accumulation, there can never be the movement of learning, for it is only when the mind is free to explore that it can learn. If the mind really sees this fact, not argumentatively, verbally, or so-called intellectually, but deeply and truly, then such a mind is capable of finding that which may be called bliss, truth, God, or what you will.

So it seems to me very important that you should understand right from the beginning of these talks that I am not teaching you anything; otherwise, we shall be moving in opposite directions. I know literally nothing except such things as how to drive a car, how

to write letters, and so on. Therefore, being in a state of not-knowing, the mind is capable of complete investigation. A mind that knows cannot investigate, and only a mind that is free from the known can find the unknown.

These talks are not meant to guide you, to tell you what to do, but rather to liberate the mind so that it will find out for itself what to do, and not follow anyone. This means breaking down tradition, discarding the whole idea of worshiping somebody in order to find God. We are brought up on the notion that the guru is essential because he knows and will tell us what to do; we are soaked in that tradition, and it must be cut away immediately if we are to understand all this. You see, we are frightened not to have leaders because we are so confused, and when we act out of our confusion, the confusion is increased. But this confusion can only be cleared up by each one of us, and that is why it is so important for the individual to understand himself. With the understanding of oneself, there comes an action which is not confused or confusing. So self-knowledge is essential—but not the kind taught in books, for that is not self-knowledge at all; it is merely vain repetition. What has value is not to assume anything—that you are the atma, the paramatma, and so on—but to discover in your relationships from day to day what you actually are, which is to learn about yourself. But you cannot learn about yourself if you have stored up what you learned yesterday because then you compare yesterday with today, and this comparison destroys further discovery. Self-knowledge is a living thing, not the accumulated debris of yesterday's gathering.

If one really sees this thing, how extraordinarily simple it is! And the mind must be simple, innocent, in the sense that it has no accumulations of yesterday. It is only such a mind that can discover the significance of this whole process of living, which is now so chaotic, miserable, violent. That is why it is essential to understand, from the very beginning, that life is not a school in which there is a teacher and the taught. The significance of life is to be found in living, but the moment you accumulate, you are dead, like a pool of stagnant water. So it is essential for the mind to be like the living waters of the river, ever moving on, which means that there must be freedom at the very beginning.

Before we consider together some of these questions, let us again understand our intent. I am not answering these questions, for there is no answer. Please understand this; otherwise, you will be wasting your time in listening to what I am saying. There is no answer; there is only the unfolding of the problem, and therefore the beauty of the discovery of the truth in the problem. A mind that is searching for an answer will never investigate the problem because it is occupied with the answer, and it is very difficult for the mind not to be occupied with the answer because it longs to be satisfied. Most of us want a pleasant and easy answer to our problems. But here we are not answering; we are unrolling the problem, uncovering all its facets, its subtleties, discerning the extraordinary thing that lies behind the problem. After all, the mind is our only instrument of perception, and when it is occupied with an answer, it has blocked itself. The mind that is concerned with a result, a conclusion, hinders its own action, its own living; it is enclosed by the walls of its own arguments, its own determined efforts. So, please bear in mind that I am not answering these questions. We are together trying to find out the truth of the problem, not the answer; because the mind wants to be satisfied, it wants a convenient and agreeable answer, and such an answer is not truth.

Question: After having listened eagerly to you for so many years, we find ourselves exactly where we were. Is this all we can expect?

KRISHNAMURTI: The difficulty in this problem is that we want a result to convince ourselves that we have progressed, that we have been transformed. We want to know that we have arrived, and a man who has arrived, a man who has listened and got a result, has obviously not listened at all. (Laughter) Sirs, this is not a clever answer. The questioner says he has listened for many years. Now, has he listened with complete attention, or has he listened in order to arrive somewhere and be conscious of his arrival? It is like the man who practices humility. Can humility be practiced? Surely, to be conscious that you are humble is not to be humble. You want to know that you have arrived. This indicates, does it not, that you are listening in order to achieve a particular state, a place where you will never be disturbed, where you will find everlasting happiness, permanent bliss. But as I said previously, there is no arriving; there is only the movement of learning—and that is the beauty of life. If you have arrived, there is nothing more. And all of you have arrived, or you want to arrive, not only in your business, but in everything you do; so you are dissatisfied, frustrated, miserable. Sirs, there is no place at which to arrive; there is just this movement of learning which becomes painful only when there is accumulation. A mind that listens with complete attention will never look for a result because it is constantly unfolding; like a river, it is always in movement. Such a mind is totally unconscious of its own activity, in the sense that there is no perpetuation of a self, of a 'me', which is seeking to achieve an end.

Question: In every direction, inwardly as well as outwardly, we see incitement to violence. Hatred, ill will, meanness, and aggression are rampant, not only in India, but in every corner of the world and in the very psyche of man. What is your answer to this crisis?

KRISHNAMURTI: This problem, like every other human problem, is very complex. There is no yes or no answer. Why are we violent as individuals and, therefore, as a group, as a nation? Look what has happened recently in this town. Why are we violent, and over what? Whether you call yourself a Gujarati or a Maharashtrian, who cares? What's in a name? But behind the name lie all the pent-up prejudices, the narrow, stupid, isolating provincialism; and overnight you hate, you knife your neighbor with words and with steel. Why do we do this? Why are we, as a group of Hindus, opposed to Christians; and why are the Germans or the Americans, as a group, opposed to some other group? Why are we like this? You and I can invent excuses and explanations by the score, and the cleverer we are, the more argumentative our explanations. But apart from explanations, do you know you are like this? Are you aware that you will suddenly turn on your neighbor over a division of land on the map because certain politicians are eager to get more power, and you are eager to support them because you also are seeking power? Why are you like this? The Muslims and the Hindus are mutually opposed. Why? And are you aware of this in yourself? Is it not important to know that you are like this, and not idealistically pretend to be nonviolent, and all that nonsense? The actual fact is that you are violent, and I think the problem is that you do not realize you are violent because you are always pretending to be nonviolent. You have been brought up, bred, nurtured, on the ideal of nonviolence, but the ideal is

phony; it does not exist at all. What exists is what you are, which is violent, and the gap between the ideal and the fact creates this hypocritical dual existences, which is one of our misfortunes in this country. You are all such idealistic persons, always talking about nonviolence, and butchering your neighbor. (Laughter) Sirs, don't laugh, it is not funny. These are facts. Do you mean to say you would tolerate the poverty, the degradation, the horrors that exist in every town and village in India, if you were really merciful? You are not merciful and compassionate actually, only theoretically, and that is why you live double lives.

The fact is much more important than what should be. The fact is that you are violent, and you refuse to face that fact because you say you must not be like that; you decry violence, you push it away, but it is still there. When you recognize the fact that you are violent instead of pursuing the ideal of nonviolence, which does not exist, only then can you deal with violence. Then your attention is not diverted; it is given wholly to understanding violence, and therefore you can do something about it; you can concern yourself attentively, diligently, with the fact of violence, ill will, meanness, cruelty. That is why it is very important that the ideal should be put away, abolished completely.

You all know that cruelty is going on in every part of this country—cruelty not only to the neighbor, to the villager, but also to the animals. If you realized the falseness of the ideal, do you mean to say you could not face that fact and put a stop to it? Then you would be a different people altogether; you would bring into being a different culture, a different society; you would not be imitative of the West; you would be something real, and reality is original, not imitative. But you cannot see the original, the real, as long as your attention is diverted by the ideal.

The ideal has no significance; what has significance is the fact. Through the ideal you hope to get rid of the fact, but it cannot be done, and I think this is again very important to understand. The mind that pursues an ideal is an unreal mind; it is a mind that escapes, that avoids the fact. But to face the fact is very difficult for a mind that has been trained for centuries to accept the ideal as something worthwhile. You practice nonviolence, ahimsa, and all the rest of it—which to me is utter nonsense because it is not a fact. The fact is that you are violent; it is being proved over and over again, which means you have no compassion; and you cannot have compassion as an ideal. Either you are compassionate or you are not. Violence exists in the world because it exists in your heart, and to reject violence should be your only concern, not to pursue the ideal of nonviolence. To reject violence, you must apply your attention to it in everyday life; you must be aware of it in your words, in your gestures, in the way you talk to your servants, to your neighbors, to your wife and children. Your violence indicates that you have no love, and that is a fact. If you can look at the fact, then that very looking will transform, will do something to the fact.

Question: Granted that religion is of the highest importance in life, will not the truly religious person be concerned with the plight of his fellow man?

KRISHNAMURTI: It all depends on whom you call a religious person and what you mean by being concerned. Please follow this, sirs. Should the religious man be occupied with social reform? What is actually happening in the world? The so-called religious person is concerned with the misery, the troubles, the poverty of his fellow man, which is called social reform. This is happening here in India and elsewhere.

Now, as we know, production is on the increase, and it is fairly certain that in 50 or 100 years we are all going to have enough food, clothing, and housing because the communists are aiming at that in their own brutal, tyrannical way, and the capitalists are also aiming at it for their own purposes. We are all working to lessen poverty and bring about more production through increased efficiency, mechanical inventions, and so on. All this is happening and will happen more extensively, as it should. But what is of first importance, surely, is to see poverty, to see degradation, to see how man treats man, which is something appalling—and to feel it, not ask what to do about it. What to do about it will come later. But most of us lose the love for man in the action of doing something to reform man. This reformation is going to take place through communism, with its disruptive elements, through socialism, through capitalism, and through the constant pressure of the poverty-ridden countries on those that are rich. That very pressure is going to bring about change, revolution.

Now, the problem is: Who is a religious man? And should a religious man be concerned with this social reformation, which is a matter of doing away with poverty and bringing about an equitable distribution of worldly goods? It is obviously essential to do away with poverty, to have good health, sufficient food, adequate houses to live in, and all the rest of it; and this is going to take place through legislation, through pressure, through mass production, and so on.

But what do we mean by a religious man? Surely, a religious man is one who is helping to free the individual, and himself, from all the cruelty and suffering in life—which means that he is free from all belief. He has no authority; he does not follow anyone because he is a light unto himself, and that light arises from self-knowledge; it is the liberation that comes into being when the individual completely understands himself. The religious man is one who is creative, not in the sense of painting pictures or writing poetry, but there is in him a creativity which is everlasting, timeless.

Now, will that religious man, who is discovering from moment to moment, be occupied with social reform? Or will he remain outside of society and help the individual who is caught in its ceaseless struggle? Surely, the truly religious man is outside of society because for him there is no authority. He is not seeking a result; therefore, results happen in spite of him, and such a man is not concerned with social reform.

Mind you, social reform is essential. But there are many people who are active in social reform, and why are they? Is it out of love? Or is that particular activity, which is called social reform, a means of their own self-fulfillment? To be aware of the beggar in the street, to see the appalling poverty and degradation in the villages, and to feel it, to have love, compassion for the beggar, for the villager, is not to fulfill yourself in the activity of social reform, though you may be socially active. But when you become important in social work, is it not because you are fulfilling yourself through that action? When you do that, you cease to love; and to love, to have compassion, to be sensitive to beauty and to ugliness, is far more important than to fulfill yourself in some tawdry work which you call social reform.

So it is the religious man who is the real revolutionary, not he who seeks to bring about a revolution in the economic sense. The religious man has no authority; he is not greedy, ambitious; he is not seeking a result; he is not a politician; therefore, it is only the religious man who can bring about the right kind of reformation. That is why it is important for all of us, not as groups, but as individuals, to liberate ourselves immediately from beliefs and dogmas, from greed and ambition. Then you will find that the mind becomes astonishingly alive, and such a man is a reformer in an entirely different sense; his action has a totally different significance because he helps to free the mind to find out, to be creative. The mind that is occupied can never be creative; the mind that is concerned with fulfilling itself can never find the unknown. Only the mind that is completely unoccupied can discover and comprehend the eternal, and such a mind will produce its own action on society.

March 4, 1956

Second Talk in Bombay

We were discussing last Sunday the question of the individual freeing himself from all the limitations imposed upon him by society, and from the conditioning of religion, because it is only when he is free from his conditioning that the individual can be creative. I mean by creativeness the instant of being liberated from time, which is the only state that can bring about the right kind of social transformation and the total well-being of man.

I do not think we realize the full significance of individual freedom from the collective, nor do we see its importance. And is it possible for the individual to emerge from the collective? After all, though we have different names, private bank accounts, separate houses, distinctive personal qualities, and so on, we are really not individuals; we are merely the result of the collective. Century upon century of traditional values, of beliefs and dogmas, either conscious or stored away in the unconscious, guide our path and compel the mind, which we think is individual. But the mind is a result of the totality of these compulsions, these urges and desires, and though a separate name is given to it as Mr. X, it has no real individuality; and I do not think we realize how essential it is that the individual should emerge from this total conditioning of man. It is in the instant of being liberated from the collective that there is the creative individual, and the releasing of this creativity is the fundamental issue, because it is only then that one can find out if there is a timeless reality, a state which may be called God. Mere assertion that there is or is not such a state has no value at all; what has value is direct experience uncontaminated by the past.

As I was explaining last time we met, liberation must be at the beginning, not at the end. Freedom must come first, not last, and there can be freedom only when the mind begins right at the start to liberate itself from its own conditioning. So it is important for each one of us to bring about that freedom in ourselves, and to demand it for our children through right education, and so on, which is what I would like to discuss this evening.

Now, we are obviously not free as long as we are following another. There must be freedom from the teacher, from the guru, which implies, does it not, that one must become a light unto oneself and not depend for that light on anyone. And can we really experience the unburdening of the mind, the freeing of the mind from the leader, from the teacher, from the guru? Can we actually experience that state as we are discussing it now, so that the mind does not depend upon another for its guidance?

All your so-called religious teachings create an ideal which you follow, and which again is another form of teacher. And surely, this total freedom from the concept of a leader, a teacher, from following in any form, is essential because following a teacher implies the accumulation of knowledge, and there can be liberation only when there is the total renunciation of knowledge. After all, it is knowledge that we are actually seeking in everyday life, is it not? We want knowledge to do things, knowledge to act, knowledge

which will guide us towards the goal, towards success, achievement; and that very knowledge becomes the binding factor. Now, can the mind free itself from knowledge? I think this is an important question to consider, so let us investigate and not brush it aside as impossible, or merely assert that it can be done.

All following implies the accumulation of knowledge, does it not? And where there is the accumulation of knowledge, there must be imitation. After all, when you are asked a familiar question, your response is immediate. When you are asked where you live, what is your job, your name, and so on, memory responds instantaneously because you are familiar with all that. But if a more complex question is asked, there is hesitation, which implies that the mind is searching in the storehouse of memory for the correct answer. And if a question is asked of which you know practically nothing at all, you refer to a book or search more deeply in that part of consciousness which is memory. So you are always being guided by memory. Memory must exist; otherwise, you would not know how to get back to your house, how to do your job, how to build a bridge, and so on. We learn a multitude of necessary things, and obviously such knowledge is not to be forgotten. But I am talking of a totally different kind of knowledge—the knowledge that the psyche accumulates in order to guard itself in the future and achieve whatever it wants to achieve psychologically, spiritually. It is this knowledge that makes us self-centered because the mind uses it as a means to its own continuity, which is the expansion of the 'me', and it is this knowledge that must be totally renounced. That is the only real renunciation—not giving up a little property, a house, or a bit of land, and putting on a loincloth.

So there is this accumulated knowledge on which the psyche builds and sustains itself, and can the mind, which is a result of the past, renounce all that? Surely, until the mind puts all that aside, it can never find out what is new; it can never know that instant of timelessness which is creativity. You see, what we need in this world is not more physicists, scientists, engineers, bureaucrats, politicians, but individuals who have felt this creativity, for they are the truly religious people—which means that they do not belong to any society, to any group, to any classification. That is why it is very important to understand this whole process of the accumulation of knowledge, by which I mean identification and the sense of evaluation. Can the mind be free to observe without evaluation, without judgment? Surely, its evaluations, its comparisons, its condemnations are all based on knowledge, and such a mind is incapable of understanding what is true.

If you observe the process of your own thinking, you will see that the mind is concerned only with accumulating more and more knowledge, and therefore there is never a moment of freedom to explore, and I think it is important to understand, which is actually to experience on the instant, this state of freedom without the continuity of the past, and not merely assert that the mind can or cannot be free. This will be fairly simple if we can listen to exactly what is being said, because it is a thing to be experienced, to be felt, and not to be argued about.

After all, the mind is the result of the past, of many yesterdays, which is fairly obvious; it is the residue of the known—the known being the experienced, the word, the symbol, the name, the whole process of recognition. Surely, such a mind is incapable of discovering or experiencing the unknown. It can speculate, but its speculation will be based on the known, on what it has read. The mind can experience that state only when knowledge—by which I mean the memory of the many experiences, the whole process of

recognition which is the self, the 'me'—has come to an end.

Now, if you can not only listen to what is being said but actually put aside everything you have known—the conclusions, the evaluations, the determinations, the ideals—then you will find that there comes a state which has no continuity as memory, but which on the instant is the totality of being. It is this moment that is the highest, the supreme, and that must be experienced; but it can be experienced only when the mind is completely still through understanding the totality of its own structure. It is through self-knowledge that there is quiescence of the mind, not through discipline, not through compulsion; and in that total stillness you will find there is a moment unrelated to the past, an instant in which all creation takes place. It is this creativity that is essential, for its releases the mind from the collective and makes for individuality.

The collective is the mind which is conditioned by society, by innumerable influences, by the values and beliefs which the multitude hold and the few discard, only to add another belief. Seeing all this, is it possible for the mind, without effort, to renounce the past? Until it does, there must be the following of tradition, whether it is the tradition of yesterday or of a thousand yesterdays, and a mind that follows tradition is imitative; it is dependent on a teacher, and therefore it maintains inequality, not only at the physical level, but at the psychological level as well. To such a mind, creativity is merely a word without any significance. To bring about a different state, a different culture, a different way of life, there must be the release of the individual, of this inner creativity, which will then produce its own society, its own values.

Question: Day follows day in this futile journey of existence. What does it all mean? Has life any significance?

KRISHNAMURTI: Most of us ask this question, do we not? Most of us are confused; and when we ask if life has any significance, we want to be assured that it has, or we want to be told the purpose, the goal of life.

Now, has life a goal, a purpose? And what is the state of the mind that asks such a question? Surely, this is much more important to find out than if life has significance. After all, what is life? Can it be comprehended by the mind? Life is sorrow and joy, the smiles, the tears, and the endless struggle; it is the extraordinary depth and beauty of everything and of nothing. Life is immense; it cannot be comprehended by a little mind, and it is the little mind that asks this question. Because the little mind is confused, as most of us are, it wants to know what is the purpose of life. Being confused politically, economically, and also spiritually, inwardly, we want a directive, we want to be told what to do; and when we ask, the answer we receive is invariably confused because the confused mind projects or translates the answer.

So the question is not what is the purpose, the significance of life—because you cannot hold the wind in your fist, nor put the vastness of life in a frame and worship it. But what you can do is to see the state of confusion you are in and find out how to tackle it. Once we understand our own confusion, we shall never ask what is the significance of life, for then we shall be living—we shall not be bound by the tyrannical pattern of a particular society, whether communist or capitalist, and that very living will find its own answer.

A confused mind seeking clarity will only find further confusion. That is so, is it not? If I am confused and I seek a way, a directive, the way or the directive will also be confused. It is only a clear mind that can find the way—if there is a way—not a confused mind. Surely, that much is simple and obvious.

Now, if I realize that it is futile to seek a directive as long as I am confused, will I go on seeking it? Or will I refuse to go to anybody to ask for a directive because I see that my choice of a guru, of a politician, of a book, or of certain values, being based on my own confusion, must also be confused? So I think it is essential to realize the totality of one's own confusion, not theoretically, but as an actual experience.

The fact is that you are confused, only you are frightened to acknowledge it; you are nervous, apprehensive, because if you admit you are confused, you will not know what to do, so you get carried away by immediate action. But if you become aware of the totality of your own confusion, what happens? Knowing that any movement of a confused mind can only create further confusion, don't you stop? Then all seeking ceases, and when a confused mind ceases to seek, confusion also ceases, and there is a new beginning. It is quite simple, but the difficulty is to acknowledge to oneself that one is confused.

So, are you experiencing, actually and not merely verbally, this state of confusion in which you are caught? If you are, then you will not ask anybody what the significance of life is. If you really see your own confusion, actually experience it as a fact, a reality, you are bound to stop asking, demanding, searching; and that very act of stopping is the beginning of an entirely new kind of inquiry. Then the mind will discover the extraordinary significance of life without being told.

At present we want to be led out of our confusion by another, but no one can lead us out of our confusion. As long as choice exists, there must be confusion. Choice indicates confusion, yet we are very proud of that choice, which we call free will. It is only the mind that does not choose but sees directly, without interpretation, without being influenced—it is only such a mind that is not confused and can therefore proceed to discover and explore the unknowable.

Question: Is there any way to build goodwill? Can you tell us how to live together in peace rather than in this bitter antagonism that exists between us?

KRISHNAMURTI: Surely, peace and goodwill are very difficult to build. You may construct a bridge or work in an office together because you have a boss over you, somebody to tell you what to do; but real cooperation cannot be compelled, nor does it come into being by following the blueprint laid down by an architect. Peace and goodwill can be built only when we feel that this earth is ours—not that of the communists, the socialists, or the capitalists, but yours and mine. It is our earth to enrich, to share together, and not to divide nationalistically, racially, or according to the beliefs, the creeds and dogmas, of the various organized religions.

Please listen to all this, sirs; it is not just a tirade of words. If you really want to build goodwill and live together in peace, you must remove all class differences and religious barriers—the barriers of dogma, tradition, and belief. You cannot look to government legislation to bring about this peace of goodwill because the peace of the politicians is not the same as that of a religious man; they are two entirely different things. It is a matter of actually feeling peace and goodwill every day, of being really good, and not being ashamed of that word, and of not getting caught in organizations which are supposed to bring peace, but which in fact destroy it through the pursuit of their own vested interests. When there is this feeling of peace and goodwill within each one of us, it will create its own world. But unfortunately, most of us are not concerned with building this feeling together. What brings us together

mostly is not love, not sympathy, not compassion, but hatred—identifying ourselves with one group in opposition to another. When our particular group is threatened by another in what is called war, it brings us together, and we separate again when the threat is over—which is being proven from day to day.

So what is necessary is not the ideal of peace and goodwill, but the actual facing of the fact that you are violent. When you call yourselves Maharashtrians, Gujaratis, or who knows what else, you are violent because you have separated yourselves with a word, and that word stimulates antagonism; it builds a barrier between you and somebody else. But we are all human beings with essentially the same troubles, worries, miseries, suffering; and what matters, surely, is to realize this obvious fact, to put away easily, happily, our nationalism, our petty little organizations and communities, and be simply human. But most of us would rather spend our days speculating about God, discussing the Gita, and all the rest of that stuff learned from books, which has no meaning at all; therefore our antagonism continues. What has meaning is relationship, and if together we would build peace and goodwill, we must cease to be merely idealistic and actually shed the absurd stupidities of nationalism, provincialism, strip ourselves of beliefs and vanities, and begin anew, freely and happily.

This is not a talk or an answer to encourage you to do these things. An intelligent man will act out of his own understanding. It is only the stupid man who seeks encouragement and if he is encouraged, he will still be stupid. But if he knows he is stupid, then he can do something about it. If he is aware of his own pettiness, jealousy, violence, and sees that to pursue ideals is another form of stupidity, then he can bring about a transformation in himself. If I know I am arrogant, I can deal with it, or not, as the case may be.

But the man who is arrogant and pretends to be humble, or who pursues the ideal of humility, is stupid, because he is escaping from the fact into unreality. Nonarrogance is an unreal state for the man who is arrogant, but we are brought up with this division in ourselves of the fact and the ideal, and therefore we are hypocritical. Whereas, to know that one is arrogant, and to face that fact, is the beginning of the end of arrogance.

In the same way, if we really wish to build peace and goodwill together, there must be love—not the ideal love, but just love, kindliness, compassion, which means breaking away from a particular community and shedding all our national, racial, and religious prejudices. We are human beings, living together on this earth, this earth which is ours; and to feel the truth of that, one must be extraordinarily humble. To feel anything deeply, there must be humility, but humility ceases when we are pursuing the ideal.

Question: You say that, do what we will, the state of reality can never come into being through our own efforts, and that even the desire for it is a hindrance. Then what can we do which will not create an obstacle?

KRISHNAMURTI: Now, you are not listening to me, and I am not replying, but together let us inquire into this problem. The problem is: How can we experience the real, the unknown, if the mind cannot capture it through its own effort, striving? So we have to understand the mind and why we make effort.

If we did not make effort at the physical level, we would not survive. If there were not the effort of working at a job, eating the right kind of food, taking exercise, and so on, the body would disintegrate. That is an obvious fact. So we make effort in order to survive physically.

Now, similarly, we make effort in order to survive psychologically, that is, in order to achieve what we call reality. We think that reality is a state to be attained through discipline, control, suppression, through various forms of compulsion, and we force the mind to conform to a pattern in the hope of arriving at that state. All this implies, does it not, that the mind is continually seeking security; being afraid of uncertainty, it wants to find certainty—a certainty which is permanent, and which it calls reality, God, truth, or what you will. That is what most of us are concerned with. We want a state in which there will be no disturbance of any kind and which will never come to an end, a permanent state which we call peace; and the mind is making a constant effort to capture that state, to enter into it. So we have to understand the process that is involved in this effort.

As I said, just as we make effort to survive physically, so also we make effort to continue as the 'me'. Do you understand? As long as I want to survive spiritually, I must make an effort towards the attainment of that which I call reality. Now, what is the 'me' which is making this effort? What are you? Surely, you are a name attached to a bundle of memories, experiences; you are an accumulation of hidden motives and outward pursuits, of various qualities, passions, fears, virtues. All that is the 'you', is it not? And that 'you', you want to continue in a direction which will lead to reality, so you make an effort, you meditate, you practice some form of discipline. Surely, only when the mind ceases to make this effort and is completely still without being induced or compelled to be still, only when it does not want anything and is therefore not seeking any experience—only then is there a possibility of the coming into being of the unknown.

The mind, after all, is the result of the known, and any effort which the mind makes must be within the field of the known; therefore, it cannot make an effort towards the unknown. No movement in the field of the known can ever lead to the unknown. This again is very simple and clear. The mind is still only when it has totally renounced the known; in that stillness there is no effort, and only then is it possible for the unknown to come into being.

March 7, 1956

Third Talk in Bombay

One of our great difficulties in communicating with each other is to understand the content, the intention of the words we employ, is it not? The depth of our words depends, surely, on the way we think, feel, and act. If we speak the word superficially, or if the word is merely an abstraction, it has very little significance; whereas, if the word is not merely an abstraction but has a referent which we both understand, a referent which we have established together with balance, with sanity, with clarity, then there is a possibility of communicating with each other, and a meeting of this kind will be useful. But the difficulty generally is that you have a certain referent while I have quite another, or I may be speaking merely abstractly and have no referent at all; therefore, communication, a deep exchange of thought between us, becomes almost impossible. So it seems to me very important, in a meeting of this kind, to communicate on the same level, at the same time; and such communication can take place only when we both understand the full content of the words we use. Understanding, surely, is instantaneous; it is not tomorrow, or after you have heard the talk.

To understand each other, I think it is necessary that we should not be caught in words; because, a word like *God,* for example, may have a particular meaning for you, while for me it may represent a totally different formulation, or no formulation at all. So it is almost impossible to communicate with each other unless both of us have the intention of understanding and going beyond mere words. The word *freedom* generally implies being free from something, does it not? It ordinarily means being free from greed, from envy, from nationalism, from anger, from this or that. Whereas, freedom may have quite another meaning, which is a sense of being free, not from anything, but the realization of the fact of being free; and I think it is very important to understand this meaning.

Most of us are not familiar with the feeling of being free, and it seems to me that we have to become familiar with it; we have to get acquainted with that feeling because throughout the world, tyranny is spreading. Whether under the guise of fascism, communism, socialism, or what you will, society is being more and more organized to fit a blueprint, a five-year plan, or a ten-year plan, which means that there must be an executive body vested with the authority to carry it out—and thereby tyranny begins. And yet society has to be organized. So the problem of what is freedom is very complex, and I think it is really quite important to go into it.

Without freedom, there is obviously no possibility of exploring and finding out what is truth. But how difficult it is for the mind to be free, to actually experience that state, and not just think it is free! To explore and to discover, the mind must have this quality of freedom, which is not the negative state of being free from something. I think there is a difference between the two. When I am merely free from something, that state of freedom is negation, it is a vacuum; but the realization of the fact of freedom, not from something, is a positive state. So I think we must understand the content of this word *freedom.*

From childhood we are not educated to be free, but we are conditioned, shaped to the pattern of society. Because we are afraid that freedom will make the child go wrong, spill over, we in our turn establish various rules and regulations, do's and don't's, thinking that these will guide the child in the right direction, lead him towards bliss, God, truth, or whatever it may be called. From the very beginning we assert that the mind must be conditioned, molded, so we have never inquired into this problem of freedom. If we had, our values, our action, our whole outlook on life would be entirely different.

The question is, then: Can the mind, which is the result of innumerable influences—of the books it has read, of the social, cultural, and religious environment in which it has been brought up, of the memory which has shaped it and made it what it is—can such a mind free itself, not abstractly, or as an ideal, but actually free itself from the past? And what is the continuity of the past? Do you understand the problem?

At present the mind is obviously a storehouse of memory—memory being accumulation, association, recognition, and response. It is very interesting to observe that there are now machines which can do all this much quicker than the human mind, which shows that it is a purely mechanical process; and a mind caught in that process, whatever its activity, must also be mechanical. So, can the mind, realizing all this, be in a state of freedom though it may employ the machine?

I do not know if I am explaining this issue clearly, but I think it is significant because it seems to me that our existence as individuals—if we are individuals at all, which perhaps we are not—is mechanical, routine, and that as individuals we are not creative. I do not mean creativity in the narrow sense of mere production; I am talking of creativity in a totally different sense, which we shall go into presently.

Now, what gives the mind this sense of continuity in which there is not a moment of freedom but merely a constant modification, a mechanical process of adding or subtracting? Surely, creativity is possible only when the mind is not occupied with the machinery of memory. I think this is very clear if you will follow it, though verbally it may be difficult. If you observe your own mind in operation, you will see that it is continually responding from the background of memory, and such a mind cannot know the state of freedom, in which alone there is creativity. To me, this is the supreme problem because it is only at the instant of being free that the mind is capable of discovering something totally new, unpremeditated, uncontaminated by the past.

So, what gives the mind this mechanical continuity, and why is the mind afraid to let it go? And what creates time—not chronological time, but time as this feeling of moving from yesterday, through today, to tomorrow? Surely, as long as the mind is seeking the 'more', there must be this sense of continuity. Being dissatisfied with myself as I am, I want to change; and to change, I say I must have time. Changing is always in terms of the 'more', and the moment I demand the 'more', there must be continuity. The demand for the 'more' is envy, and our social structure is based on envy. There is envy, not only in our worldly relationships, but also in our desire to be more spiritual. As long as the mind thinks in terms of the 'more', either inwardly or outwardly, there must be envy, and freedom from envy is not a denial of or an abstraction from envy but the total absence of envy without struggling to be nonenvious.

Can we go into this a little? You know what envy is, do you not? I think most of us are quite familiar with that feeling, and perhaps we have noticed that our whole society is based on it. There is a constant struggle to be something more, not only in the hierarchical social structure, but also inwardly. I see a car, and I want to possess it; I see a saint, and I want to become like him. This constant struggle to have or to become something, indicates an extraordinary dissatisfaction with what we are, but if we would understand what we are, we could not compare it with what we would like to be. The understanding of *what is* does not come about through comparing *what is* with 'what should be'.

I do not know if you have ever tackled this problem of envy. In our jobs, in our daily life and work, envy is rampant; it shows in the respect we pay to the man who knows more, to the man who has power, position, prestige, and in the constant struggle for the 'more' within ourselves. We all know this feeling of envy, and as long as it exists, there must be frustration and sorrow.

Now, can the mind be totally free from envy? I think this is a very important question because if the mind can never be totally free from envy, we shall perpetuate a society based on acquisitiveness, on ambition, and all the rest of the horrors, and there will be ceaseless conflict between us, the meaningless struggle to become something, at all levels of our existence. So, can the mind be free from envy? If I struggle to be free from envy, through discipline, through practicing a method, surely I give continuity to envy in a different form. There is still the desire to be something, and I have merely changed the object of that desire. I now want to be what I call nonenvious; but the want is still the same, the demand for the 'more' is still there. So, being aware of this fact, can the mind be free from envy? If you will go slowly with me, step by step, I think you will see it.

When am I conscious of envy? Does not envy come into being through comparison? Surely, I am envious because you have, and I have not. The very process of comparison is envy. I am a petty, little being, and you are a big saint, and I want to be like you. So where there is comparison, there is envy, and if you observe, you will see that we are brought up on this; our education, our culture, our whole manner of thinking is based on comparison and the worship of capacity. And do we understand anything through comparison? Through comparison we may extend knowledge, but knowledge, surely, is not understanding.

So the word *envy* implies ambition, greed, the desire to be something, not only socially, but psychologically. And can the mind be entirely free from this demand for the 'more'? Why do we demand the 'more'? And does that demand lead to progress? When we demand a refrigerator, a better car, and so on, it brings about progress at one level, obviously. But when we demand more power, more fulfillment, greater virtue, when psychologically we want to achieve a result, that inner demand destroys the benefits of technical progress and brings misery to man. As long as we psychologically demand the 'more', our society will be acquisitive, and there must be conflict and violence. This does not mean that we should do away with physical comforts, the mechanical aids produced by technology; but it is the psychological urge to use these things for self-expansion, which is the demand for the 'more', that is destroying us.

So, can the mind free itself from envy? It can free itself from envy only when comparison ceases, that is, when the mind is directly confronted by the fact that it is envious. Do you understand, sirs? To be directly confronted by the fact that I am envious is not the same as the realization of that fact which comes through comparison. I hope you are listening, not merely to my verbal expression, the description of what I am trying to convey, but listening in the sense that you are actually experiencing what I am saying—

which is to observe the activity of your own mind and come to the point where you are aware, directly conscious, of the fact that you are envious.

Now, when do you know that you are envious? Do you know you are envious only when comparison exists, and when you employ the word *envy?* Do you know that you are envious when you see something which you want, and there is the demand for the 'more': more pleasure, more prestige, more money, more virtue, and so on? Or do you know that you are envious without the process of demanding the 'more'? That is, can the mind look at the fact that it is envious without this demand? Can the mind free itself from the word envy?

After all, the mind is made up of words, amongst other things. Now, can the mind be free of the word envy? Experiment with this, and you will see that words like *God, truth, hate, envy,* have a profound effect on the mind. And can the mind be both neurologically and psychologically free of these words? If it is not free of them, it is incapable of facing the fact of envy. When the mind can look directly at the fact which it calls envy, then the fact itself acts much more swiftly than the mind's endeavor to do something about the fact. As long as the mind is thinking of getting rid of envy through the ideal of nonenvy, and so on, it is distracted, it is not facing the fact; and the very word envy is a distraction from the fact. The process of recognition is through the word, and the moment I recognize the feeling through the word, I give continuity to that feeling.

Surely, a man who is concerned with the total freedom from envy must go into all this; he has to see that our whole cultural background is based on envy, on acquisitiveness, spiritually as well as mundanely. That is, most of us want to be something, in this life or the next. We want more knowledge, greater power, a higher position, more virtue; so the continuity of the mind as the 'me' is through the demand for the 'more', which is envy. Envy is also the process of dependence.

Now, seeing the extraordinarily complex ways of envy, can the mind totally free itself from envy? If it does not, it cannot be free to explore, to discover, to understand. It can be free of envy only when it is directly aware of the fact that it is envious, and it cannot be directly aware of that fact as long as it condemns or compares. This is really quite simple. If you want to understand your son, you must study him, must you not? Studying your son implies watching him, and not comparing him with his elder brother or anybody else; it means looking at him directly, and not thinking of him comparatively. The moment you think comparatively, you are destroying him because the image of the other then becomes more important than your son.

So, can the mind watch in itself this unrolling of envy, but without condemnation or comparison? Can it be cognizant of the fact that it is envious, and not act upon that fact? The action of the mind upon the fact is also envy because the mind then wants to change the fact into something else. Unless the mind is totally free from envy, we shall always be in bondage; there will always be suffering, and whatever the mind's activity, it will only create more mischief. The mind that is concerned with total freedom from envy has to be aware of the fact, and not act upon the fact. Then you will see how swiftly the fact itself brings a result, an action, which is not the action of a mind distracted from the fact; and only then can the mind be still. No amount of control or self-hypnosis can ever make the mind really quiet, and it is essential for the mind to be quiet, unoccupied with itself, for only then is there a possibility of discovering or experiencing something new.

Any experience which has continuity is based on envy, on the demand for the 'more'; so the mind must die to everything it has learned, acquired, experienced. Then you will find that the mind is silent, and this silence has its own movement, uncontaminated by the past; therefore, it is possible for something totally new to take place.

In considering these questions together, again I think it is important to realize that there is no answer, and this realization is in itself an extraordinary experience. But to realize that there is no answer is very difficult for most of us because the mind is seeking a result. When the mind is seeking a result, it will find what it seeks, but that very result creates problems.

Question: When I listen to you, it appears to create and intensify my perplexity. Eight days ago I was without a problem, and now I am swamped by confusion. What is the reason for this?

KRISHNAMURTI: It may be very simple. Perhaps you have been asleep, and now you are beginning to think. Coming and sitting here casually, perhaps you have been pushed, cornered, stimulated; therefore, you are confused; but if you are merely stimulated, when you leave here, you will fall back into the same old condition. Stimulation makes the mind dull, it does not awaken the mind; it may awaken it for a minute or a second, but the mind will fall back into its habitual dullness. Depending on these meetings as a means of stimulation is like taking a drink—in the end it will make the mind dull. If you depend on a person to stimulate you to think, you become his disciple, his follower, his slave, with all the nonsense of it; and so you are bound to be dull. Whereas, if you realize that you have problems—they may be dormant for the moment, but they are there—and begin directly to confront them, then you won't have to be stimulated by me or by anyone else. Then you won't have to seek out the problems, for you will see them in yourself, and in everything about you as you go down the street: tears, disease, poverty, death.

So the question is how to tackle, how to approach the problem. If you approach any problem with the intention of finding an answer, then the answer will create more problems—which is so obvious. What is important is to go into the problem and begin to understand it; and you can do that only when you don't condemn, resist, or push it away. The mind cannot solve a problem as long as it is condemning, justifying, or comparing. The difficulty is not in the problem, but in the mind that approaches the problem with an attitude of condemnation, justification, or comparison. So first you have to understand how your mind is conditioned by society, by the innumerable influences that exist about you. You call yourself a Hindu, a Christian, a Muslim, or what you will, which means that your mind is conditioned; and it is the conditioned mind that creates the problem. When a conditioned mind seeks an answer to a problem, it is going around in circles, its search has no meaning; and your mind is conditioned because you are envious, because you compare, judge, evaluate, because you are tethered to beliefs, dogmas. That conditioning is what creates the problem.

Question: How can I be active politically without being contaminated by such action?

KRISHNAMURTI: Sir, what do we mean by political action? What is politics? Surely, it is one segment, one part of a vast complex, is it not? Life consists of many parts, political, social, religious, and if you pursue one part, which you call political action, irrespective of the whole—that is, without considering the totality of life—then, whatever you do, your action will be contaminating. I think that is so obvious. Only the mind that is seeking, groping, that does not think in compartments, either political, social, or religious, can understand the totality of life. A man who is thinking as a Maharashtrian, or a Gujarati, cannot perceive the significance of that totality; he does not see that this earth is ours. He can think only in terms of Poona or Bombay, which is so silly; and his separative thinking must eventually lead to mischief and murder, as it has already done. The mind is always setting itself apart as an Indian, a Hindu, a Muslim, a communist, a Christian, this or that, and holding on to its separation, its provincialism, thereby creating ever-increasing misery. Whereas, the man who does not feel himself to be an Indian, a Christian, or a Hindu, but only a human being, and who thinks in terms of the totality of life—it is such a man whose action will not be contaminating. But this is very difficult for most of us because we are always thinking in segments, and we hope by putting these segments together to make the whole. That can never happen. One must have a feeling for the totality of life, and then one can work differently.

Unfortunately, the politically minded want to cling to their politics and introduce religion into it, but that is an impossibility because religion is something entirely different. Religion is not dogma, it is not ritual, it is not knowledge of the Gita, of the Bible, or of any other book. Religion is an experience, on the instant, of that state of mind which is without the continuity of time. It is a single second of being free from time, and that state cannot act politically or in terms of social reform. But when a man has that feeling which is without the continuity of time, his action, whatever it be, will have quite a different meaning. Through the part, you cannot come to the whole, and you don't realize

this. To truth there is no path, neither Hindu, Christian, Buddhist, nor Muslim. Truth has no path; it must be discovered from moment to moment, and you can discover it only when the mind is free, unburdened with the continuity of experiences.

Question: We listen to all that you say to the point of surfeit. Can there be such a thing as listening too much to you? Don't we become dull by excess of stimulation?

KRISHNAMURTI: Is there such a thing as too much listening? What do we mean by listening? If I listen in order to store up, and from that stored-up knowledge to act, then listening can become too much because it is merely a stimulation to further action. That is what most of us do. We listen in order to learn, to acquire; we retain in the mind what we have learned, and from there proceed to act. As long as listening is a process of accumulation, naturally there can be too much, a surfeit; but if I am listening without any sense of acquisition, without storing up, then listening has quite a different significance. Listening is learning, but if I am storing up what I learn, then learning becomes impossible. What I learn is then contaminated by what I have stored up; therefore, it is no longer learning. It is in the process of accumulation that listening becomes wearisome, excessive, and like any other stimulant, it soon makes the mind dull; you know that what is going to be said, has already been said, and you are at the end of the sentence before I finish it. That is not listening. Listening is an art; it is to hear the totality of a thing, not just the words—and of such listening there can never be too much.

Question: Is God a reality to you? If so, tell us about God.

KRISHNAMURTI: It is the indolent mind that asks this question, is it not? It is like a man sitting comfortably in the valley and wanting a description of what lies beyond the mountains. That is what we are all doing. The words we read in the so-called sacred books satisfy the mind. The descriptions of the experiences of others gratify us, and we think we have understood; but we never bestir ourselves, we never move out of the valley, climb the steep hills, and find out for ourselves. That is why it is very important to start anew, to put aside all the books, all the guides, all the teachers, and take the journey by oneself. God, the unknown, is a thing to be discovered, not to be told about or speculated upon. What is speculated upon is the outcome of the known, and a mind that is crippled, burdened, occupied with the known, can never find the unknown. You may practice virtue, sit meditating by the hour, but you will never know the unknown because the unknown comes into being only through self-knowledge. The mind must free itself from the sense of its own continuity, which is the known—and then you will never ask if God is a reality. The man who says he knows what God is does not know. It is only the mind that frees itself from the experience it had a second ago that can know the unknown. God or truth has no abiding place, and that is the beauty of it; it cannot be made into a shelter for the petty, little mind. It is a living, dynamic thing, like the moving waters of a river. It is only a mind that is not tethered to any organized religion, to any dogma or belief, that is not burdened with the known—it is only such a mind that can discover if there is or there is not God. To state that there is, or there is not, cripples all discovery. But because the mind itself is impermanent, it wants to be assured that there is something permanent, so it says there must be the eternal, the everlasting. Out of its own quality of time, it projects a thing which it calls the timeless and then speculates about it, but only the mind that frees itself from time can know the unknown.

March 11, 1956

Fourth Talk in Bombay

We may theoretically or verbally agree that it is very important for the individual to emerge from the collective, but I do not think we pay sufficient attention to the problem, because it is only when there is the creative release of the individual that there is a possibility of discovering and living a totally different kind of life from that which we are living now. At present our life, our thinking, is collective; we are part of the collective; and if we are to bring about a different kind of society, with different values, it seems to me that the individual must begin to understand all the collective impressions that the mind has gathered through the centuries. And as I was saying, it is only when there is freedom at the very beginning that the true individual can emerge. After all, most of us are the result of environment; our thoughts, our activities, our beliefs, our various pursuits are conditioned by the many influences that exist about us; and to discover what is truth, one has to free the mind from this conglomeration of influences, which is extraordinarily arduous and difficult. I do not think we give sufficient importance to this. It is not until the mind frees itself from these many influences that it is uncorrupted, and only then is there a possibility of discovering something entirely new—something which has not been premeditated, which is not a self-projection, which is not the result of any culture, society, or religion.

Propaganda is the cultivation of prejudices, and all of us are prejudiced because we have been educated to accept or to reject, but never to inquire into this whole problem of influence. We say that we are seeking truth, but what is it that most of us are really seeking? If you are at all aware, self-observant, you will know that you are seeking a result of some kind; you want some form of satisfaction, an inward stability or permanency which you call by different names, according to the environment in which you have been brought up. And are you not seeking success? You want to be successful, not only in this world, but also in the next. It seems to me that this desire to be successful, to arrive, to become something, is a result of the wrong kind of education. And can the mind totally free itself from this desire?

I do not think we ask ourselves this question because all we are concerned with is to follow a method, a system, or an ideal, which we hope will produce a result, lead us to certainty, to success, to definite and permanent happiness, bliss, or what you will. So our minds are always occupied in the effort to arrive at something; and as long as the mind is seeking a goal, an end, a result, which will give it complete satisfaction, there must be the creation and following of authority. That is so, is it not? As long as I think that bliss, happiness, God, truth, or what you will, is an end to be reached, there will be the desire to reach it; so I must have a guru, an authority, who will help me to achieve what I demand. Therefore I become a follower; I depend on another, and as long as there is dependence, there is no question of the individual's emerging from the collective and finding out for himself what is truth, or what is the right thing to do.

So, if you observe, you will see that we are always seeking someone to tell us what to do. Being confused, we go to another to seek advice. The result is that we are always following, thereby psychologically setting up authority which invariably blinds our thinking and prevents the creativity which is so essential. Outwardly, in this competitive, ac-

quisitive society, we are ambitious, ruthless; otherwise, we shall be driven out, pushed aside. Inwardly, psychologically, we are equally ambitious; there also we want to arrive at a certain height, so we pursue an end, either self-projected or created by another. Seeing all this, what is one to do? How is one to find out what is right action?

Surely, this must be a problem to all of us. We see confusion within us and around us; the old values, beliefs, and dogmas, the leaders we have followed, no longer satisfy us; they have lost their grip; and seeing all this chaos, what is one to do? How is one to find out what is right action? To go into this problem, we must ask ourselves what we mean by search, must we not? We all say we are seeking—at least, those of us do who are serious, earnest; but before we go on with our search, surely we must find out what we mean by that word and what it is that each one of us is seeking.

Sirs, can you find anything new by seeking it? Or in your search, can you only find that which you have already known and projected into the future? I think this is an important question. What is it that we are seeking? And can a mind that is seeking ever find something beyond time, beyond its own projections? That is, I say I am seeking truth, God, bliss; but to find it, I must be able to recognize it, must I not? And to be able to recognize it, I must have already experienced it. Previous experience is necessary for recognition, so what I can recognize has already existed in my mind; therefore, it is not truth, it is my own projection. And yet that is what most of us are doing. When we seek, we are seeking something which the mind has already experienced and wants to recapture; therefore, what we are really after is the permanency of an experience of pleasure, gratification. So, as long as the mind is seeking, obviously it can never find out what is truth. It is only when the mind is no longer seeking—which does not mean that it becomes dull, distracted—and understands this whole process of search that there is a possibility of discovering something which is not of its own projection, of its own evaluation.

For example, you read in the Gita or the Upanishads a description of something permanent, an everlasting bliss, or what you will; and because this life is transient and your thinking, your activities, your relationships, are confused, disturbing, miserable, you want that other state about which you have read. That is what you are seeking. In the search for that state, you cultivate the acceptance of authority; you go to someone who promises to lead you to what you want. Therefore you become a follower, and as long as you follow, you are part of the collective, the mass. You have already recognized; you have established in your mind what that other state is, and you are seeking it through following a guru, through meditation, through the practice of various forms of discipline, and so on. What you are really seeking is something which you already know or have been taught, a state which you have read about or vaguely experienced; so your search is for the continuance of a gratifying experience, or for the discovery of a pleasurable state which you hope exists, is it not? And I say this search will never reveal the unknown; therefore, all seeking must cease.

Please do listen to all this with a little attention, if you kindly will. As they are now, our lives are contradictory, shallow, empty, and we are very confused. We go from one guru to another, from one book to another; all about us there are specialists in what we call spirituality, each offering a particular form of meditation, discipline, and we have to choose what is the right thing to do. Now, as long as there is choice, there must be confusion; and it seems to me that before we choose, seek, it is imperative to find out for ourselves what is freedom. For it is only the

free mind that can inquire, and not the mind that is caught in tradition, that is conditioned, influenced; nor the mind that is seeking a result; nor the mind that is filled with the activity of the immediate in relation to a projected future.

Surely, then, we must discover for ourselves the full significance of freedom, not as a goal, not at an end, but now. What does freedom mean to all of us? As long as the mind is conditioned by society, by culture, as long as it is burdened with its own loneliness, emptiness, as long as it is a slave to any kind of influence, it is not free. So, can the mind be fully aware of the influences that exist outside of and within itself, and which cause it to think in a particular direction, thereby making it incapable of straight thinking? As long as there is pressure behind thinking, thinking can never be straight; and can the mind remove all this pressure? That is, can it be free of motivation, of all compulsion to be this or to be that? We may not be conscious of the pressures that lie behind our thinking, the compulsions of fear, of motive, of dogma, and belief; but they are there. Now, can we be fully aware of these influences and allow the mind to think very smoothly and straightly for itself? Surely, that is one of our greatest problems, is it not? Can we find out what are the pressures on and in the mind that are making us think and act in a certain direction? Let us look at the problem differently.

You live here in Bombay. Are you to take the side of Maharashtra, or Gujarat? To which state is Bombay to go? You all sit up and take interest now, do you not? (Laughter) It is very surprising. Now, what are you to do? If you say, ''As a citizen I must choose,'' and you act either as a Maharashtrian, or a Gujarati, that action is bound to lead to further misery. Whereas, if you act neither as a Maharashtrian nor a Gujarati, but as a human being who is not involved in any of this business—with all its stupidity and narrow prejudice, with its clinging to caste, and all the rest of that nonsense—then your action will obviously be entirely different.

So we have to inquire what are the pressures, the motives that are compelling us to act in this way or that; for unless we understand these influences and are free of them, our action will invariably lead to greater sorrow and confusion. That is why it is very important to have self-knowledge, which is to understand the background, the conditioning of one's own mind, and to be freeing oneself from it all the time. You see, when we are merely concerned with immediate action, we get carried away by it, without inquiring into the whole problem of conditioning, how the mind is shaped as a Hindu, as a Christian, or what you will; and unless the mind is liberating itself from its conditioning, whatever action we may take is bound to be disintegrating and can only create more chaos. So our concern is not to choose this or that course of action but to understand how the mind is conditioned; for in freeing the mind from its conditioning, there comes an action which is sane, rational, intelligent.

What is important, then, is to find out for ourselves what each one of us is seeking, and whether what we are seeking has any validity or is merely an escape. It is imperative to have self-knowledge, to know oneself—not as the atma, and all the rest of it, but to know what one is from day to day, which is to observe how one thinks, to see what are the influences behind one's thought, and to be aware of the conscious as well as the unconscious movements of the mind. Then the mind is capable of being very quiet, and it is only in that quietness that something real can take place.

Question: One of the dominant ideas in Hinduism is that this world is an illusion. Do you not think that this idea, through the centuries, has been a strong contributing factor to the present misery?

KRISHNAMURTI: I do not know what the doctrines of Hinduism are because I am not a Hindu, nor am I a Christian or a Buddhist. But I know, as we all do, that the mind has the power to create illusion. It can mesmerize itself into believing that the trees and the houses do not exist, or that suffering is not; it has the extraordinary faculty of believing whatever it likes, irrespective of facts—which is the power to create illusion. Illusion is of different kinds. We have created the illusion of the ideal. We say this world does not matter; it is only the next world that matters, and this world is merely a passage to that. Or we say, "I am rich now because I lived a good life last time." So we can explain anything away, but the fact remains that the mind has the power to create illusion.

Now, can the mind free itself from that power and see facts as they are, instead of its opinion about the facts? Is it possible to see that one is cruel, and not explain cruelty away, or speculate about what it is that has made one cruel? Can one see the starvation, the degradation, the misery, the conflict, the brutality that exists in the world, and not explain it? Can we be simply aware of the fact that we are brutal, violent, cruel, not only outwardly, but inwardly? If we just see that fact without explaining it, what happens? Then the fact begins to operate on the mind; the mind does not operate on the fact. The mind operates on the fact only when we evaluate the fact, when we have opinions about it. Being cruel, I have the ideal of kindliness, compassion, which is over there, away from the fact. What is over there is an illusion created by the mind; the fact is, I am cruel. Now, can the mind remain with the fact, not morbidly, but just remain with the fact that I am cruel—full stop? The ideal has been created by the mind, and it is a total illusion; it exists because I want to escape from the fact. But if the mind is free from that illusion which it calls the ideal, then the mind can be operated on by the fact. Let us make it more clear and simple.

Most of you, I am sure, have ideals; and ideals exist because the mind has the power to create them. They have no validity, they are not facts; they are the mind's conception of 'what should be', which is entirely different from *what is*. *What is* is the fact, not 'what should be'; but unfortunately we are all idealistic, and so there is the split personality. We are always talking about nonviolence, ahimsa—how easily this word slips out of us!—and yet we are Maharashtrians, Gujaratis, Telugus, and God knows what else. (Laughter) Sirs, why have ideals, which have no value at all? If we have no ideals, then the fact of misery, of starvation, and the appalling cruelty we indulge in, will force us to do something.

As long as we belong to any religion, to any caste, to any particular group, as long as we make the family or the nation the most important unit, there must be cruelty; and we never face this fact, we never look at it, but are always attempting to reach the ideal, and never do. When the mind frees itself from the idea of 'what should be', it can look at the fact of *what is,* and then the fact will obviously do something to the mind. As long as I only speculate about there being a poisonous snake in my room, I can go on speculating indefinitely, and there is no action; but if there is an actual snake, then action is immediate; I do not have to think about action.

So it may be partly because we have thought of this world as illusory, or as a steppingstone to something much greater, that we are not very concerned with its social horrors and utter misery—but this does not mean that each one of us should immediately enter the field of social reform, which would only increase the present chaos. What is important is to find out how your mind works, which means seeing the pressures, the compulsions, that make you do a certain thing, and freeing the mind from its conditioning. As long as the mind thinks as a Hindu, a Brahmin, a Catholic, or what you will, its conditioning prevents it from facing the fact; but the moment it frees itself from that conditioning and faces the fact, there is an action uninfluenced by the past.

Sirs, the problem is very complex. You see, any ideas the mind creates are the outcome of its background, of its prejudice, bias; and a mind that would find out what is the right thing to do in all this chaotic misery must understand and free itself from its background—which is much more important than to find out what to do. The "what to do" will come with the understanding of the background. As long as you think as a Brahmin or a non-Brahmin, as long as you follow this path or that path, any action born of such thinking inevitably creates more confusion, more wars, more hatred. But if you begin to understand the background, there is bound to be right action; and the understanding of the background comes only through awareness in relationship.

Question: Can there be a synthesis of the East and the West, and is not that the only way of bridging the gulf between them?

KRISHNAMURTI: Sir, what are the East and the West? You see, we are asking a wrong question and trying to find a right answer. Is there an East and a West, except geographically? Is there an Eastern culture and a Western culture? Is there an Eastern way of thinking and a Western way of thinking? Superficially there may be, but whether it is called Eastern or Western, communist or Catholic, each one of us is conditioned by the culture in which he is brought up. You may live in the East, and another in the West; but he is conditioned by his society, by the climate, by the food he eats, by the innumerable impressions, pressures, influences, that exist around him, just as you are. In the West, people wear a certain type of clothing, and here they wear something else; but the human being is the same throughout the world, whatever he wears, and regardless of whether his skin is brown, white, black, or yellow. We are all ambitious, greedy, envious, wanting success—though "success" may take one form there, and a different form here. We are human beings, not Easterners and Westerners; this is our world, it is not the world of the communists, the Catholics, or of any other group, however much they may want it to be. Large groups of people are deliberately being conditioned to think in a certain way. But there is no "better" conditioning; there is only conditioned thinking, and as long as our minds are conditioned and act according to that conditioning, we are bound to create wars. As long as you think as a Hindu, opposed to Americans or Russians or Muslims or what you will, you must inevitably bring about antagonism; as long as you think of yourself as a Gujarati or a Maharashtrian, you are going to have appalling brutalities.

So there is only the human mind; there is only thinking, whether here or in the West; and it is the primary job of every serious person to inquire into the whole process of thinking because all action springs from thought. Without thinking, there is no action; and thinking is now divided as Indian, European, this or that, which means that it is conditioned, influenced, shaped by a particular culture. Having produced its own culture, the mind then gets caught in that culture, in that society; and to understand this process, to go into it and break it down is the function of every responsible human being. It

is only when we free the mind from its conditioning that we can know what love is, what compassion is; and as long as we remain Hindus, Maharashtrians, or what you will, it is all nonsense to talk about God, truth, love, compassion.

A new world cannot come into being unless each one of us feels that this earth is ours to live on, yours and mine; and we cannot live on it peacefully if I think of myself as a Brahmin, or a great saint, and look upon you as a little man, a servant to be abused. We are human beings together, and the change of heart is much more important than the change of legislation. Laws cannot change the heart, and the heart or mind which is ambitious can utilize or circumvent any form of legislation to enrich itself. That is why it is very important to understand all this, and not divide the world as the East and the West.

Question: According to you, the known can never discover the unknown. How then can one recognize the unknown? Is it so utterly different?

KRISHNAMURTI: Surely, the mind is the result of the known. The mind only knows as a fact what has been; it can never know as a fact what will be. It can conjecture, but there are innumerable influences which are constantly changing the future, so no man can say what the future will be; and I think it is very important to understand this politically. No group of people, whether communist, Catholic, socialist, or any other can know the future. To assume that the future can be known is to have a pattern, from which arises the effort to force man to fit into that pattern, liquidating him if he does not, or destroying him in prison camps, and all the rest of the horrors. What can be known is the process of one's own thinking. The known is the past;

recognition is the whole process of the known.

The questioner asks, in effect, "Can I recognize the unknown? Can I experience, and know that I am experiencing the unknown?" Now, what do we mean by recognition? Surely, we can only recognize something we have known. Having met you before, I recognize you; if I have not previously met you, I cannot recognize you—recognition being familiarity with the name, the quality and shape of the face, the manner of speech, the gesture, and all the rest of it. So recognition is always the result of the known. I recognize because I have experienced before that that is a house, that is a tree, that is a man, a woman, or a child; I know because I have been told, and also because it is my own experience. I know through experience, so the mind is the result of the known. From the known it can project the unknown, calling it God, truth, or what you will, but it is still a projection of the known.

So, can the known experience the unknown? Obviously not. Such a question is a contradiction; it has no validity. The question is not whether the mind can recognize or experience the unknown but whether the mind can free itself from the known. Being the result of the known, can the mind free itself from the known? This is an extraordinary question if you really put it to yourself and go into it. The mind has become mechanical because it functions from the known to the known. Like the electronic machines which have been invented, it can function only through association. Our thinking is the result of the known; otherwise, there is no thinking; it is the reaction of memory, which is the past; and it is the past that asks, "Can I know or experience something which is timeless, something without measure, beyond recognition?" The answer is obvious.

So, all that we can do is to understand the operations of the known, to see how the mind thinks, feels, inquires—which is meditation; and only then is the mind completely still. Stillness of the mind may be induced by drugs or by discipline, suppression, but that is not meditation; it is just a trick, and such a mind is not still. It is only through inquiring into the known that the mind can be quiet, completely still—the totality of the mind, the conscious as well as the unconscious, not just the superficial mind which says, "I must be still in order to experience the unknown." The totality of the mind must be still, which means that the whole process of thinking must come to an end; and it cannot come to an end by chopping it off, or operating upon it, but only by understanding it. When the whole process of thinking is understood, there comes a stillness of mind in which there is neither the experiencer nor the experienced; there is no movement, and only then is there a possibility of the coming into being of something which is beyond the measure of time.

Our job, then, is not to inquire into the unknown but to find out whether the mind can be free from the known. If you really put this question to yourself, factually and not theoretically, you will find out whether the mind can or cannot be free. I cannot tell you; it is for you to discover the truth of the matter. And you are bound to put this question to yourself because, as it is now, your mind is mechanical; it endlessly repeats what it has been taught, what it has learned, what it has read—the eternal gossip about the known. Only when the mind understands itself is there the possibility of freedom from the known.

March 14, 1956

Fifth Talk in Bombay

The last four times we have met here, I have been talking about how important it is for the individual to free himself from the many social, cultural, and religious influences, for it is only then that there can take place the creative release of the good mind. It seems to me very important to understand the quality of the mind and to bring about that which is good. Most of us are not concerned with bringing about the good mind but only with what to do; action has become much more important than the quality of the mind. To me, action is secondary. If I may so put it, action does not matter; it is not important at all because when there is the good mind, the mind that is creatively explosive, then from that creative explosiveness comes right action; it is not "doing is being," but "being is doing."

For most of us, action seems vital, important, and so we get caught in action; but the problem is not action, though it may appear to be. Most of us are concerned with how to live, what to do in certain circumstances, whether to take this side or that side in politics, and so on. If you observe, you will see that our search is generally to find out what is the right action to take, and that is why there is anxiety, this pursuit of knowledge, this search for the guru. We inquire in order to find out what to do; and it seems to me that this approach to life must inevitably lead to a great deal of suffering and misery, to contradiction, not only within oneself, but socially—a contradiction that invariably breeds frustration. To me, action inevitably follows being. That is, the very state of listening is an act of humility. If the mind is capable of listening, that very listening brings about the good mind, from which action can come into being. Whereas, without the good mind, without that strange, explosive quality of creativity, mere search for action leads to pettiness, to shallowness of heart and mind.

I do not know if you have noticed how most of us are occupied with what to do, and

probably we have never had this quality of mind which immediately perceives the totality. The very perception of the totality is its own action, and I think it is important to understand this because our culture has made us very shallow; we are imitative, traditionally bound, incapable of wide and deep vision because our eyes are blinded by the immediate action and its results. Observe your own mind and you will see how concerned you are with what to do, and this constant occupation of the mind with what to do can only lead to very shallow thinking. Whereas, if the mind is concerned with the perception of the whole—not with how to perceive the whole, what method to use, which is again to be caught in the immediate action—then you will see that from this intention comes action, and not the other way around.

What is it that most of us are now concerned with? With violence and non-violence, with acquiring a little virtue, with the particular caste or nation we belong to, with whether there is God or not, with what kind of meditation to practice, and so on—all of which is on a limited, petty scale. So the mind gets lost in little things, but this does not mean that one must not inquire into what is meditation. To discover what meditation is, is quite a different matter. But the mind is concerned with what system of meditation to use in order to arrive, and this preoccupation with a system makes the mind petty, shallow, empty—which is what is happening to most of us. We repeat the Gita, the Bible, the Koran, or some Buddhist book, or we quote Lenin or Marx, and think we have solved all the issues. Whereas, it seems to me that what is important is to bring about the good mind, that extraordinary quality of the mind that captures instantaneously the totality of feeling, the totality of being; and I think that the good mind is not possible as long as there is effort. As long as one is striving in any direction, making an effort to be or not to be this or that, the good mind, the mind that is capable of perceiving the whole, is not possible. It is only the mind that is freeing itself from effort, from striving, that can understand the totality of being.

Why do we make effort? Please, this is a serious question; let us think it out together. Effort is obviously necessary at a certain level of our existence—the struggle to acquire knowledge in school, to learn a technique, and so on; but why does the mind make an effort to be something, to be nonviolent, or to be peaceful? Is it not because being aware that it is violent, greedy, or stupid, the mind wants to transform that state into something else? The desire to change from *what is* to 'what should be', brings about a process of effort, does it not? I am ignorant, and I must have knowledge; I am envious, and I must be nonenvious. So the desire to be nonenvious breeds effort, the struggle to be something. To me, this effort, in which most people are caught, is the deteriorating factor. As I said, the very act of listening is humility, but we do not listen. We say to ourselves, "What is he talking about? What will happen to me if I make no effort to be something? How shall I live? How shall I get a job, or be promoted?" All life as we know it is struggle, effort, drive, compulsion; we are used to that rhythm, to that way of thinking, and so we never listen. We are listening through the objection of our own opinions.

Now, can we put all that aside and merely listen? When we are merely listening, what has happened? That very act of listening is humility. There is no effort involved; the mind has done nothing to be humble, it is humble; therefore, it is capable of listening. Do you follow? Because I want to understand what another is talking about, I am not offering my opinion, my objections, my arguments; that is all laid aside, and I listen to what is being said. That very listening is humility; the mind is humble in that very act; therefore, there is no effort to be humble. The arrogant mind cannot listen. The mind that is full of knowledge, argumentation, that has acquired, experienced—such a mind is incapable of listening because it is full of vanity, conceit. So the problem is not how to get rid of conceit but whether the mind is able to listen. When it can listen, the mind is in a state of humility, and then it is capable of perceiving totally, from which action follows. But what are we concerned with now? Most of us are concerned with the accumulation of a little virtue, a little knowledge, and with multiplying it, making it bigger, wider; but it is still an additive process. We have knowledge; we know what the Gita says, what our guru says, but the good mind is not; therefore, the mind with its everlasting struggle is incapable of perceiving, of understanding the whole.

So its seems to me that the greatest factor in the deterioration of the mind is this struggle to be something. After all, when you desire to be something, when you have a goal, an end in view, you struggle towards that end and your whole life is molded by it; therefore, your mind is not concerned with its own quality and depth but only with the result of effort.

Do think about this and you will see how uncreative we are throughout the world. We are merely imitative; we are shaped by the pattern of society, by the blueprint of a particular culture; and can such a mind be creatively explosive? Obviously it cannot. Yet all we are concerned with is what to do. There is starvation in the world; there is misery, suffering, both outwardly and inwardly, and we are concerned only with how to put an end to it all. So the mind gets caught in the "how," the answer, the explanation: how to find God, how to meditate, whether or not there is a continuity after death, what is the right action, who is the right guru, which is the right book, and so on. That is all you are concerned with, is it not? You are not concerned with the quality of the mind but only with the many "hows," which obviously make the mind shallow. You may have the best guru, read all the sacred books, be extraordinarily virtuous; but if you have not this creatively explosive quality of the good mind, your virtue becomes very shallow, respectable; therefore, it has no validity because virtue is not an end in itself.

So it seems to me that what is important is really to inquire into the quality of the good mind—which is a mind that is not imitative, that does not merely follow, but is literally creatively explosive—because without that quality, of what value is your virtue, your knowledge, your search for truth? And can the shallow, mediocre mind, the mind that is educated merely to fit into society, that is beaten, broken, suffering—can such a mind find this creatively explosive quality?

Sirs, first we must realize that our minds are shallow, empty; we may fill them with a lot of words, with the knowledge of books, but they are still empty. And can a petty, shallow mind break up its pettiness, its shallowness? Can it make itself vast and deep? Now, when you ask this question, with what intention do you ask it? Is it in order to arrive at a result, to find a method? Or do you ask it merely as the gardener plants a seed, waters it, and lets it grow? I do not know if I am making this issue clear. To me, the explanation of why the mind is petty is of no importance; what is important is for the mind to find out why it is putting this question.

Realizing that it is empty, what does the mind do? It proceeds to acquire more knowledge; it makes effort to fill, to enrich itself. Because it feels shallow, the mind wants to be deep, and then the problem arises of how to be deep; so it practices a method which promises what it wants, and thereby it

gets caught in the method. To me, this is a totally wrong process; it is most destructive because it leads to further shallowness, emptiness. The mind that is caught in a method is still petty because it is concerned only with its own enrichment; it has not understood itself. Whereas, if the mind realizes that it is shallow and asks of itself why it is shallow without seeking an explanation, an answer, then quite a different process takes place. As I said, it is like a gardener planting a seed and watering it. If the water and the soil are good, and if the seed has vitality, it puts out a shoot. Similarly, if the mind asks itself why it is shallow and does not seek an answer or try to find ways and means of enriching itself, then that very question brings about its own explosion. Then you will find that there comes a totally different state in which the mind is no longer struggling to achieve, to accumulate; and such a mind knows no deterioration.

At present our minds are all deteriorating, and what matters, surely, is to put an end to that deterioration. This cannot be done by merely searching out the cause of deterioration and explaining it. But if one is aware of this inner deterioration, and without seeking an answer, one asks oneself why it exists, then that very questioning is an act of listening. To listen, there must be humility, and humility cleanses the mind of the past; then the mind is fresh, innocent, and is therefore capable of perceiving the totality, the whole. It is only such a mind that can bring about order and create a new society with values entirely different from those that exist now.

Question: What do you say regarding tapas, *and the* sadhana *mentioned in Hindu books for bringing about the cessation of thought?*

KRISHNAMURTI: I think it is a great mistake to interpret what the books tell you. Please follow this; I am not saying anything irrational. The books tell you to do this or that, and the books may be wrong, and it is also possible that thought can never cease. But what you can do is to find out directly for yourself, without depending on a single person or book, whether or not thought can come to an end. That is much more vital, much more significant, than practicing some method that promises the cessation of thought.

Now, why do you want thought to cease? Is it because thought is very disturbing, contradictory, transient? And how do you know thought can cease? Do you know because the books have said so? Or is your mind inquiring into the whole process of thinking? Do you follow, sirs? Our problem is to understand the process of thinking, and not how to end thought. You can end thought by taking a drug, or by learning a few tricks which you call meditation, but the mind will still be dull, shallow. Whereas, if you begin to inquire into what is thinking, then you will find out whether or not thought can come to an end.

Let us be very clear about this. A method, however noble, however promising, can only stifle thinking or hold it in a static state, but that is not the cessation of thought. You have only smothered, put a lid on thinking. Whereas, if you begin to inquire into the whole process of thinking, then you will find out what that process is.

Thinking, surely, is the response of memory to challenge—memory being the continuity of the past. Behind thinking there are certain pressures, compulsions, which make thought crooked. When there is pressure of any kind behind thinking—pressure being motive, compulsion, urge—thought must invariably be crooked. But if the mind can free itself from all pressures, from all motives, then you will find that the mind becomes extraordinarily quiet, and that in this quietness there is the cessation of what you

call thinking. If you merely wish for the cessation of thinking because you hope it will solve all your problems, or because the books promise a reward, you may succeed in making your mind very still, but it is still a petty mind. So, what we are concerned with is not how to put an end to thought, but with putting an end to pettiness, to shallowness; and for the mind to cease to be petty, it must be free from all authority, from all following, so that it is capable of thinking anew.

Sirs, to put the problem differently, a collective belief is very destructive. Many of you call yourselves Hindus, which means that you are still bound by the collective dogmas, traditions, and influences that have made you what you are. Where there is a collective belief, there is deterioration; a destructive process is going on, and that is exactly what is happening throughout the world at the present time. We are all communists or socialists, Hindus or Christians, this or that, which is the collectivity of belief, so there is no individuality at all; and that is why it is very important to see the evil of collective belief. In the very perception of that evil, the individual emerges. It is only the mind that is neither communist nor capitalist, neither Christian nor Hindu, the mind that has no compulsion, no pressure or motive behind it—it is only such a mind that can be without thought. With the ceasing of thought there comes a quietness like that of living waters, and in that quietness there is a vast movement which cannot be comprehended by the mind that is urged through pressure, through motive. Any practice by a mind which is petty will only make the mind still more petty because it does not understand itself; it is not aware of its own pettiness; it may learn new tricks, new ways or methods, but it will still be petty. All that a petty mind can do is to be aware that it is petty, and not do a thing about it. When the mind is aware that it is petty, it has done everything that it can do.

Question: You say that the past must totally cease for the unknown to be. I have tried everything to be free from my past, but memories still exist and engulf me. Does this mean that the past has an existence independent of me? If not, please show me how I can be free of it.

KRISHNAMURTI: First of all, is the past different from the 'me'? Is the thinker, the observer, the experiencer, different from the past? The past is memory, all one's experiences, one's ambitions, the racial residue, the inherited tradition, the cultural values, the social influences—all that is the past, all that is memory. Whether we are conscious or unconscious of it, it is there. Now, is the totality of all that different from the 'me' who says, "I want to be free from the past"?

Please follow this patiently with me. There is this continuance of memory, which is extensive and has great depth, and which is responding all the time to challenge. Now, is this memory different from the 'me', or is it the 'me'? Do you understand? If there were no name, no association with the family, with the past, with the race, and all the rest of it, then would there be a 'me'? Would there be a 'me', a thinker, if there were no thinking? Or do you say that above the 'me' there is the atma, an independent entity who is watching all the time? If there is an independent entity, surely the mind which is dependent is incapable of knowing it. Do you follow? The mind which is both dependent on and a result of the past has said there is the atma, the watcher from above, who is free, independent; but it is still the dependent mind that has said it; therefore, what it calls the atma is part of the mind; it is within the field of memory, of tradition. That is fairly obvious, is it not? You are educated through tradition, through repetition, through reading, and all the rest of it, to believe that there is something independent of this 'me', something beyond this field of memory; but a man educated in Russia will say there is no such thing, it is all nonsense; there is only this 'me'. So we are all the result of our education; we are conditioned by our past, by the culture in which we live, by the religious, political, and social influences in which we have been brought up; and to assume, to postulate, to suppose, that there is something superior to this 'me', though there may be, is a most infantile and immature way of thinking which has led to a great deal of confusion and misery.

So, there is no 'me' separate from the past. The 'me' is the past; it is the quality, the virtue, the experience, the name, the family association, the various tendencies, both conscious and unconscious, the racial inheritance—all that is the 'me', and the mind is not separate from it. The soul, the atma, is part of the mind because the mind has invented these words.

The problem is, then: How can the mind, which is a result of the past, free itself from its own shadow? Do you understand? How can the mind, which is the totality of memory, free itself from the past? Is that a right question, sirs? I think it is a wrong question. All that the mind can do is to be aware of the past, how every reaction, every response derives from the past—just be totally aware of it without the desire to alter it, without choosing out of the past what is good and rejecting what is bad. If the mind struggles to end, to forget, or to alter the past, it separates itself from the past and so creates a duality in which there is conflict, and that very conflict is the deterioration of the mind. Whereas, if the mind sees the totality of this memory and is simply aware of it, then you will find that something strange happens. Without effort, the past has come to an end.

Try it, not because I say so, but because you see it for yourself. A mind which is the result of the past cannot free itself from the past through its own effort. All that it can do is to be aware of its reactions, aware of how it accumulates resentment, and then forgives; of how it acquires, and then renounces; of how it chooses, and then gets confused in choice. A mind that chooses is a confused mind. Be aware of all this, and you will find that the mind becomes astonishingly quiet. Then there is no choice because the mind sees the falseness of doing something to free itself from the past. Out of that perception there comes, not a freedom from the past, but a sense of freedom which can deal with the past.

Question: The strongest underlying commandment in all religions is: Love your fellow man. Why is this simple truth so difficult to carry out?

KRISHNAMURTI: Why is it that we are incapable of loving? What does it mean to love your fellow man? Is it a commandment? Or is it a simple fact that if I do not love you, and you do not love me, there can be only hate, violence, and destruction? What prevents us from seeing the very simple fact that this world is ours, that this earth is yours and mine to live upon, undivided by nationalities, by frontiers, to live upon happily, productively, with delight, with affection and compassion? Why is it that we do not see this? I can give you lots of explanations, and you can give me lots more, but mere explanations will never eradicate the fact that we do not love our neighbor. On the contrary, it is because we are forever giving explanations, causes, that we do not face the fact. You give one cause, I give another, and we fight over causes and explanations. We are divided as Hindus, Buddhists, Christians, this or that. We say we do not love because of social conditions, or because it is our karma, or because somebody has a great deal of money while we have very little. We offer innumerable explanations, lots of words, and in the net of words we get caught. The fact is that we do not love our neighbor, and we are afraid to face that fact, so we indulge in explanations, in words, in the description of the causes; we quote the Gita, the Bible, the Koran—anything to avoid facing the simple fact.

Do you understand, ladies and gentlemen? What happens when you face the fact and know for yourself that you do not love your neighbor? Your son is your neighbor, so you do not have to go very far. You do not love your son, and that is a fact. If you loved your son, you would educate him entirely differently; you would educate him not to fit into this rotten society but to be self-sufficient, to be intelligent, to be aware of all the influences around him in which he is caught, smothered, and which never allow him to be free. If you loved your son, who is also your neighbor, there would be no wars between Pakistan and India, or between Germany and Russia, because you would want to protect him and not your property, your petty, little belief, your bank account, your ugly country, or your narrow ideology. So you do not love, and that is a fact.

The Bible may tell you to love your neighbor, and the Gita or the Koran may tell you the same thing, but the fact is that you do not love. Now, when you face that fact, what happens? Do you understand? What happens when you are aware that you are not loving, and being aware of that fact, do not offer explanations or give causes as to why you do not love? It is very clear. You are left with the naked fact that you do not love, that you feel no compassion, that you have not a single thought of another. The contemptuous way you talk to your servants, the respect you show to your boss, the deep, reverential salute with which you greet your guru, your pursuit of power, your identification with a country, your seeking after the great ones—all this indicates that you do not love. If you start from there, then you can do something. Sirs, if you are blind and really know it, if you do not imagine you can see, what happens? You move slowly, you touch, you feel; a new sensitivity comes into being.

Similarly, when I know that I have no love, and do not pretend to love; when I am aware of the fact that I have no compassion, and do not pursue the ideal, which is all nonsense—then with the facing of that fact, there comes a different quality; and it is this quality that saves the world, not some organized religion, or an ideology invented by the clever. It is when the heart is empty that the things of the mind fill it, and the things of the mind are the explanations of that emptiness, the words that describe its causes.

So, if you really want to stop wars, if you really want to put an end to this conflict within society, you must face the fact that you do not love. You may go to a temple and offer flowers to some stone image, but that will not give the heart this extraordinary quality of compassion, love, which comes only when the mind is quiet, and not greedy, envious. When you are aware of the fact that you have no love and do not run away from it by trying to explain it, or find its cause, then that very awareness begins to do something; it brings gentleness, a sense of compassion. Then there is a possibility of creating a world totally different from this chaotic and brutal existence which we now call life.

March 18, 1956

Sixth Talk in Bombay

It seems to me that one of the most difficult things in our life is to understand the whole implication of living and what it is all about. With its pleasure and sorrow, its varieties of experience, its strife and strain, this enormous process that we call living becomes extremely complex, and perhaps very few of us understand it completely. In this vast process, there are many problems, some impersonal, outside of us, and others that are intimately related to the individual, which we almost never consider. Why do we perform any action, and what is its significance, what are its implications? Is there such a thing as the absolute, the immeasurable, and is there any relation between that immensity and our everyday living? We keep all these things in watertight compartments and then try to find a relationship between them. Unfortunately, we are educated not to understand the whole significance of life but only to have a job, to perform some immediate action, to earn a livelihood; and so the mind is incapable of thinking deeply on any issue.

Now, I do not think that the problem of immediate action, the problem of what to do, whether in this or in any other country, can be divorced from the inquiry into whether there is such a thing as the absolute, the immeasurable, something beyond the field of the mind—because without this inquiry, I feel that mere action, however satisfactory and necessary, will lead only to further misery. If we would understand each other, I think this point must be made very clear. Our fundamental problem is not what to do but rather how to awaken the creativity of the individual; that is, how not to get so involved in the immediate action that the immense significance of this creative release is denied or put aside.

After all, why is it that we are listening? Surely, not to be told what to do, but rather, if we are at all serious and thoughtful, to find out together—not as pupil and teacher, but together—how the mind gets caught in all the various influences to which it is subjected and so becomes incapable of deep inquiry. Without deep inquiry, without search, one may bring about immediate results which produce temporary alleviation, but this may be the cause of further misery, further strife.

So I think it is very important for each one of us to find out for himself what it is that he ultimately wants, and whether there is such a thing as the immeasurable, in the understanding of which his present activity will have quite a different significance. To me, most definitely, the immediate activity has significance only in the understanding of that immensity, call it God, truth, reality, or what you will; and to be concerned with immediate change or reformation, divorced from the other, has no meaning at all.

For most of us, life is chiefly a process of earning a livelihood, with its constant economic and social pressures, and the complex demands of individual relationships. We are caught in this process, and we are trying to do something within its field—trying to be noble, nonviolent, and all the rest of it. We seem to be incapable of inquiring into this whole issue, of searching out its significance at a deeper level. So, why is one not capable of deep inquiry? I think that is a legitimate question for all of us to ask ourselves. Why is it that we are apparently incapable of penetrating into the deeper issues of life? Why is it that we do not even ask fundamental questions? Is it that we are blocked by so-called education, by society, by our relationships, by our own miseries and conflicts? What actually blocks or hinders this inquiry? And are we blocked, or are we just incapable of real inquiry?

We are trying to find out if there can be a creative release of the individual so that the mind is capable of constant inquiry, of penetrating to extraordinary depths, not theoretically, abstractly, but actually. Is this capacity to probe, to penetrate deeply, blocked by our own thinking? Or does it not exist in us at all?

We know when we are blocked; we know what that word signifies. When I want to do something, I am consciously blocked, pre-vented, hindered by society, by some relationship, or by a particular act; or there is an unconscious hindrance. This conscious or unconscious blockage may be the factor which is preventing the mind from penetrating to great depths. Is there a blockage because our education is so superficial that we cannot inquire profoundly? Is it because our so-called intellectual training is so limited or specialized that our minds cannot penetrate deeply or ask really fundamental questions?

Our education at present is merely the cultivation of memory; it is the repetition of phrases, words, the learning of techniques; it is as superficial as lighting a lamp. With a mind so educated, we try to inquire; and we feel blocked, incapable of asking a really serious question and going into it alone. Now, is there a blockage, or is it that we have not the capacity to inquire? I think there is a difference between the two. It may be that I block my own inquiry through various fears, frustrations, and all the rest of it; or I may simply not have the capacity to inquire persistently, to dig very deeply and discover something extraordinarily significant which will give light to my daily activities.

What do we mean by the capacity to inquire? Can a mind which has been trained, educated to think only superficially, penetrate to great depths? Obviously not. After all, the man who has read the Gita, the Koran, or what you will, and knows all the ready-made answers, the man who has compared the various teachers and learned a cunning way of approaching every problem, has acquired knowledge which is very superficial. He repeats what others have written, and this repetition, which is traditional, makes the mind very shallow. If one talks with a man who is erudite, who has read all the *shastras,* who is familiar with the teachings of Buddha and Shankara, who has great knowledge as well as the power of expression, and who has therefore become a leading authority—if one talks with such a man, one sees that his mind is very shallow. Such a man has never put a fundamental question to himself and found the truth of it on his own; he is always quoting some authority. We also are trained to be like that; therefore, the mind is very shallow, limited, petty; and with such a mind we try to inquire. But I say a shallow mind cannot penetrate very deeply or ask questions that have profound significance. So what is one to do? I think this is your problem if you really think about it.

Let us put it differently. We see great confusion around us, not only among the experts, the authorities, but also among ourselves and in our own thinking. There are many political, sociological, and so-called religious organizations, and most of us join one or the other of these, throwing ourselves into its work because we think it has the final answer. So we come to depend on organizations, or on leaders who give us an assurance; they know, therefore we follow, we imitate, we belong to these various groups. All this indicates, does it not, a mind that is not solitary, alone, a mind that is incapable of thinking out a problem completely for itself because it is dependent. The moment the mind becomes dependent, it is made incapable of inquiry; like a child who is dependent on its mother, such a mind is not free to inquire.

So, through dependence on organizations and authority, through so-called education, culture, through our own constant ambition, our desire for power, position, and prestige, the mind is made incapable of deep penetration. If you actually observe your own mind—I am repeating this most respectfully—you will see how incapable it is of real penetration into what may be called truth or God. Probably your mind has never asked what life is all about, and when it does ask, it has an answer according to Buddha, Christ, Shankara, the Upanishads, or what you will; so it is satisfied. Only the mind that is alone,

that is really free, can penetrate to great depths without seeking some stupid result. But our minds are not like that, and until they are, our life has very little meaning; it can only produce more war, more despair, more chaos—which is being shown in the world at the present time.

So, is it possible for you and me, who have no capacity for it, to penetrate deeply? And without that capacity, has it any significance for us to inquire into that which may be the final answer to all our problems? Surely, you must have asked yourself this question. If not, I am asking it now. After all, if you have no capacity to inquire, what is the good of following somebody? By that very following, you are made more dependent, and therefore less capable of inquiry. To be capable of inquiring profoundly, you need a mind which is completely alone—alone in the sense that it is not being pushed in any direction, not being driven by the anxiety of immediate action, immediate reformation, immediate demand. So what is one to do?

You see, the difficulty with most of us is that we want tangible evidence that we have arrived; we want to be assured of a result; we want to be told that we have changed, that we are good, or that we are effective social entities. To me, all these things are unimportant because I see that the capacity to inquire, to discover what is truth, cannot be cultivated. All that the mind can do is to be aware that it is incapable of inquiry, and not keep on imitating, copying. Sirs, it is like leaving the window open; then the fresh air comes in as it will, if there is fresh air. Similarly, all that one can do is to leave the window of the mind open—not ask how to leave it open, but actually leave it open. I hope you see the difference between the two. To ask, "How am I to leave the window of the mind open so that reality can come into being?" only makes you incapable of leaving it open. When you want to know the "how," the method, you are a follower of the method, and to the method you become a slave. Any method can produce only its own result, which is not the opening of the mind; the moment you really understand this, the mind is open. Then you will see that your inquiry no longer has a particular object, and because the mind is open, free of any system, it is capable of receiving something immeasurable. That immeasurable thing is not to be talked about; it has no meaning if it is merely read about and repeated. It must be experienced; and that very experience brings about an action in the world without which this existence has no significance at all, except that it produces more misery.

After all, what is it we all want? Life, with its constant change, its strife, its varieties of experience, is very fleeting; and the mind says, "Is this all?" When it asks that question, it generally turns to a book, or to a person, and thereby gets caught in authority because the mind is very easily satisfied with words. But when the mind is not satisfied with words, with explanations, but proceeds to delve, to inquire freely, easily, without any pressure, then there comes into being that extraordinary something—the name does not matter—which will solve all the complexities of our life.

Sirs, what is a problem? Does not the problem exist only when the mind has given soil for it to take root? If there is no soil for the problem to take root, then you can deal with the problem. The mind at present has so many rooted problems that it is nothing but a seedbed of problems. So the question is not how to solve any particular problem but whether it is possible for the mind not to give soil to problems. The moment the mind gives soil to a problem, the problem takes root and spreads. Now, listen to this and understand it. Do not ask how not to give soil to problems, but see that a problem exists only when there is soil in the mind for the

problem to take root. Just to see and to understand that fact is sufficient to dissolve the problem.

Question: From what you said last Sunday, I gather that you think we do not love our children. Do you not know, sir, that the love of our children is one of the greatest and most deep-rooted of human affections? Surely you realize how helpless we are individually to do anything about war and peace.

KRISHNAMURTI: If we loved our children, there would be no wars, for our education would be entirely different, and we would create a totally different kind of society; but since there are wars and our society is in perpetual conflict within itself, with each man against another, it indicates that we do not love our children. That is what I said last Sunday, and I think it is a fact. You say that your love for your children is deep-rooted and great, but the fact is that you are at each other's throats. There is ambition, and when man is ambitious, there is no love in his heart; when he encourages his son to climb the ladder of success and reach the top, obviously he is encouraging him to be ruthless. Surely, all this indicates that there is no love, does it not?

After all, as a parent, you are also a teacher because your child lives with you; you train him, he follows you, he builds himself in your image. There is the teacher at school, but you are the teacher at home, and you train the child in the do's and don't's, compelling him to imitate, to copy, to follow in your footsteps and become somebody in society. All you are concerned with is the child's security, which is your own; you want him to be respectable, to earn a livelihood, to adjust himself to the demands of the existing social order. You call that love, and is it love? What does it mean to love a child? Surely, it does not mean encouraging him to become your little image, shaped by society, by so-called culture; it means, rather, helping him to grow freely. He has acquired certain tendencies, inherited certain values from you, and so he cannot be free at the beginning; but to love him is to help him from the beginning to free himself constantly, so that he becomes a real individual, not merely an imitative machine.

If you love your child, you will educate him not to conform to society but to create his own society, which may be entirely different from the present one; you will help him to have not a traditional mind but a mind that is capable of inquiring into the significance of all the cultural, social, religious, and national influences by which he is surrounded, and not be caught in any of them, so that his mind is free to find out what is true. Surely, that is right education. Then the child will grow into a free human being, self-sufficient and capable of creating his own world, a totally different kind of society; having confidence, the capacity to work out his own destiny, he will not want your property, your money, your position, your name. But now it is the reverse; you expect your son to carry on your property, your wealth, your name, and that is what you call love.

What can the individual do about all this? Surely, it is only the individual who can alter the world, the individual who feels very strongly that a new kind of education, a new way of living must be brought about. It begins with the individual, with those of you who really feel the importance of these things. You may not prevent an immediate war, but you can prevent future wars if you see for yourself, and help your children to see, the stupidity of wars, of class divisions, of social conflict. But unfortunately, most of us are not aware of the implications of all this, which means that the coming generation is an imitation of ourselves in a modified form, and so there is no new world. It is only when we love our children in the true sense of the word that we shall bring about the right kind of education and thereby put an end to war.

Question: What is beauty?

KRISHNAMURTI: In exploring this question, are we looking for an explanation, the dictionary meaning of that word? Or are we trying to feel out the full significance of beauty? If we are merely looking for a definition, then we shall not be sensitive to that which we call beauty. Surely, the mind must be very simple to appreciate what is beautiful. Please follow this a little bit. I am thinking aloud, exploring as I go along. The mind must be sensitive not only to that which it thinks is beautiful but also to that which is ugly; it must be sensitive to the dirty villages, to hovels, as well as to palaces and beautiful trees. If the mind is sensitive only to what is beautiful, then it is not sensitive at all. To be sensitive, it must be open to both the ugly and the beautiful. That is obviously so. To pursue beauty and deny that which is not beautiful makes the mind insensitive. To feel that which is ugly—which may not be ugly—and that which is beautiful—which may not be beautiful—there must be sensitivity: sensitivity to poverty, to the dirty man sitting in the bus, to the beggar, to the sky, to the stars, to the shy, young moon.

Now, how is this sensitivity to come into being? It can come into being only when there is abandonment—not calculated abandonment, but the abandonment that comes when there is no self-fulfillment. You see, there can be no abandonment without austerity. But it is not the disciplined austerity of the ascetic, because the ascetic is seeking power, and therefore he is incapable of abandonment. There can be abandonment only when there is love, and love can come into being only when the 'me' is not dominant. So the mind must be very simple, innocent—not made innocent. Innocency is not a state to be brought about through discipline, through control, through any form of compulsion or suppression. The mind is fresh, innocent, only when it is not cluttered up with the memories of many centuries; and this implies, surely, an extraordinary sensitivity, not merely to one part of life which is called beauty, but also to tears, to suffering, to laughter, to the hovels of the poor, and to the open skies—that is, to the totality of life.

Question: You are helping us to understand the workings of our own minds and to see how unintelligently we are living; but in an industrial society, is it possible to practice what you say?

KRISHNAMURTI: Sir, what I say cannot be practiced because there is nothing to practice. The moment you practice something, your mind is caught in that practice; therefore, it is made dull, stupid. Practice creates habit, and whether good or bad, it is still habit; and a mind that is merely the instrument of habit is not sensitive; it is incapable of penetration, inquiry, deep search. Yet your whole tradition and education is to practice, practice, practice, which means that you are concerned not with helping the mind to be sensitive, profound, supple, but with learning a few tricks so that you will not be disturbed. If anyone offers a method which will enable you not to be disturbed, that method you practice, and in practicing it, you are putting the mind to sleep. Surely, the mind that is alert, watchful, inquiring, does not need any practice.

And what is it that we are talking about? We are saying that unless you understand yourself, any society, industrial or otherwise,

is going to destroy you—and you are being destroyed, crushed, made uncreative. Unless you understand the whole content of your being, the motives, the urges, the ways of your thought, unless you know the total substance and depth of your mind, you will gradually become just another machine—which is what is actually happening. Slowly, inescapably, you are being made into machines—machines which are creating problems.

So, what matters is to understand yourself, the ways of your own mind—but not through introspection or analysis, whether by an analyst or by yourself, nor through reading books about the mind. The ways of the mind are to be understood in our relationships from day to day, which means seeing what we actually are without distortion, as we see our faces in the mirror. But we destroy the understanding of what we are the moment we compare or condemn, reject or accept. It is by just seeing *what is* that the mind makes itself free, and only in freedom is there the coming into being of that which may be called God, truth, or what you will.

Sirs, as one begins to understand oneself, that very beginning is the moment of freedom, and that is why it is very important not to have a guru, or make any book into an authority—because it is you who create authority, power, position. What is important is to understand yourself. You may say, "Well, that has been said before; many teachers have said it," but the fact is that we do not know ourselves. When you begin to discover the truth about yourself, there is something totally new, and this quality of newness can come into being only through self-discovery from moment to moment. There is no continuity in discovery; all that you have discovered must be lost in order to find the new again. If the mind really does this, then you will see that there comes an extraordinary quality—the quality of a mind that is completely alone, uninfluenced, a mind that has no motive; and it is only such a mind that can receive something which has never been known before. There must be freedom from the known for the unknown to be, and this whole process is meditation. It is only the meditative mind that can discover something beyond itself.

March 21, 1956

Seventh Talk in Bombay

It seems to me that all over the world there is very little respect for the individual, and without this respect, the individual is totally crushed—which is what is happening in modern society. A different social environment must obviously be brought about, but I do not think we realize how important it is for the individual to be free; that is, we do not see the significance of individual inquiry, search, and release. It is only the individual who can ultimately find reality; it is only the individual who can be a creative force in this disintegrating society; and I do not think we fully comprehend how urgent it is that we as individuals should discover for ourselves a way of life dissociated from the cultural, social, and religious influences which surround us. If we did perceive the importance of the individual, we should never have leaders and be followers. We follow only when we have lost our individuality. There are leaders only when we as individuals are confused and are therefore incapable of clearly thinking out our own problems and acting upon them. At present we are not individuals; we are merely the residue of collective influences, of cultural impressions and social restrictions. If you observe very closely and carefully the operation of your own mind, you will see that your thinking is according to tradition, according to books, according to leaders or gurus, which means that the individual has

completely ceased; and surely, it is only the individual who can create anything new.

Now, why is it that we have lost respect for the individual? We talk a great deal about the importance of the individual; all the politicians talk about it, including those in the collective, tyrannical society, just as the various religious leaders talk about the importance of the soul. But how does it happen that in actual practice the individual is ground down, totally lost? I do not know if this is a problem to any of you, but if we can pay sufficient attention this evening, perhaps we shall be able to emerge from the mass of collective influences—actually emerge from it and discover for ourselves what it is to be real individuals, totally integrated human beings.

I think one of the fundamental reasons for our having ceased to be individuals is the fact that we are pursuing power; we all want to be somebody, even in the house, in the flat, in the room. Just as nations create the tension of power, so each separate human being is everlastingly seeking to be something in relation to society; he wants to be recognized as a big man, as a capable bureaucrat, as a gifted artist, as a spiritual person, and so on. We all want to be something, and the desire to be something springs from the urge to power. If you examine yourself, you will see that what you want is success and the recognition of your success, not only in this world, but in the next world—if there is a next world. You want to be recognized, and for that recognition, you are dependent on society. Society recognizes only those who have power, position, prestige; and it is the vanity, the arrogance, of power, position, prestige, that most of us are seeking. Our deep underlying motive is the pride of achievement, and this pride asserts itself in different ways.

Now, as long as we are seeking power in any direction, real individuality is crushed out—not only our own individuality, but that of others. I think this is a basic psychological fact in life. When we seek to be somebody, it means that we desire to be recognized by society, therefore, we become slaves to society, mere cogs in the social machine, and hence we cease to be individuals. I think this is a fundamental issue, not to be quickly brushed aside. As long as the mind is seeking any form of power—power through a sect, power through knowledge, power through wealth, power through virtue—it must invariably breed a society which will destroy the individual, because then the human mind is caught and educated in an environment which encourages the psychological dependence on success. Psychological dependence destroys the clear mind which is alone, uncorrupted, and which is the only mind capable of thinking problems right through individually, independent of society and of its own desires.

So, the mind is everlastingly seeking to be something and thereby increasing its own sense of power, position, prestige. From the urge to be something springs leadership, following, the worship of success; and hence there is no deep individual perception of inward reality. If one actually sees this whole process, then is it possible to cut at the root of one's search for power? Do you understand the meaning of that word *power?* The desire to dominate, to possess, to exploit, to depend on another—all that is implied in this search for power. We can find other and more subtle explanations, but the fact is that the human mind is seeking power, and in the search for power it loses its individuality.

Now, how is this demand for power—which breeds arrogance, pride, vanity—to be put away? The mind is constantly seeking flattery; its emphasis is on itself, all its activities are self-centered; and how is the mind to cut at the root of this thing? I do not know if you have thought about this problem

of how to be totally rid of the drive to power, but I think it would be worthwhile if we could go into it this evening.

There is the desire to be somebody in this world, or to be somebody spiritually. Now, is it at all possible to get at and uproot this thing so that we never follow a leader, have no sense of self-importance, and do not want to be somebody in the political or any other world? Can we be nobody even though the whole stream of existence is moving the other way, urging us from childhood to be somebody? All our education is comparative; we are always comparing ourselves with somebody, which is again the search for power and position. And can this competitive spirit be got rid of, not little by little, not gradually through time, but completely and instantaneously, like cutting at the root of a tree and destroying it? Can this be done, or must we have time to bridge the gap between *what is* and 'what should be'?

I think we all realize the significance of this desire to be something, which produces imitation and destroys real individuality, clear perception; so I need not go into further details this evening. Now, can this desire be destroyed, wiped away instantaneously, or does it need time, which we call evolution? As we are at present educated, we say that it is a matter of time, of gradually approaching the ideal state in which there is no desire for power, and in which the mind is totally integrated. That is, we are here, and we must reach there, which is somewhere in the far distance; so there is a gap, an interval between the two, and hence we must struggle; we must move away from here to arrive there, which demands time. To me, this idea that the root of the desire to be something can be destroyed through time is utterly false. It must be wiped away immediately, or it can never be; and if you will give this your full attention, you will see it for yourself. Please listen, not merely to what I am saying, but to what is actually happening in your own mind as I am talking—to the reaction, the psychological process, awakened in you by my words, my description.

It is obvious that each one of us wants to be something, and we see that the desire to be something does breed antagonism, arrogance, crime. We also see that it brings about a social structure which encourages that very desire, and in which the individual ceases to exist, because the mind gets caught up in the organization of power. Seeing this whole process, can the desire to be something utterly disappear? Surely, it is only when the mind is capable of complete and direct thinking, uninfluenced by any self-centered activity, that it can find out what is real; and being caught in this extraordinarily complex desire to be something, is it possible for the mind totally to free itself? If the problem and its implications are clear, we can proceed. But if you say, "It will take time to get rid of the desire to be something," then you are already looking at the problem with a prejudice, with a so-called educated mind. Your education or the Gita or your guru has told you it will take time, so when you approach the problem, you already have a preconceived opinion about it.

Now, is it possible for the mind instantaneously to wipe away this desire to be something and hence never again create a leader by becoming a follower? It is the follower who creates the leader; there is no leader otherwise, and the moment you become a follower, you are an imitative entity; therefore, you lose creative individuality. So, can the mind wipe away totally this sense of following, this sense of time, this wanting to be something? You can wipe it away only when you give it your whole attention. Please see this. When you give your undivided attention to it and are completely observant, fully aware of the fact that the mind is seeking power, position, that it wants to be

something—only then can you be free. I shall explain what I mean by complete attention.

Attention is not to be forced, put together; the mind is not to be driven to pay attention to something. Please look at this, if you kindly will. The moment you have a motive for attention, there is no attention because the motive is more important than paying attention. For the total cessation of the desire to be something, complete attention must be given to that desire. But you cannot give complete attention to it if there is any motivation, any intention to wipe away that desire in order to get something else; and our minds are trained, not to pay attention, but to derive from attention a result. You pay attention only when you get something out of it, but here such attention is an obstruction, and I think it is very important to understand this right from the beginning. Any form of attention which has an objective becomes inattention; it breeds indolence, and indolence is one of the factors which prevent the immediate wiping away of the desire we are talking about. The mind can wipe away a particular desire only when it gives it complete attention, and it cannot give it complete attention as long as it is seeking a result. That is one factor of inattention, and any form of explanation, verbalization, is another. That is, there can be no attention as long as the mind has explanations of why it is seeking power, position, prestige. When you are trying to explain the cause of all that, there is inattention; therefore, through explanation you will never find freedom.

There is no attention as long as you are comparing what has been said about this problem by various authorities, by Shankara, Buddha, Christ, or X, Y, Z. When your mind is full of other people's knowledge, other people's experience, when it is following guides, sanctions, there can be no attention. Neither is there attention if you judge or condemn—which is fairly obvious. If you condemn a thing, you cannot understand it. And there can be no attention when there is an ideal because the ideal creates duality. Please see this. The ideal creates duality, and in that duality we are caught, especially in this unfortunate country where we all have ideals. Everybody talks about the ideal of the guru, the ideal of nonviolence, the ideal of loving your neighbor, the ideal of one life—and all the time you are denying that very thing in your living. So why not scrap the ideal? The moment you have an ideal, you have duality, and in the conflict of that duality the mind is caught. The fact is that there is this desire for power, this pride in being something, and it can only be wiped away instantaneously, not through the process of time; that is, only when the mind is aware of it without being distracted by the ideal. The ideal is a distraction, breeding inattention.

I hope you are giving your complete attention to the problem now, not because I am telling you to, but because you see for yourself the full significance of this desire to be something. If the mind is giving complete attention to the problem, it is not creating the opposite; therefore, there is humility. The fact is that your mind is seeking power, position, mundanely or spiritually, and is thereby causing all this mess, the chaos, confusion, and misery in the world. When the mind really sees that fact, which is to give complete attention to it, then you will find that pride and arrogance totally cease, and this cessation is an entirely different state from that brought about by the desire to be humble. Humility is not to be cultivated, and if it is cultivated, it is no longer humility; it is merely another form of arrogance. But if you can look at the problem very clearly and directly, which is to give it your undivided attention, you will discover that to wipe away this desire to be something—with its arrogance, vanity, and disrespect—is not a matter of time, for then it is wiped away immediately. Then you are

a different human being who will perhaps create a different society.

Question: It seems to me that the most notable thing about India is the all-pervading sense of timelessness, of peace, and religious intensity. Do you think this atmosphere can be maintained in the modern industrial age?

KRISHNAMURTI: Who do you think has created this sense of timeless peace and religious intensity? You and I? Or was it set going by some ancient people who lived quietly, anonymously, who felt these things intensely and perhaps expressed them in poems, in religious books? Because they felt intensely this religious spirit, it has remained; but it is not in our life; it is outside somewhere, and it has become our tradition. We are inclined to be so-called idealistic, which is a most unfortunate thing; and somewhat surreptitiously we have maintained this sense of timelessness—or rather, we have not maintained it, but it has gone on in spite of us. We are now caught in this modern industrial society. It is right that we should have machines to produce what is necessary in a country which is poverty-stricken, but because we have had nothing for so long, now that we can have things, if we are not very alert, individually clearsighted and aware of the whole problem, we shall probably become more materialistic than America and the other Western nations—while America and Europe may perhaps become more spiritual, more timeless, more gentle, more compassionate. That may happen.

So, what is the problem? Is it how to maintain the sense of timelessness, the sense of peace and religious intensity, in spite of this modern industrial society? This industrial society has to exist, and production must be stepped up still more; but unfortunately, in bringing about greater production, in mechanizing farms and industries, the danger is that the mind will also become mechanized. We think science is going to solve all our difficulties. It is not. The solution of our difficulties depends not on machines and the inventions of a few great scientists but on how we regard life. After all, though we may talk about religion, we are not religious people because the religious person is free of dogma, of belief, of ritual, of superstitions; he is not bound by class or caste, which means that he is free of society. The man who belongs to society is ambitious; he is seeking power, position; he is proud, greedy, envious, and such a man is not religious though he may quote *shastras* by the dozen. It is the religious person who will create this sense of timelessness, this sense of peace, even though living in an industrial society, because he is inwardly intense in his discovery from moment to moment of that which is eternal. But this requires astonishing vigor, mental clarity; and you cannot be mentally clear if your mind is cluttered up with knowledge gathered from the *shastras,* the Gita, the Koran, the Bible, the Buddhist scriptures, and all the rest of it. Knowledge is the past; it is all that the mind has known, and as long as the mind is burdened with knowledge, it is incapable of discovering what is real. Only the religious mind can be timelessly creative, and its action is peace, for it reflects the intensity and the fullness of life.

Question: Is there anything new in your teaching?

KRISHNAMURTI: To find out for yourself is much more important than my asserting yes or no. It is your problem, not my problem. To me, all this is totally new because it has to be discovered from moment to moment; it cannot be stored up after discovery; it is not something to be experienced and then retained as memory—which would be putting new wine in old bottles. It must be discovered as one lives from day to day, and it is new to the person who so discovers it. But you are always comparing what is being said with what has been said by some saint, or by Shankara, Buddha, or Christ. You say, "All these people have said this before, and you are only giving it another twist, a modern expression"—so naturally it is nothing new to you. It is only when you have ceased to compare, when you have put away Shankara, Buddha, Christ, with all their knowledge, information, so that your mind is alone, clear, no longer influenced, controlled, compelled, either by modern psychology or by the ancient sanctions and edicts—it is only then that you will find out whether or not there is something new, everlasting. But that requires vigor, not indolence; it demands a drastic cutting away of all the things that one has read or been told about truth and God. That which is eternal, new, is a living thing; therefore, it cannot be made permanent, and a mind that wants to make it permanent will never find it.

Question: Listening to you, one feels that you have read a great deal and are also directly aware of reality. If this is so, then why do you condemn the acquisition of knowledge?

KRISHNAMURTI: I will tell you why. It is a journey that must be taken alone, and there can be no journeying alone if your companion is knowledge. If you have read the Gita, the Upanishads, and modern psychology, if you have gathered information about yourself from the experts, and about what they say you should strive after—such knowledge is an impediment. The treasure is not in books but buried in your own mind, and the mind alone can discover this treasure. To have self-knowledge is to know the ways of your mind, to be aware of its subtleties with all their implications, and for that you don't have to read a single book. As a matter of fact, I have not read any of these things. Perhaps as a boy, or a young man, I casually looked at some of the sacred books, but I have never studied them. I do not want to study them; they are tiresome because the treasure is somewhere else. The treasure is not in the books, nor in your guru; it is in yourself, and the key to it is the understanding of your own mind. You must understand your mind, not according to Patanjali, or according to some psychologist who is clever at explaining things, but by watching yourself, by observing how your mind works, not only the conscious mind, but the deep layers of the unconscious as well. If you watch your mind, play with it, look at it when it is spontaneous, free, it will reveal to you untold treasures; and then you are beyond all the books. But that again requires a great deal of attention, vigor, an intensity of pursuit—not the dilettantism of lazy explanations. So the mind must be free from knowledge because a mind that is occupied with knowledge can never discover *what is*.

Question: I have tried various systems of meditation, but I don't seem to get very far. What system do you advocate?

KRISHNAMURTI: I do not advocate any system because every system makes the mind a prisoner, and I think it is very important really to understand this. It does not matter what system you practice, what posture you take, how you control your breathing, and all the rest of it, because your mind becomes a prisoner of whatever system you adopt. But there must be meditation, for meditation is a sweet thing—it clarifies the mind, bringing order and revealing the significance, the fullness, the depth and beauty of life. Without

meditation, the mind is shallow, empty, dull, dependent on stimulation. So meditation is necessary—but not the meditation that you do now, which has no value at all; it is a form of self-hypnosis. The problem is not how to meditate, or what system to follow, but to discover for yourself what meditation is.

Now, we are going to enter into this question of what meditation is, so don't shut your eyes and go to sleep over it, thinking you are meditating. We are inquiring, and inquiry demands attention, vigor—not closing your eyes and going into a trance, which you are apt to do when you hear that word *meditation*. We are trying to find out what meditation is, and to find out what meditation is requires meditation. (Laughter) Sirs, please don't laugh it off. To find out what meditation is, your mind must be meditating, not just following some stupid system based on the teaching of a guru, of Shankara or Buddha. All teachings are stupid the moment they become systems. You and I are trying to find out together what meditation is and what it means to meditate; we are not concerned with where meditation is going to lead. If you are intent upon finding out where meditation is going to lead, then you will never discover what meditation is because you are interested in the result, not in the process of meditation.

So we are setting out on a journey to find out what is meditation; and to find out, to discover what is meditation, the mind must first be free of systems, must it not? If you are tied to a system, it does not matter whose system it is, you obviously cannot find out what is meditation. You follow a system because you want a result out of it, and that is not meditation; like practicing the piano, it is merely the development of a certain faculty. When you follow a system, you may learn a few tricks, but your mind is caught in the system, which prevents you from finding out what is meditation; therefore, to find out, the mind must be free of systems. It is not a question of how to be free because the moment you say, "How am I to be free of the system in which my mind is caught?" the "how" becomes another system. But if you see the truth that the mind must be free of systems, then it is free; you don't have to ask how.

So, being free of systems, the mind must then inquire into the whole problem of concentration. This is a little more abstract, but please follow it. When a child is playing with a toy, the toy absorbs his mind, it holds his attention. He does not give attention to the toy, but the toy attracts him. That is one form of what you call concentration. Similarly, you have phrases, images, symbols, pictures, ideals, which attract and absorb you—at least, you want to be absorbed by these things, as the child is absorbed by the toy. But what happens? You are not as absorbed as the child; other thoughts come in, and you try to fix your mind on the chosen image or symbol, so you have a battle. There is contradiction, strife, a ceaseless effort to concentrate, but you never quite achieve it. This effort is what you call meditation. You spend your time trying to concentrate, which any child can do the moment he is interested in something; but you are not interested, so your concentration is a form of exclusion.

Now, is there attention without anything absorbing the mind? Is there attention without concentrating upon an object? Is there attention without any form of motive, influence, compulsion? Can the mind give full attention without any sense of exclusion? Surely it can, and that is the only state of attention; the others are mere indulgence or tricks of the mind. If you can give full attention without being absorbed in something, and without any sense of exclusion, then you will find out what it is to meditate because in that attention there is no effort, no division,

no struggle, no search for a result. So meditation is a process of freeing the mind from systems and of giving attention without either being absorbed or making an effort to concentrate.

Meditation is also a process of freeing the mind from its own projections, and its projections take place when the mind is occupied with the past. That is, when the mind is full of experiences, which are a result of the past, it inevitably projects and is caught in the images or ideations of the past. To project an image of Rama, Seeta, Christ, Buddha, or Mataji, and then worship that projection, is a form of self-hypnosis which does bring extraordinary visions, a state of trance, and all the rest of that nonsense; but meditation is the process of freeing the mind from the past so that there are no such projections at all.

So the worshiping of a projection, however noble, is not meditation. And meditation is not prayer—the prayer which demands, petitions, begs for some result. Nor is meditation the pursuit of virtue, which becomes a self-centered activity. When the mind is free from the hypnosis of the past, from the pursuit of its own activities, its own projections, when it is no longer experiencing the things it has learned, then you will find out what meditation is. Then you will never ask how to meditate because from morning till night, in whatever you are doing, subtle, hidden, the perfume of meditation is there. But merely closing your eyes, repeating some phrases, fingering the beads, is utterly vain. These things do not free the mind at all; on the contrary, the mind becomes a slave to them. It is the inquiry into what is meditation that has significance, that has great depth and vision, not the inquiry into what system to follow. It is only the stupid, arrogant mind that wants a system. The free mind never asks how, but is always discovering, moving, living.

March 25, 1956

Eighth Talk in Bombay

This is the end of the present series of meetings, and I wonder what most of us have made of these talks and discussions. What have we understood; how far have we penetrated into our problems and comprehended them? Have we merely listened to find an answer, a solution to our problems, a practical way of dealing with everyday suffering and the trials of existence? Or have we broken through to a wider and deeper awareness of ourselves so that independently and freely we can resolve the problems which inevitably arise in our life? I think it is very important, after having listened to these talks and discussions, to discover for oneself what one has understood and how that understanding operates in one's daily activities. Obviously, mere listening, divorced from action, has very little meaning; and I feel it would be utterly useless and vain to attend these meetings without having something come of it—not something that is put together, a conclusion logically arrived at, or a plan systematically thought out for future activity, but rather the breaking down of the mind's narrow walls of conditioning which make it incapable of seeing the totality of things. Whether those walls have been broken down in listening to these talks is the only significant question, not how much one has learned from whatever has been said. What matters is to discover for ourselves our own conditioning and to break it down spontaneously, easily, almost unconsciously, because it is not the deliberate thought, with its particular action, but rather the spontaneous and almost unconscious falling away of this conditioning that is going to free the mind.

So, considering the present state of society, the utter confusion we are in—with wars, inequality, various forms of degradation, and the constant battle within and without—it seems to me very important for those of us who have taken these talks seriously to find out if we have brought about a radical change in ourselves because, after all, it is only the individual, not circumstances, that can bring about a radical change. When we merely yield to the change of circumstances, the mind resolves its problems on a very superficial level; therefore, it becomes petty and incapable of seeing the whole. I think it is the comprehension of the whole, of the total, the limitless, or even a slight opening in the conditioned mind that is going to resolve our problems, and not the process of dissecting and analyzing our problems one by one. A tree is made up not only of the trunk, the branches, the leaves, the blossoms, and the fruit but also of the roots hidden deep in the earth; and without understanding all that, without having a feeling for the totality of it, you can never experience the fullness, the beauty of the tree.

Now, it seems to me that what most of us are doing is very unfortunate. By trying to understand our daily struggles and miseries separately, that is, through the gradual accumulation of knowledge, we think we shall understand the totality of life. But putting many parts together does not make the whole. By putting together leaves, branches, a trunk, and some roots, you will not have a tree; and yet that is what we are doing. We are approaching the problems of life separately, not as a unitary process; and the whole cannot be comprehended through analytical, cumulative knowledge. Knowledge has its place; but knowledge becomes a hindrance, a complete barrier to the discovery of the truth in its totality, in its beauty, for which the mind must be extraordinarily simple.

Most of you are concerned with what to do; you want to know what practical results you have gained by listening to these talks. I am sure many of you have asked yourselves that question, and others have put it to me. I sincerely hope that you have gained nothing practical because the mind seeks what is practical, what can be used or carried out, only when it is concerned with the little activities of its own momentum. "How can I practice what I have heard? In what way can I use it?"—all such questions seem to me so superficial, and it is the small mind that puts them, not the mind that sees the totality, the immensity of life, with all its many problems. When one really sees the immensity, the extraordinary depth and width of life, that very perception produces action which is not of the petty mind. What the small, conditioned mind does is to produce activity in its own dimension, and so there is more and more confusion.

Why is it that we think in parts, that is, in terms of a particular segment of society? Have you ever asked yourself this question? Is it not because our minds are conditioned by the literature we read, the education we get, the cultural and religious influences we are exposed to from childhood? All these factors condition the mind, and it is this conditioning that makes us think in parts. We think of ourselves as Hindus or Christians, Americans or Russians, as belonging to the Asiatic or the Western world. Here in India we divide ourselves still further; we are Malabaris, Madrasis, or Gujaraties; we belong to this caste or that caste; we read this book or that book.

Sir, would you mind not taking photographs now? I do not know what you think these meetings are for. It is too bad that you have to be reminded what kind of gathering this is. When you take photographs, watch people coming in, look to see where your friends are sitting, converse with each other—all this indicates such disrespect, not to me, but to your neighbor and to yourself. When you cannot diligently and purposively pursue a thought to the end, it shows to what extraordinary superficiality you have reduced yourself. If you will just

listen, I feel very strongly that in that very listening you will break down your conditioning; the act of listening is all that is needed. The afterthought, the thought which you accumulate and take away with you to think over, is not going to liberate you. What will break down the wall is giving your full attention now; and you cannot give your full attention if your mind is wandering, if you are distracted. When you are listening to a song which you love, to your favorite music, there is no effort; you just listen and let the music have its own action on you. Similarly, if you will listen now with that kind of attention, with that ease, you will find that the very act of listening does something which has much greater significance than any deliberate effort on your part to hear, to rationalize, and to carry out what is said.

I was asking why it is that all of us are thinking in parts, in little segments, when all over the world human beings are struggling with more or less the same problems, having the same anxieties, the same fears and transient joys. Why do we not take this extraordinary life on our earth as a whole, as something which you and I have to understand, not as Indians or Englishmen, Chinese or Germans, communists or capitalists, but as human beings? Is it not because we think in these little segments that we are forever quarreling, fighting, destroying each other? And this partial thinking, this divided comprehension, takes place because through education, through social influences, through so-called religious instruction, through books and the interpretation thereof, our minds are conditioned. Only the mind that is unconditioned can be free, and you cannot uncondition the mind by deliberately setting about it. You have to understand the whole process of conditioning and why the mind is conditioned. Every act, every thought, every movement of the mind is limited, and with that limited mind we are trying to comprehend something which has the depth and width of all existence.

So, the question is not what to do or whether one has learned anything practical by attending these meetings. It is not merely by trying to find an answer, a solution to the problem, but rather by listening, by discussing, by deep inquiry, by putting serious and fundamental questions that the mind's conditioning is broken down. But the conditioning must break down of its own accord; the mind cannot do anything about it. Being conditioned, the mind cannot act upon its own conditioning. A narrow mind trying to be broad will still be narrow. A petty mind may conceive of God, truth, but its conception can only be a projection of its own pettiness. When once the mind realizes this, it no longer formulates what God is or struggles to be free. It leaves all that entirely alone because it is now only concerned with inquiring into the whole process of conditioning, and if you are at all serious, you will find that this very inquiry opens the door so that your conditioning is revealed and destroyed. You don't destroy your conditioning, but the very perception of the fact that you are conditioned brings a vitality which destroys your conditioning. I do not think we see this. The very fact that I am greedy, and know it, has its own vitality to destroy greed.

So if we can really inquire into and comprehend why the mind thinks in parts, then I feel we shall have discovered a very important fact about ourselves; and it is out of this questioning that individuality comes into being. At present we are not free individuals; we are conditioned by society and are merely the playthings of environment; but if the mind can inquire into and thereby free itself from that conditioning, then there emerges the free individual who does not follow, who has no authority, no leader; and with this uninfluenced state of mind, there comes the creativity which is not of time.

So, if I may suggest, don't inquire to find out what you can learn. If you are merely listening in order to learn, then you create a teacher whom you follow. Surely, what matters is to be very clear that your mind is limited, conditioned, which is an obvious fact, and that whatever solution the petty mind may find, it is still petty. The very realization of this fact—that you are conditioned and that your values, your opinions, your learning, your judgments, are petty, dull, empty—is the beginning of humility. It is not the mind that has cultivated humility but the mind that is simple, humble, that is ever in a state of not-knowing—it is only such a mind that can find the unknowable. The mind that is pursuing virtue, respectability, that is seeking a system or a practical philosophy to live by in this world, will never find the unknowable. But the mind that understands its own conditioning, and so becomes simple, humble, the mind that is not accumulating, that is uncertain, always in a state of not-knowing, and is therefore a living, moving, dynamic thing—it is such a mind that can experience the unknowable, or allow the unknowable to be.

Question: It often seems to me that you give the gloomy rather than the happy side of life. Do you deliberately do this?

KRISHNAMURTI: Sir, our life is both gloomy and cheerful, dark and light. It would be terrible and destructive if life were nothing but light, good cheer, happiness, or nothing but darkness; but life is not like that, is it? Life has extraordinary variety. But unfortunately, you want to cling to the light, to the pleasurable, to the beautiful, and put all the rest away; and you call gloomy any man who says, "Look, there is also the other side, and if you really understand it, I think there will come into being an entirely different state." You see, we have divided life as happiness and unhappiness, so we are all the time battling between these two. We know that life sometimes has delight, but for most of us, life is sorrow. For those who have money, position, authority, respectability, life may be gay; but that makes the mind very superficial, as is shown in modern civilization. Whereas, if each one of us understands the whole significance of sorrow and joy as a total process, not as opposites in conflict with each other, then perhaps we shall find that life is neither sorrow nor joy but something entirely different which is not of this dualistic quality; and if we have never tasted or experienced that state, it is only because we are caught in this ceaseless struggle between the opposites.

That state beyond the opposites is not a formula, a mere conception, and it must be directly experienced; but you see, it cannot be directly experienced as long as the mind is seeking happiness. Happiness is a by-product; like virtue, it is of secondary importance. The man who is pursuing happiness will never be happy, for happiness comes upon us suddenly, obscurely, unexpectedly. Have you not noticed that the moment you know you are happy, you have lost happiness? When you say, "I am joyous," it is over, finished. Happiness, like love, is something of which the mind can never be conscious. The moment the mind is conscious that it loves, there is no longer love. It is very strange, and very interesting, that a mind which is deliberately trying to experience something loses the whole perfume of life. This is not a poetical saying to be brushed aside but rather a fact to be realized. The mind must not seek anything because what it seeks, it will experience; and what it then experiences is not the truth, for in its very search it has projected what it wants. That projection is out of the past; it has already been tasted; therefore, the projection and the attainment of that projection are not

happiness but a delusion, a process of self-hypnosis. Once you realize this, if you are at all serious and deeply interested, you will find that your mind is always empty, ever experiencing and never gathering.

But our minds are full, are they not? They are full of acquired virtue; they are constantly occupied with pursuing the ideal, seeking God, truth, this or that; therefore, there is always a conditioned response. So what matters is to understand that in its very search, the mind creates its own hindrance because what it finds will be the projection of its own desire. When the mind deeply realizes this, all seeking comes to an end; the mind is very quiet, alert, and then there comes into being a different state altogether. When you begin to understand sorrow, to observe how it arises; when you go into it, cherish it, and do not merely resist it, then you will find that the mind is not caught in sorrow, or in its opposite, because such a mind is empty in the deep sense of that word. Most minds are empty in the superficial sense that they are perpetually occupied with problems. I do not mean that kind of emptiness. I am talking of the emptiness which has extraordinary depth and width, and a mind that is everlastingly occupied with problems and immediate solutions cannot be empty in that deep sense of the word.

Question: What is psychosomatic disease, and can you suggest ways to cure it?

KRISHNAMURTI: I do not think it is possible to find ways to cure psychosomatic disease, and perhaps the very search for a way to cure the mind is producing the disease. To find a way, or to practice a method, implies inhibiting, controlling, suppressing thought, which is not to understand the mind. It is fairly obvious that the mind does create disease in the physical organism. If you eat when you are angry, your tummy is upset; if you violently hate somebody, you have a physical disorder; if you restrict your mind to a particular belief, you become mentally or psychically neurotic, and it reacts upon the body. This is all part of the psychosomatic process. Of course, not all diseases are psychosomatic, but fear, anxiety, and other disturbances of the psyche do produce physical diseases. So, is it possible for the mind to be made healthy? Many of us are concerned with keeping the body healthy through right diet, and so on, which is essential; but very few are concerned with keeping the mind healthy, young, alert, vital, so that it does not deteriorate.

Now, if the mind is not to deteriorate, it must obviously never follow; it must be independent, free. But our education does not help us to be free; on the contrary, it helps us to fit into this deteriorating society; therefore, the mind itself deteriorates. We are encouraged from childhood to be fearful, competitive, to think always about ourselves and our own security. Naturally, such a mind must be in everlasting conflict, and that conflict does produce physical effects. What is important, then, is to discover and understand for ourselves, through our own vigilant watchfulness, the whole process of conflict, and not depend on any psychologist or guru. To follow a guru is to destroy your mind. You follow him because you want what you think he has; therefore, you have set going a process of deterioration. The effort to be somebody, mundanely or spiritually, is another form of deterioration, because such effort always brings anxiety; it produces fear, frustration, making the mind unhealthy, which in turn affects the body. I think this is fairly simple. But to look to another for the cure of the mind is part of the process of deterioration.

Question: You have suggested that through awareness alone, transformation is possible. What do you mean by awareness?

KRISHNAMURTI: Sir, this is a very complex question, but I shall try to describe what it is to be aware, if you will kindly listen and patiently follow it step by step, right through to the end. To listen is not just to follow what I am describing but actually to experience what is being described, which means watching the operation of your own mind as I describe it. If you merely follow what is being described, then you are not aware, observant, watchful of your own mind. Merely to follow a description is like reading a guidebook while the scenery goes by unobserved; but if you watch your own mind while listening, then the description will have significance, and you will find out for yourself what it means to be aware.

What do we mean by awareness? Let us begin at the simplest level. You are aware of the noise that is going on; you are aware of the cars, the birds, the trees, the electric lights, the people sitting around you, the still sky, the breathless air. Of all that you are aware, are you not? Now, when you hear a noise or a song, or see a cart being pushed, and so on, what is heard or observed is translated, judged by the mind; that is what you are doing, is it not? Please follow this slowly. Each experience, each response, is interpreted according to your background, according to your memory. If there were a noise which you were hearing for the first time, you would not know what it was; but you have heard the noise a dozen times before, so your mind immediately translates it, which is the process of what we call thinking. Your reaction to a particular noise is the thought of a cart being pushed, which is one form of awareness. You are aware of color, you are aware of different faces, different attitudes, expressions, prejudices, and so on. And if you are at all alert, you are also aware of how you respond to these things, not only superficially, but deeply. You have certain values, ideals, motives, urges, on different levels of your being; and to be conscious of all that is part of awareness. You judge what is good and what is bad, what is right and what is wrong; you condemn, evaluate, according to your background, that is, according to your education and the culture in which you have been brought up. To see all this is part of awareness, is it not?

Now, let us go a little further. What happens when you are aware that you are greedy, violent, or envious? Let us take envy and stick to that one thing. Are you aware that you are envious? Please go with me step by step, and bear in mind that you are not following a formula. If you make it into a formula, you will have lost the significance of the whole thing. I am unfolding the process of awareness, but if you merely learn by heart what has been described, you will be exactly where you are now. Whereas, if you begin to see your conditioning, which is to be aware of the operation of your own mind as I go on explaining, then you will come to the point where an actual transformation is possible.

So you are aware, not only of outward things and your interpretation of them, but you have also begun to be aware of your envy. Now, what happens when you are aware of envy in yourself? You condemn it, don't you? You say that it is wrong, that you must not be envious, that you must be loving, which is the ideal. The fact is that you are envious, while the ideal is what you should be. In pursuing the ideal, you have created a duality, so there is a constant conflict, and in that conflict you are caught.

Are you aware, as I am describing this process, that there is only one thing, which is the fact that you are envious? The other, the

ideal, is nonsense; it is not an actuality. And it is very difficult for the mind to be free of the ideal, to be free of the opposite, because traditionally, through centuries of a particular culture, we have been taught to accept the hero, the example, the ideal of the perfect man, and to struggle towards it. That is what we have been trained to do. We want to change envy into nonenvy, but we have never found out how to change it, and so we are caught in everlasting strife.

Now, when the mind is aware that it is envious, that very word *envious* is condemnatory. Are you following, sirs? The very naming of that feeling is condemnatory, but the mind cannot think except in words. That is, a feeling arises with which a certain word is identified, so the feeling is never independent of the word. The moment there is a feeling like envy, there is naming, so you are always approaching a new feeling with an old idea, an accumulated tradition. The feeling is always new, and it is always translated in terms of the old.

Now, can the mind not name a feeling like envy but come to it afresh, anew? The very naming of that feeling is to make it old, to capture it and put it into the old framework. And can the mind not name a feeling—that is, not translate it by calling it a name, and thereby either condemning or accepting it—but merely observe the feeling as a fact?

Sir, experiment with yourself, and you will see how difficult it is for the mind not to verbalize, not to give a name to a fact. That is, when one has a certain feeling, can that feeling be left unnamed and be looked at purely as a fact? If you can have a feeling and really pursue it to the end without naming it, then you will find that something very strange happens to you. At present the mind approaches a fact with an opinion, with evaluation, with judgment, with denial or acceptance. That is what you are doing. There is a feeling, which is a fact, and the mind approaches that fact with a term, with an opinion, with judgment, with a condemnatory attitude, which are dead things. Do you understand? They are dead things, they have no value, they are only memory operating on the fact. The mind approaches the fact with a dead memory; therefore, the fact cannot operate on the mind. But if the mind merely observes the fact without evaluation, without judgment, condemnation, acceptance, or identification, then you will find that the fact itself has an extraordinary vitality because it is new. What is new can dispel the old; therefore, there is no struggle not to be envious— there is the total cessation of envy. It is the fact that has vigor, vitality, not your judgments and opinions about the fact; and to think the thing right through, from the beginning to the end, is the whole process of awareness.

Question: Why is there such fear of death?

KRISHNAMURTI: Again, if I may suggest it, let us think the problem right through to the end, and not stop halfway, or wander off at a tangent. We know that the body deteriorates and dies; the heart beats only so many times in so many years, and the whole physical organism, being in constant use, must inevitably wear out and come to an end. We are not afraid of that; it is a common, everyday event, and we often see the body being carried away to be burned. But then we say, "Is that all? With the ending of the body, will the things I have gathered, my learning, my love, my virtue, also end? And if all that does end, then what is the good of living?" So we begin to inquire; we want to know whether there is annihilation or continuity after death.

This is not a problem merely for the superstitious or the so-called educated; it is a problem for each one of us, and we must find out for ourselves the truth of the matter, neither accepting nor rejecting, neither believing nor being skeptical. The man who is afraid of death and therefore clings to belief in reincarnation, in this or that, will never find out the truth of the matter; but a mind that really wants to know and is trying to find out what is true is in quite a different state; and that is what we are doing here.

Now, what is it that continues? Do you understand, sirs? How do you know you have continued from yesterday, and that, if all goes well and there is no accident, you will continue through today to tomorrow? You know that only through memory, do you not? Let us keep it very simple, and not philosophize or introduce a lot of words. So I know I exist only because of memory. The mere statement that I exist has no meaning, but I know I exist because today I remember having existed yesterday, and I hope to exist tomorrow. So the thread of continuity is memory—the memory which has been accumulating for centuries, which has gone through a great many experiences, distortions, frustrations, sorrows, joys, the endless struggle of ambition. We want all that to continue, and because we do not know what is going to happen to it when the body dies, fear comes into being. That is one fact. And why do we divide death from living? It may be altogether wrong to divide them. It may be that living is dying—and perhaps that is the beauty of living. But living is something which most of us have not fully grasped or understood, nor have we understood what death is; so we are afraid of living, and we are afraid of death.

Now, what do we mean by living? Living is not merely going to the office or passing examinations or having children or the everlasting struggle for bread and butter; that is only part of it. Living also implies seeing the trees, the sunlight on the river, a bird on the wing, the moon through the clouds; it is to be aware of smiles and tears, of turmoils and anxieties; it is to know love, to be gentle, compassionate, and to perceive the extraordinary depth and width of existence. Do we know all that? Or do we know only a little part of it, the part which is made up of my struggle, my job, my family, my virtue, my religion, my caste, my country? All we know is the 'me' with its self-centered activities, and that is what we call life.

So we do not know what living is. We have divided living from dying, which shows that we have not understood the whole depth and width of life, in which death may be included. I think death is not something apart from life. It is only when we die every day to all the things we have gathered—to our knowledge, our experiences, to all our virtues—that we can live. We do not live because we are continuing from yesterday, through today, to tomorrow. Surely, only that which comes to an end has a beginning, but we never come to an end. Again, this is not just a poetical saying, so don't brush it aside. We have no beginning because we are not dying; we never know a timeless moment, and so we are concerned about death. For most of us, living is a process of struggle and tears; and what we are frightened of is not the unknown, which we call death, but of losing all that we have known. And what do we know? Not very much. This is not cynical but factual. What do we actually know? Hardly anything. Our names, our little bank accounts, our jobs, our families, what other people have said in the Gita, the Bible, or the Upanishads, the various preoccupations of a superficial life—these things we know, but we do not know the depths of our own being.

So we are covering the unknown with the known, and we are afraid to let go of, to renounce, the known. But to renounce in order to find God is not renunciation; it is merely another form of seeking a reward. A man who renounces the world in order to find God will never find God because he is still out to get something. There is total renunciation only when there is no asking for anything, no laying up for tomorrow, which is to die to everything of yesterday. Then you will find that death is not something to be afraid of and run away from, nor does it demand belief in the beyond. It is the known that captures and holds us, not the unknown; and the mind is full of the known. It is only when the mind is free from the known that the unknown can be. Death and life are one; and death is to be experienced, not at the last moment through disease and corruption, or accident, but while we are living and the mind is vigorous.

You see, sirs, timelessness is a state of mind, and as long as we are thinking in terms of time, there is death and the fear of death. Timelessness is not to be glibly talked about but to be directly experienced, and there can be no experiencing of timelessness as long as there is a continuity of all the things that one has gathered. So the mind must be free from all its accumulations, and only then is there the coming into being of the unknown. What we are afraid of is letting go of the known, but a mind that is not dead to the known, free from the known, can never experience the extraordinary state of timelessness.

March 28, 1956

Index for Questions

Amsterdam, 1955

London, 1955

Sydney, 1955

Banaras, 1955

Madras, 1956

Madanapalle, 1956

Bombay, 1956

Index